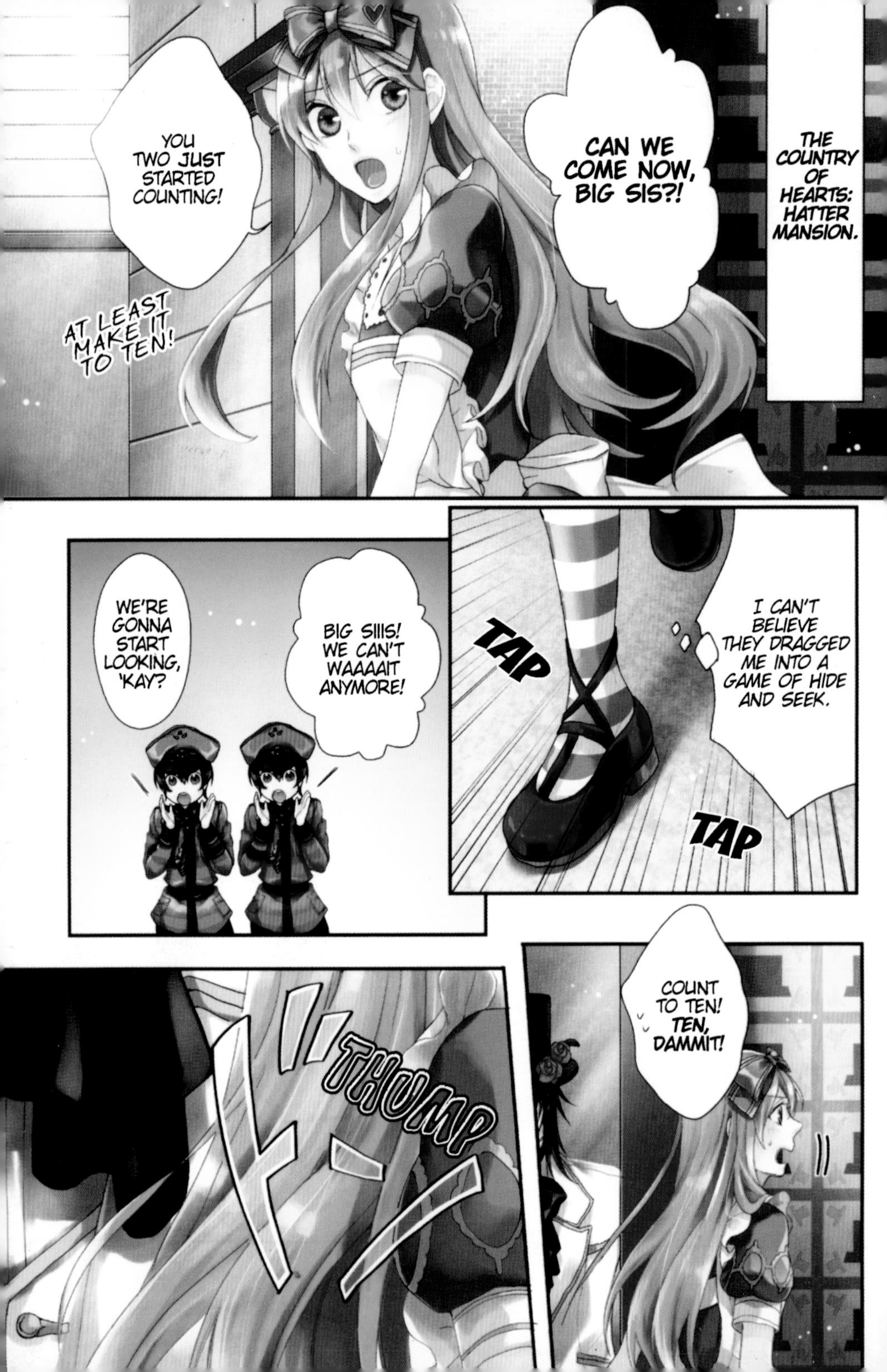
THE COUNTRY OF HEARTS: HATTER MANSION.
CAN WE COME NOW, BIG SIS?!
YOU TWO JUST STARTED COUNTING!
AT LEAST MAKE IT TO TEN!
I CAN'T BELIEVE THEY DRAGGED ME INTO A GAME OF HIDE AND SEEK.
TAP
TAP
BIG SIIIS! WE CAN'T WAAAAIT ANYMORE!
WE'RE GONNA START LOOKING, 'KAY?
COUNT TO TEN! TEN, DAMMIT!
THUMP

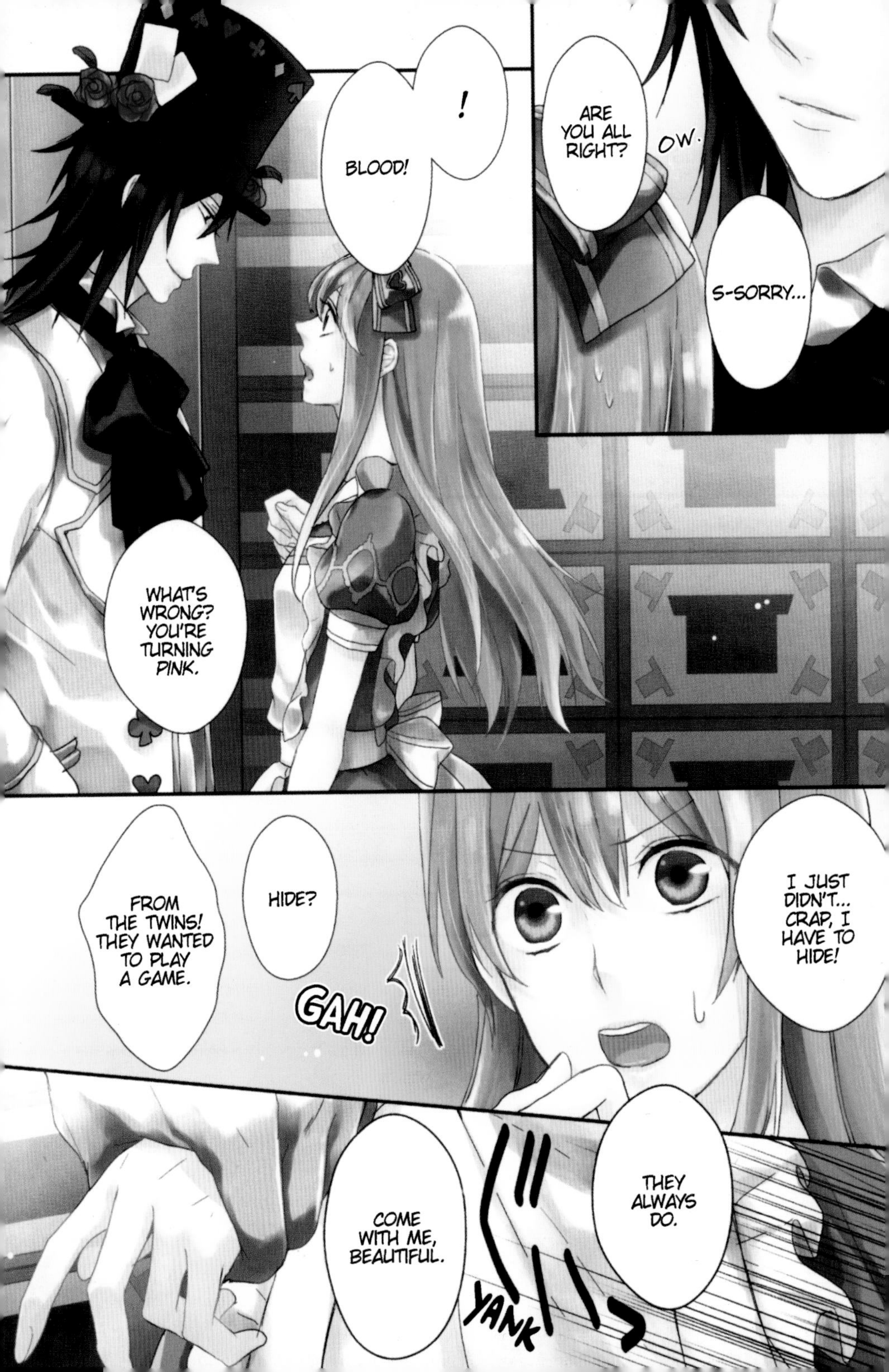
OW.
ARE YOU ALL RIGHT?
S-SORRY...
!
BLOOD!
WHAT'S WRONG? YOU'RE TURNING PINK.
I JUST DIDN'T... CRAP, I HAVE TO HIDE!
GAH!
HIDE?
FROM THE TWINS! THEY WANTED TO PLAY A GAME.
THEY ALWAYS DO.
YANK
COME WITH ME, BEAUTIFUL.

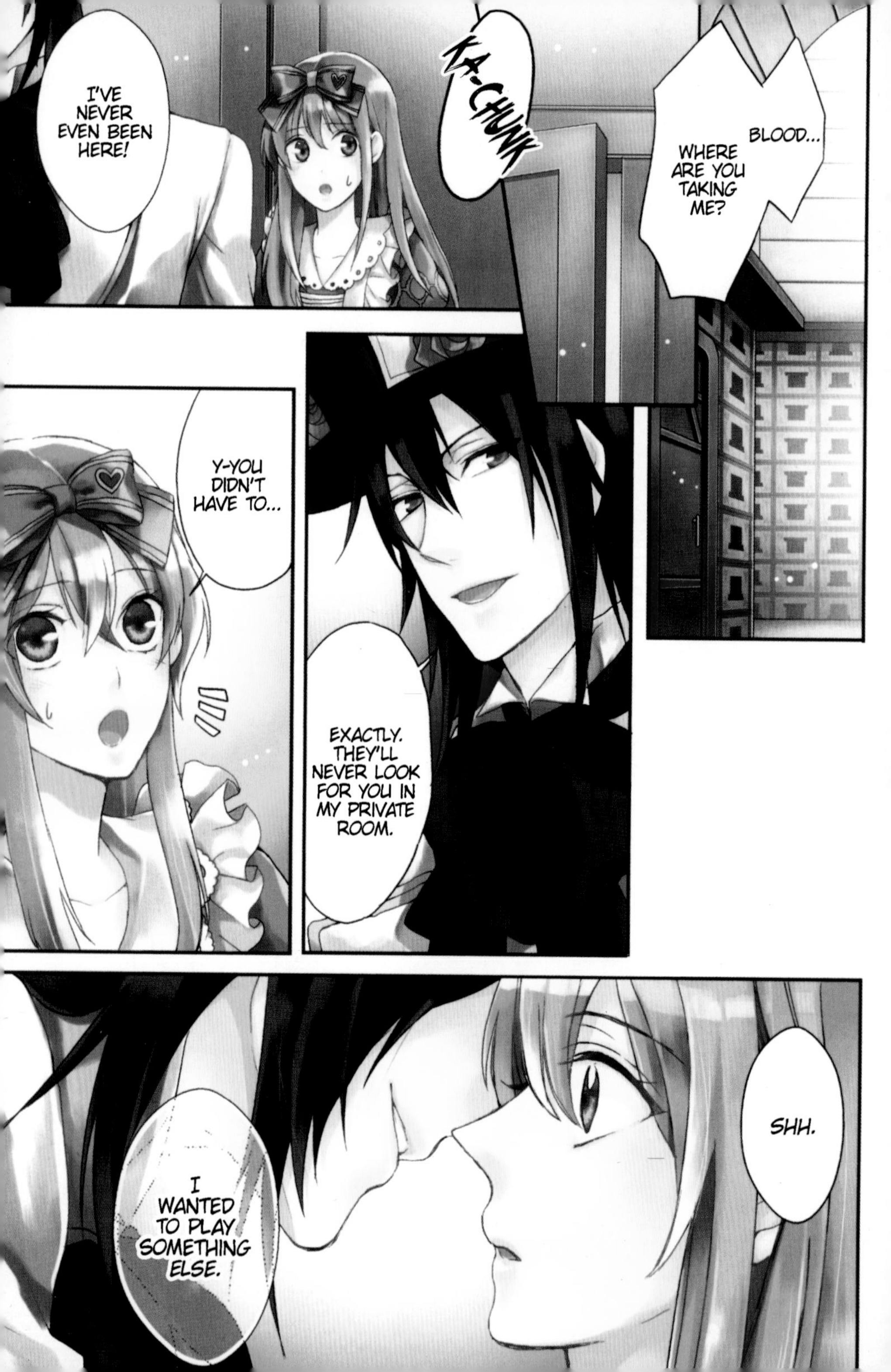
BLOOD... WHERE ARE YOU TAKING ME?
KA-CHUNK
I'VE NEVER EVEN BEEN HERE!
EXACTLY. THEY'LL NEVER LOOK FOR YOU IN MY PRIVATE ROOM.
Y-YOU DIDN'T HAVE TO...
SHH.
I WANTED TO PLAY SOMETHING ELSE.

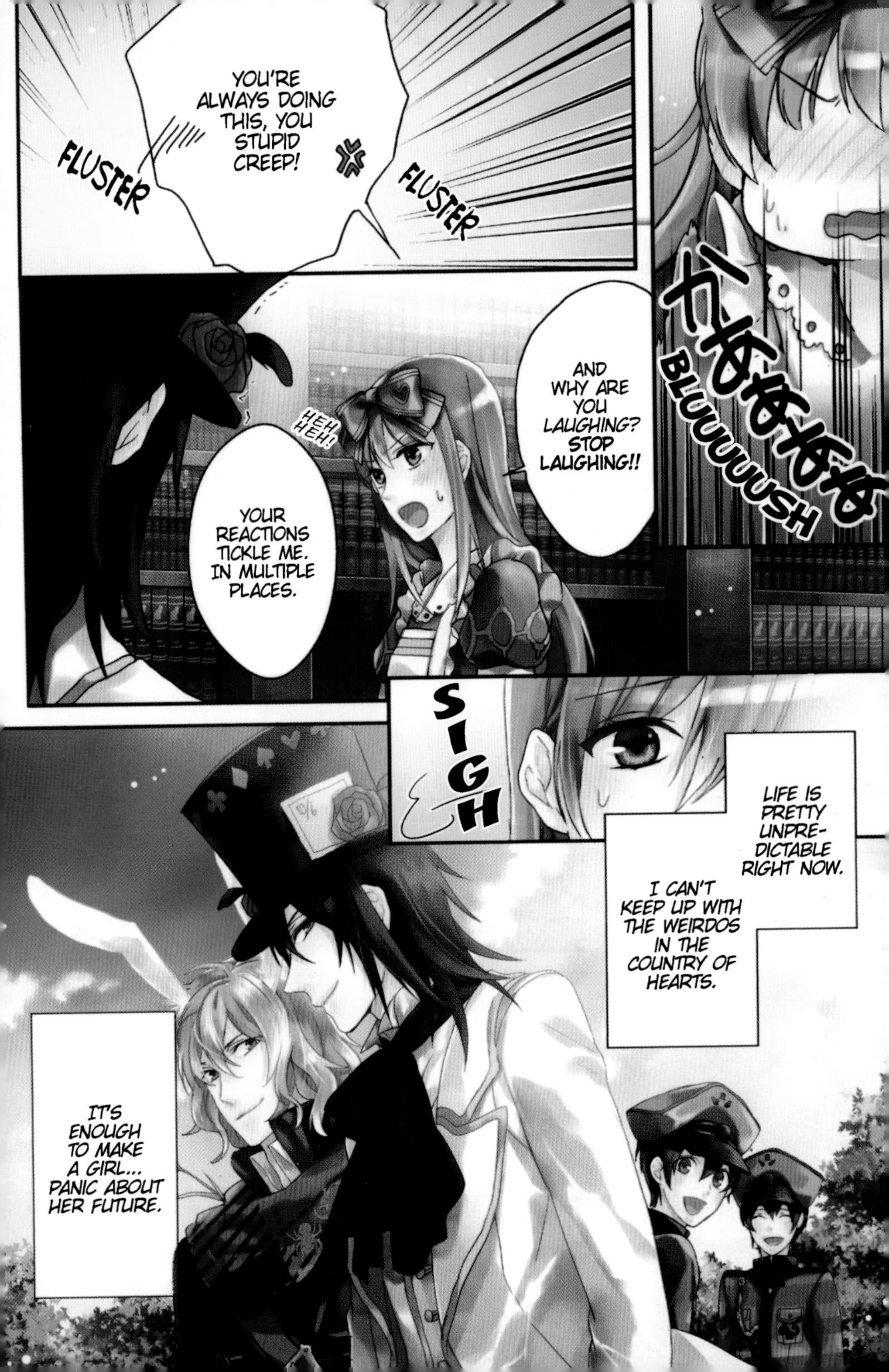
かああああ
BLUUUUUSH
FLUSTER
YOU'RE ALWAYS DOING THIS, YOU STUPID CREEP!
FLUSTER
AND WHY ARE YOU LAUGHING? STOP LAUGHING!!
HEH HEH!
YOUR REACTIONS TICKLE ME. IN MULTIPLE PLACES.
SIGH
LIFE IS PRETTY UNPRE-DICTABLE RIGHT NOW.
I CAN'T KEEP UP WITH THE WEIRDOS IN THE COUNTRY OF HEARTS.
IT'S ENOUGH TO MAKE A GIRL... PANIC ABOUT HER FUTURE.

ALICE IN THE COUNTRY OF HEARTS
~The Mad Hatter's Late Night Tea Party~

1

RIKO SAKURA

佐倉 リコ

STAFF CREDITS

translation	**Angela Liu**
adaptation	**Lianne Sentar**
lettering	**Laura Scoville**
cover design	**Nicky Lim**
proofreader	**Shanti Whitesides,**
	Katherine Bell
editor	**Adam Arnold**
publisher	**Jason DeAngelis**
	Seven Seas Entertainment

ALICE IN THE COUNTRY OF HEARTS:
THE MAD HATTER'S LATE NIGHT TEA PARTY VOL. 1
Copyright © Riko Sakura / QuinRose 2011
First published in Japan in 2011 by ICHIJINSHA Inc., Tokyo.
English translation rights arranged with ICHIJINSHA Inc., Tokyo, Japan.

ISBN: 978-1-937867-78-2
Printed in Canada
First Printing: November 2013
10 9 8 7 6 5 4 3 2 1

Alice IN THE COUNTRY OF Hearts
THE MAD HATTER'S LATE NIGHT TEA PARTY
VOLUME 1

story by **QuinRose**
art by **Riko Sakura**

FOLLOW US ONLINE: **www.gomanga.com**

READING DIRECTIONS

This book reads from *right to left*, Japanese style. If this is your first time reading manga, you start reading from the top right panel on each page and take it from there. If you get lost, just follow the numbered diagram here. It may seem backwards at first, but you'll get the hang of it! Have fun!!

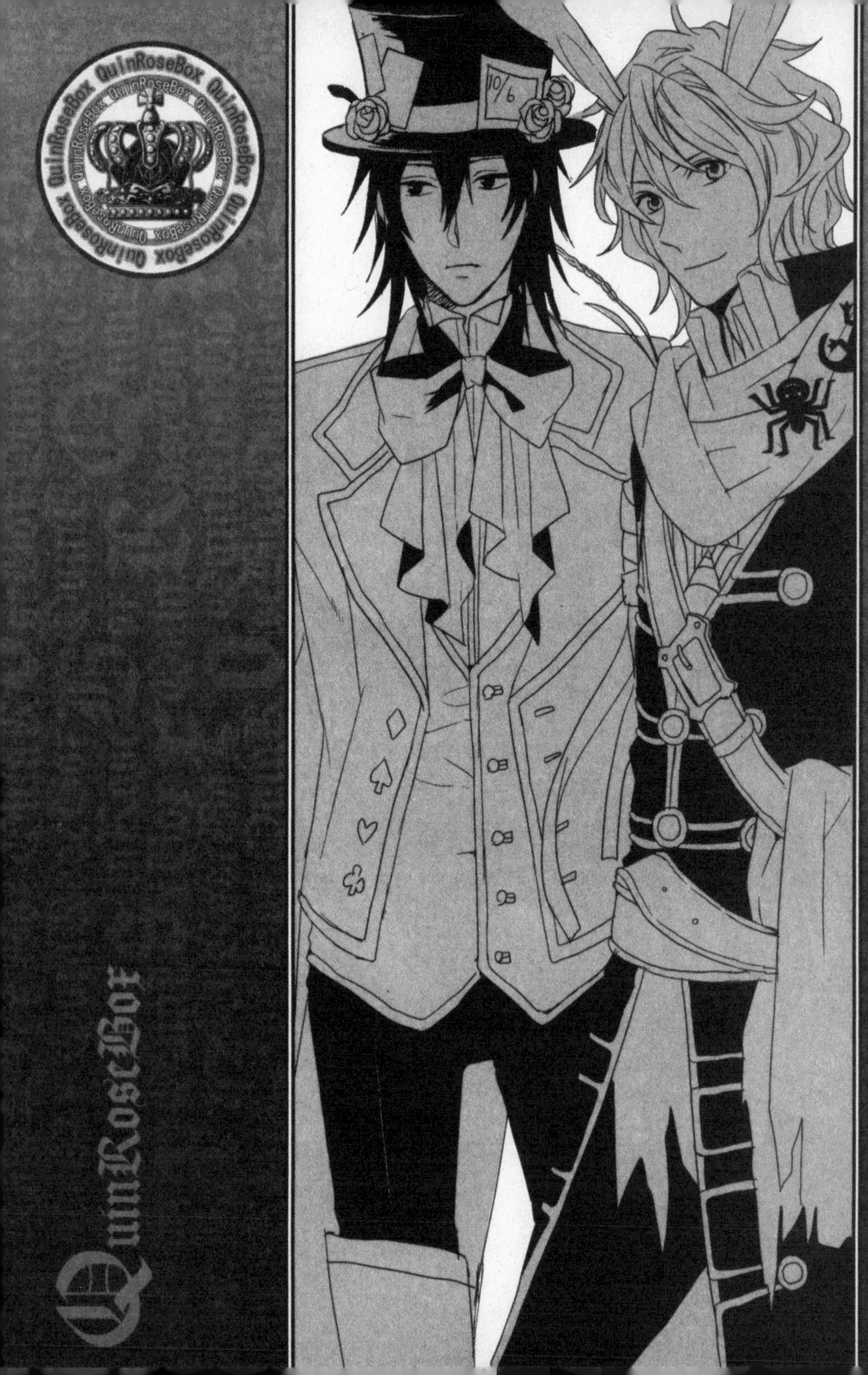
10/6

QuinRoseBox

Alice in the Country of Hearts

ハートの国の
アリス

~ Wonderful Wonder World ~

- STORY -

This is a love adventure game. It is based on *Alice in Wonderland,* but evolves into a completely different story.

The main character is far from a romantic. In fact, she's especially sick of love relationships.

She's pulled (against her will) into the dangerous Country of Hearts, which is not as peaceful as the name makes it sound. The Hatters are a mafia family and even the employees of the Amusement Park carry weapons.

The leaders of the three domains are constantly trying to kill each other. Many of the skirmishes are the result of territory grabs by three major powers trying to control more land: the Hatter, the Queen of Hearts, and Gowland.

After drinking some strange medicine (again, against her will), the main character is unable to return to her world. She quickly decides that she's trapped in a dream and allows herself to enjoy(?) the extraordinary experience she's been thrown into.

What territory will she stay with and who will she interact with to get herself home? And will this girl, so jaded about love, fall into a relationship she doesn't expect?

Alice in Country of Hearts
Character Information

Elliot March
VA: Tsuguo Mogami

The No. 2 of the Hatter Family and Blood's right-hand man, Elliot is an ex-criminal and an escaped convict. Very short-tempered, he used to be a "very bad guy" who shot before asking questions. After partnering up with Blood, he rounded out and changed to a "slightly bad guy" who thinks for about three seconds before shooting. In his mind, this is a vast improvement.

Blood Dupre
VA: Katsuyuki Konishi

The dangerous leader of the crime syndicate known as the Hatter Family. Since he enjoys plotting more than working directly, he controls everything from the shadows. He's incredibly smart, but due to his temperamental moods and his desire to keep things "interesting," he often digs his own grave in his secret plans.

Alice Liddell
VA: Rie Kugimiya

She grew up to be a responsible young woman after losing her mother early, but Alice still carries a complex toward her older sister. She respects her older sister very much, but is frustrated about always being compared to her. Since her first love fell for her older sister, she has no confidence in herself when it comes to romance.

Vivaldi
VA: Yuuko Kaida

Ruthless and cruel, the Queen of Hearts is an arrogant beauty with a wild temper. She's enemies with the Hatter and Gowland. Impatient at heart, Vivaldi takes her fury out on everyone around her including her subordinates, whom she considers pawns. Anyone **not** working for her doesn't even register as existing.

Tweedle Dum
VA: Jun Fukuyama

The second "Bloody Twin" and a dead ringer for his brother—in both appearance and personality. As they often change places, it's uncertain which one is the older twin.

Tweedle Dee
VA: Jun Fukuyama

Gatekeeper of the Hatter territory, and one of the dark, sneaky twins. They sometimes show an innocent side, but they usually have a malicious agenda. Also known as the "Bloody Twins" due to their unsavory activities.

Ace
VA: Daisuke Hirakawa

The knight of Hearts and the ex-subordinate of Vivaldi. He's left the castle and is currently wandering. He's a very unlucky and unfortunate man, yet remains strangely positive, thus he tends to plow forward and make mistakes that only worsen his situation. He's one of the few friends of the clockmaker, Julius.

Julius Monrey
VA: Takehito Koyasu

The clockmaker, a gloomy machine expert who easily falls into depression. He lives in the Clock Tower and doesn't get out much. He always thinks of everything in the most negative way and tends to distrust people, but he gets along with Ace. He had some part in the imprisonment of the March Hare, Elliot, and is thus the target of Elliot's hatred.

Peter White
VA: Kouki Miyata

Don't be fooled by the cute ears—Peter is the dangerous guide who dragged Alice to Wonderland in the first place. He claims to always be worried about the time, despite having a strange grasp on it. Rumors say his heart is as black as his hair is white.

Nightmare
VA: Tomokazu Sugita

A sickly nightmare. He appears in Alice's dream, sometimes to guide her— and other times, to **misguide** her.

Mary Gowland
VA: Kenyuu Horiuchi

The owner of the Amusement Park. He hides his hated first name, Mary, but pretty much everyone already knows it. His full name is a play on words that sounds like "Merry Go Round" when said quickly. If his musical talent was given a numerical value, it would be closer to negatives than zero.

Boris Airay
VA: Noriaki Sugiyama

A riddle-loving cat with a signature smirk. He sometimes gives hints to his riddles, but the hints usually just cause more confusion. He also has a tendency to pose questions and never answer them.

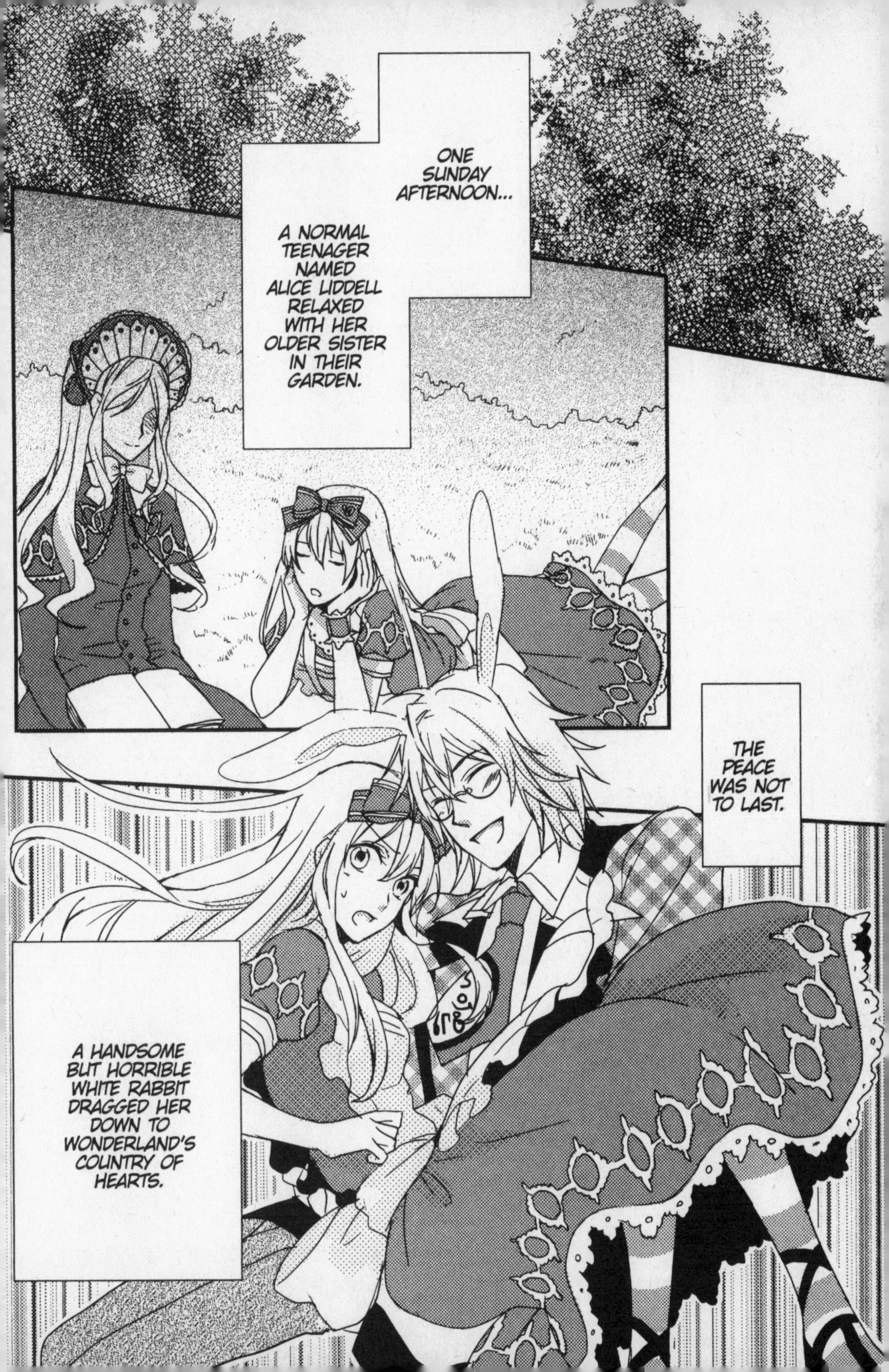
ONE SUNDAY AFTERNOON...
A NORMAL TEENAGER NAMED ALICE LIDDELL RELAXED WITH HER OLDER SISTER IN THEIR GARDEN.
THE PEACE WAS NOT TO LAST.
A HANDSOME BUT HORRIBLE WHITE RABBIT DRAGGED HER DOWN TO WONDERLAND'S COUNTRY OF HEARTS.

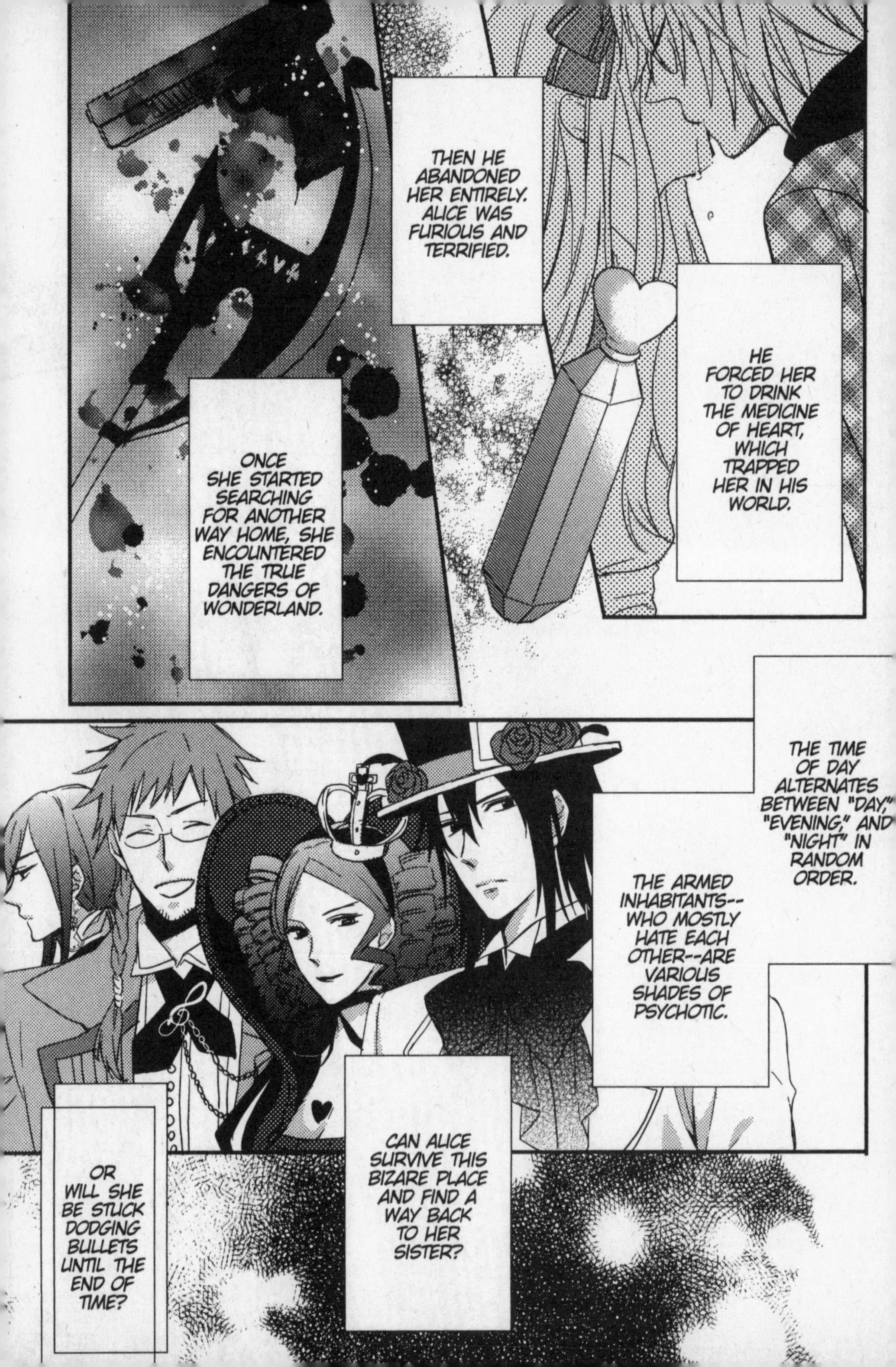
HE FORCED HER TO DRINK THE MEDICINE OF HEART, WHICH TRAPPED HER IN HIS WORLD.
THEN HE ABANDONED HER ENTIRELY. ALICE WAS FURIOUS AND TERRIFIED.
ONCE SHE STARTED SEARCHING FOR ANOTHER WAY HOME, SHE ENCOUNTERED THE TRUE DANGERS OF WONDERLAND.
THE TIME OF DAY ALTERNATES BETWEEN "DAY," "EVENING," AND "NIGHT" IN RANDOM ORDER.
THE ARMED INHABITANTS--WHO MOSTLY HATE EACH OTHER--ARE VARIOUS SHADES OF PSYCHOTIC.
CAN ALICE SURVIVE THIS BIZARE PLACE AND FIND A WAY BACK TO HER SISTER?
OR WILL SHE BE STUCK DODGING BULLETS UNTIL THE END OF TIME?

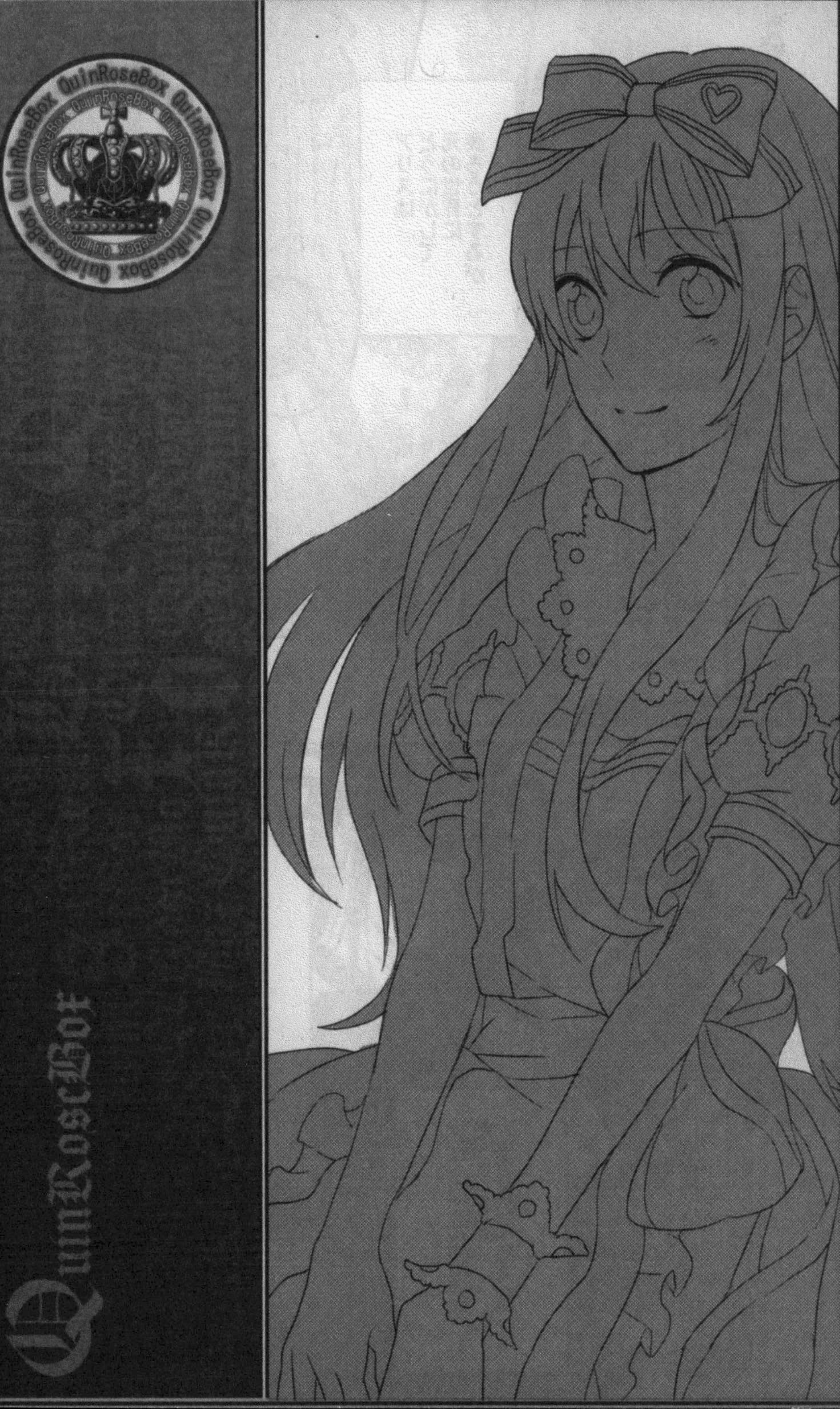

QuinRoseBox

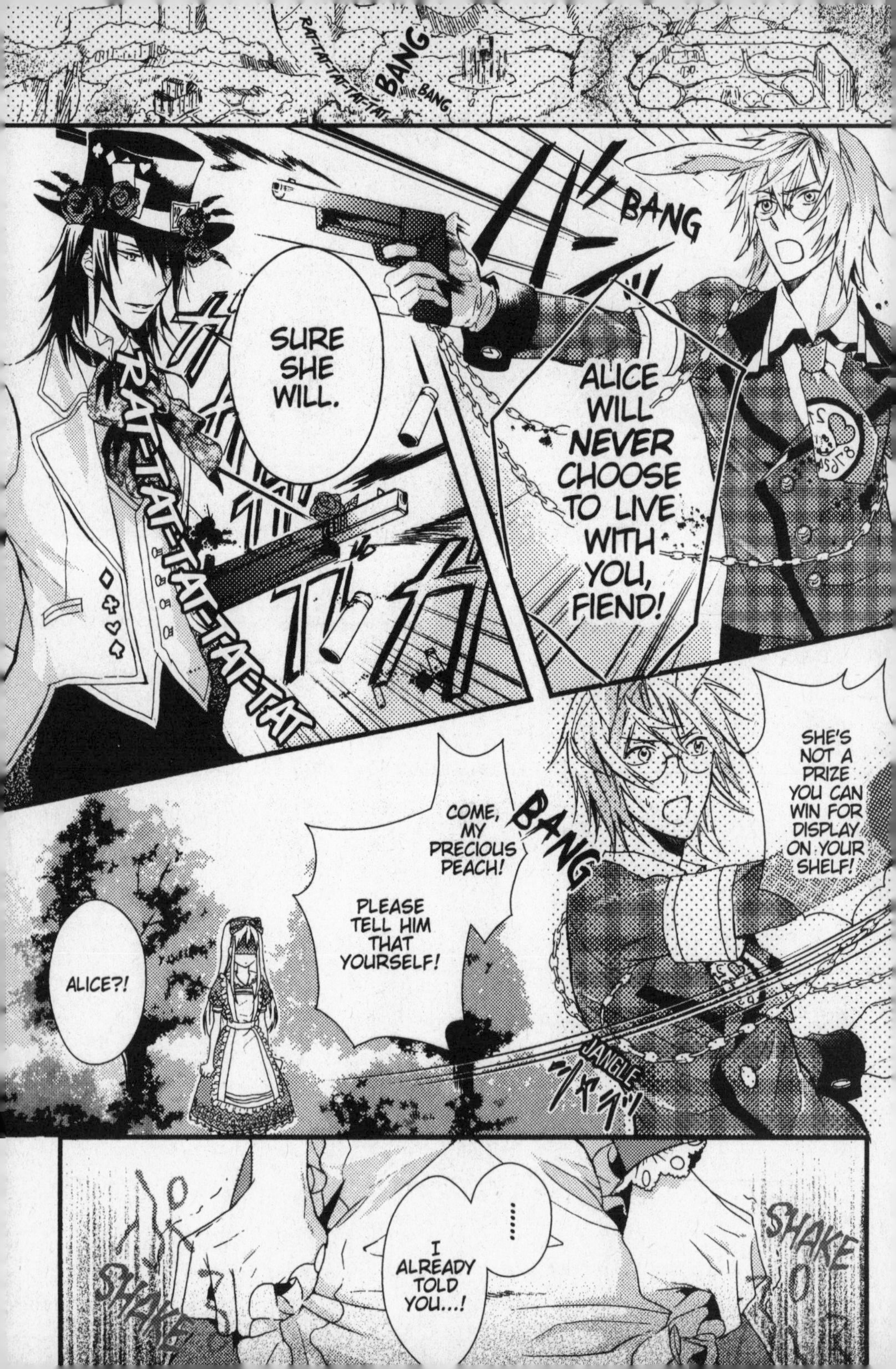

BANG
BANG
RAT-TAT-TAT-TAT-TAT
BANG
ALICE WILL NEVER CHOOSE TO LIVE WITH YOU, FIEND!
SURE SHE WILL.
RAT-TAT-TAT-TAT-TAT
SHE'S NOT A PRIZE YOU CAN WIN FOR DISPLAY ON YOUR SHELF!
BANG
COME, MY PRECIOUS PEACH!
PLEASE TELL HIM THAT YOURSELF!
JANGLE
ALICE?!
SHAKE
......
I ALREADY TOLD YOU...!
SHAKE

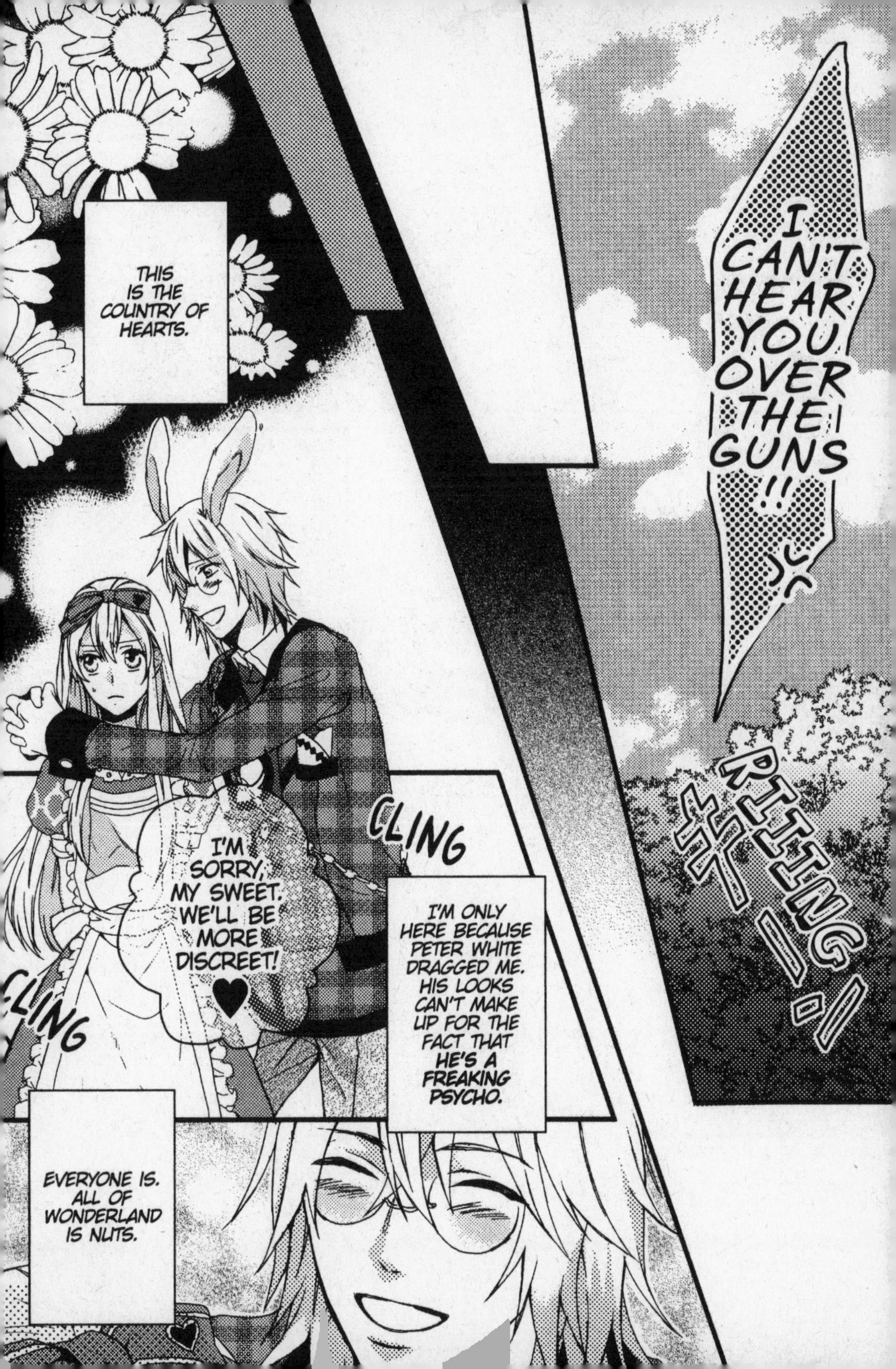
I CAN'T HEAR YOU OVER THE GUNS!!
RIIING--!
THIS IS THE COUNTRY OF HEARTS.
I'M ONLY HERE BECAUSE PETER WHITE DRAGGED ME. HIS LOOKS CAN'T MAKE UP FOR THE FACT THAT HE'S A FREAKING PSYCHO.
CLING
I'M SORRY, MY SWEET. WE'LL BE MORE DISCREET! ♥
CLING
EVERYONE IS. ALL OF WONDERLAND IS NUTS.

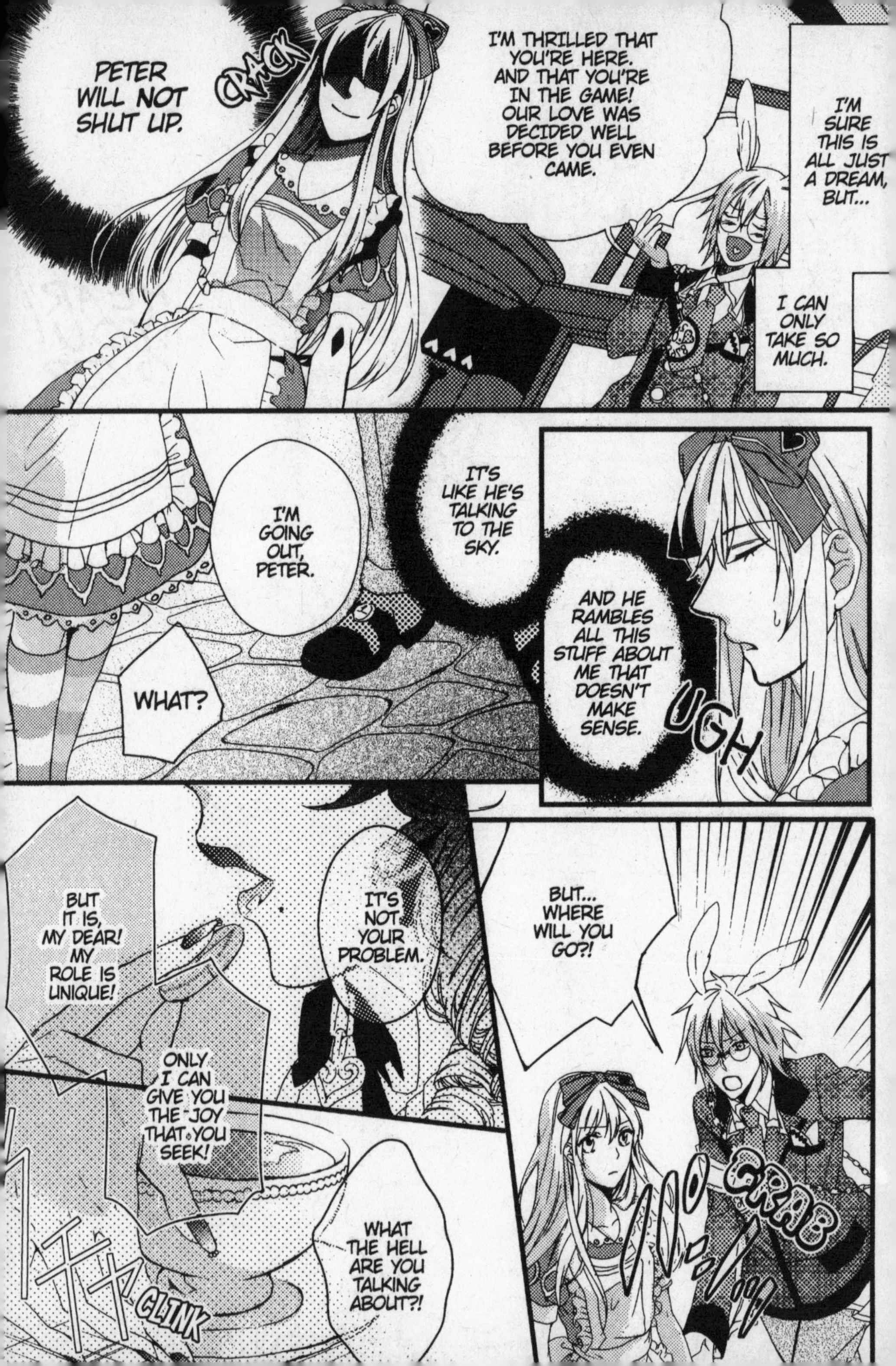
I'M SURE THIS IS ALL JUST A DREAM, BUT...
I'M THRILLED THAT YOU'RE HERE. AND THAT YOU'RE IN THE GAME! OUR LOVE WAS DECIDED WELL BEFORE YOU EVEN CAME.
I CAN ONLY TAKE SO MUCH.
CRACK
PETER WILL NOT SHUT UP.
IT'S LIKE HE'S TALKING TO THE SKY.
AND HE RAMBLES ALL THIS STUFF ABOUT ME THAT DOESN'T MAKE SENSE.
UGH
I'M GOING OUT, PETER.
WHAT?
BUT... WHERE WILL YOU GO?!
GRAB
IT'S NOT YOUR PROBLEM.
BUT IT IS, MY DEAR! MY ROLE IS UNIQUE!
ONLY I CAN GIVE YOU THE JOY THAT YOU SEEK!
WHAT THE HELL ARE YOU TALKING ABOUT?!
CLINK

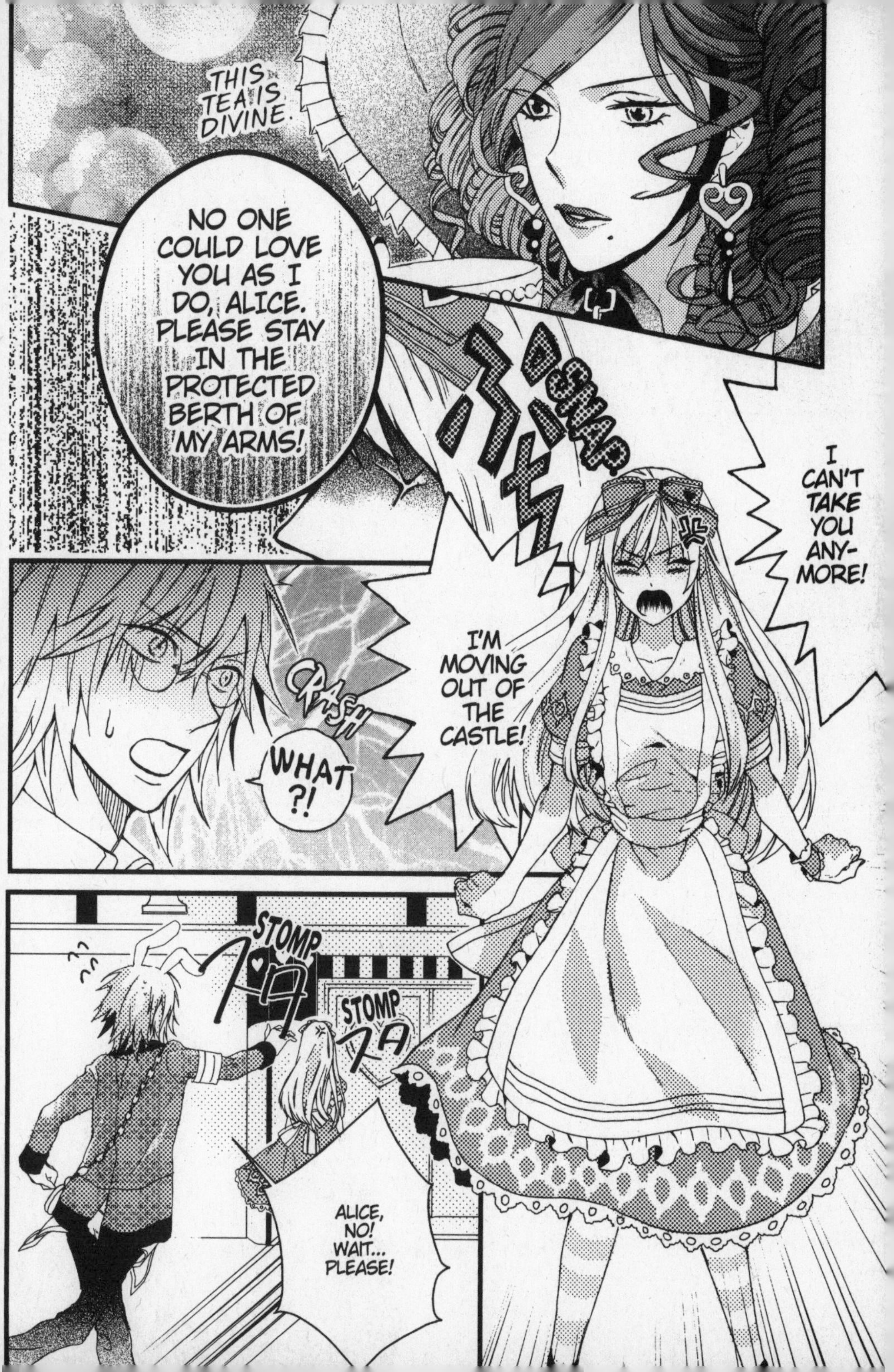
THIS TEA IS DIVINE.
NO ONE COULD LOVE YOU AS I DO, ALICE. PLEASE STAY IN THE PROTECTED BERTH OF MY ARMS!
SNAP
I CAN'T TAKE YOU ANYMORE!
I'M MOVING OUT OF THE CASTLE!
CRASH
WHAT?!
STOMP
STOMP
ALICE, NO! WAIT... PLEASE!

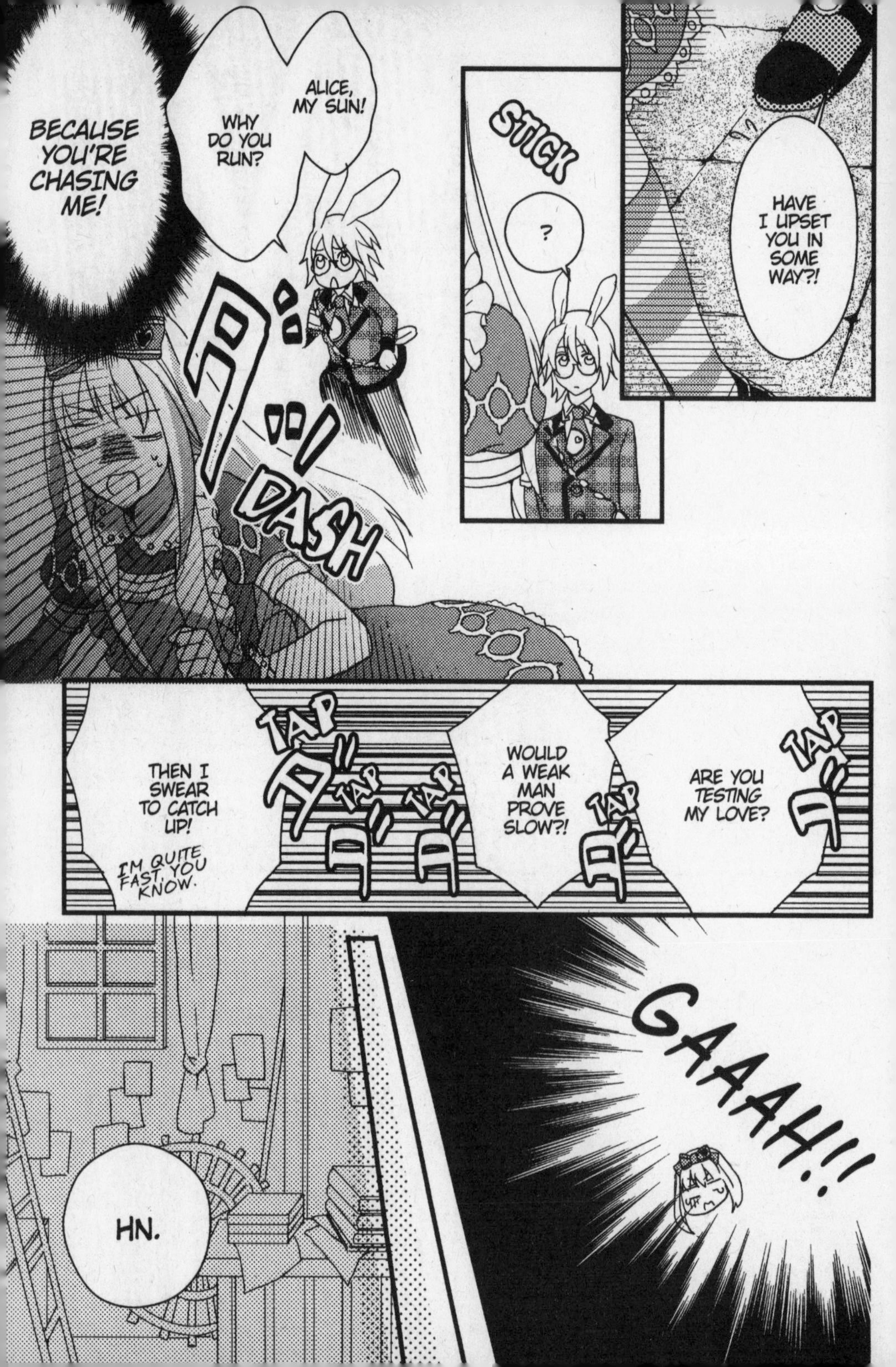
HAVE I UPSET YOU IN SOME WAY?!
STICK
?
ALICE, MY SUN!
WHY DO YOU RUN?
BECAUSE YOU'RE CHASING ME!
DASH
TAP
ARE YOU TESTING MY LOVE?
TAP
WOULD A WEAK MAN PROVE SLOW?!
TAP
TAP
TAP
THEN I SWEAR TO CATCH UP!
I'M QUITE FAST YOU KNOW.
GAAAH!!
HN.

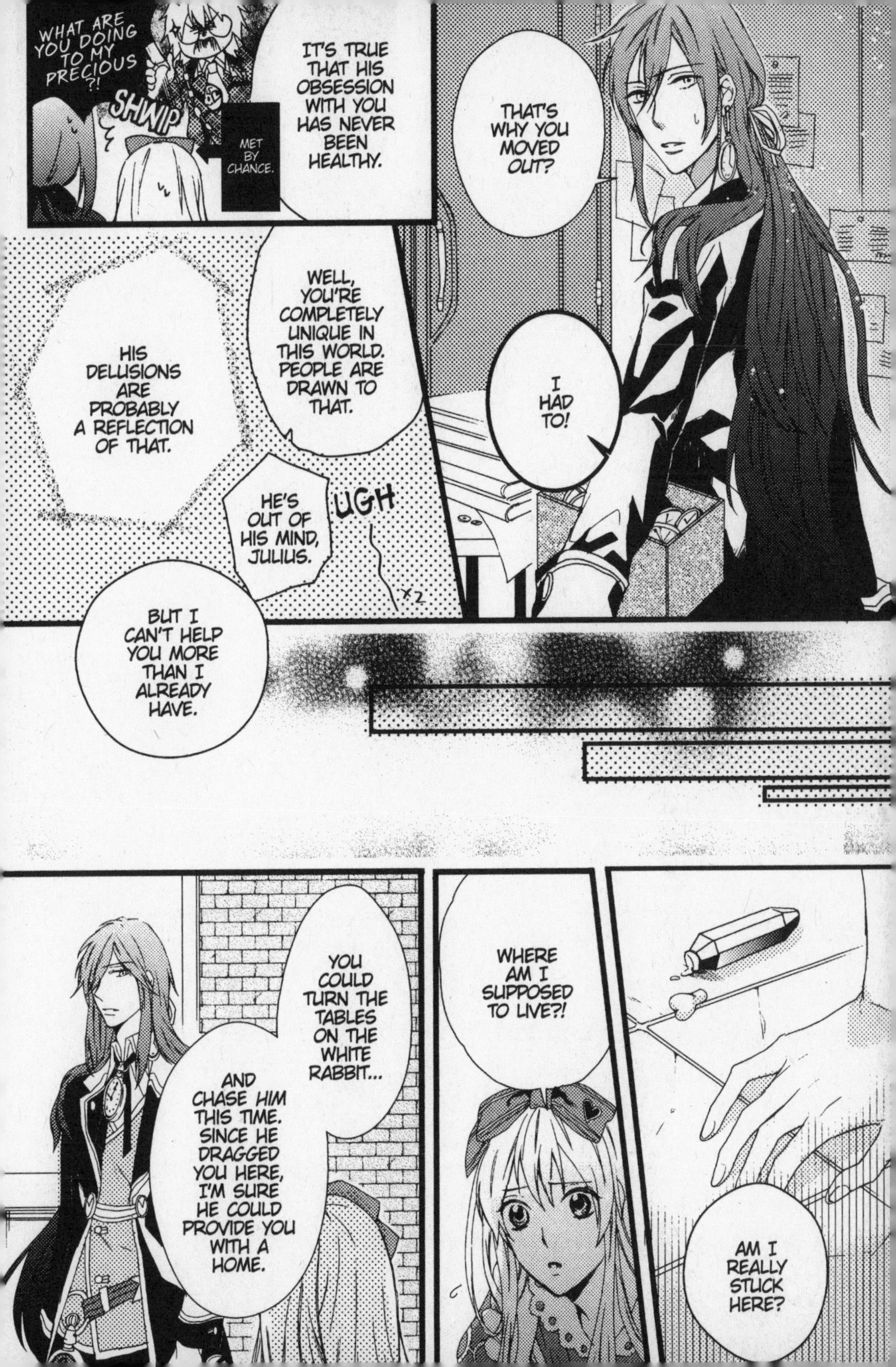
THAT'S WHY YOU MOVED OUT?
I HAD TO!
IT'S TRUE THAT HIS OBSESSION WITH YOU HAS NEVER BEEN HEALTHY.
WHAT ARE YOU DOING TO MY PRECIOUS ?!
SHWIP
MET BY CHANCE.
WELL, YOU'RE COMPLETELY UNIQUE IN THIS WORLD. PEOPLE ARE DRAWN TO THAT.
HIS DELUSIONS ARE PROBABLY A REFLECTION OF THAT.
UGH
HE'S OUT OF HIS MIND, JULIUS.
BUT I CAN'T HELP YOU MORE THAN I ALREADY HAVE.
AM I REALLY STUCK HERE?
WHERE AM I SUPPOSED TO LIVE?!
YOU COULD TURN THE TABLES ON THE WHITE RABBIT...
AND CHASE HIM THIS TIME. SINCE HE DRAGGED YOU HERE, I'M SURE HE COULD PROVIDE YOU WITH A HOME.

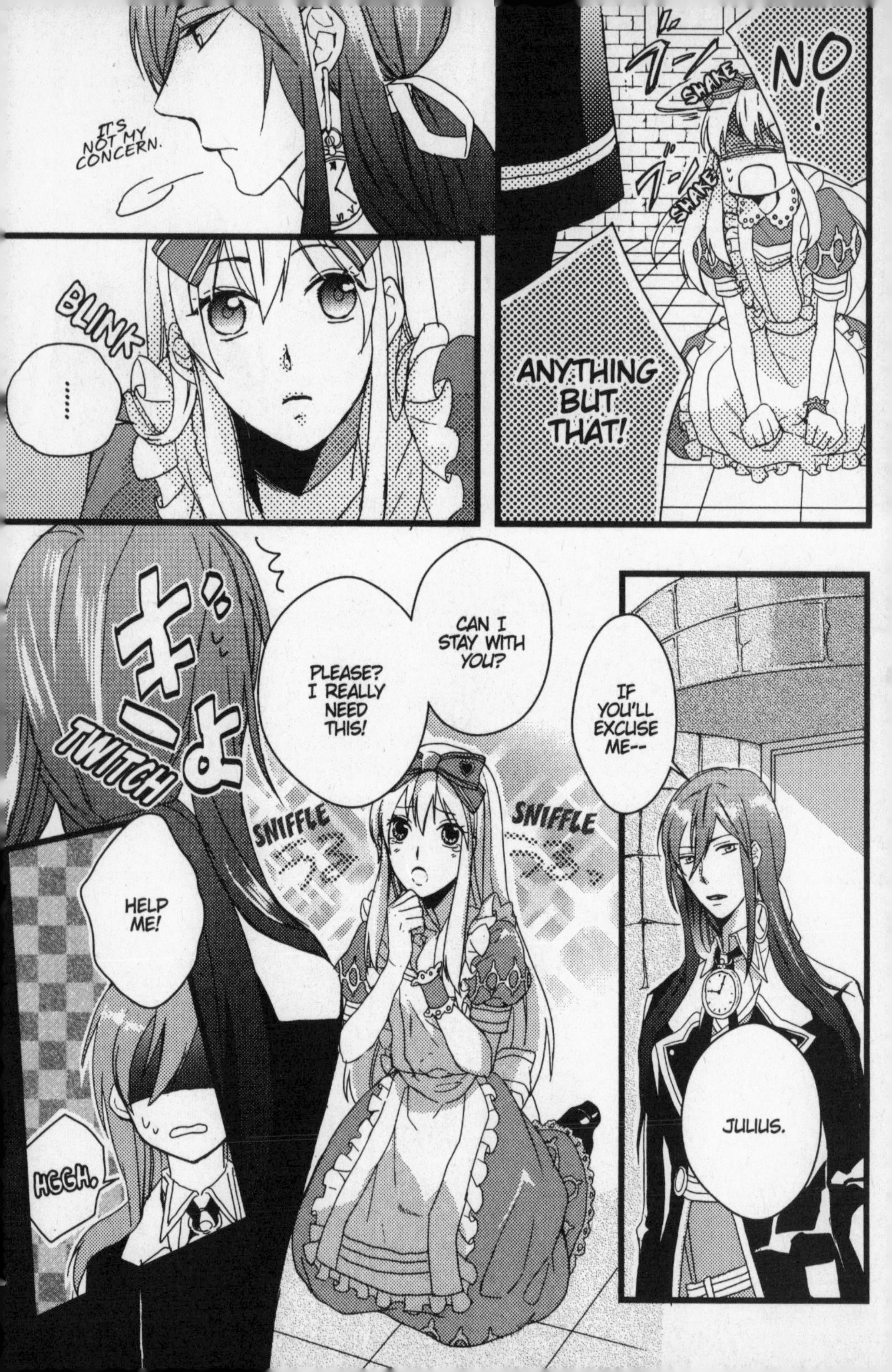
SHAKE
SHAKE
NO!
ANYTHING BUT THAT!
IT'S NOT MY CONCERN.
BLINK
......
IF YOU'LL EXCUSE ME--
JULIUS.
CAN I STAY WITH YOU?
PLEASE? I REALLY NEED THIS!
SNIFFLE
SNIFFLE
TWITCH
HELP ME!
HGGH.

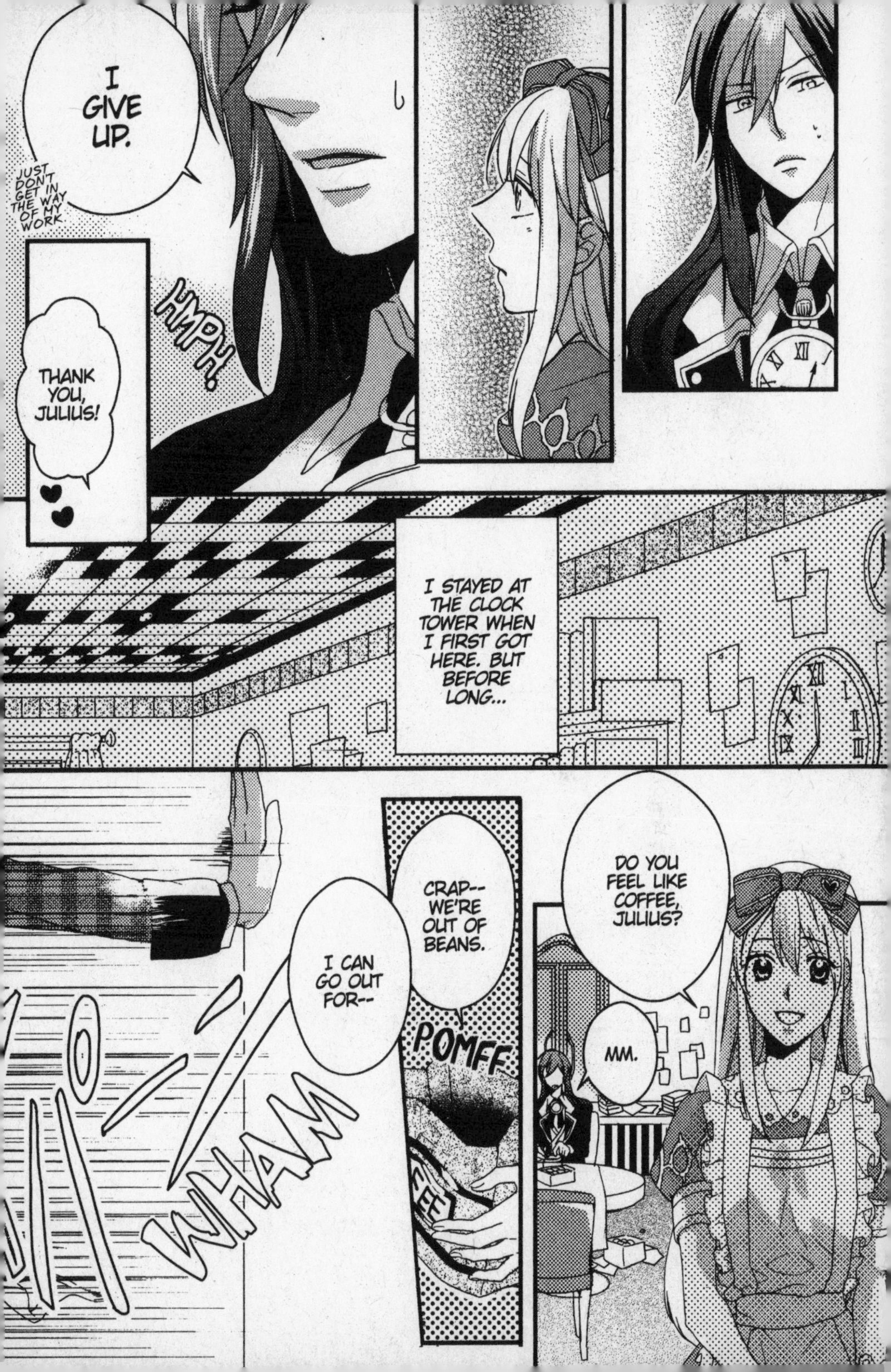

I GIVE UP.
JUST DON'T GET IN THE WAY OF MY WORK.
HMPH.
THANK YOU, JULIUS!
I STAYED AT THE CLOCK TOWER WHEN I FIRST GOT HERE. BUT BEFORE LONG...
DO YOU FEEL LIKE COFFEE, JULIUS?
MM.
CRAP-- WE'RE OUT OF BEANS.
POMFF
I CAN GO OUT FOR--
WHAM

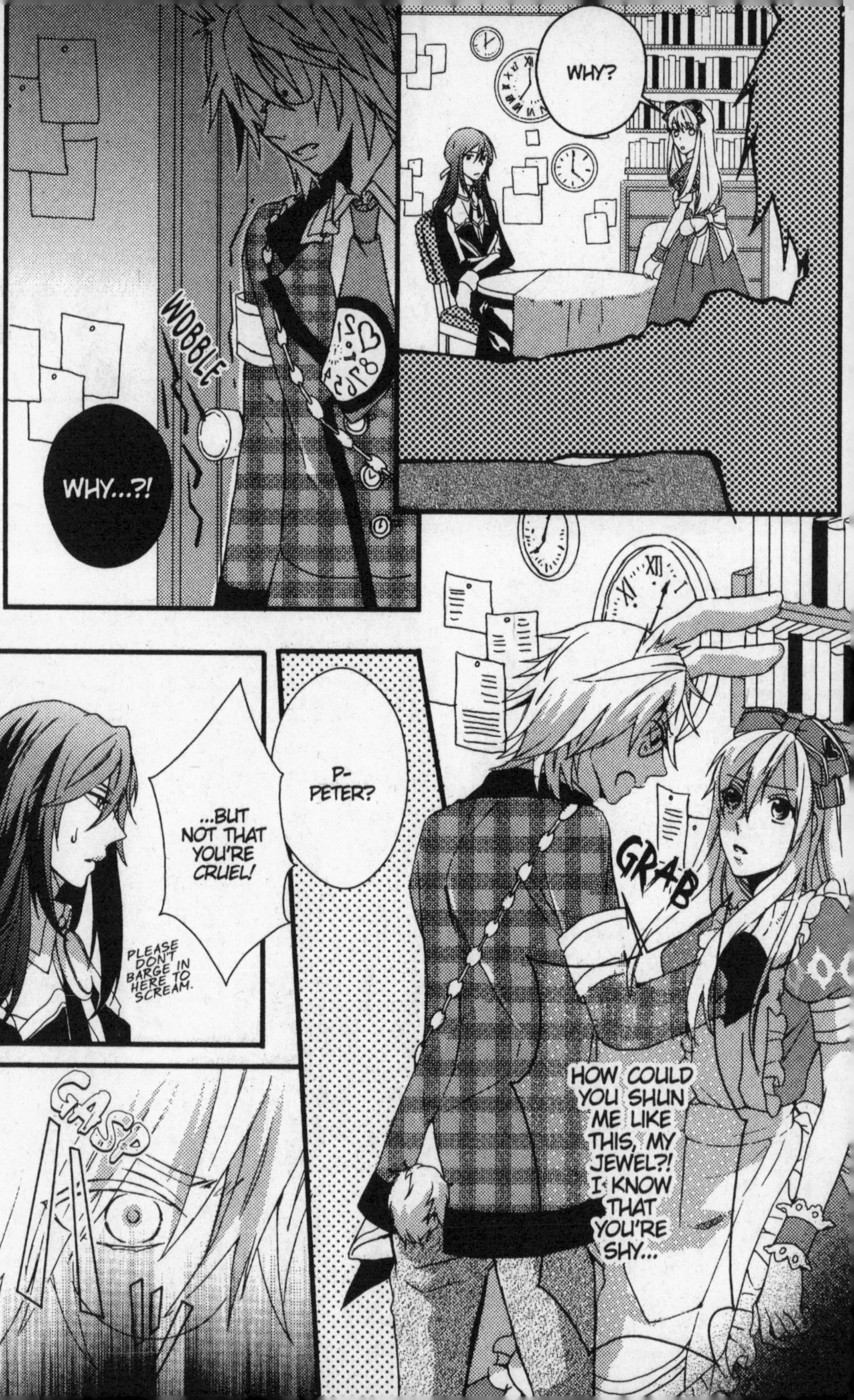
WHY?
WOBBLE
WHY...?!
GRAB
HOW COULD YOU SHUN ME LIKE THIS, MY JEWEL?! I KNOW THAT YOU'RE SHY...
P-PETER?
...BUT NOT THAT YOU'RE CRUEL!
PLEASE DON'T BARGE IN HERE TO SCREAM.
GASP

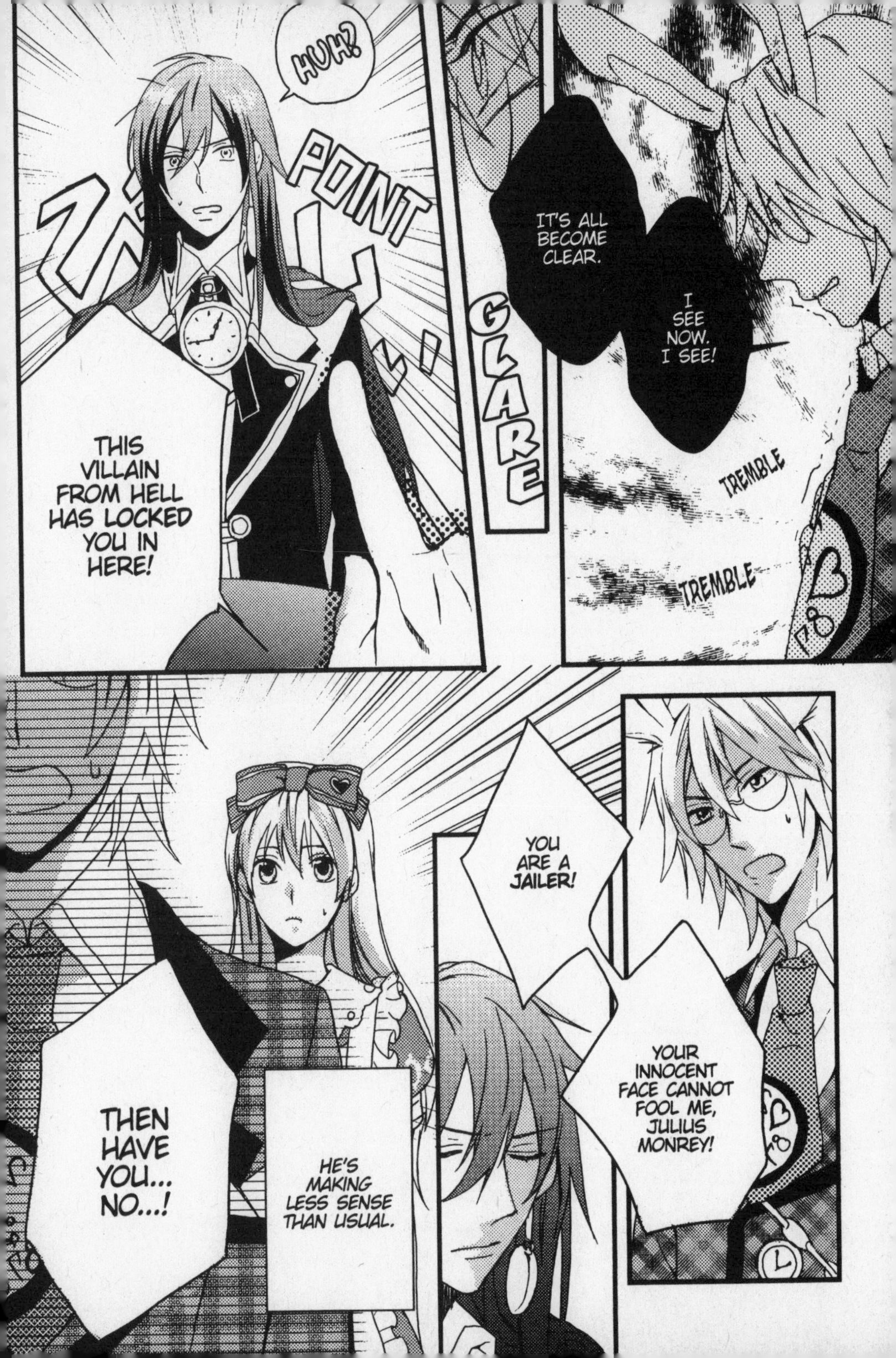
IT'S ALL BECOME CLEAR.
I SEE NOW. I SEE!
TREMBLE
TREMBLE
GLARE
HUH?
POINT
THIS VILLAIN FROM HELL HAS LOCKED YOU IN HERE!
YOU ARE A JAILER!
YOUR INNOCENT FACE CANNOT FOOL ME, JULIUS MONREY!
HE'S MAKING LESS SENSE THAN USUAL.
THEN HAVE YOU... NO...!

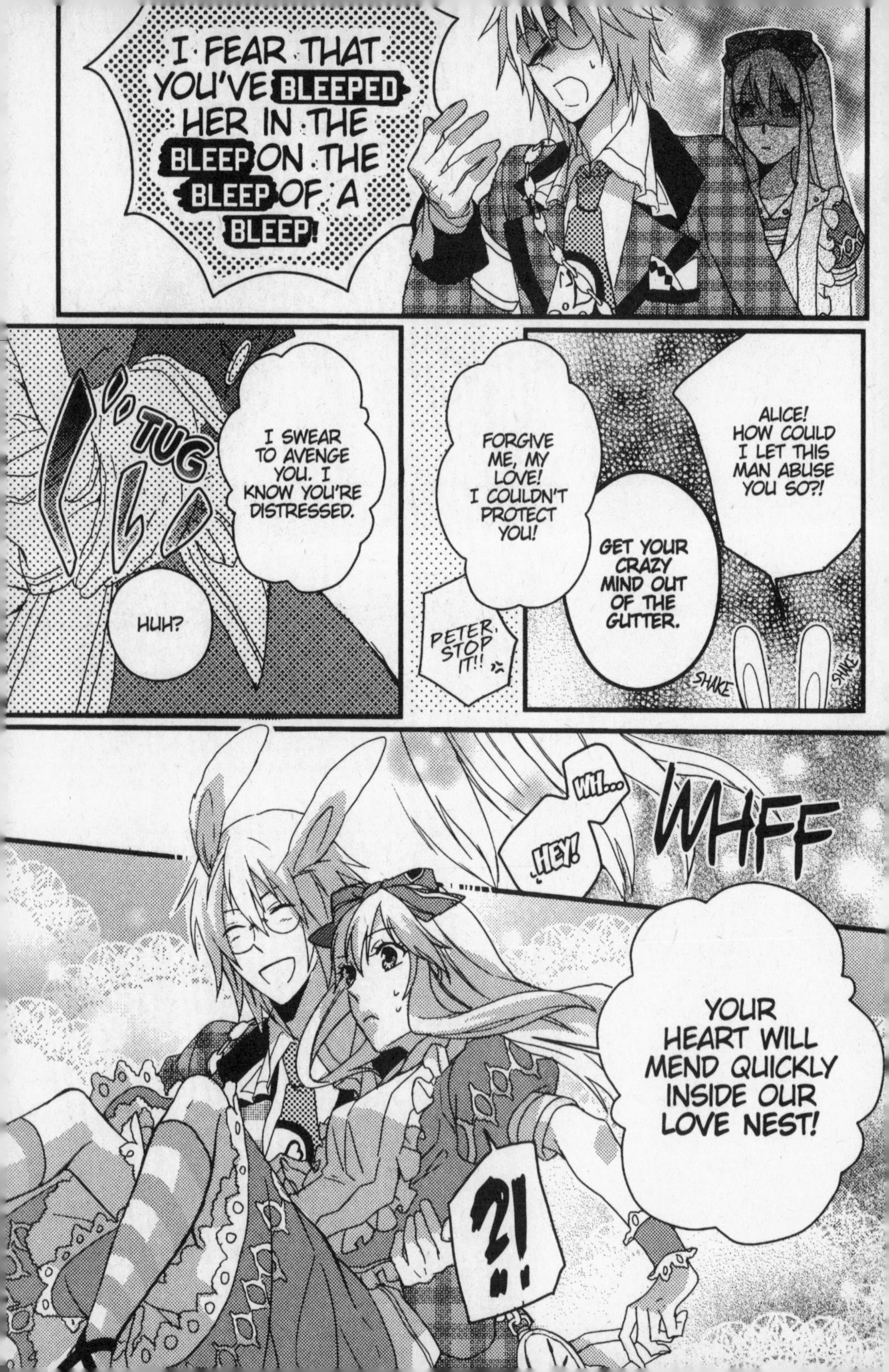
I FEAR THAT YOU'VE BLEEPED HER IN THE BLEEP ON THE BLEEP OF A BLEEP!
ALICE! HOW COULD I LET THIS MAN ABUSE YOU SO?!
GET YOUR CRAZY MIND OUT OF THE GUTTER.
SHAKE
SHAKE
FORGIVE ME, MY LOVE! I COULDN'T PROTECT YOU!
PETER, STOP IT!!
I SWEAR TO AVENGE YOU. I KNOW YOU'RE DISTRESSED.
TUG
HUH?
WHFF
WH...
HEY!
YOUR HEART WILL MEND QUICKLY INSIDE OUR LOVE NEST!
?!

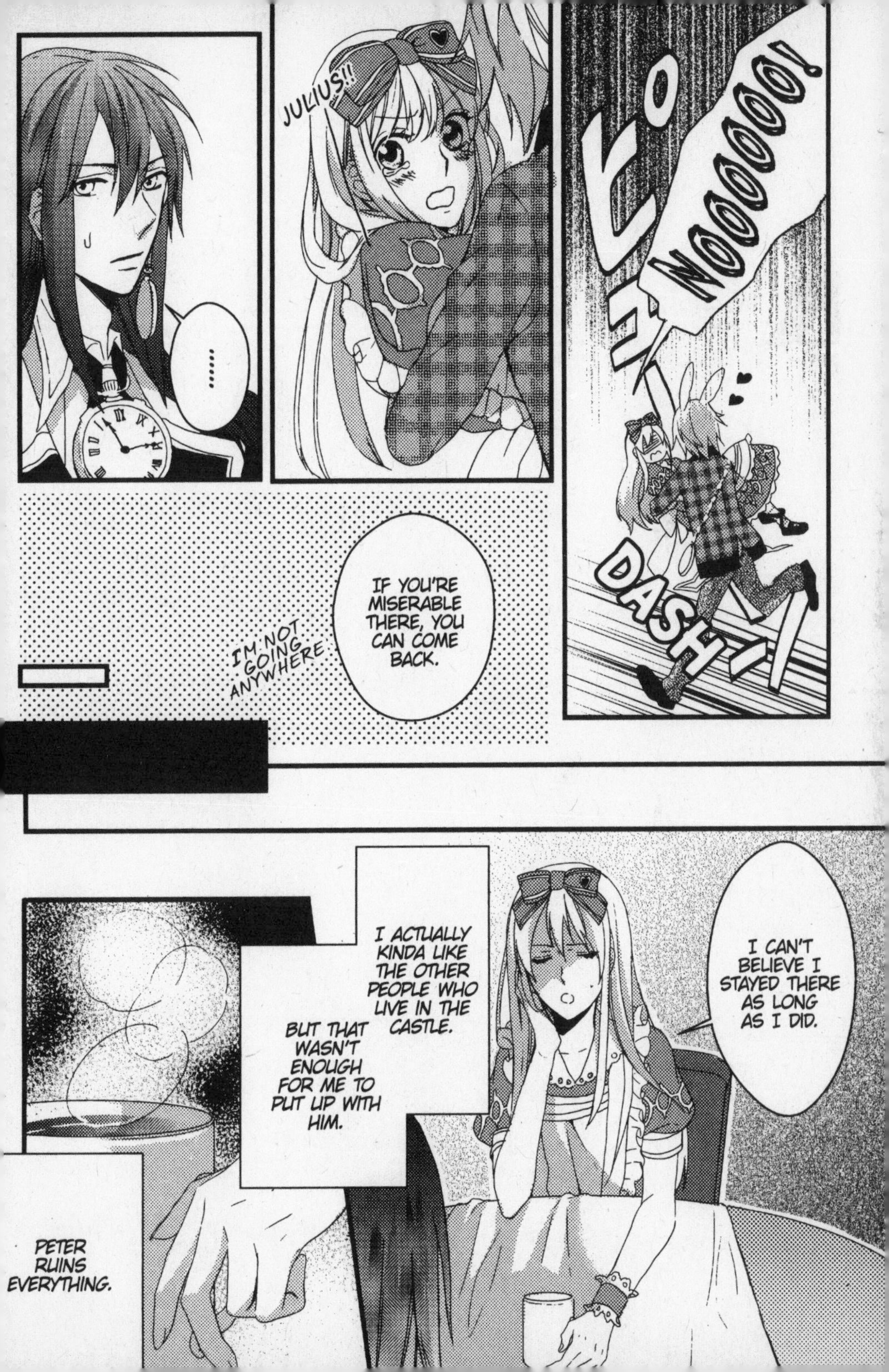
NOOOOOOOO!
DASH
JULIUS!!
......
IF YOU'RE MISERABLE THERE, YOU CAN COME BACK.
I'M NOT GOING ANYWHERE
I CAN'T BELIEVE I STAYED THERE AS LONG AS I DID.
I ACTUALLY KINDA LIKE THE OTHER PEOPLE WHO LIVE IN THE CASTLE.
BUT THAT WASN'T ENOUGH FOR ME TO PUT UP WITH HIM.
PETER RUINS EVERYTHING.

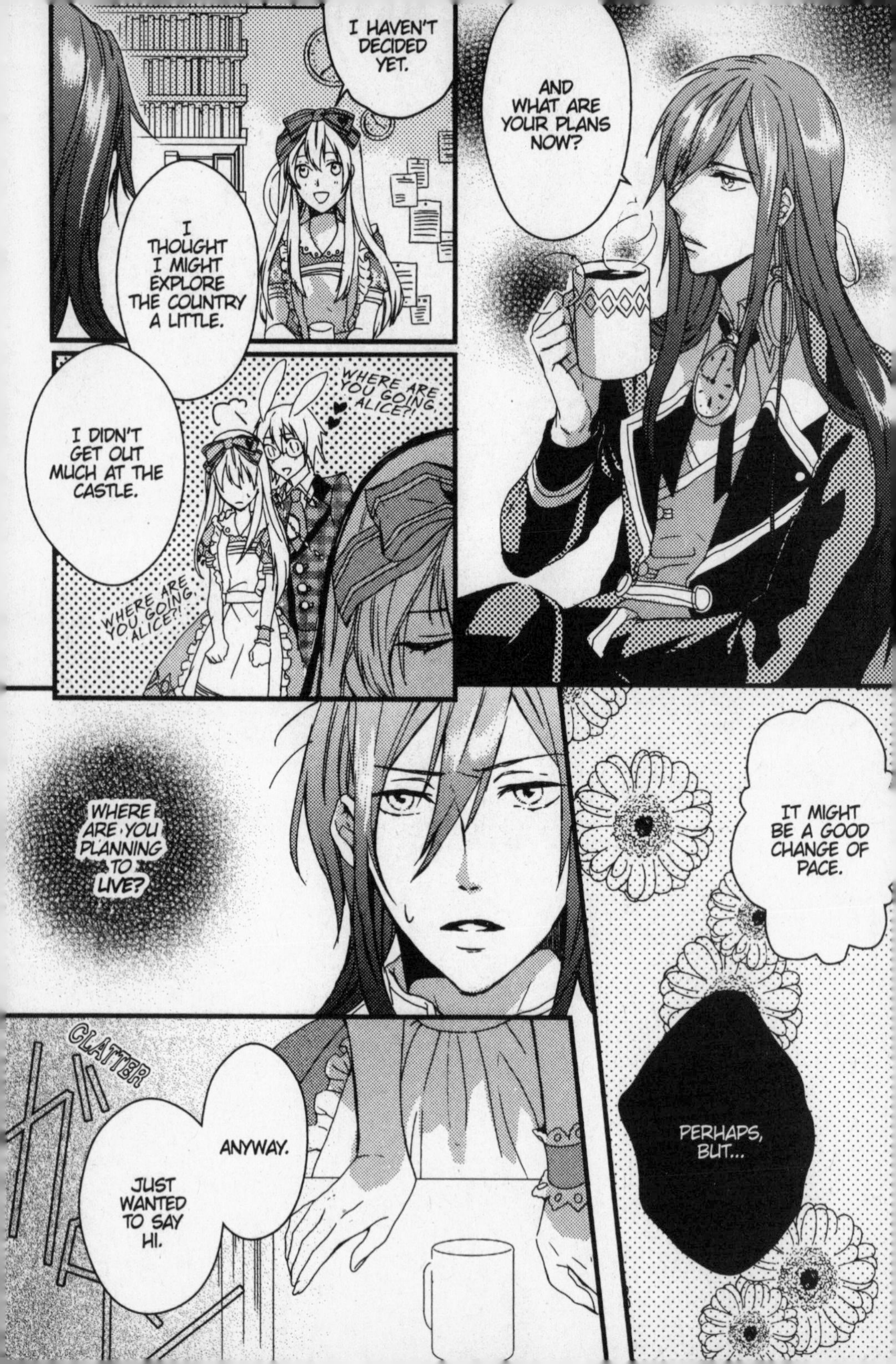

AND WHAT ARE YOUR PLANS NOW?
I HAVEN'T DECIDED YET.
I THOUGHT I MIGHT EXPLORE THE COUNTRY A LITTLE.
I DIDN'T GET OUT MUCH AT THE CASTLE.
WHERE ARE YOU GOING ALICE?!
WHERE ARE YOU GOING ALICE?!
IT MIGHT BE A GOOD CHANGE OF PACE.
PERHAPS, BUT...
WHERE ARE YOU PLANNING TO LIVE?
CLATTER
ANYWAY.
JUST WANTED TO SAY HI.

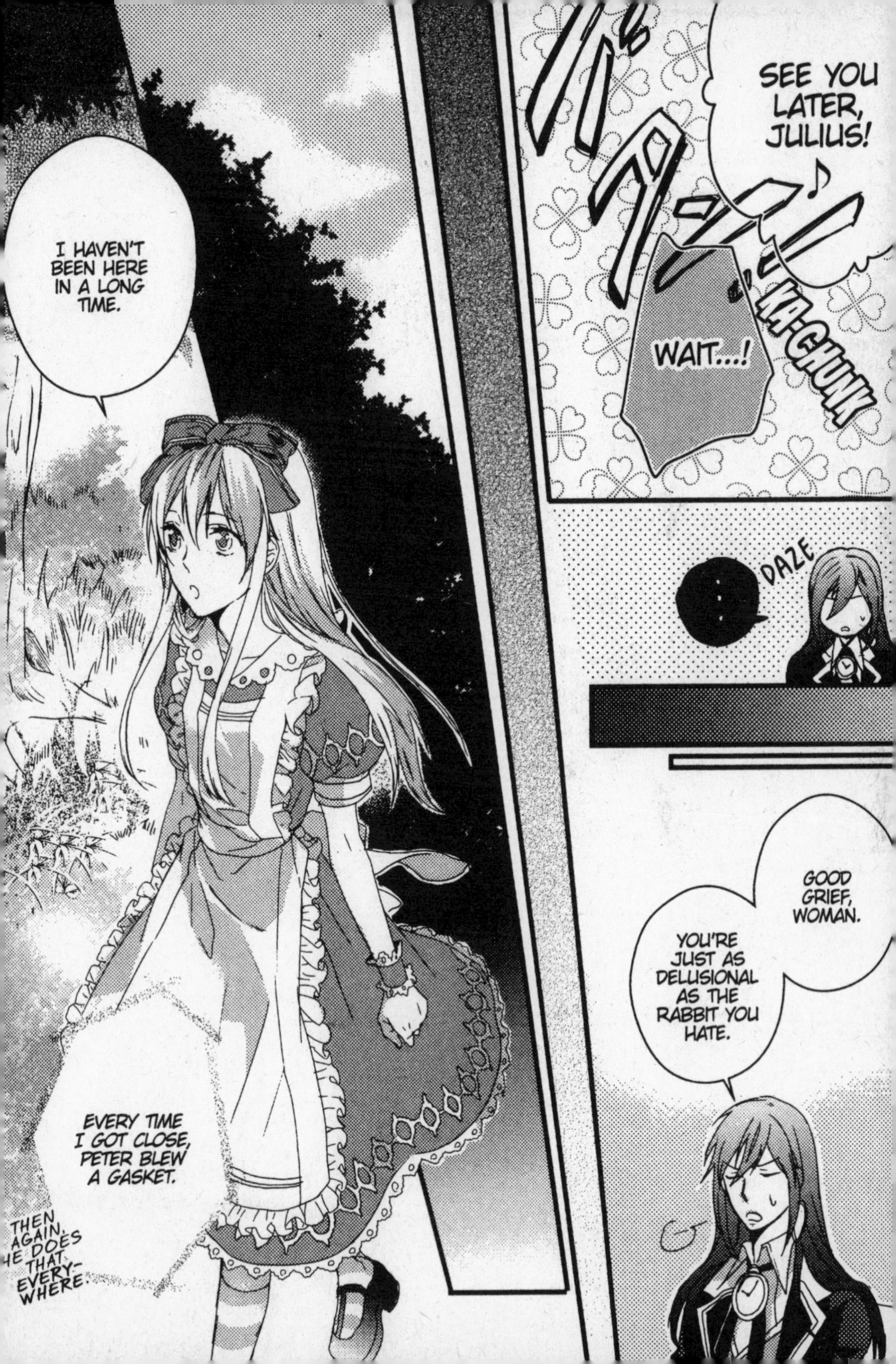
SEE YOU LATER, JULIUS! ♪
KA-CHUNK
WAIT...!
DAZE
...
GOOD GRIEF, WOMAN.
YOU'RE JUST AS DELUSIONAL AS THE RABBIT YOU HATE.
I HAVEN'T BEEN HERE IN A LONG TIME.
EVERY TIME I GOT CLOSE, PETER BLEW A GASKET.
THEN AGAIN, HE DOES THAT EVERY-WHERE.

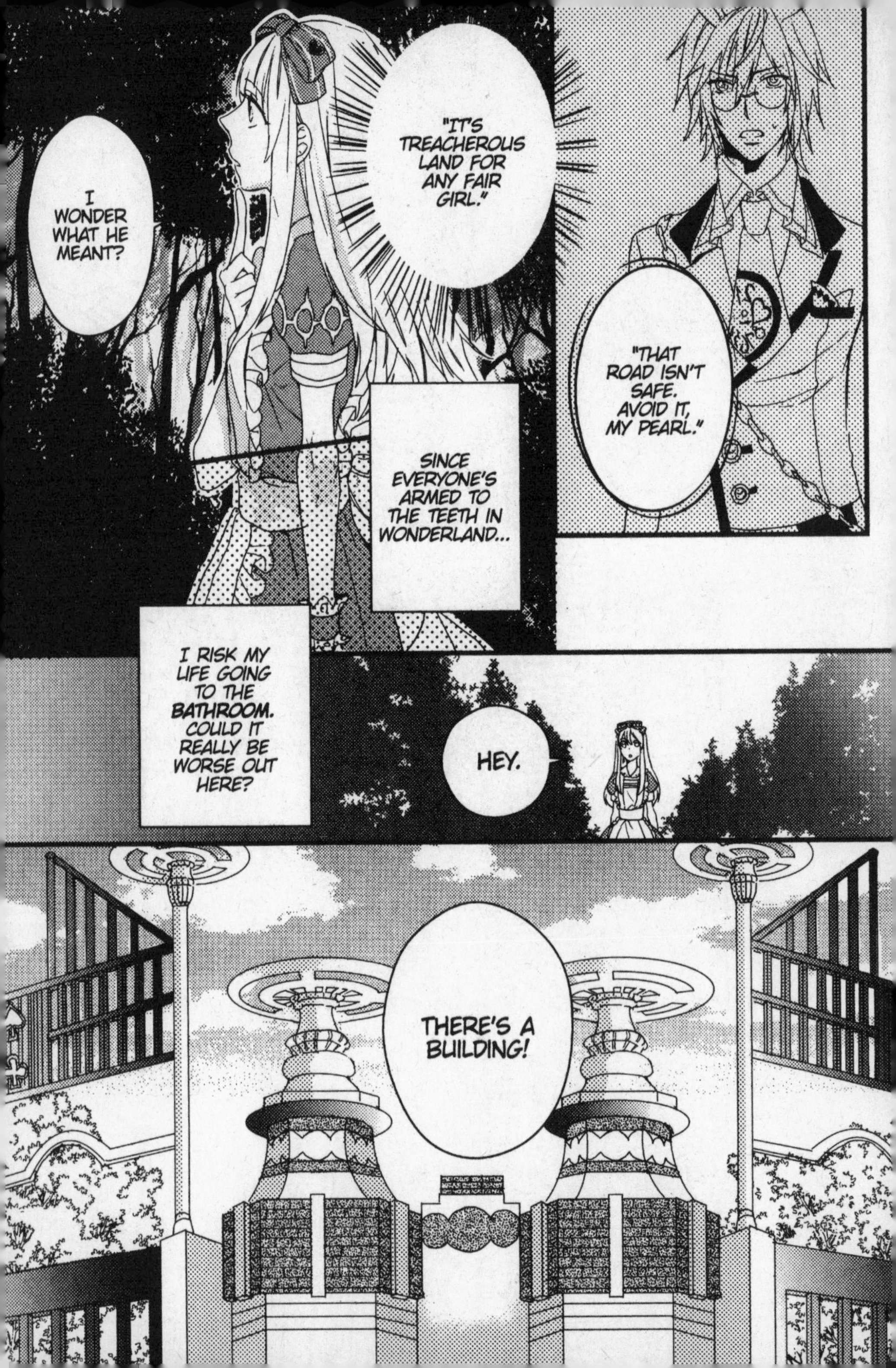
"THAT ROAD ISN'T SAFE. AVOID IT, MY PEARL."
"IT'S TREACHEROUS LAND FOR ANY FAIR GIRL."
I WONDER WHAT HE MEANT?
SINCE EVERYONE'S ARMED TO THE TEETH IN WONDERLAND...
I RISK MY LIFE GOING TO THE BATHROOM. COULD IT REALLY BE WORSE OUT HERE?
HEY.
THERE'S A BUILDING!

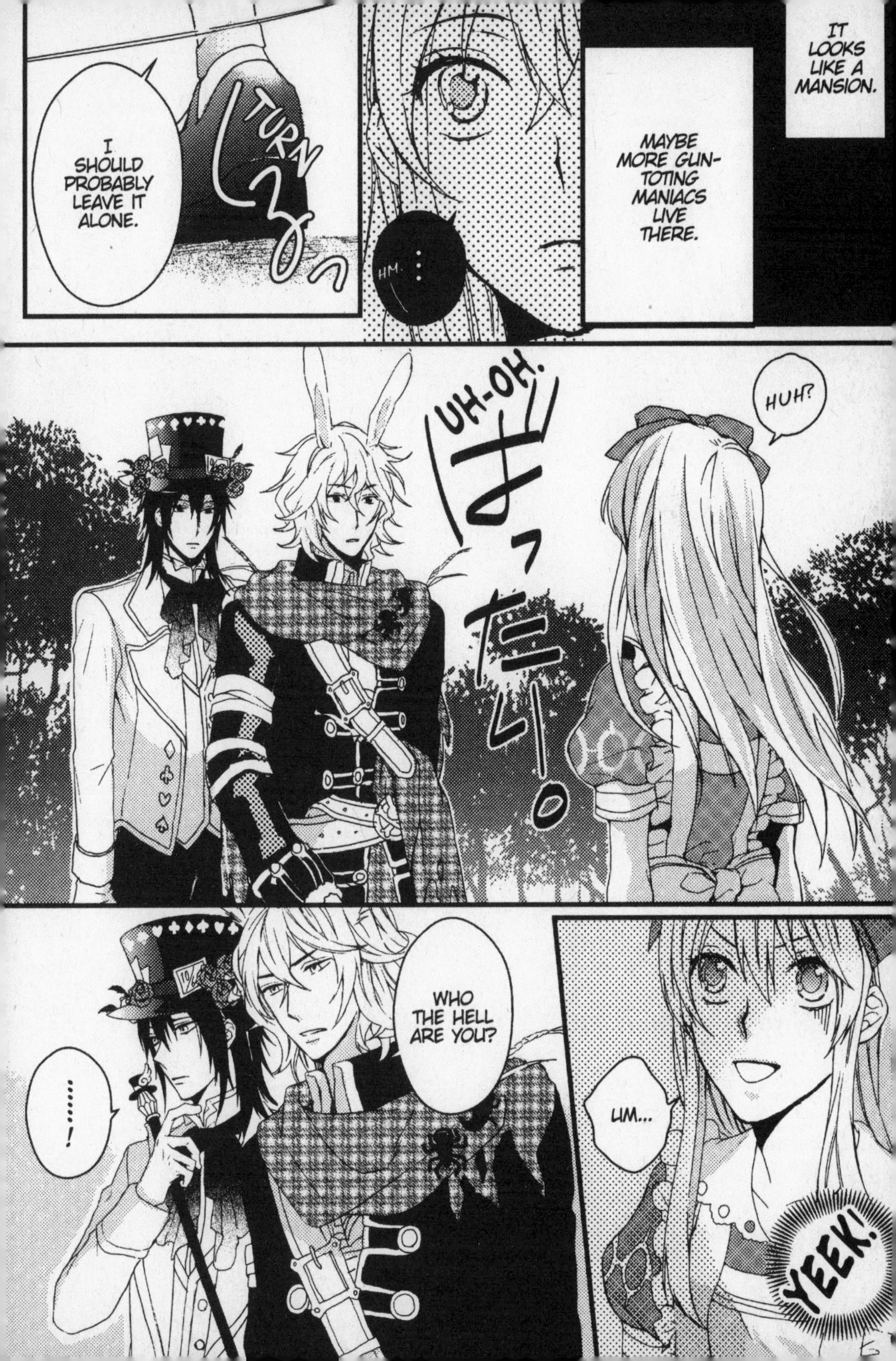
IT LOOKS LIKE A MANSION.
MAYBE MORE GUN-TOTING MANIACS LIVE THERE.
HM...
TURN
I SHOULD PROBABLY LEAVE IT ALONE.
HUH?
UH-OH.
UM...
YEEK!
WHO THE HELL ARE YOU?
......!

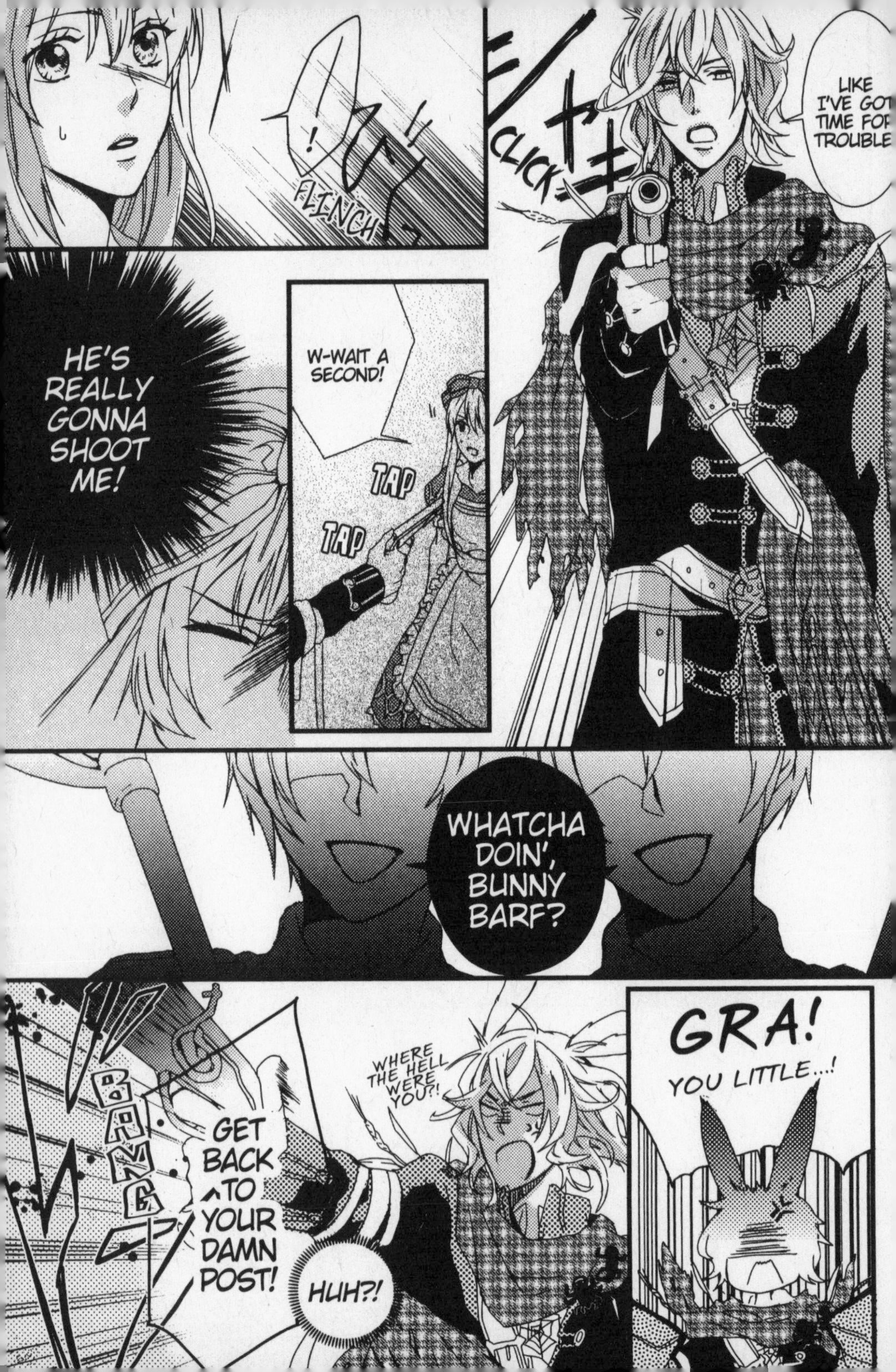
LIKE I'VE GOT TIME FOR TROUBLE
CLICK
!
FLINCH
HE'S REALLY GONNA SHOOT ME!
W-WAIT A SECOND!
TAP
TAP
WHATCHA DOIN', BUNNY BARF?
GRA!
YOU LITTLE...!
WHERE THE HELL WERE YOU?!
GET BACK TO YOUR DAMN POST!
HUH?!
BOING

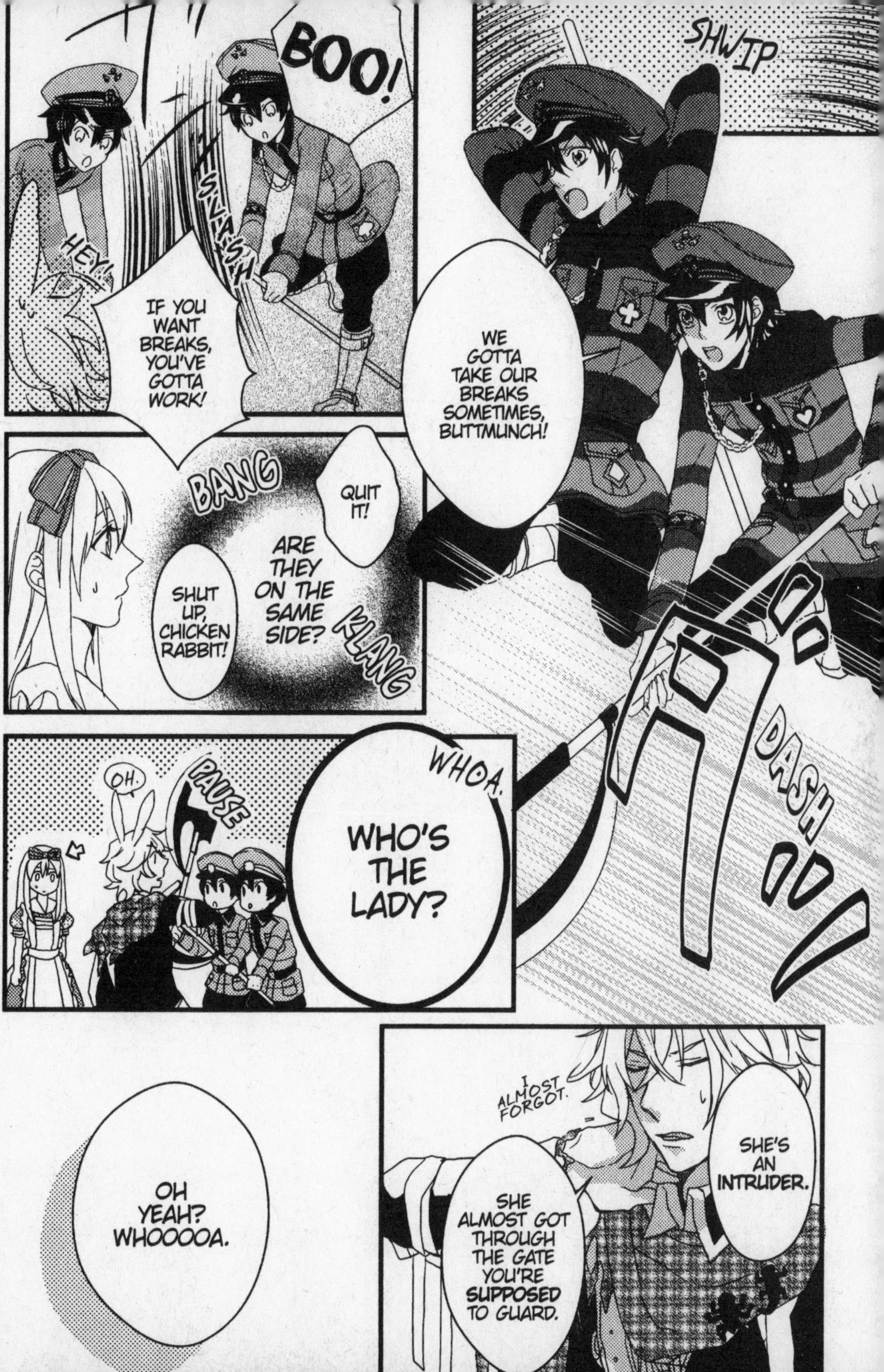
SHWIP
WE GOTTA TAKE OUR BREAKS SOMETIMES, BUTTMUNCH!
DASH
BOO!
SLASH
HEY!
IF YOU WANT BREAKS, YOU'VE GOTTA WORK!
BANG
QUIT IT!
ARE THEY ON THE SAME SIDE?
SHUT UP, CHICKEN RABBIT!
KLANG
WHOA.
WHO'S THE LADY?
PAUSE
OH.
I ALMOST FORGOT.
SHE'S AN INTRUDER.
SHE ALMOST GOT THROUGH THE GATE YOU'RE SUPPOSED TO GUARD.
OH YEAH? WHOOOOA.

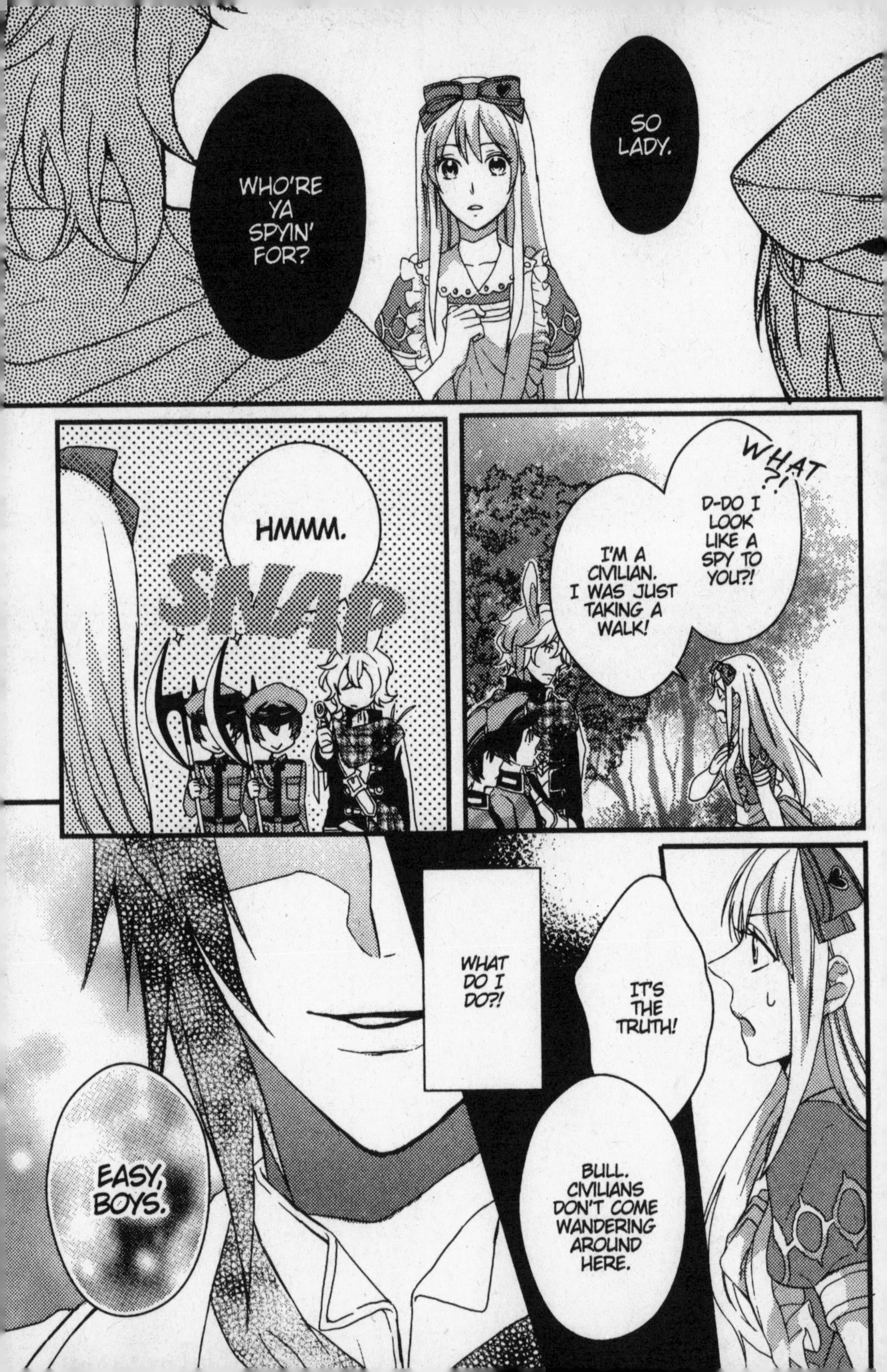
SO LADY.
WHO'RE YA SPYIN' FOR?
WHAT ?!
D-DO I LOOK LIKE A SPY TO YOU?!
I'M A CIVILIAN. I WAS JUST TAKING A WALK!
HMMM.
SNAP
IT'S THE TRUTH!
WHAT DO I DO?!
BULL. CIVILIANS DON'T COME WANDERING AROUND HERE.
EASY, BOYS.

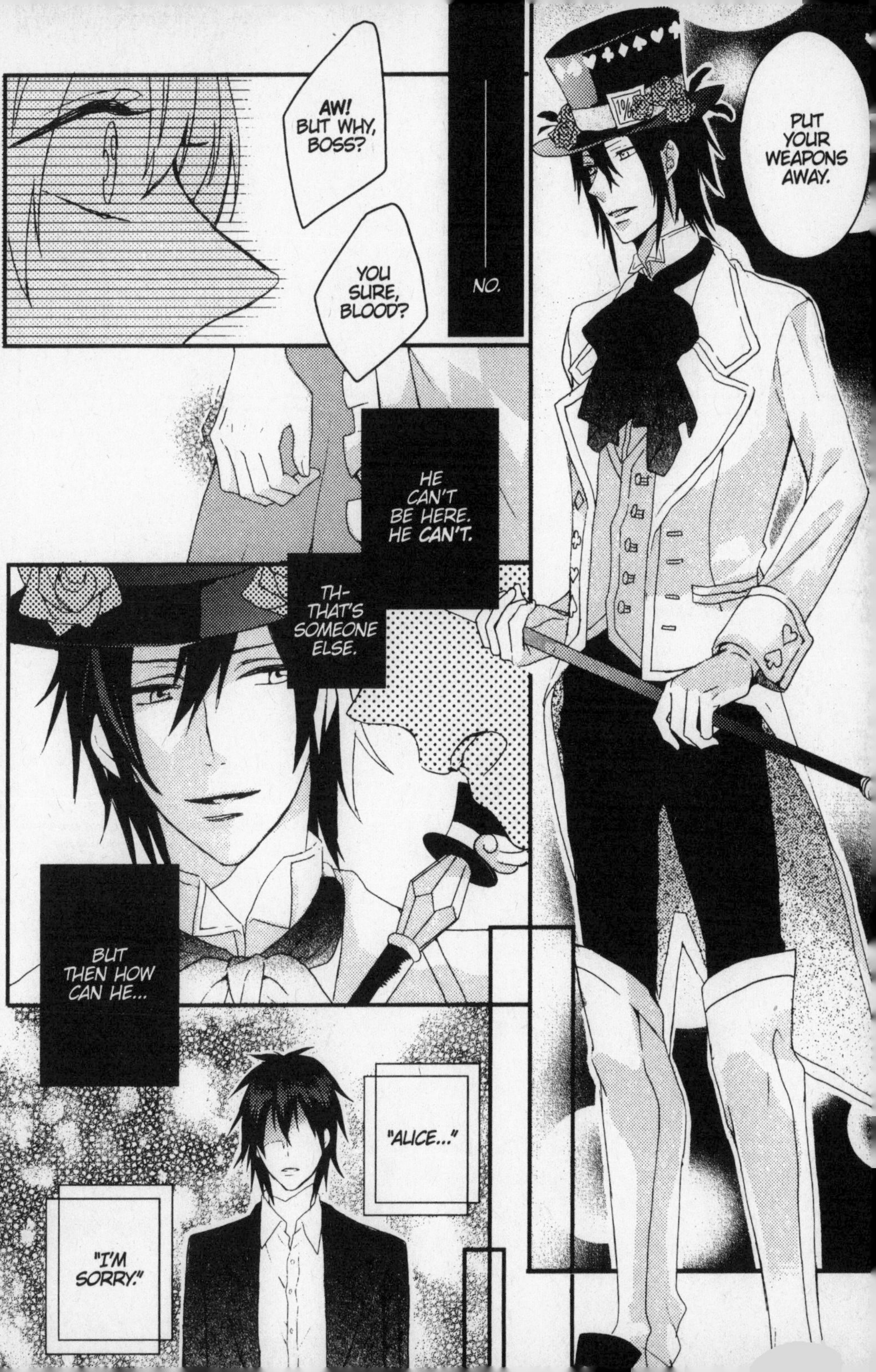
PUT YOUR WEAPONS AWAY.
AW! BUT WHY, BOSS?
YOU SURE, BLOOD?
NO.
HE CAN'T BE HERE. HE CAN'T.
TH-THAT'S SOMEONE ELSE.
BUT THEN HOW CAN HE...
"ALICE..."
"I'M SORRY."

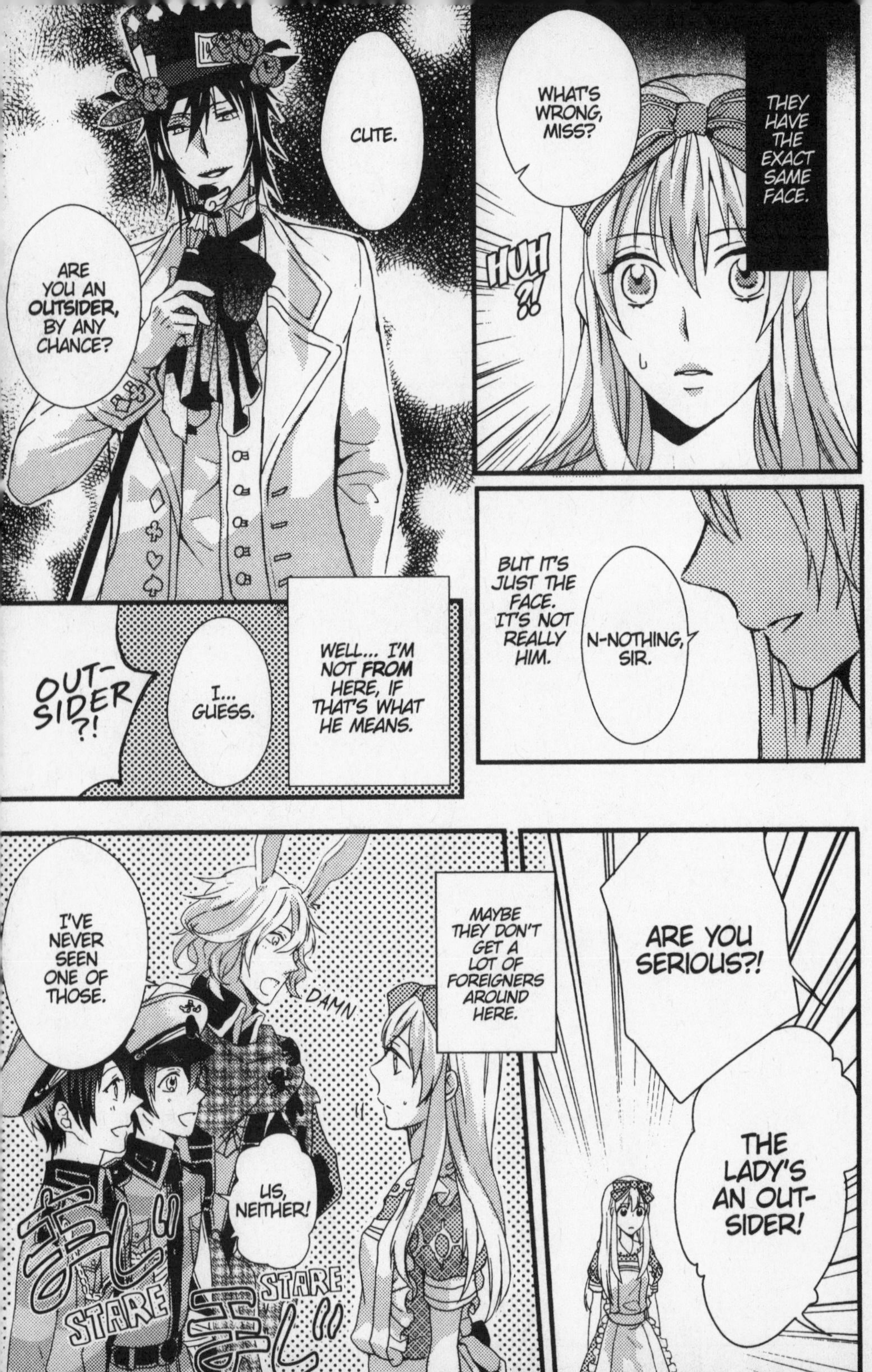
WHAT'S WRONG, MISS?
HUH?!
THEY HAVE THE EXACT SAME FACE.
N-NOTHING, SIR.
BUT IT'S JUST THE FACE. IT'S NOT REALLY HIM.
CUTE.
ARE YOU AN OUTSIDER, BY ANY CHANCE?
WELL... I'M NOT FROM HERE, IF THAT'S WHAT HE MEANS.
I... GUESS.
OUT-SIDER?!
ARE YOU SERIOUS?!
THE LADY'S AN OUT-SIDER!
MAYBE THEY DON'T GET A LOT OF FOREIGNERS AROUND HERE.
I'VE NEVER SEEN ONE OF THOSE.
DAMN
US, NEITHER!
STARE
STARE

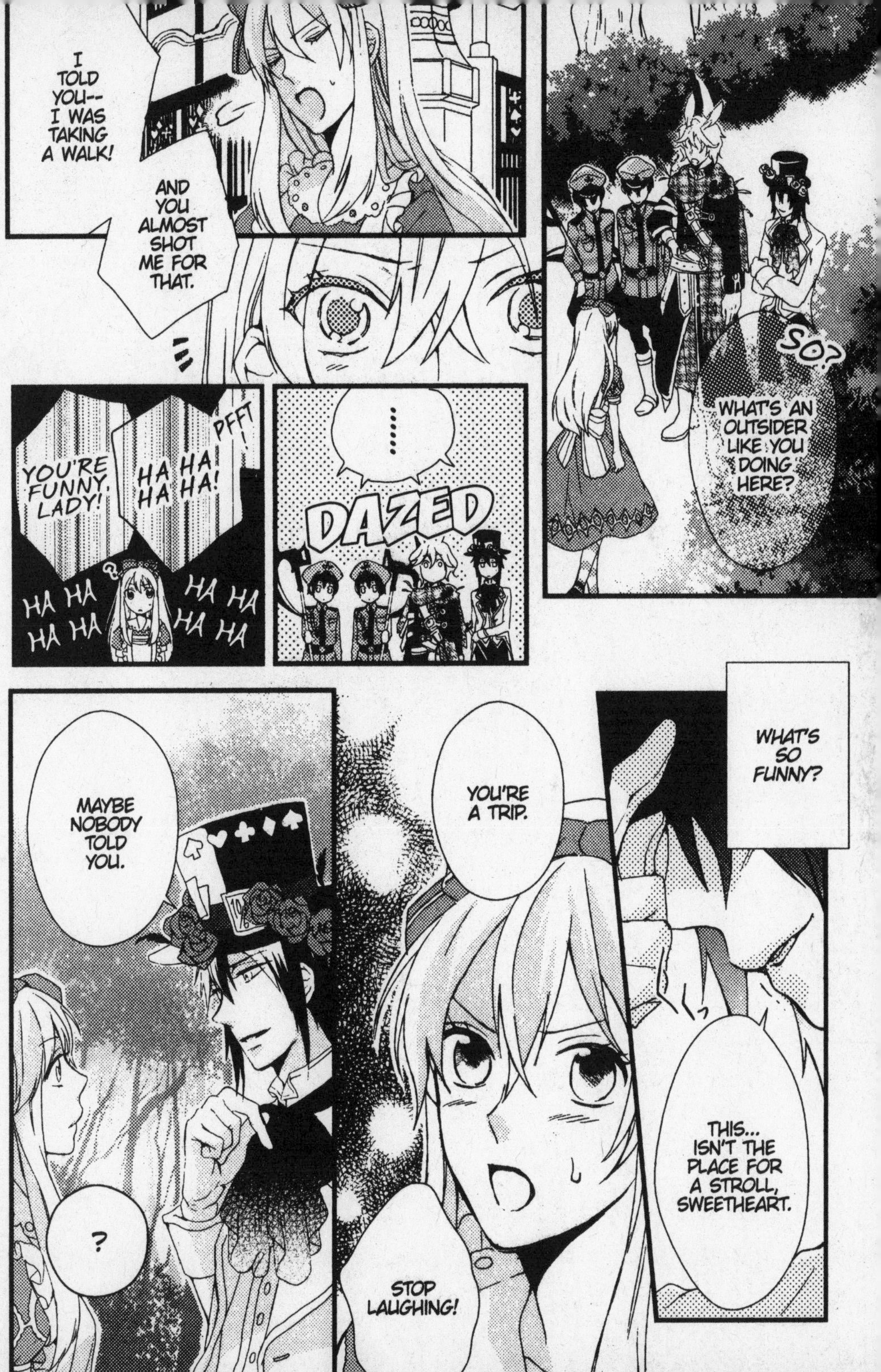
SO?
WHAT'S AN OUTSIDER LIKE YOU DOING HERE?
I TOLD YOU-- I WAS TAKING A WALK!
AND YOU ALMOST SHOT ME FOR THAT.
......
DAZED
PFFT
HA HA HA HA!
YOU'RE FUNNY, LADY!
HA HA HA HA
HA HA HA HA
WHAT'S SO FUNNY?
THIS... ISN'T THE PLACE FOR A STROLL, SWEETHEART.
YOU'RE A TRIP.
STOP LAUGHING!
MAYBE NOBODY TOLD YOU.
?

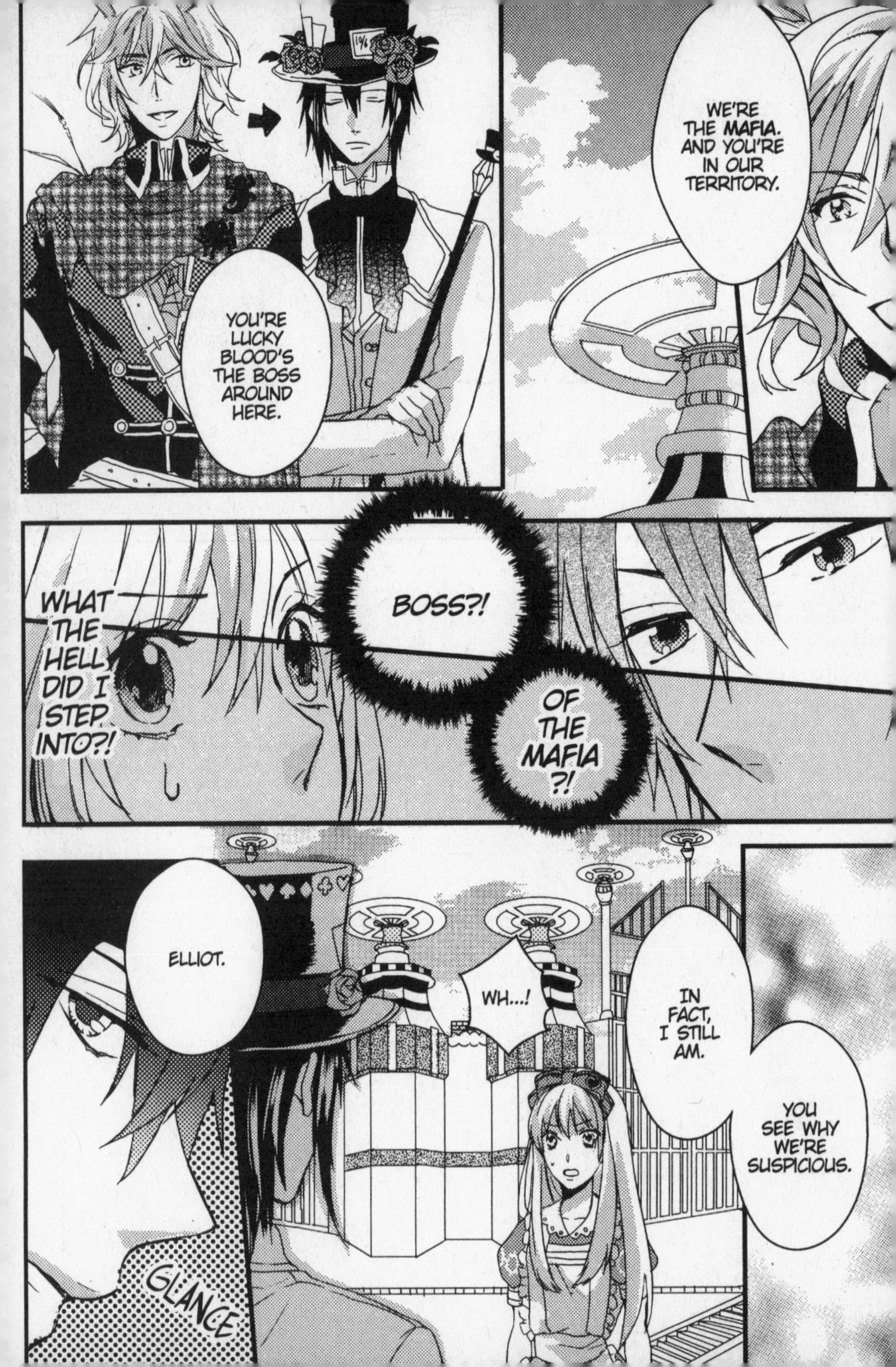
WE'RE THE MAFIA. AND YOU'RE IN OUR TERRITORY.
YOU'RE LUCKY BLOOD'S THE BOSS AROUND HERE.
BOSS?!
OF THE MAFIA ?!
WHAT THE HELL DID I STEP INTO?!
IN FACT, I STILL AM.
YOU SEE WHY WE'RE SUSPICIOUS.
WH...!
ELLIOT.
GLANCE

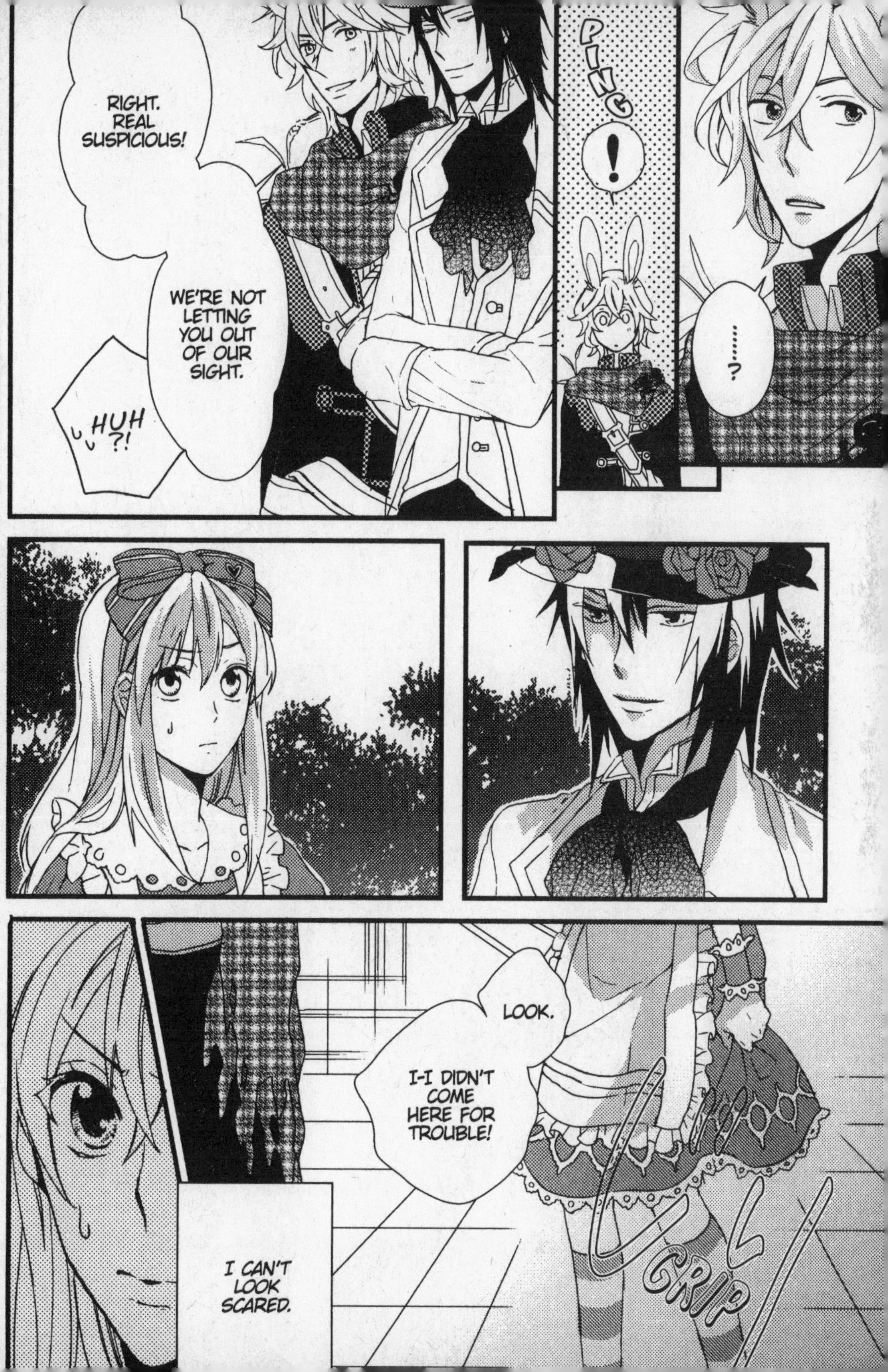
......?
PING
!
RIGHT. REAL SUSPICIOUS!
WE'RE NOT LETTING YOU OUT OF OUR SIGHT.
HUH ?!
LOOK.
I-I DIDN'T COME HERE FOR TROUBLE!
GRIP
I CAN'T LOOK SCARED.

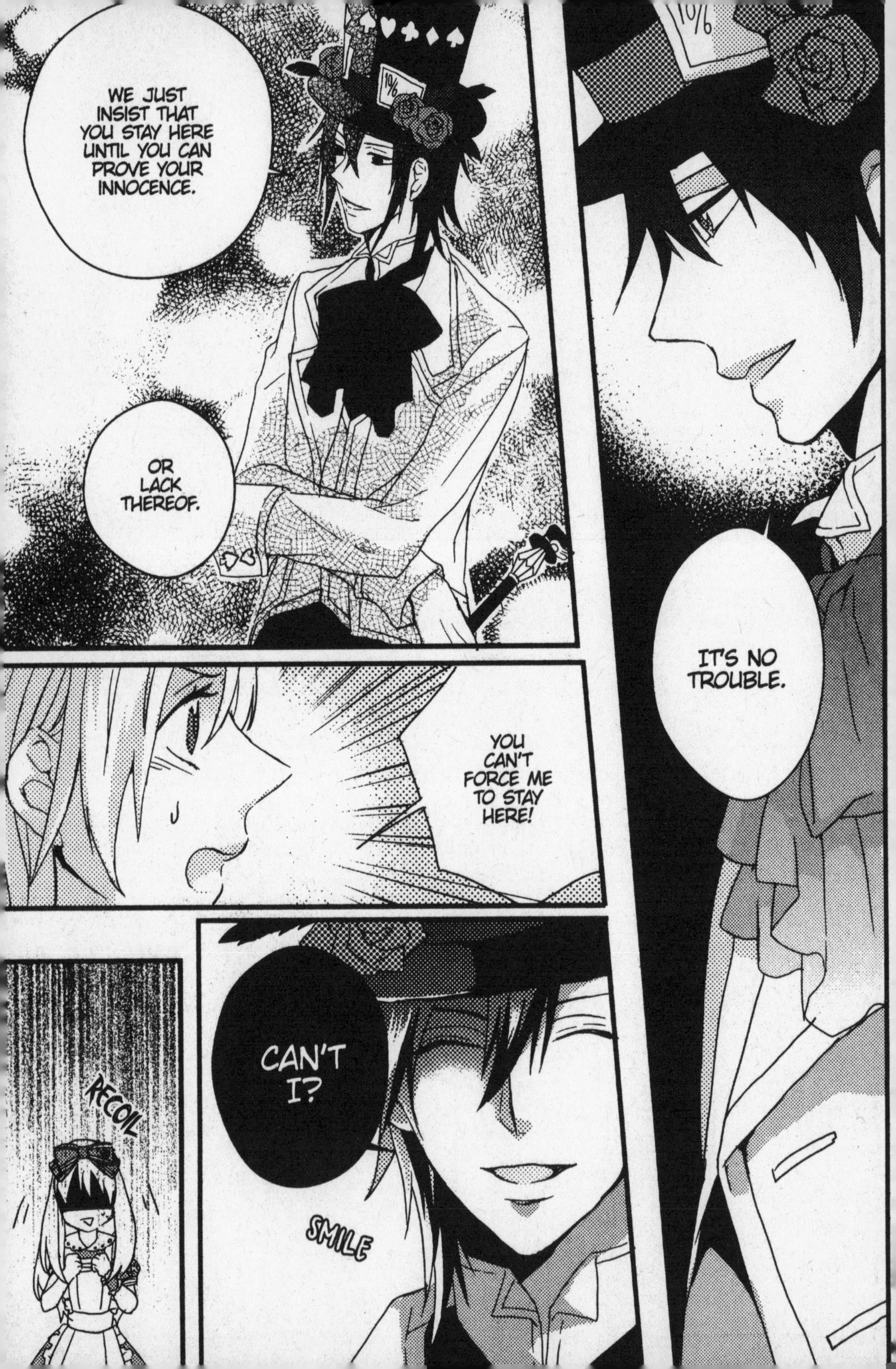
IT'S NO TROUBLE.
WE JUST INSIST THAT YOU STAY HERE UNTIL YOU CAN PROVE YOUR INNOCENCE.
OR LACK THEREOF.
YOU CAN'T FORCE ME TO STAY HERE!
CAN'T I?
SMILE
RECOIL

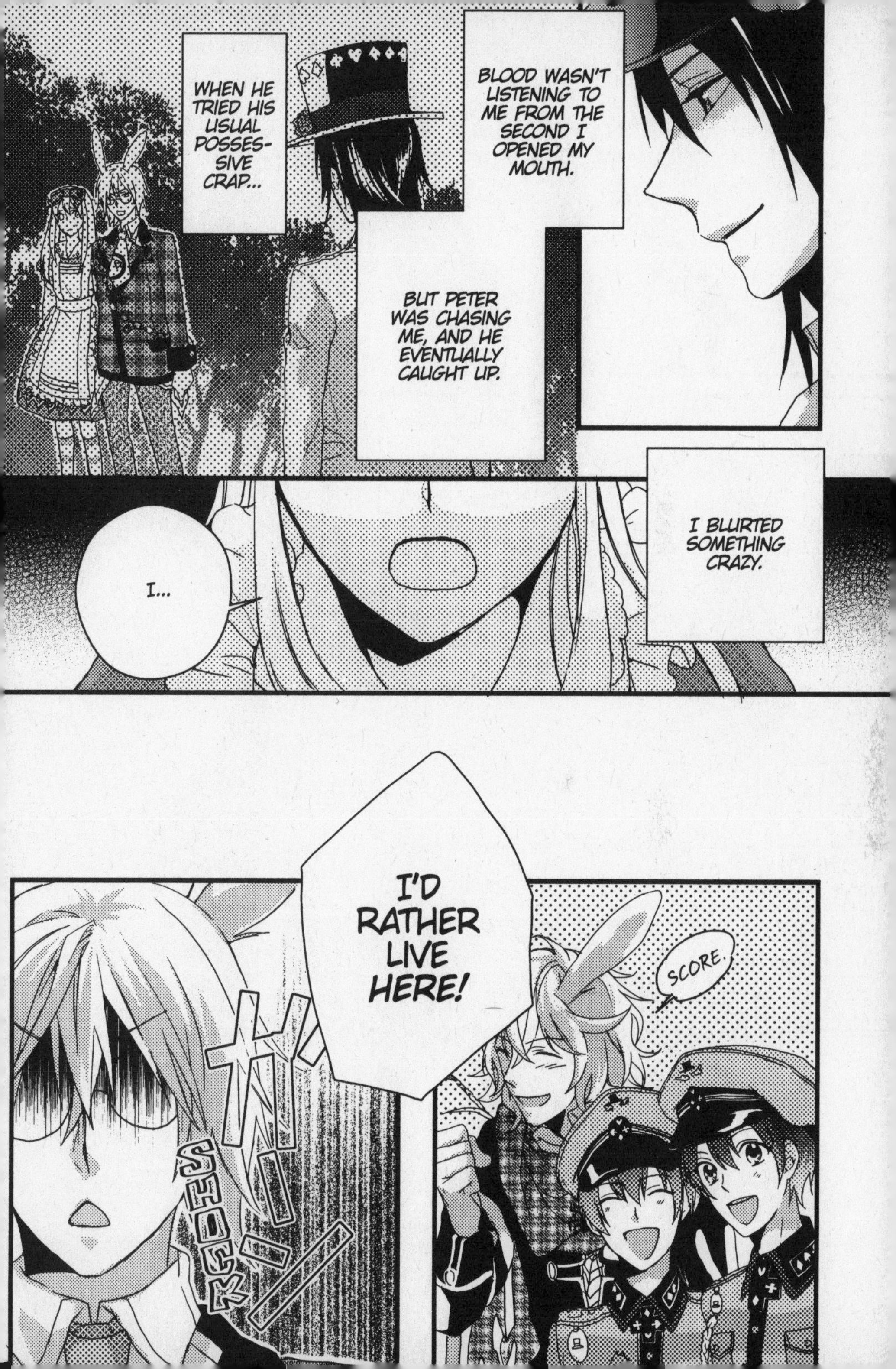
BLOOD WASN'T LISTENING TO ME FROM THE SECOND I OPENED MY MOUTH.
WHEN HE TRIED HIS USUAL POSSES-SIVE CRAP...
BUT PETER WAS CHASING ME, AND HE EVENTUALLY CAUGHT UP.
I BLURTED SOMETHING CRAZY.
I...
I'D RATHER LIVE HERE!
SCORE.
SHOCK!

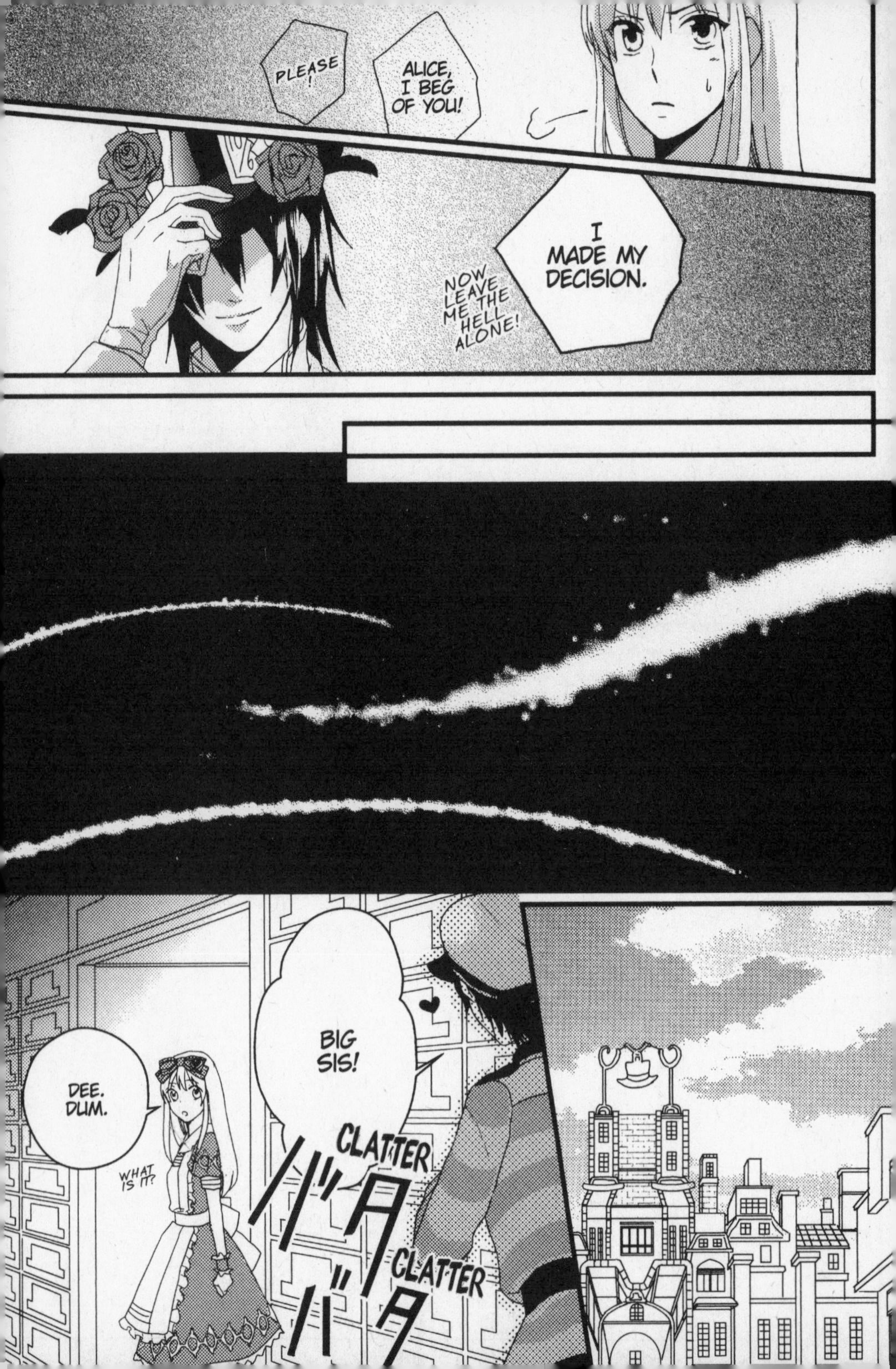

ALICE, I BEG OF YOU!
PLEASE!
I MADE MY DECISION.
NOW LEAVE ME THE HELL ALONE!
BIG SIS!
CLATTER
バタ
CLATTER
バタ
DEE. DUM.
WHAT IS IT?

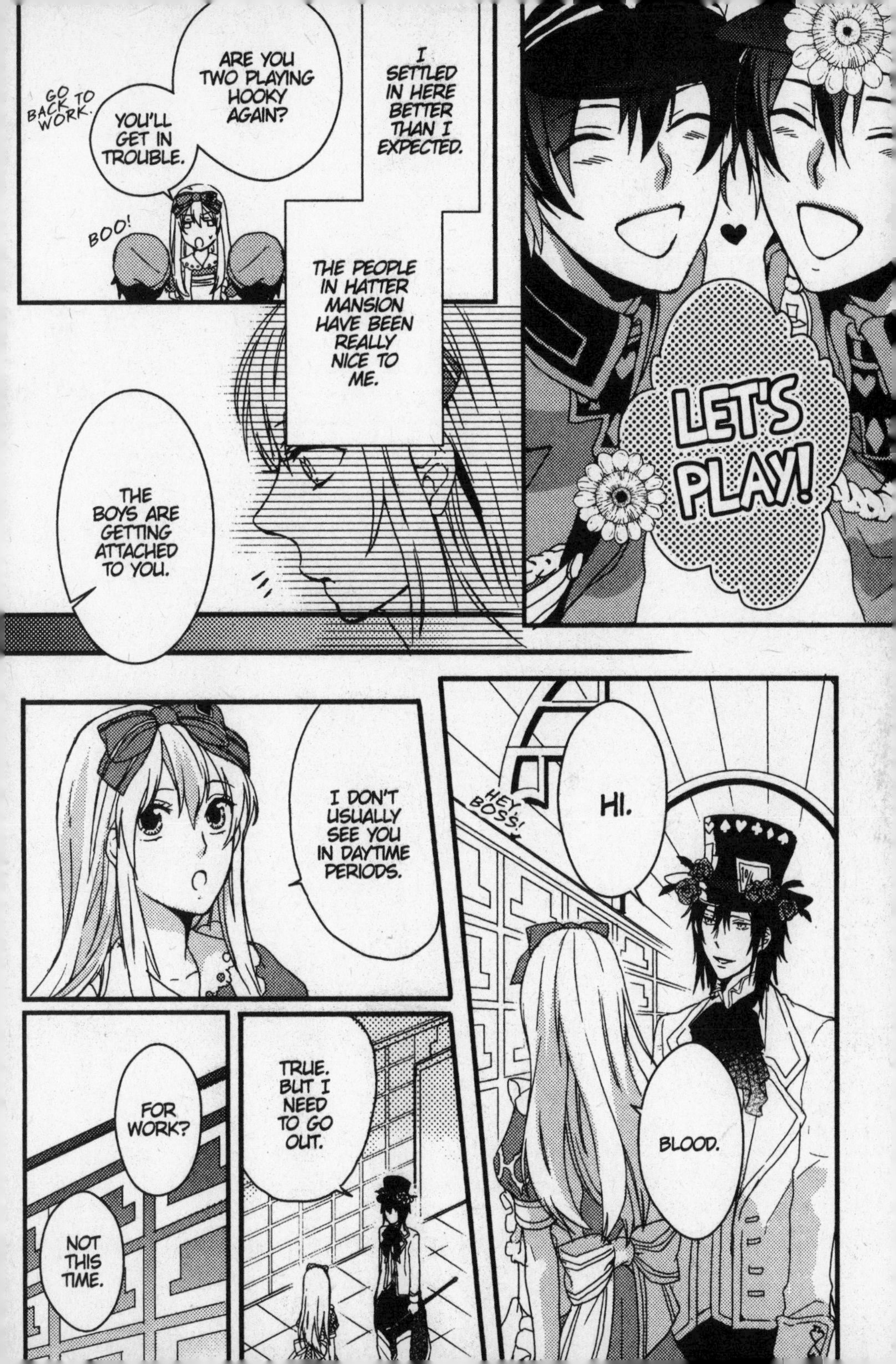
LET'S PLAY!
I SETTLED IN HERE BETTER THAN I EXPECTED.
ARE YOU TWO PLAYING HOOKY AGAIN?
YOU'LL GET IN TROUBLE.
GO BACK TO WORK.
BOO!
THE PEOPLE IN HATTER MANSION HAVE BEEN REALLY NICE TO ME.
THE BOYS ARE GETTING ATTACHED TO YOU.
HI.
HEY BOSS!
BLOOD.
I DON'T USUALLY SEE YOU IN DAYTIME PERIODS.
TRUE. BUT I NEED TO GO OUT.
FOR WORK?
NOT THIS TIME.

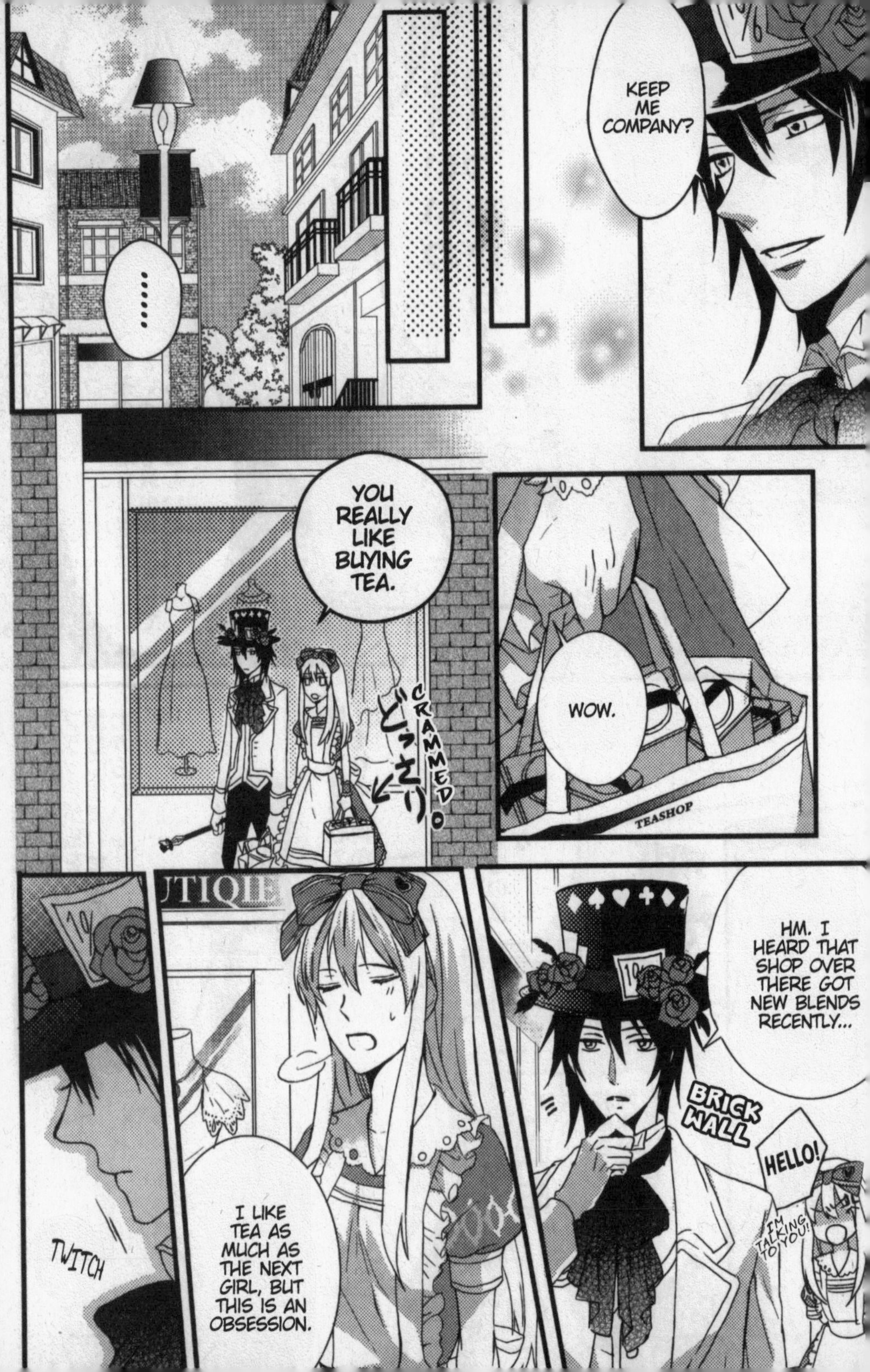
KEEP ME COMPANY?
......
WOW.
TEASHOP
YOU REALLY LIKE BUYING TEA.
どっさり
CRAMMED.
HM. I HEARD THAT SHOP OVER THERE GOT NEW BLENDS RECENTLY...
BRICK WALL
HELLO!
I'M TALKING TO YOU!
I LIKE TEA AS MUCH AS THE NEXT GIRL, BUT THIS IS AN OBSESSION.
TWITCH

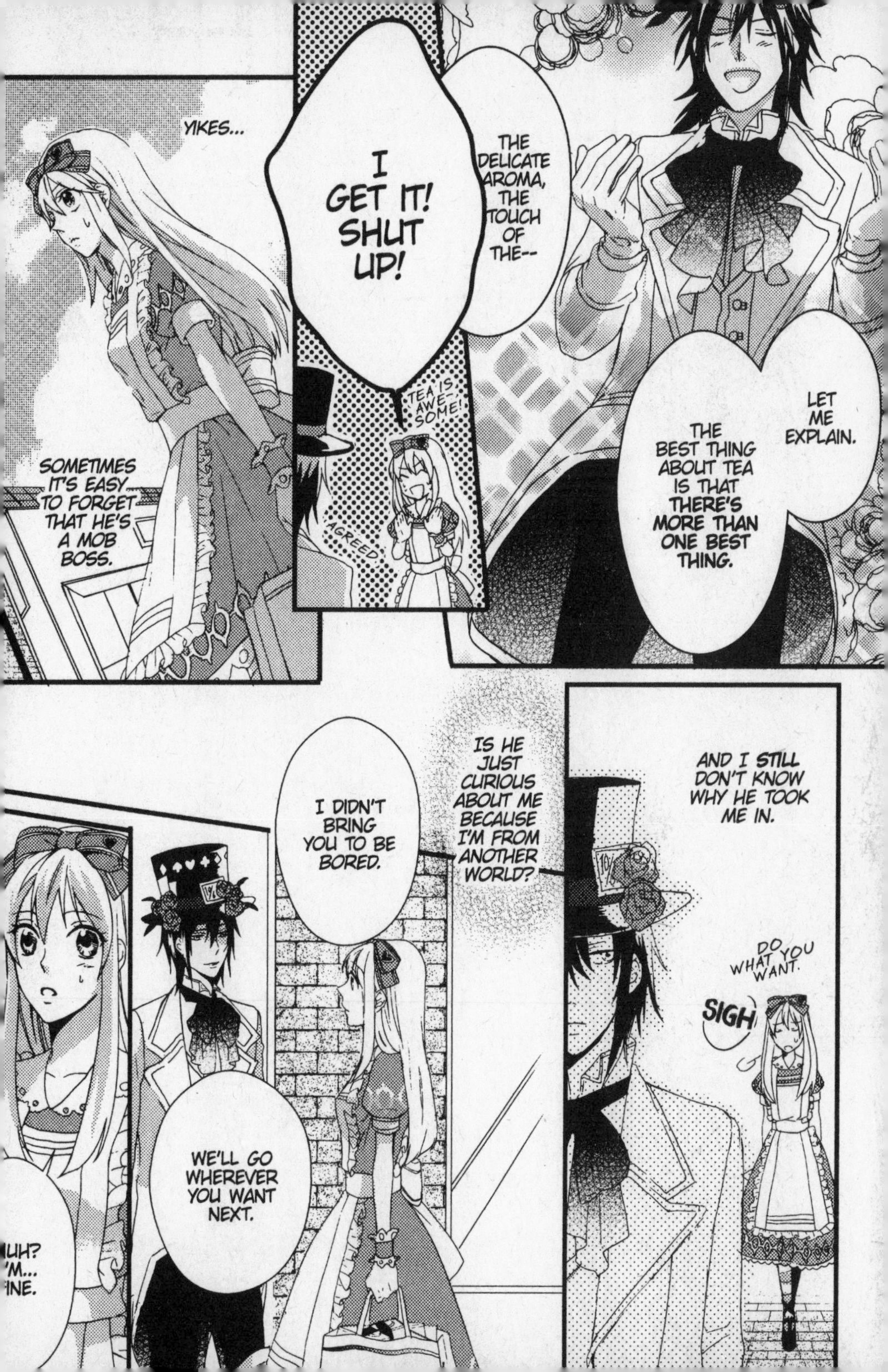
LET ME EXPLAIN.
THE BEST THING ABOUT TEA IS THAT THERE'S MORE THAN ONE BEST THING.
THE DELICATE AROMA, THE TOUCH OF THE--
I GET IT! SHUT UP!
TEA IS AWE-SOME!
AGREED
YIKES...
SOMETIMES IT'S EASY TO FORGET THAT HE'S A MOB BOSS.
AND I STILL DON'T KNOW WHY HE TOOK ME IN.
DO WHAT YOU WANT.
SIGH
IS HE JUST CURIOUS ABOUT ME BECAUSE I'M FROM ANOTHER WORLD?
I DIDN'T BRING YOU TO BE BORED.
WE'LL GO WHEREVER YOU WANT NEXT.
UH? 'M... INE.

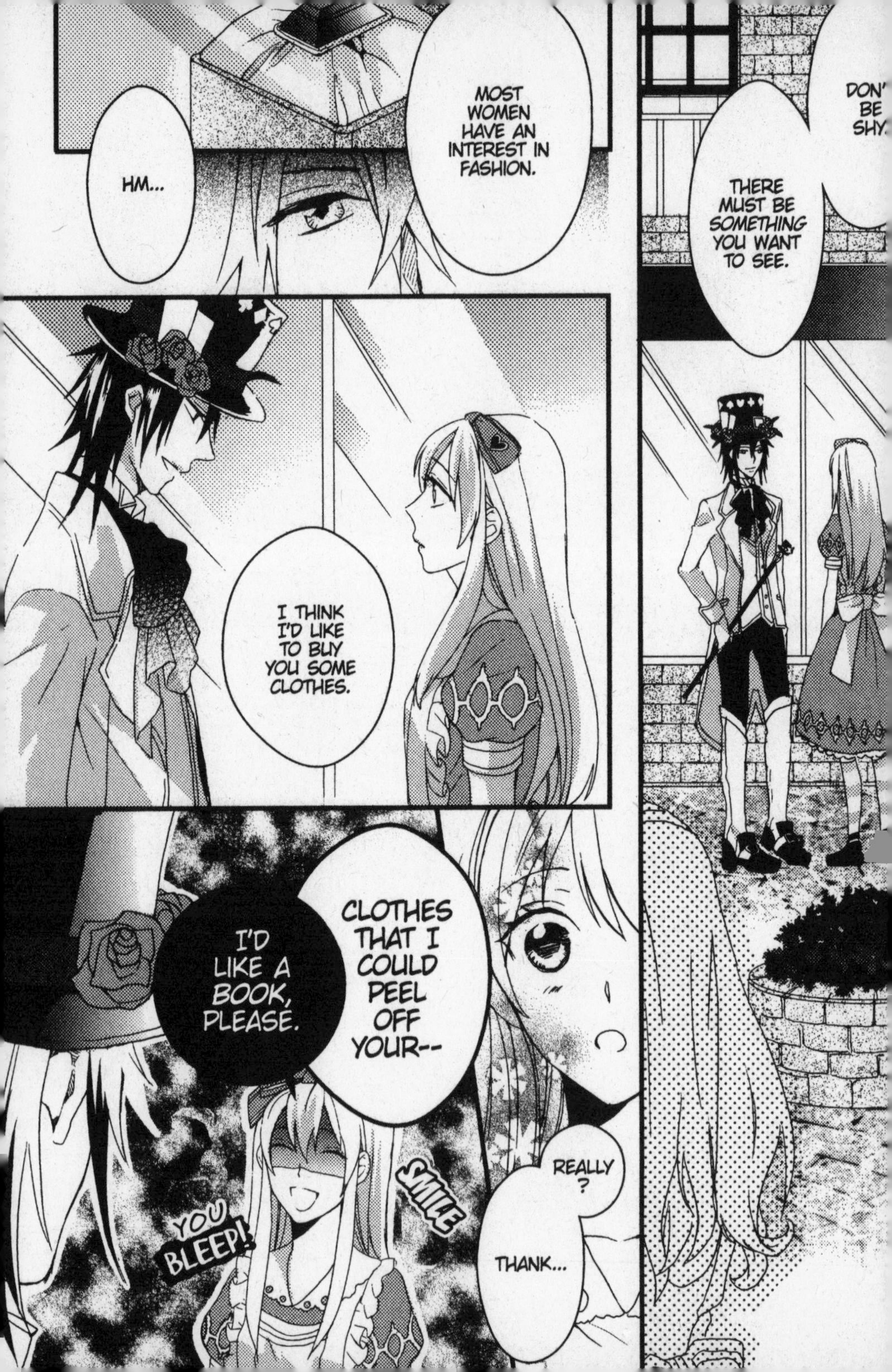
DON' BE SHY.
THERE MUST BE SOMETHING YOU WANT TO SEE.
MOST WOMEN HAVE AN INTEREST IN FASHION.
HM...
I THINK I'D LIKE TO BUY YOU SOME CLOTHES.
CLOTHES THAT I COULD PEEL OFF YOUR--
I'D LIKE A BOOK, PLEASE.
SMILE
YOU BLEEP!
REALLY?
THANK...

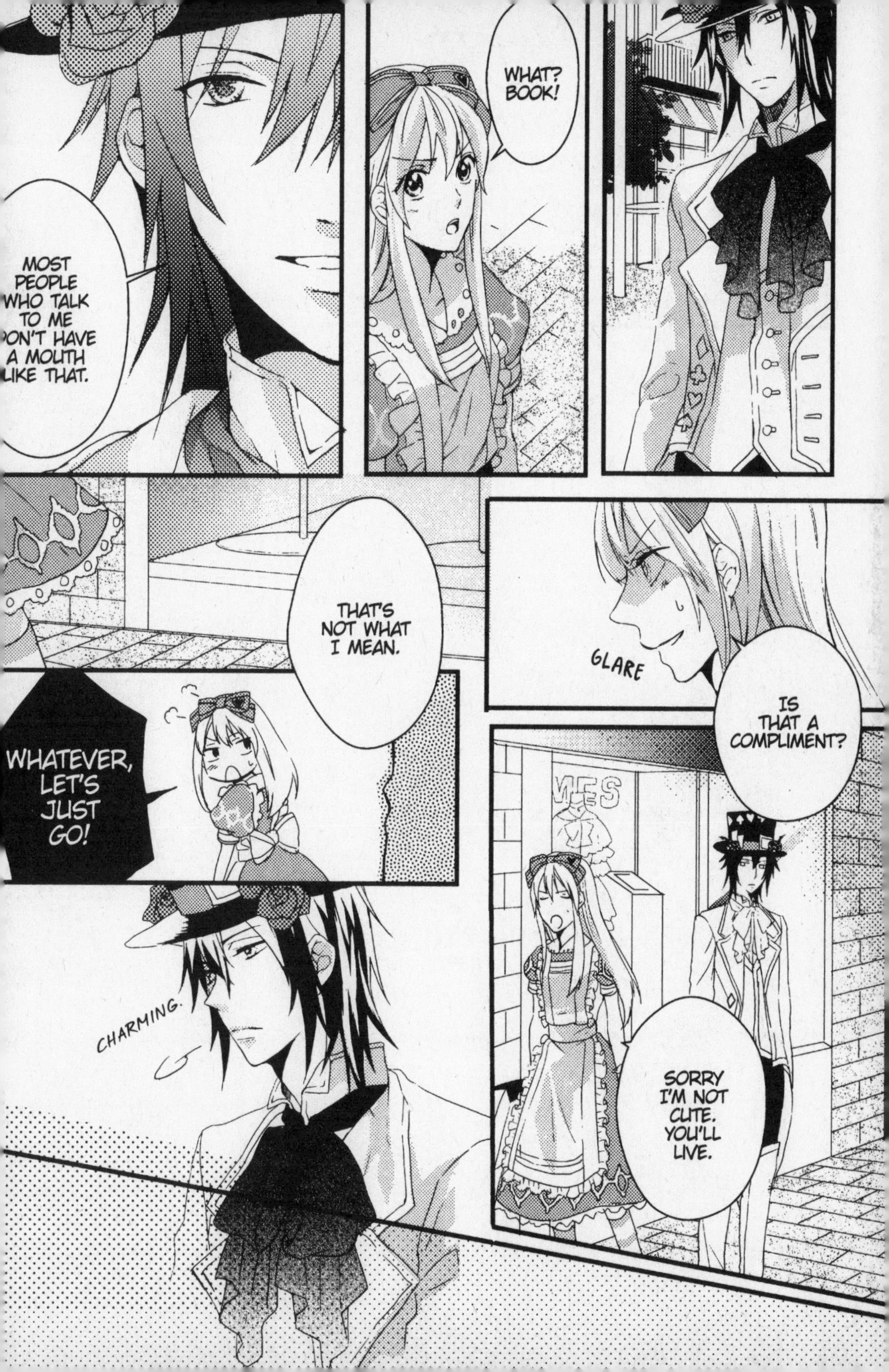
WHAT? BOOK!
MOST PEOPLE WHO TALK TO ME DON'T HAVE A MOUTH LIKE THAT.
GLARE
IS THAT A COMPLIMENT?
THAT'S NOT WHAT I MEAN.
SORRY I'M NOT CUTE. YOU'LL LIVE.
WHATEVER, LET'S JUST GO!
CHARMING.

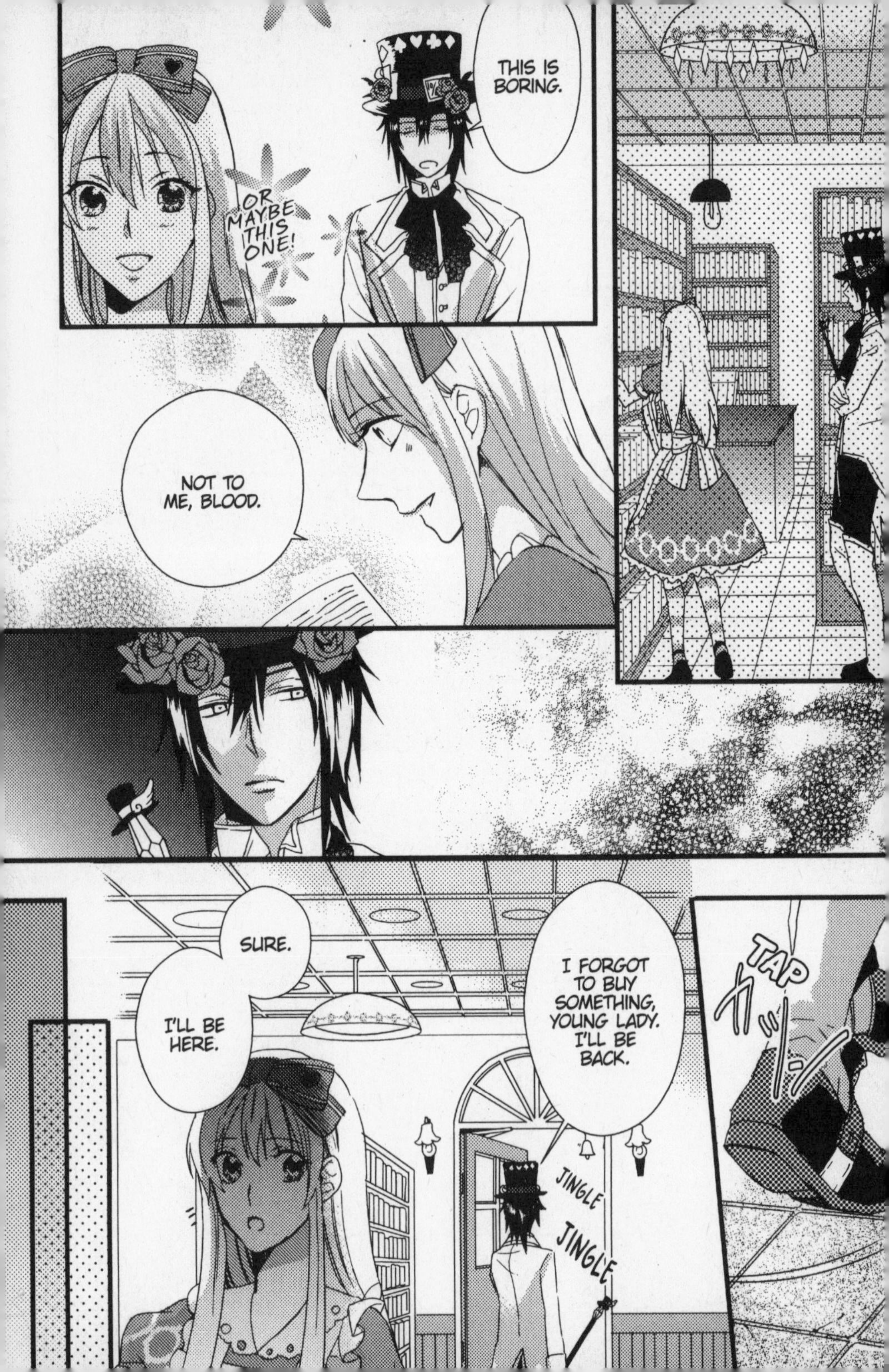
THIS IS BORING.
OR MAYBE THIS ONE!
NOT TO ME, BLOOD.
TAP
I FORGOT TO BUY SOMETHING, YOUNG LADY. I'LL BE BACK.
JINGLE
JINGLE
SURE.
I'LL BE HERE.

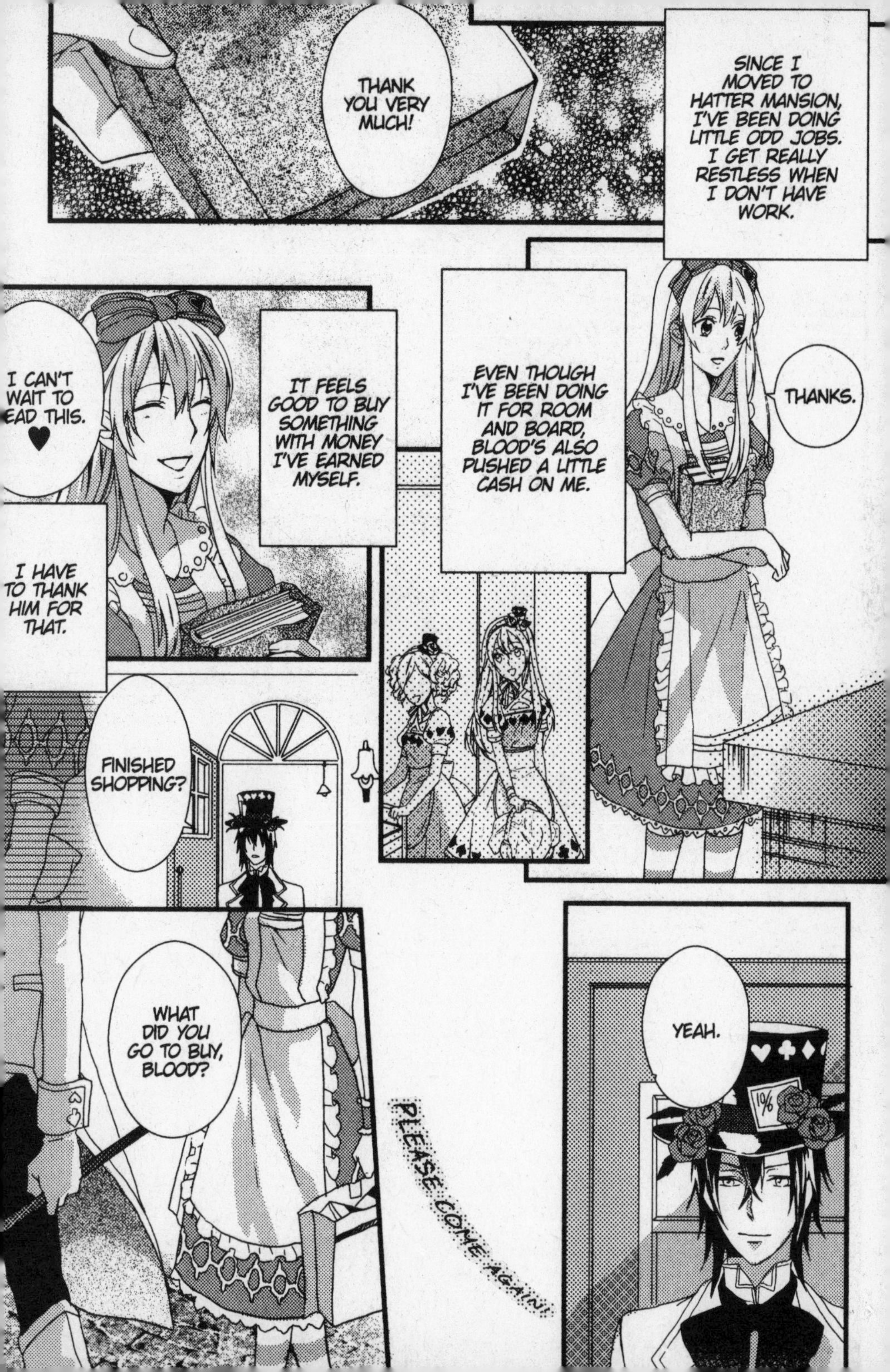
SINCE I MOVED TO HATTER MANSION, I'VE BEEN DOING LITTLE ODD JOBS. I GET REALLY RESTLESS WHEN I DON'T HAVE WORK.
THANK YOU VERY MUCH!
THANKS.
EVEN THOUGH I'VE BEEN DOING IT FOR ROOM AND BOARD, BLOOD'S ALSO PUSHED A LITTLE CASH ON ME.
IT FEELS GOOD TO BUY SOMETHING WITH MONEY I'VE EARNED MYSELF.
I CAN'T WAIT TO EAD THIS. ♥
I HAVE TO THANK HIM FOR THAT.
FINISHED SHOPPING?
YEAH.
WHAT DID YOU GO TO BUY, BLOOD?
PLEASE COME AGAIN!

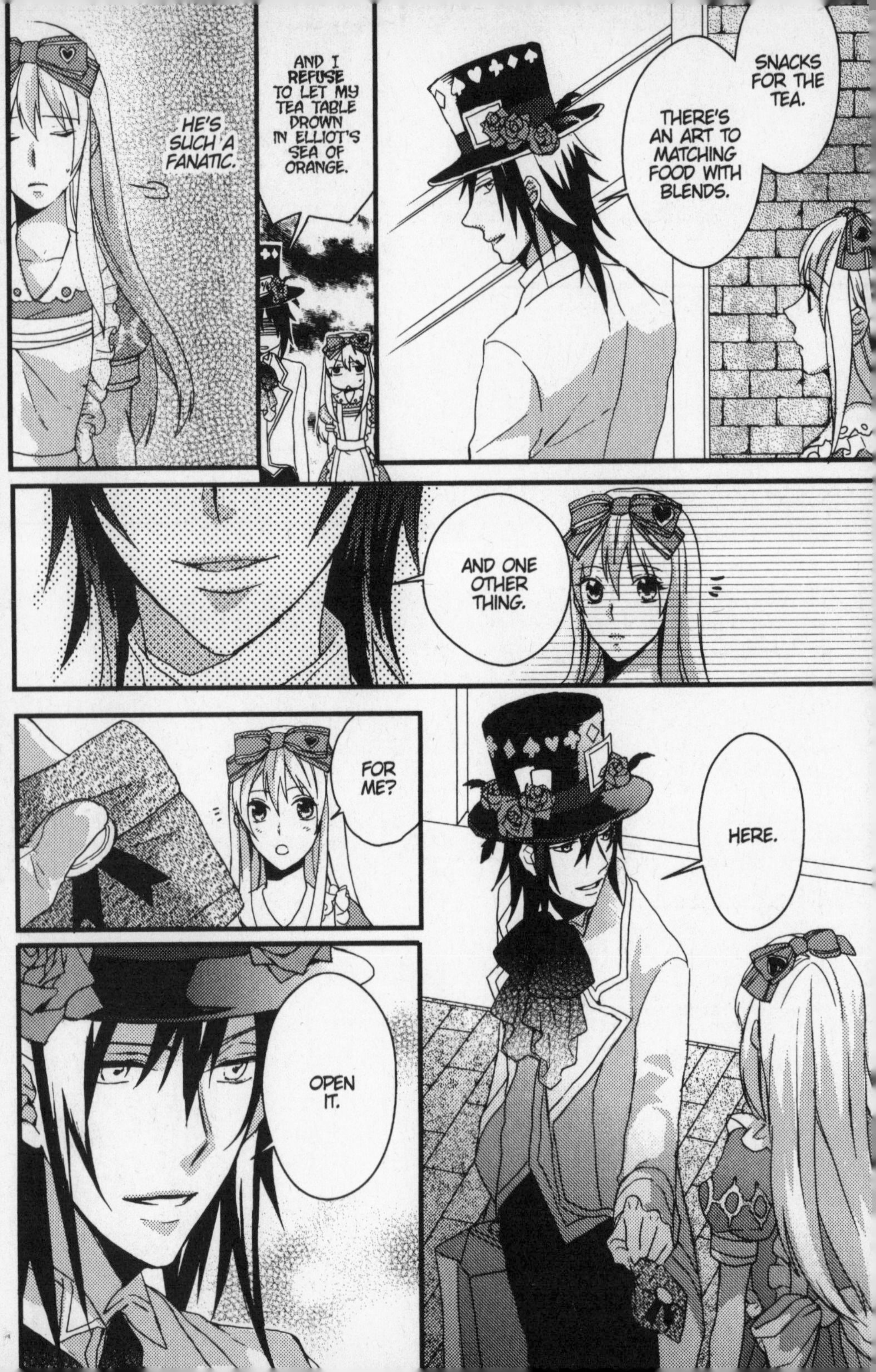
SNACKS FOR THE TEA.
THERE'S AN ART TO MATCHING FOOD WITH BLENDS.
AND I REFUSE TO LET MY TEA TABLE DROWN IN ELLIOT'S SEA OF ORANGE.
HE'S SUCH A FANATIC.
AND ONE OTHER THING.
HERE.
FOR ME?
OPEN IT.

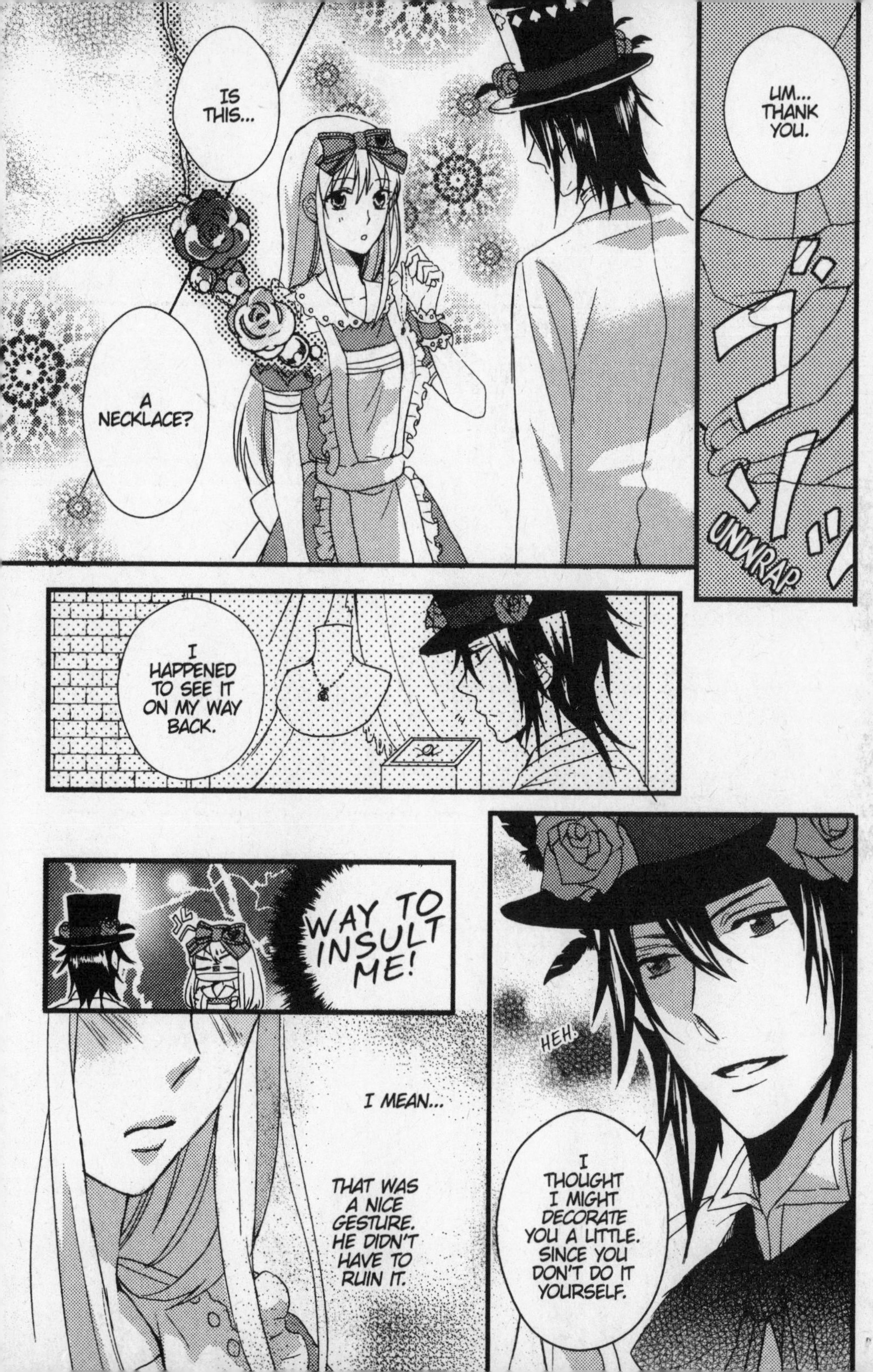
UM... THANK YOU.
UNWRAP
IS THIS...
A NECKLACE?
I HAPPENED TO SEE IT ON MY WAY BACK.
HEH.
I THOUGHT I MIGHT DECORATE YOU A LITTLE. SINCE YOU DON'T DO IT YOURSELF.
WAY TO INSULT ME!
I MEAN...
THAT WAS A NICE GESTURE. HE DIDN'T HAVE TO RUIN IT.

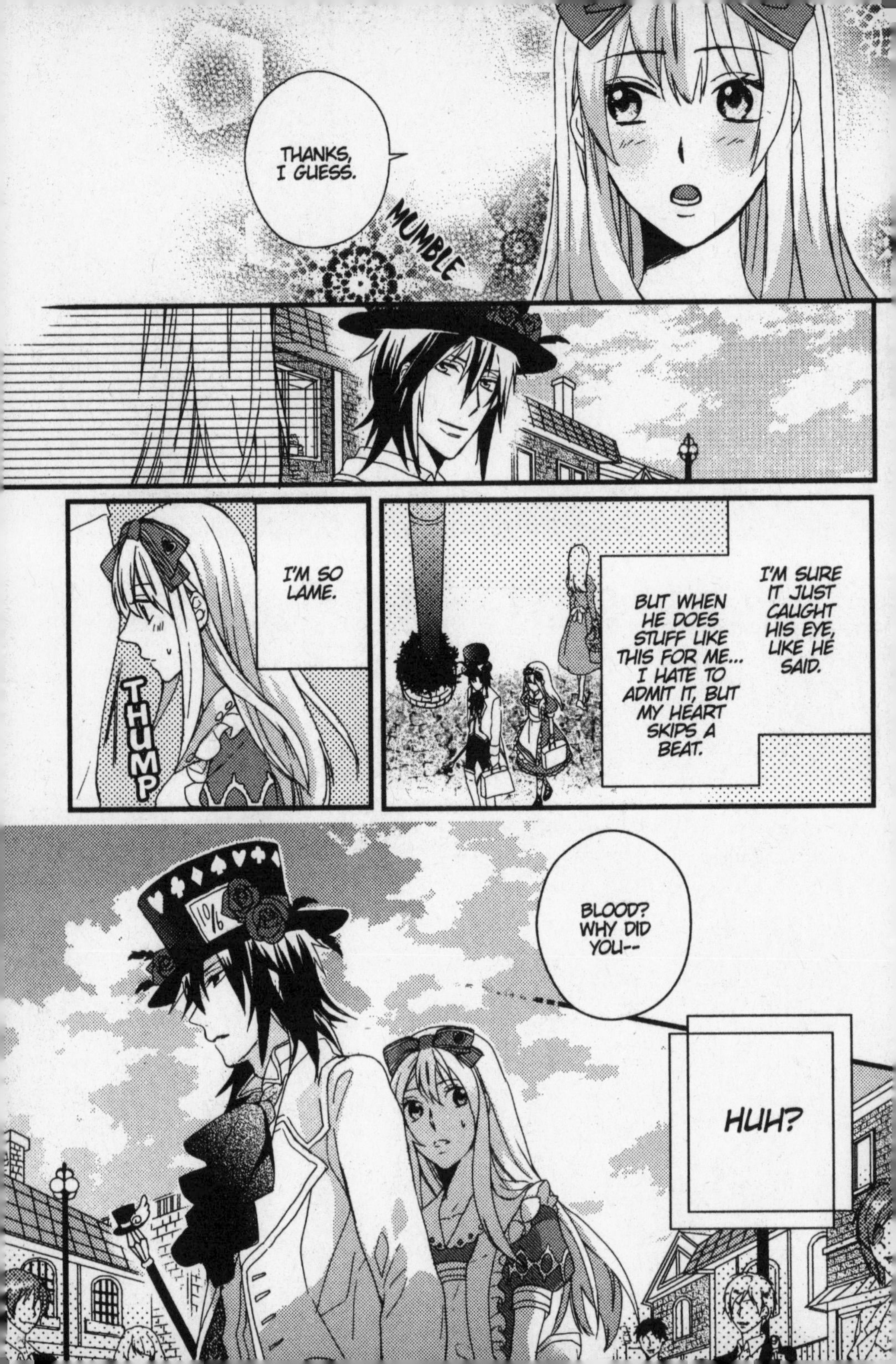
THANKS, I GUESS.
MUMBLE
I'M SURE IT JUST CAUGHT HIS EYE, LIKE HE SAID.
BUT WHEN HE DOES STUFF LIKE THIS FOR ME... I HATE TO ADMIT IT, BUT MY HEART SKIPS A BEAT.
I'M SO LAME.
THUMP
BLOOD? WHY DID YOU--
HUH?

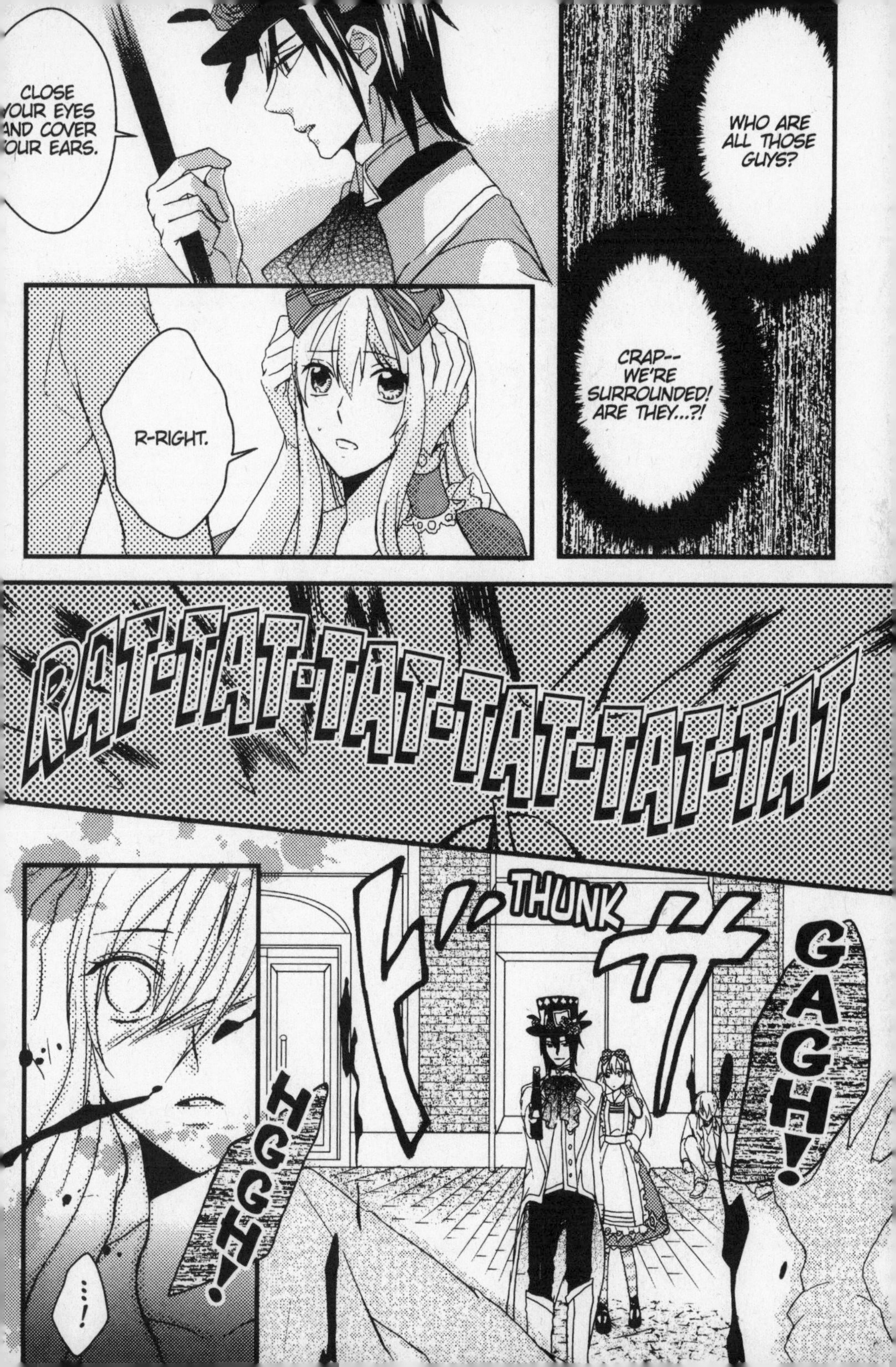
WHO ARE ALL THOSE GUYS?
CRAP-- WE'RE SURROUNDED! ARE THEY...?!
CLOSE YOUR EYES AND COVER YOUR EARS.
R-RIGHT.
RAT-TAT-TAT-TAT-TAT-TAT-TAT
THUNK
GAGH!
HGGH!
...!

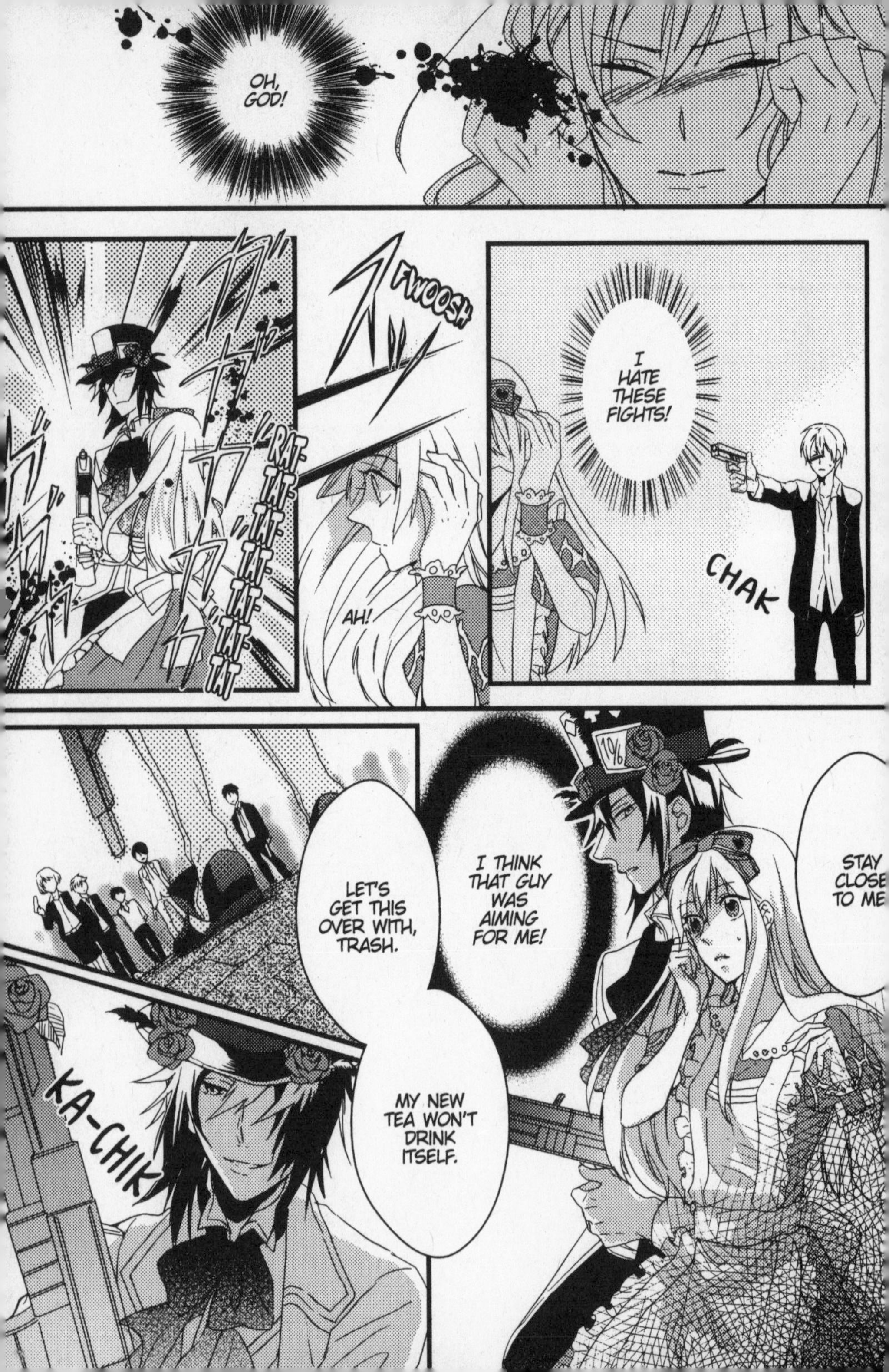
OH, GOD!
I HATE THESE FIGHTS!
CHAK
FWOOSH
AH!
RAT-TAT-TAT-TAT-TAT-TAT
STAY CLOSE TO ME
I THINK THAT GUY WAS AIMING FOR ME!
LET'S GET THIS OVER WITH, TRASH.
MY NEW TEA WON'T DRINK ITSELF.
KA-CHIK

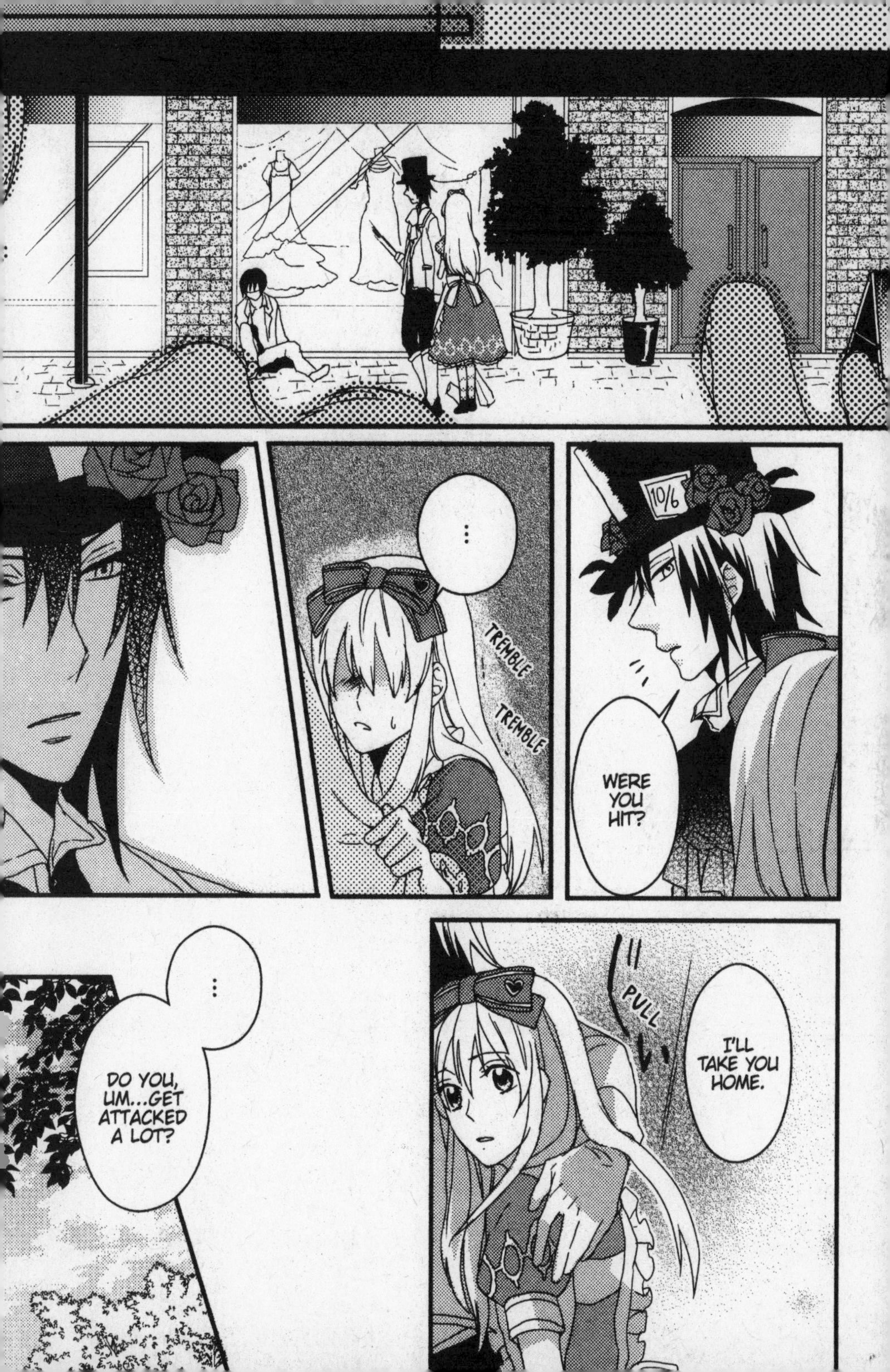
WERE YOU HIT?
...
TREMBLE
TREMBLE
PULL
I'LL TAKE YOU HOME.
...
DO YOU, UM...GET ATTACKED A LOT?

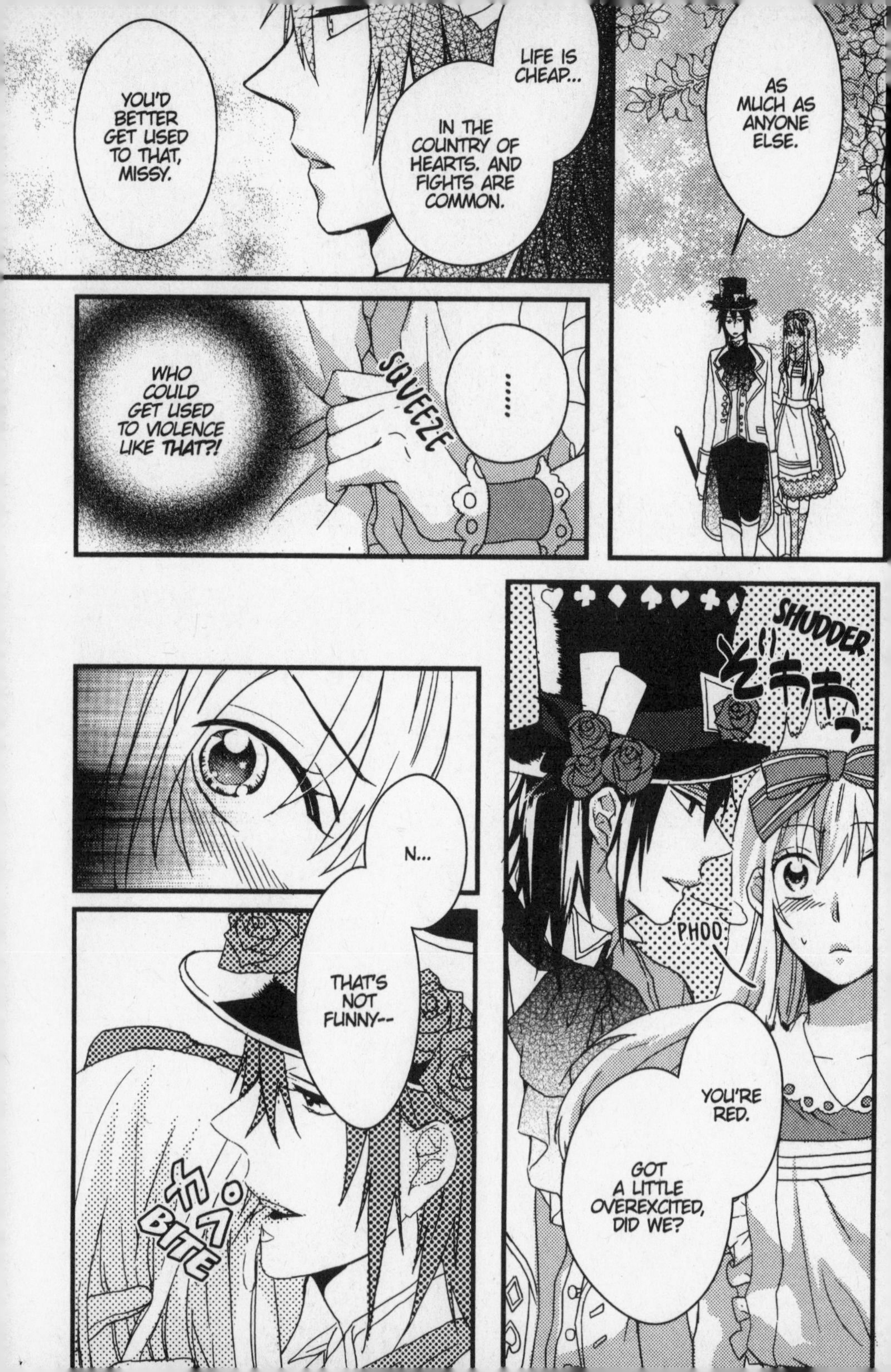
AS MUCH AS ANYONE ELSE.
LIFE IS CHEAP...
IN THE COUNTRY OF HEARTS. AND FIGHTS ARE COMMON.
YOU'D BETTER GET USED TO THAT, MISSY.
......
SQUEEZE
WHO COULD GET USED TO VIOLENCE LIKE THAT?!
SHUDDER
PHOO
YOU'RE RED.
GOT A LITTLE OVEREXCITED, DID WE?
N...
THAT'S NOT FUNNY--
BITE

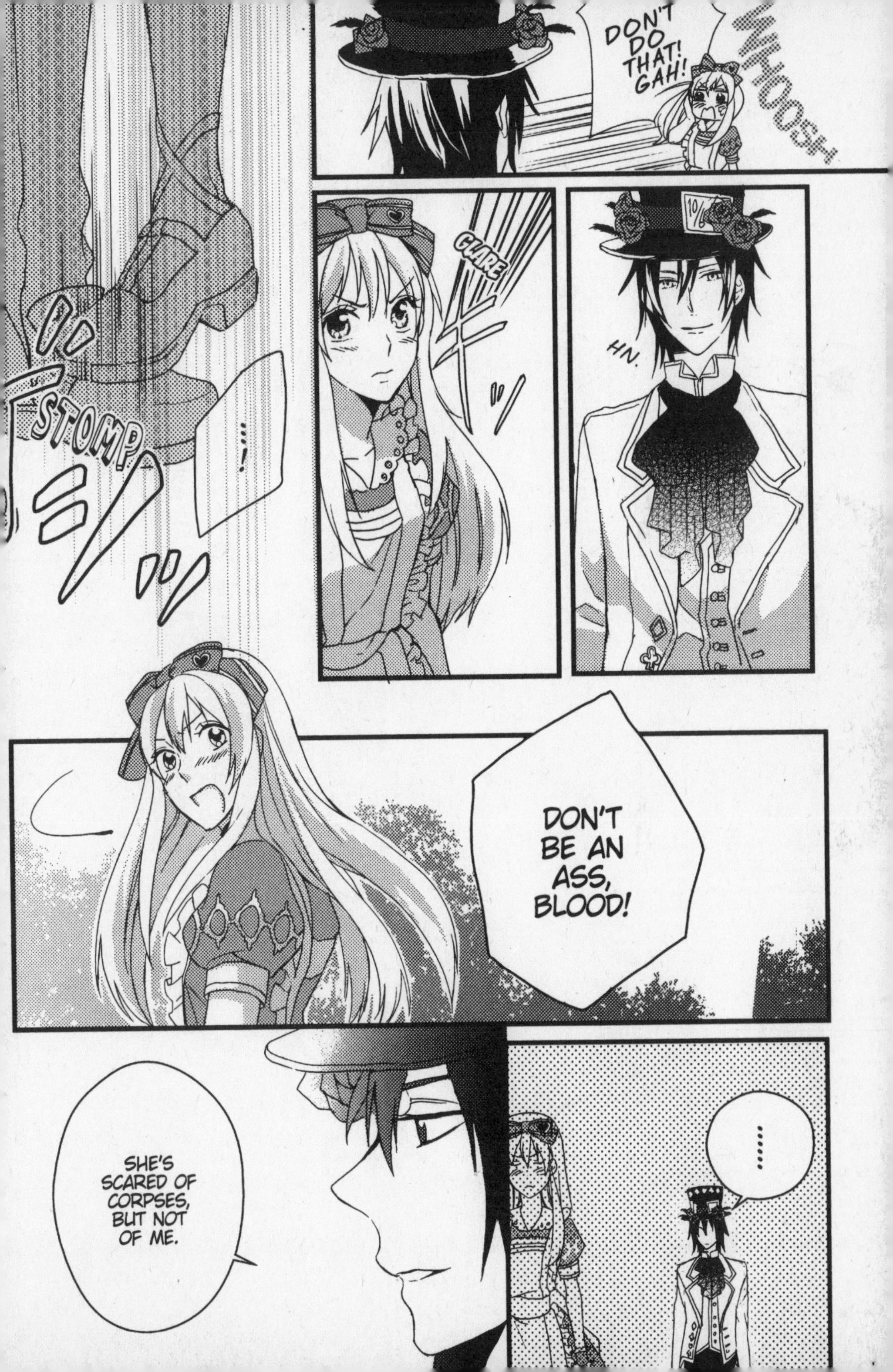
DON'T DO THAT! GAH!
WHOOSH
HN.
GLARE
STOMP
...!
DON'T BE AN ASS, BLOOD!
......
SHE'S SCARED OF CORPSES, BUT NOT OF ME.

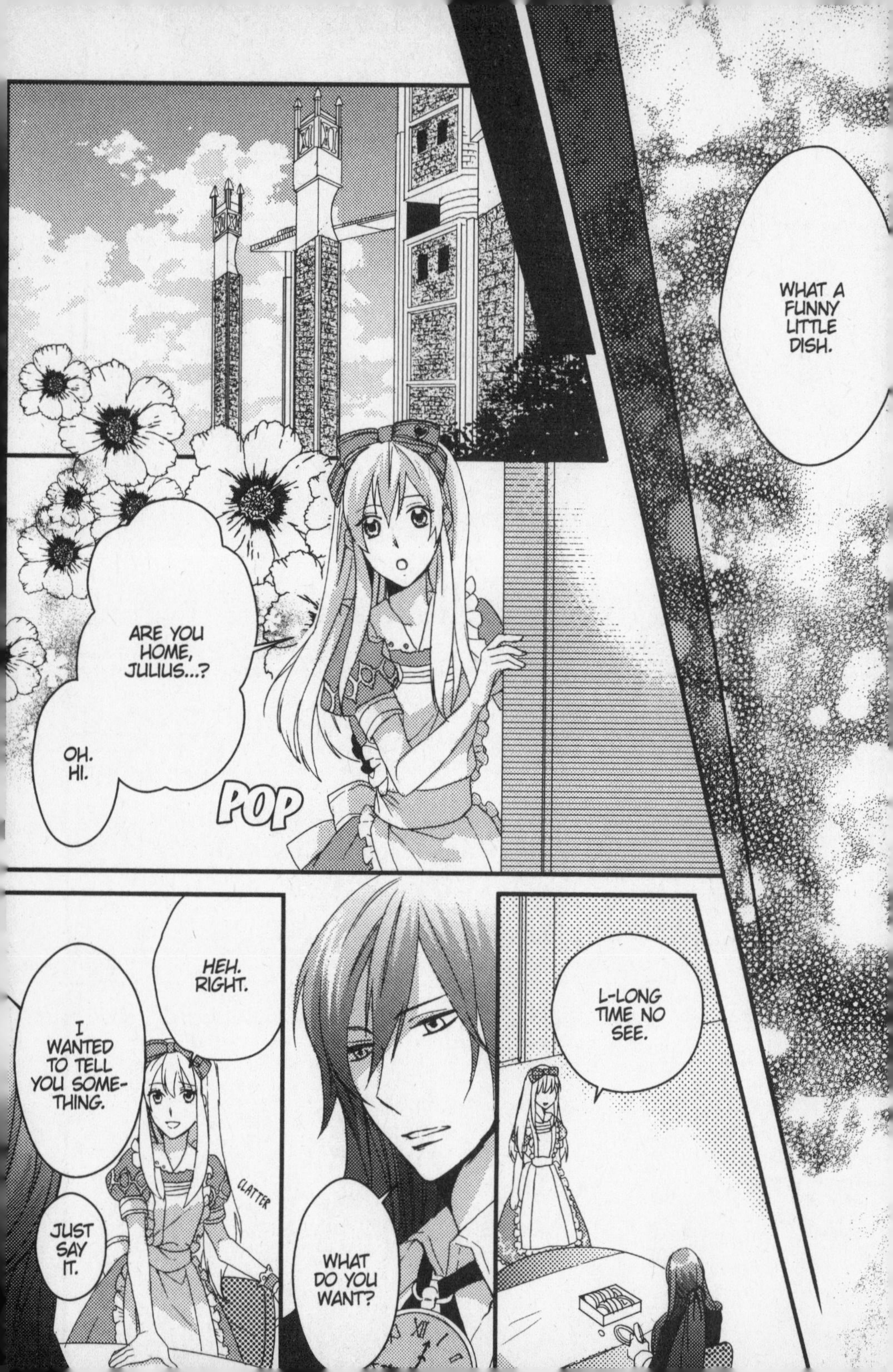

WHAT A FUNNY LITTLE DISH.
ARE YOU HOME, JULIUS...?
OH. HI.
POP
L-LONG TIME NO SEE.
HEH. RIGHT.
WHAT DO YOU WANT?
I WANTED TO TELL YOU SOME-THING.
CLATTER
JUST SAY IT.

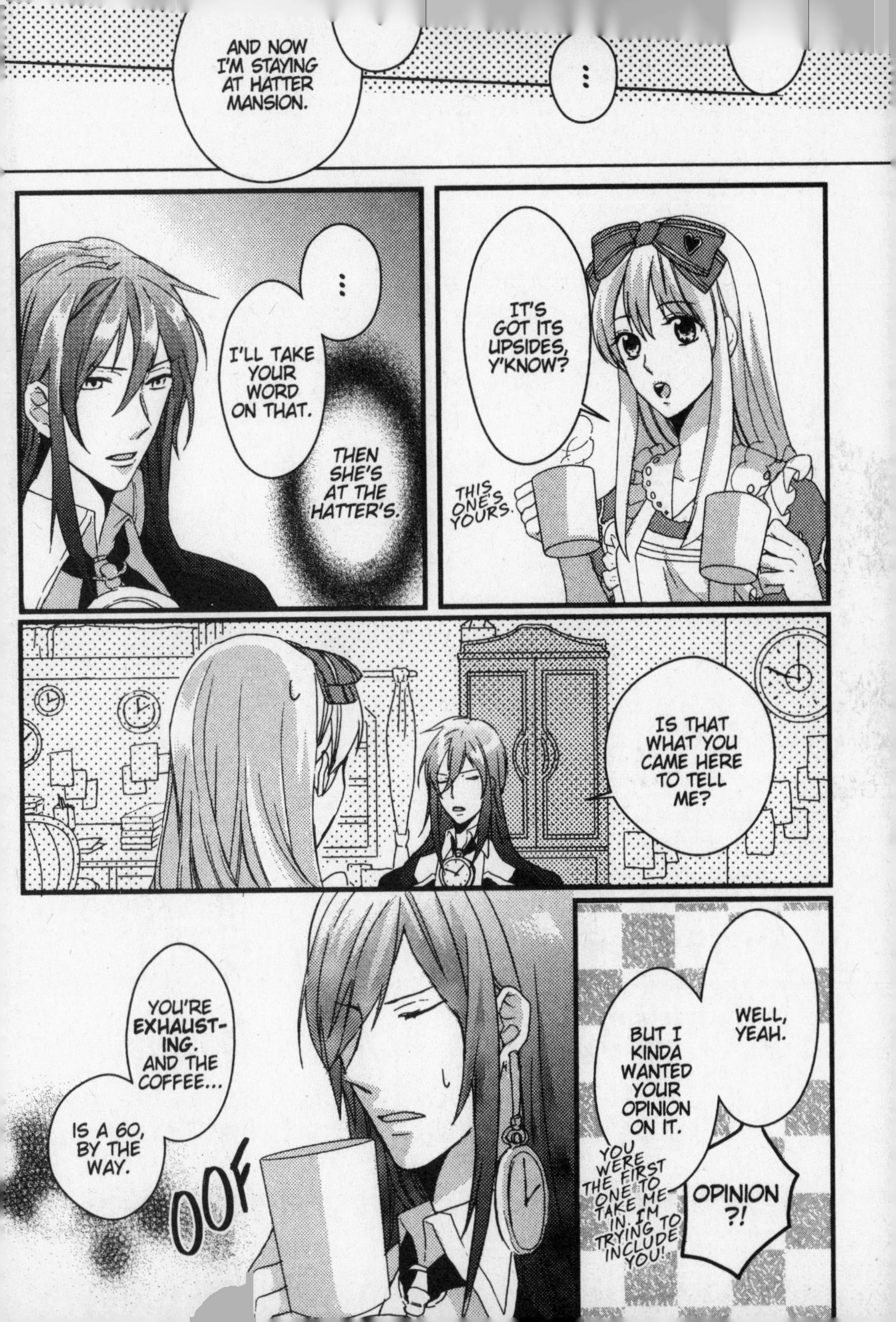
AND NOW I'M STAYING AT HATTER MANSION.
...
IT'S GOT ITS UPSIDES, Y'KNOW?
THIS ONE'S YOURS.
...
I'LL TAKE YOUR WORD ON THAT.
THEN SHE'S AT THE HATTER'S.
IS THAT WHAT YOU CAME HERE TO TELL ME?
WELL, YEAH.
BUT I KINDA WANTED YOUR OPINION ON IT.
YOU WERE THE FIRST ONE TO TAKE ME IN. I'M TRYING TO INCLUDE YOU!
OPINION ?!
YOU'RE EXHAUST-ING. AND THE COFFEE...
IS A 60, BY THE WAY.
OOF

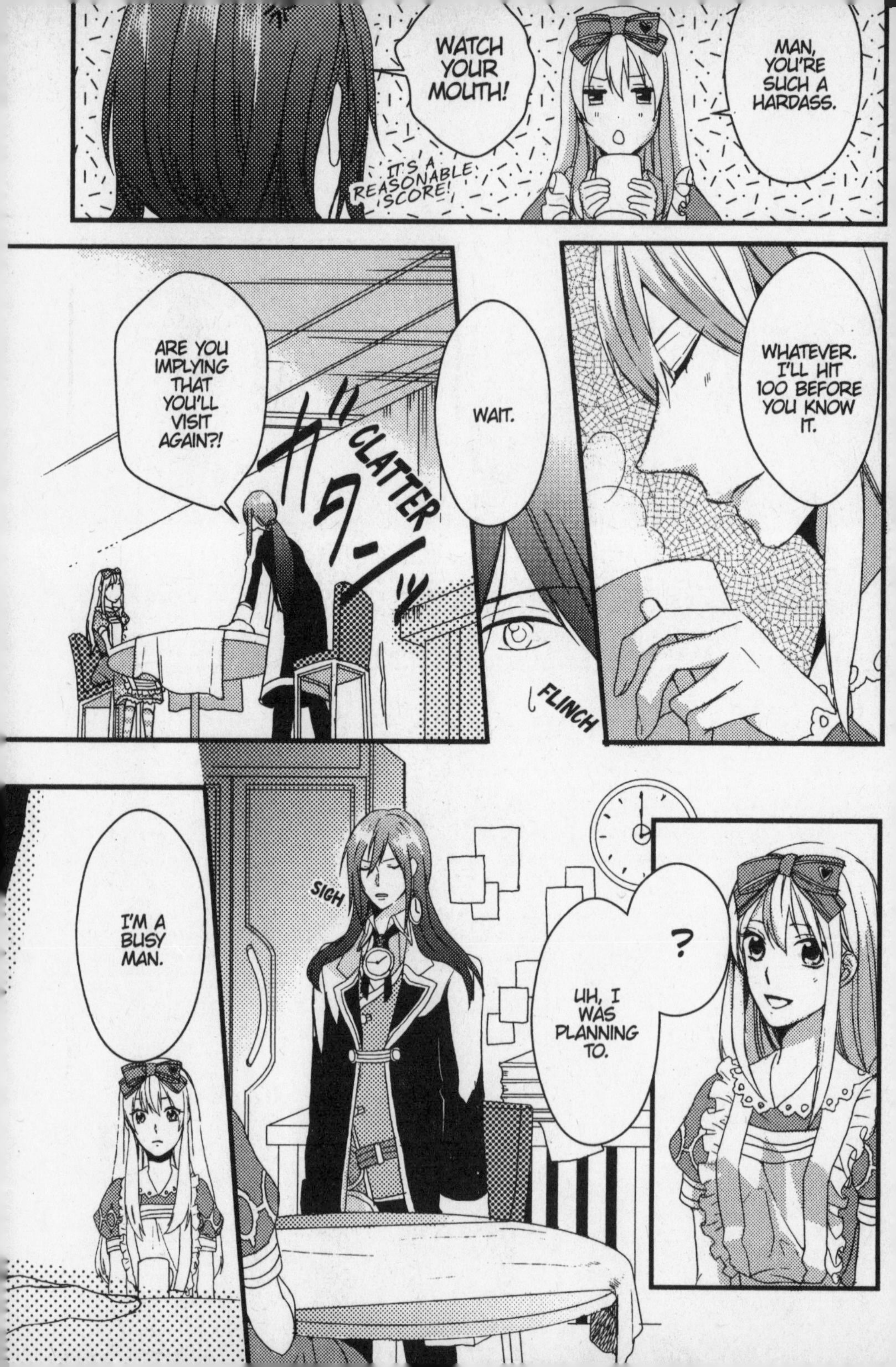
MAN, YOU'RE SUCH A HARDASS.
WATCH YOUR MOUTH!
IT'S A REASONABLE SCORE!
WHATEVER. I'LL HIT 100 BEFORE YOU KNOW IT.
WAIT.
FLINCH
CLATTER
ARE YOU IMPLYING THAT YOU'LL VISIT AGAIN?!
?
UH, I WAS PLANNING TO.
SIGH
I'M A BUSY MAN.

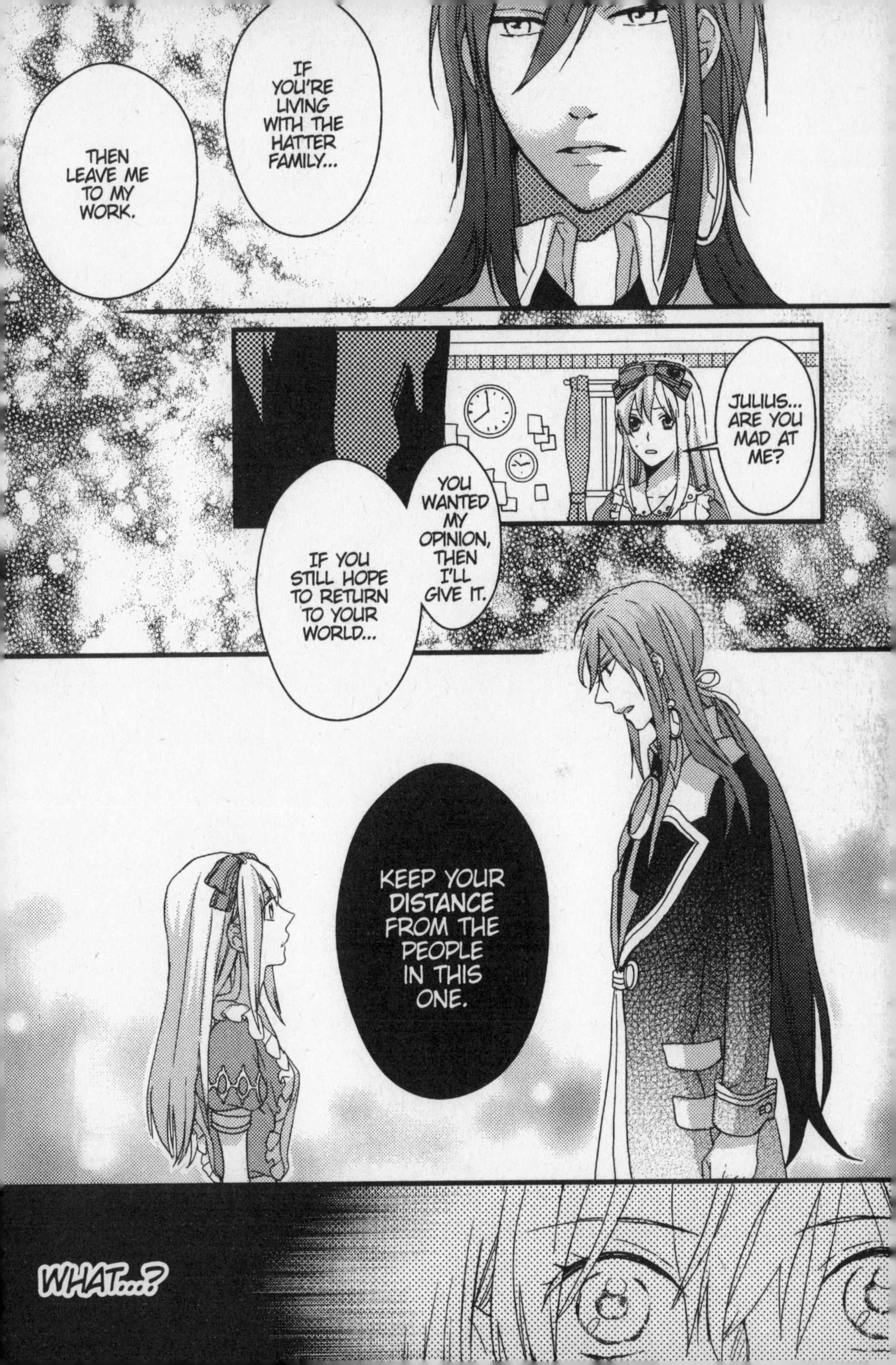
IF YOU'RE LIVING WITH THE HATTER FAMILY...
THEN LEAVE ME TO MY WORK.
JULIUS... ARE YOU MAD AT ME?
YOU WANTED MY OPINION, THEN I'LL GIVE IT.
IF YOU STILL HOPE TO RETURN TO YOUR WORLD...
KEEP YOUR DISTANCE FROM THE PEOPLE IN THIS ONE.
WHAT...?

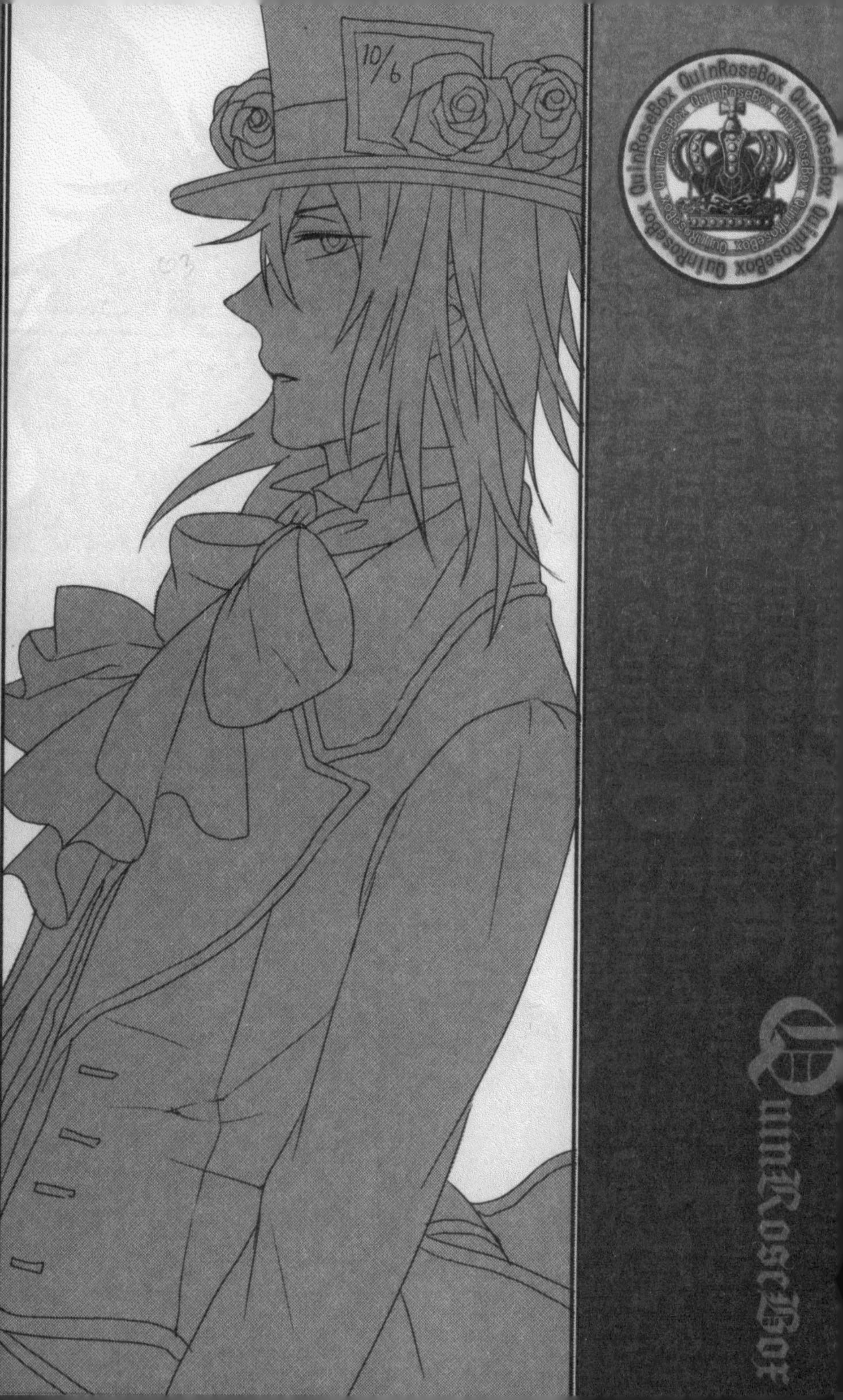
10/6

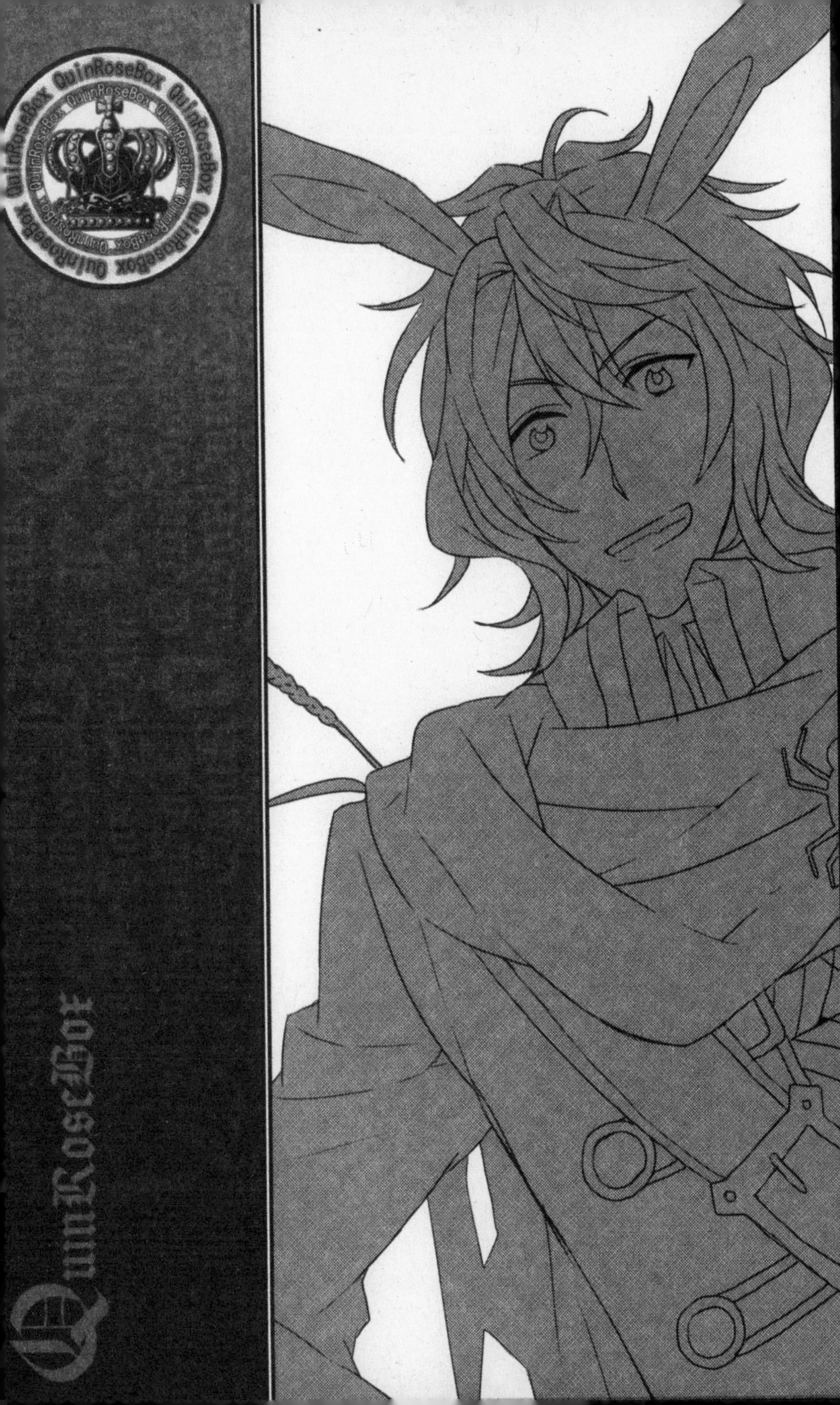

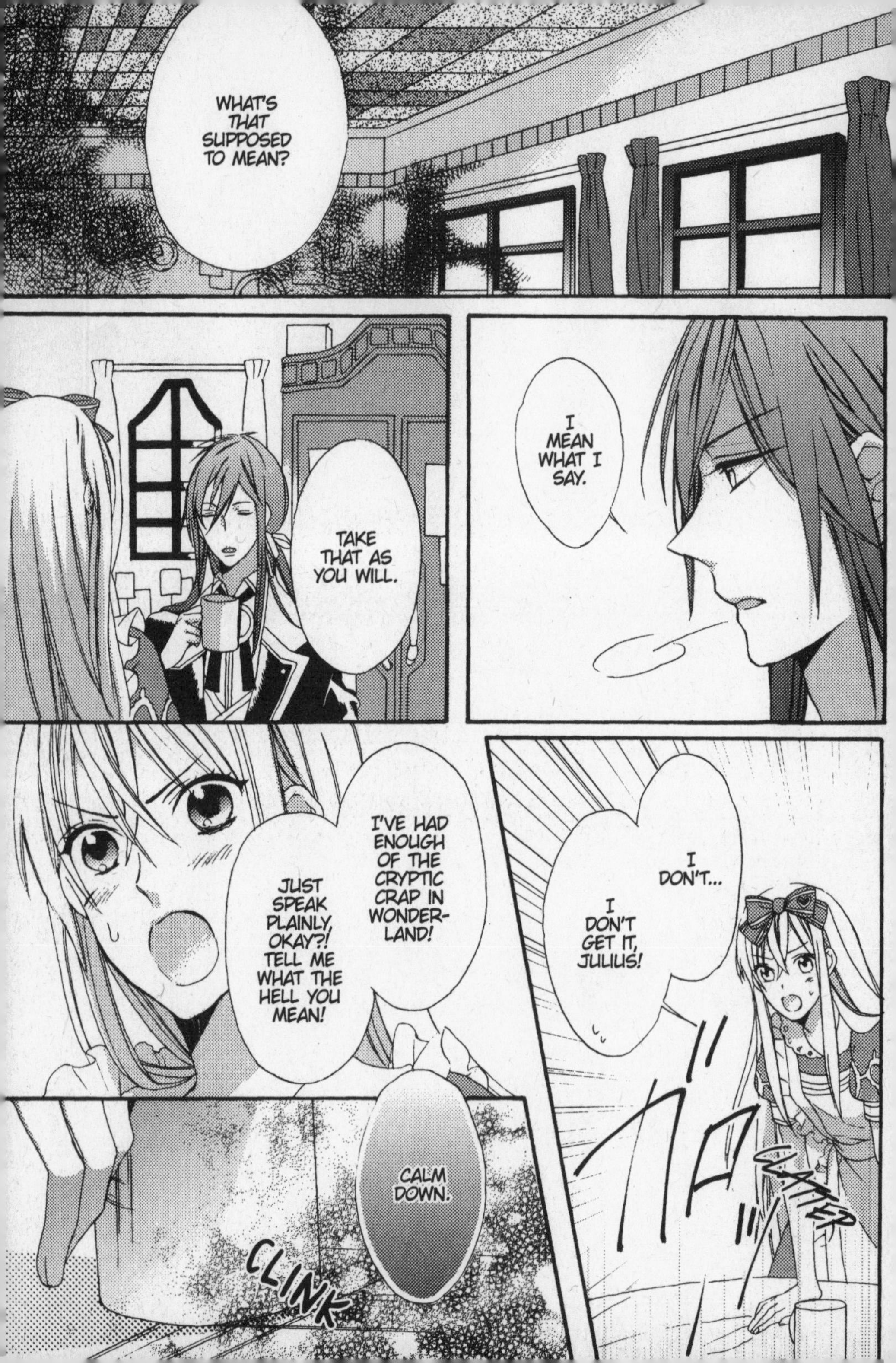
WHAT'S THAT SUPPOSED TO MEAN?
I MEAN WHAT I SAY.
TAKE THAT AS YOU WILL.
I DON'T...
I DON'T GET IT, JULIUS!
CLATTER
I'VE HAD ENOUGH OF THE CRYPTIC CRAP IN WONDERLAND!
JUST SPEAK PLAINLY, OKAY?! TELL ME WHAT THE HELL YOU MEAN!
CALM DOWN.
CLINK

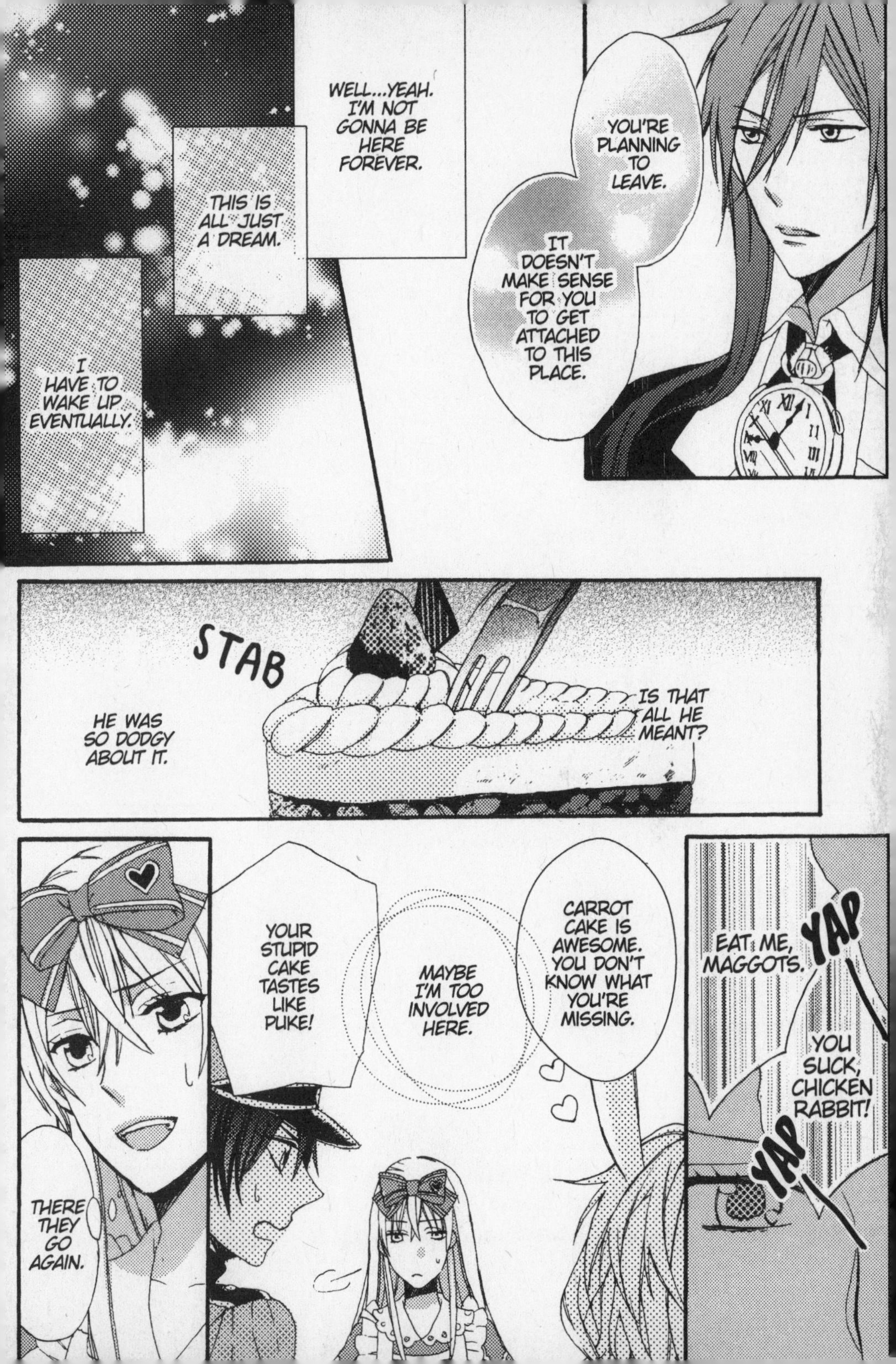

YOU'RE PLANNING TO LEAVE.
IT DOESN'T MAKE SENSE FOR YOU TO GET ATTACHED TO THIS PLACE.
WELL...YEAH. I'M NOT GONNA BE HERE FOREVER.
THIS IS ALL JUST A DREAM.
I HAVE TO WAKE UP EVENTUALLY.
STAB
IS THAT ALL HE MEANT?
HE WAS SO DODGY ABOUT IT.
YAP
EAT ME, MAGGOTS.
YOU SUCK, CHICKEN RABBIT!
YAP
CARROT CAKE IS AWESOME. YOU DON'T KNOW WHAT YOU'RE MISSING.
MAYBE I'M TOO INVOLVED HERE.
YOUR STUPID CAKE TASTES LIKE PUKE!
THERE THEY GO AGAIN.

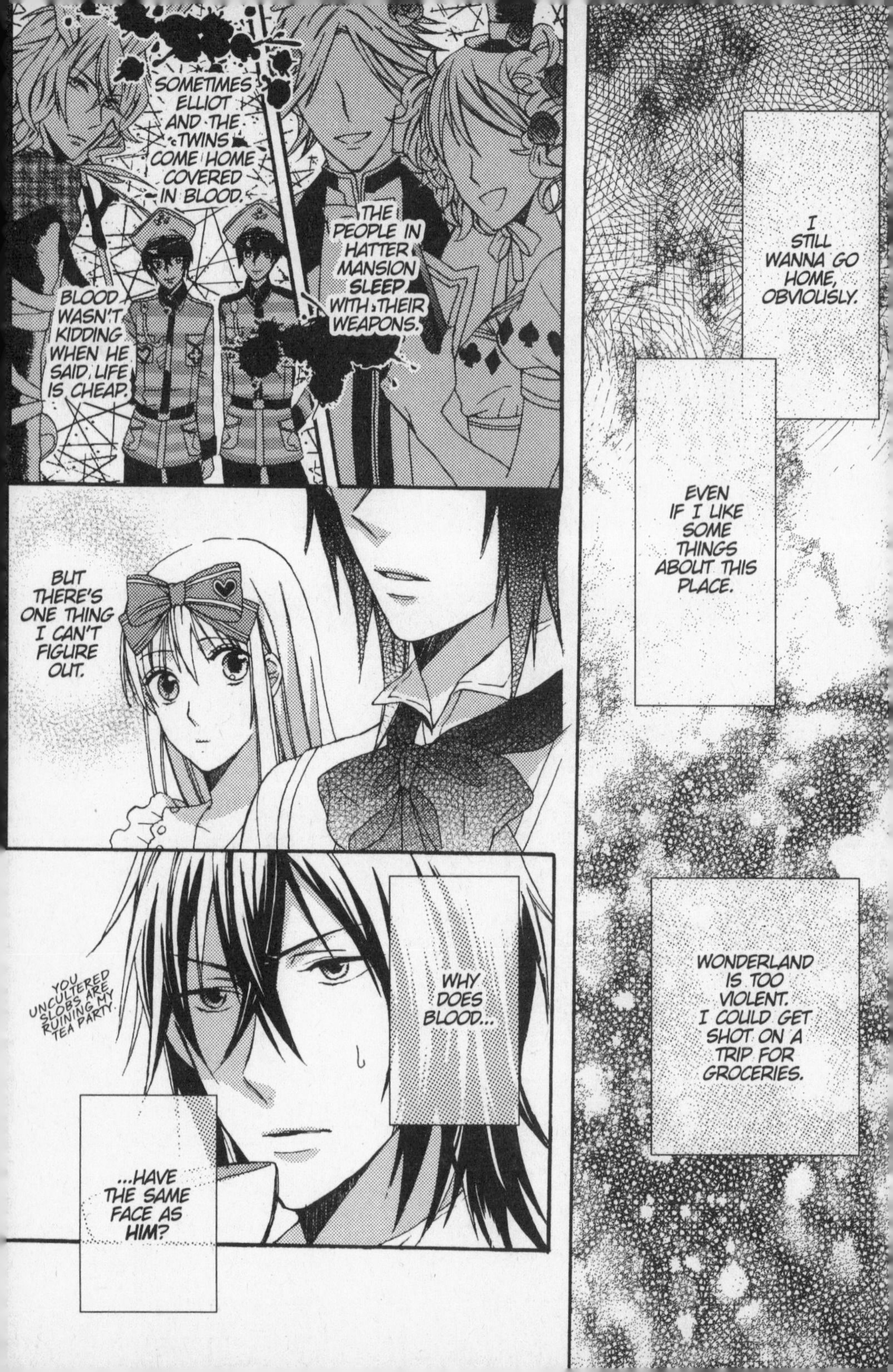
I STILL WANNA GO HOME, OBVIOUSLY.
EVEN IF I LIKE SOME THINGS ABOUT THIS PLACE.
WONDERLAND IS TOO VIOLENT. I COULD GET SHOT ON A TRIP FOR GROCERIES.
THE PEOPLE IN HATTER MANSION SLEEP WITH THEIR WEAPONS.
SOMETIMES ELLIOT AND THE TWINS COME HOME COVERED IN BLOOD.
BLOOD WASN'T KIDDING WHEN HE SAID LIFE IS CHEAP.
BUT THERE'S ONE THING I CAN'T FIGURE OUT.
WHY DOES BLOOD...
YOU UNCULTERED SLOBS ARE RUINING MY TEA PARTY.
...HAVE THE SAME FACE AS HIM?

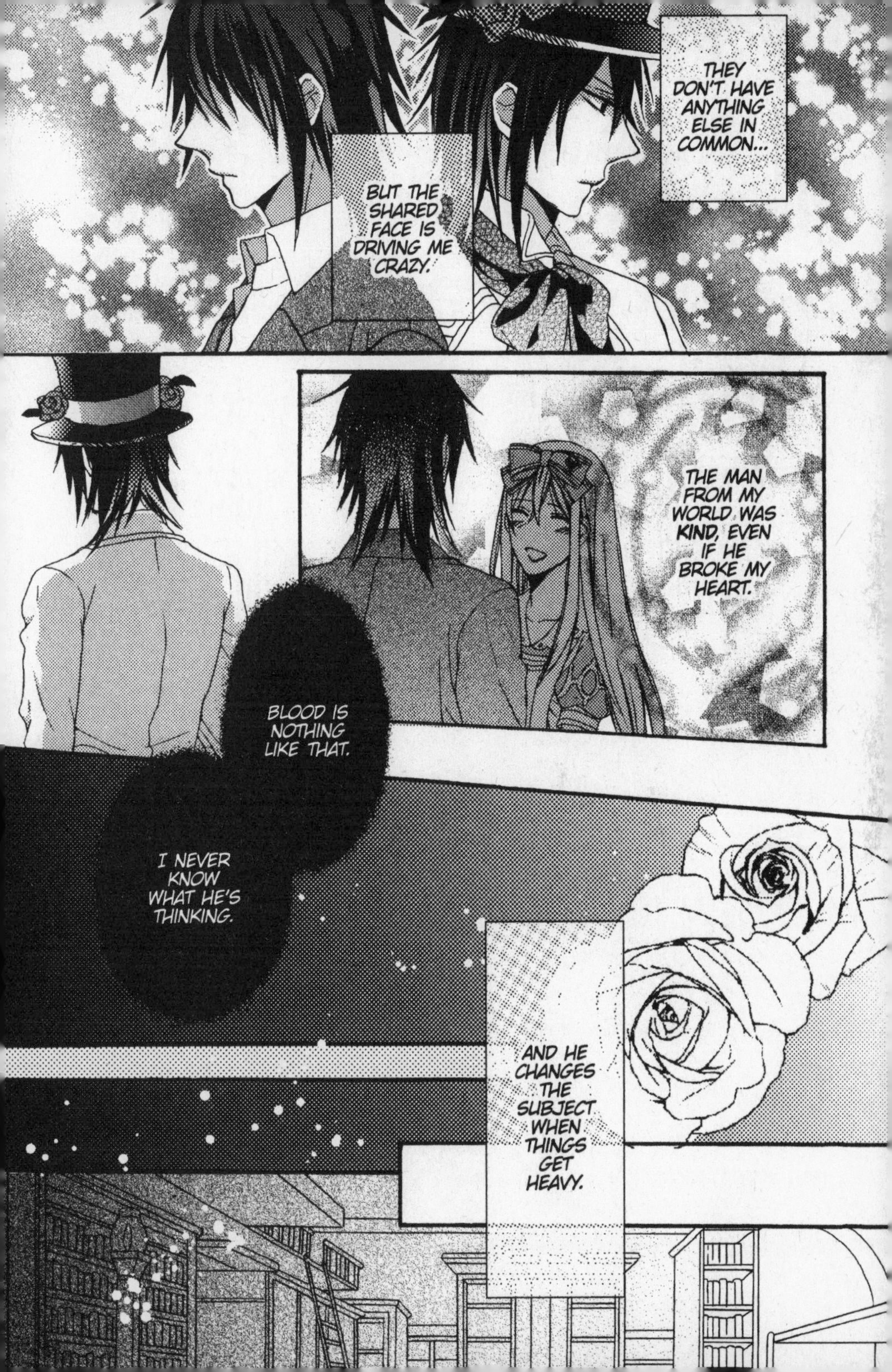
THEY DON'T HAVE ANYTHING ELSE IN COMMON...
BUT THE SHARED FACE IS DRIVING ME CRAZY.
THE MAN FROM MY WORLD WAS KIND, EVEN IF HE BROKE MY HEART.
BLOOD IS NOTHING LIKE THAT.
I NEVER KNOW WHAT HE'S THINKING.
AND HE CHANGES THE SUBJECT WHEN THINGS GET HEAVY.

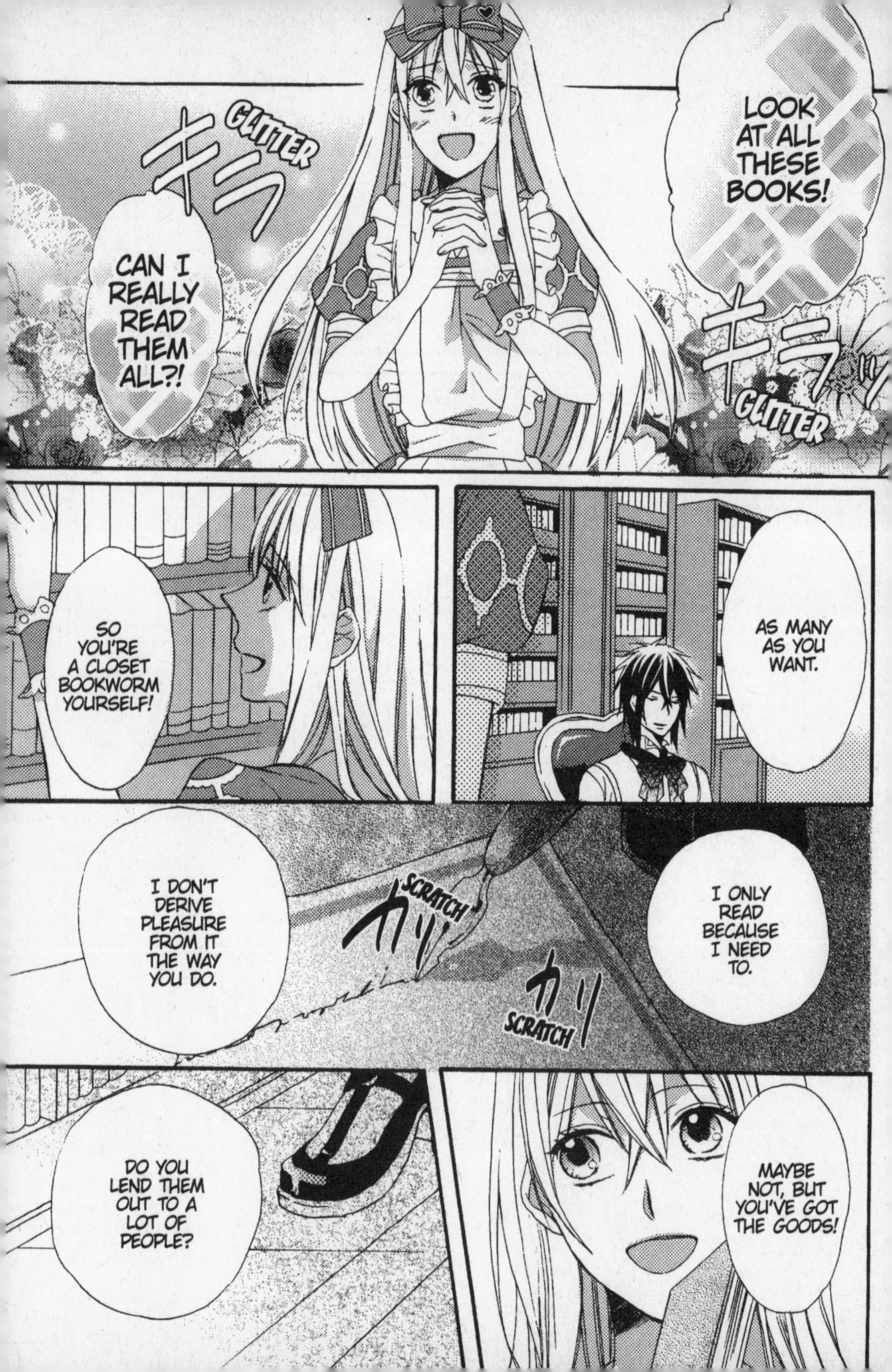
LOOK AT ALL THESE BOOKS!
キラッ
GLITTER
キラ
GLITTER
CAN I REALLY READ THEM ALL?!
AS MANY AS YOU WANT.
SO YOU'RE A CLOSET BOOKWORM YOURSELF!
I ONLY READ BECAUSE I NEED TO.
カリ
SCRATCH
カリ
SCRATCH
I DON'T DERIVE PLEASURE FROM IT THE WAY YOU DO.
MAYBE NOT, BUT YOU'VE GOT THE GOODS!
DO YOU LEND THEM OUT TO A LOT OF PEOPLE?

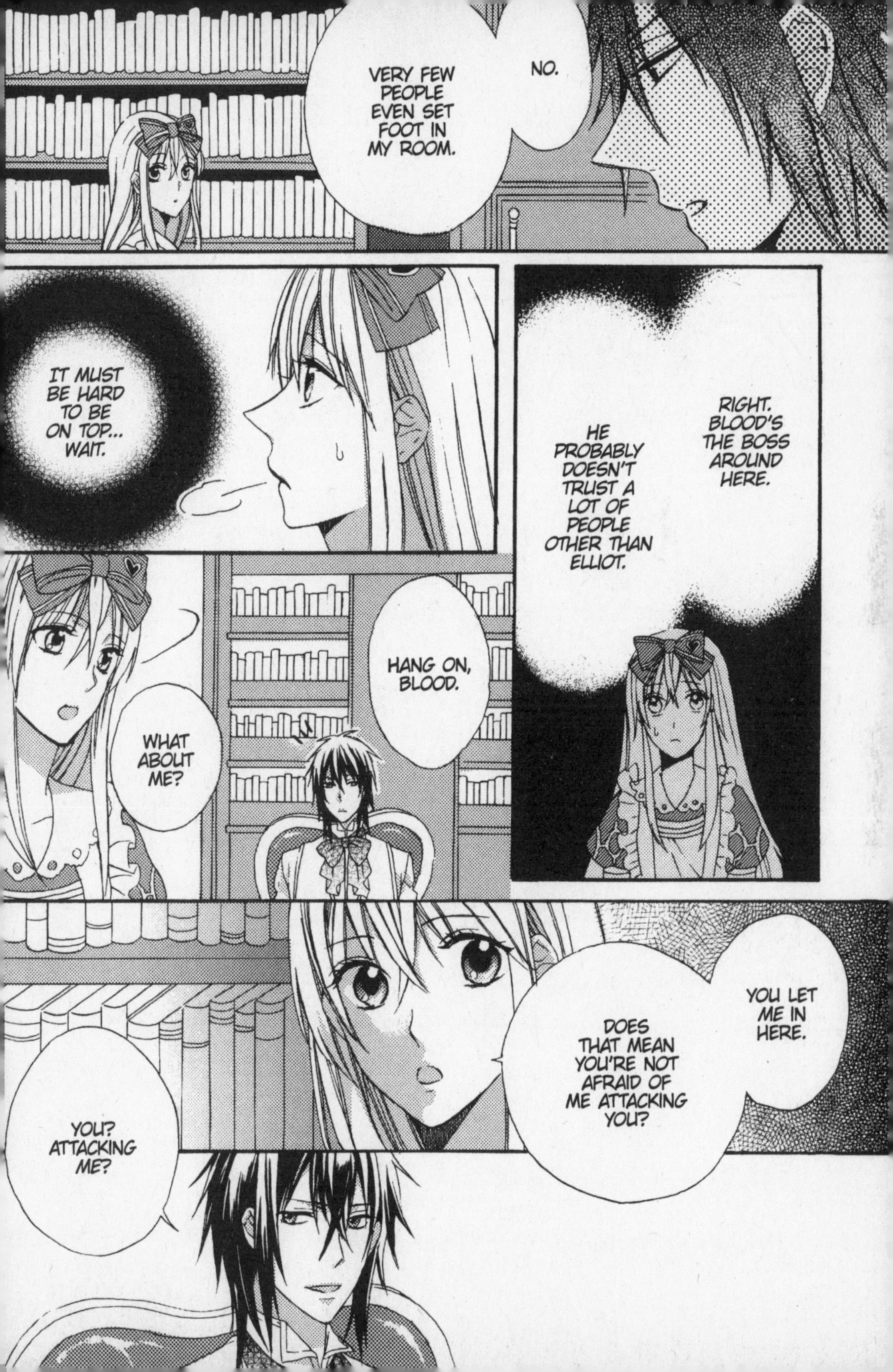
NO.
VERY FEW PEOPLE EVEN SET FOOT IN MY ROOM.
RIGHT. BLOOD'S THE BOSS AROUND HERE.
HE PROBABLY DOESN'T TRUST A LOT OF PEOPLE OTHER THAN ELLIOT.
IT MUST BE HARD TO BE ON TOP... WAIT.
HANG ON, BLOOD.
WHAT ABOUT ME?
YOU LET ME IN HERE.
DOES THAT MEAN YOU'RE NOT AFRAID OF ME ATTACKING YOU?
YOU? ATTACKING ME?

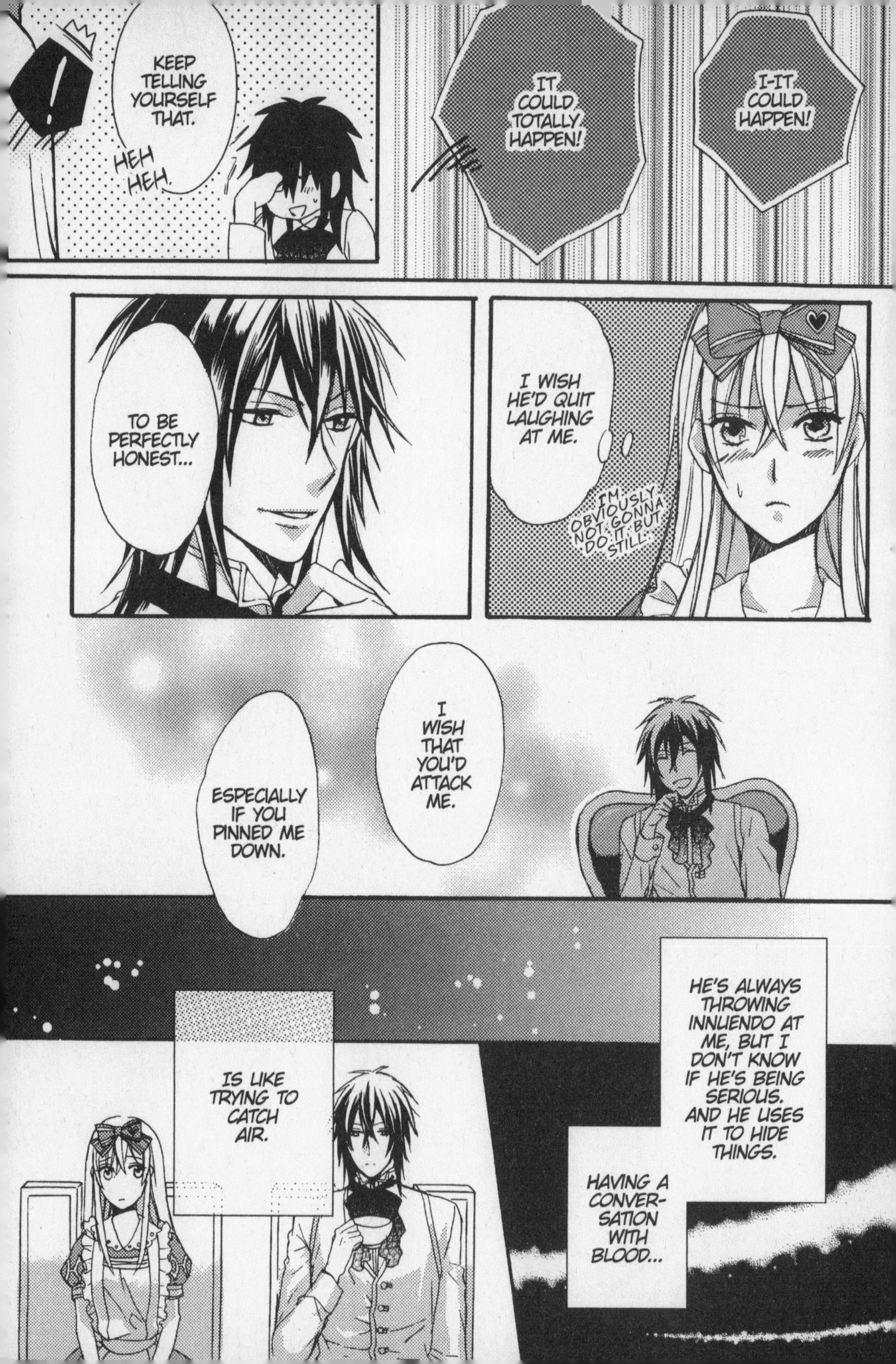
I-IT COULD HAPPEN!
IT COULD TOTALLY HAPPEN!
KEEP TELLING YOURSELF THAT.
HEH HEH.
I WISH HE'D QUIT LAUGHING AT ME.
I'M OBVIOUSLY NOT GONNA DO IT, BUT STILL.
TO BE PERFECTLY HONEST...
I WISH THAT YOU'D ATTACK ME.
ESPECIALLY IF YOU PINNED ME DOWN.
HE'S ALWAYS THROWING INNUENDO AT ME, BUT I DON'T KNOW IF HE'S BEING SERIOUS. AND HE USES IT TO HIDE THINGS.
HAVING A CONVERSATION WITH BLOOD...
IS LIKE TRYING TO CATCH AIR.

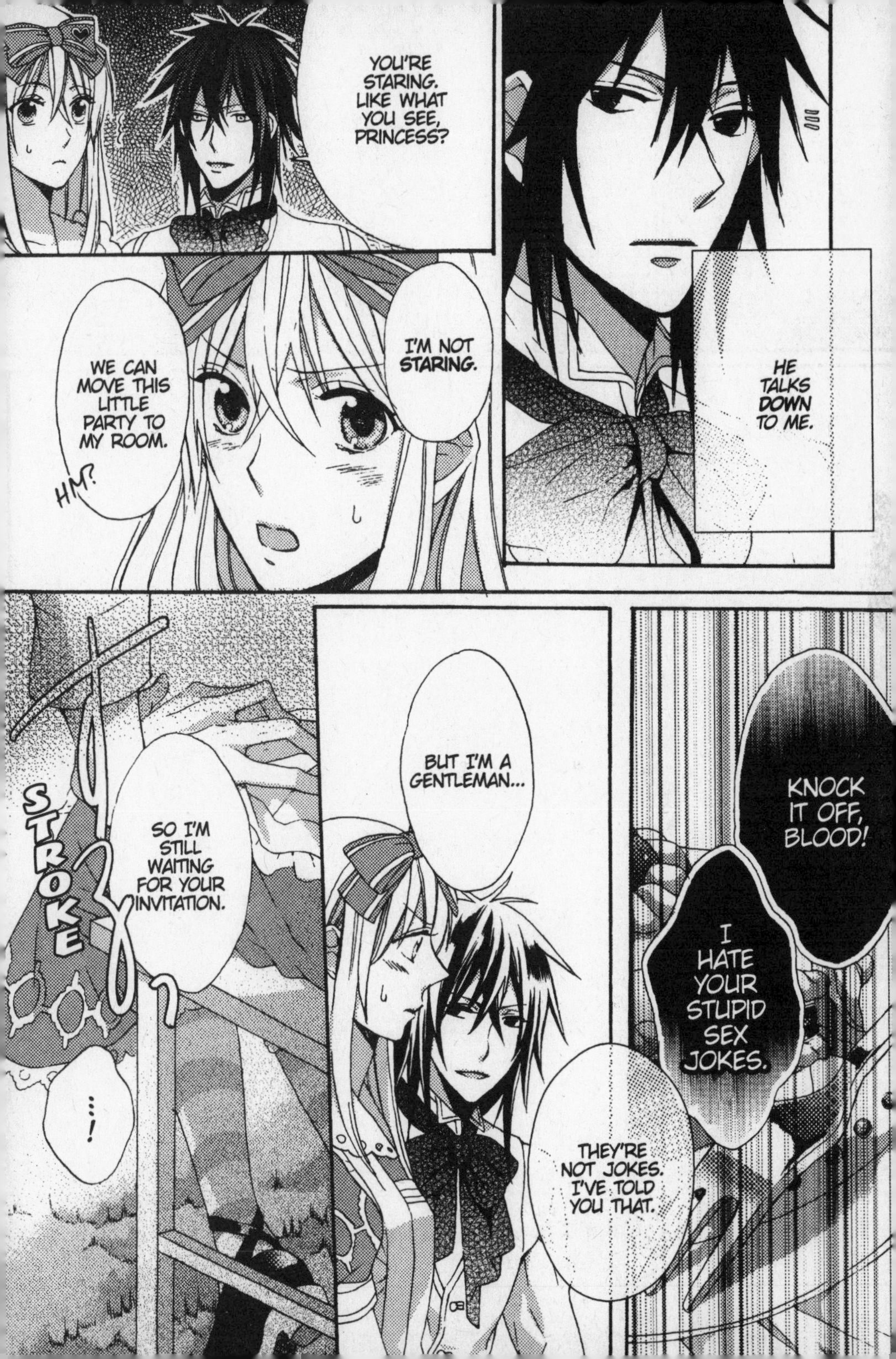
HE TALKS DOWN TO ME.
YOU'RE STARING. LIKE WHAT YOU SEE, PRINCESS?
I'M NOT STARING.
WE CAN MOVE THIS LITTLE PARTY TO MY ROOM.
HM?
KNOCK IT OFF, BLOOD!
I HATE YOUR STUPID SEX JOKES.
BUT I'M A GENTLEMAN...
THEY'RE NOT JOKES. I'VE TOLD YOU THAT.
SO I'M STILL WAITING FOR YOUR INVITATION.
STROKE
...!

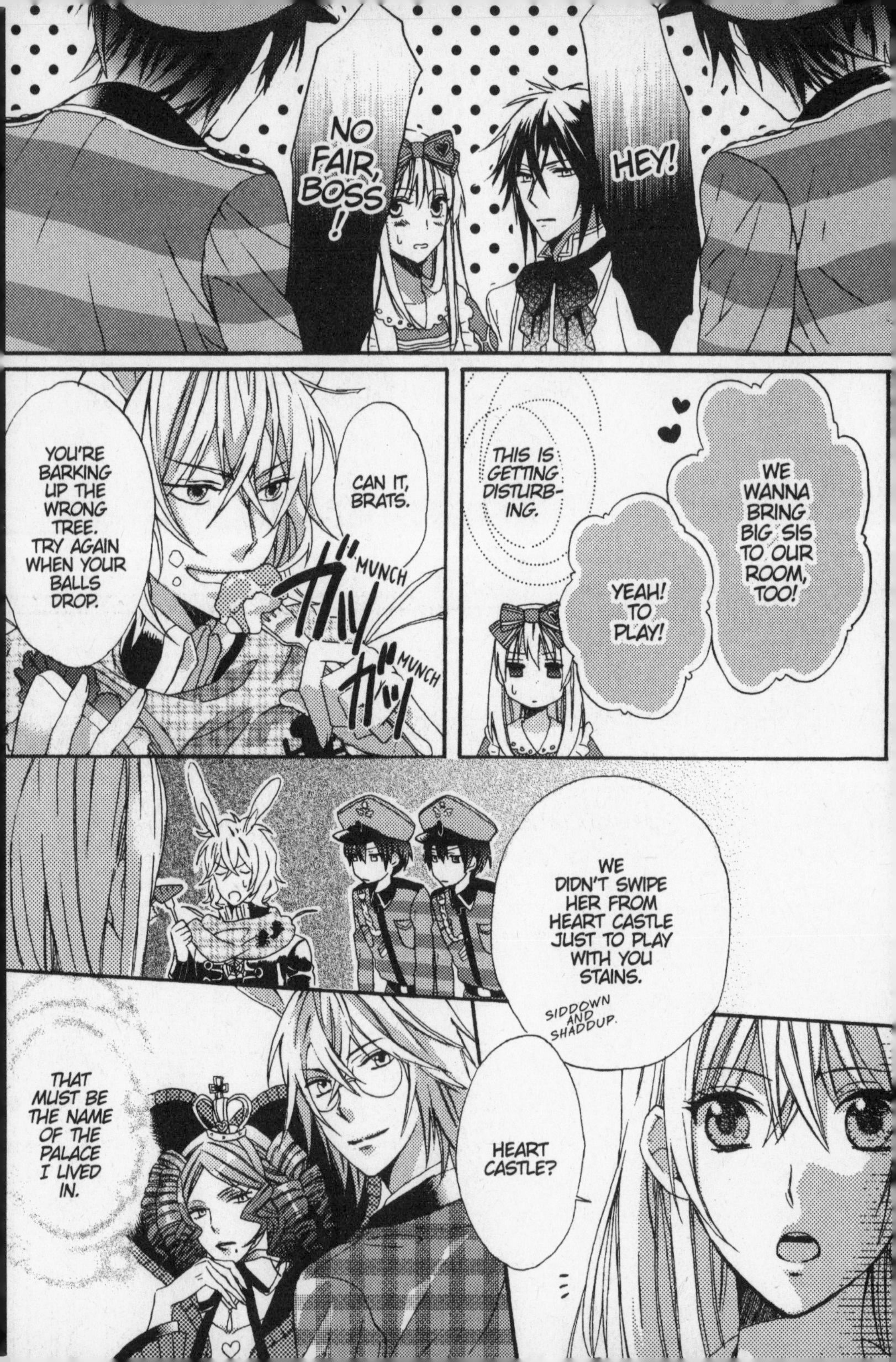
HEY!
NO FAIR, BOSS!
WE WANNA BRING BIG SIS TO OUR ROOM, TOO!
YEAH! TO PLAY!
THIS IS GETTING DISTURBING.
CAN IT, BRATS.
ガリ
MUNCH
MUNCH
YOU'RE BARKING UP THE WRONG TREE. TRY AGAIN WHEN YOUR BALLS DROP.
WE DIDN'T SWIPE HER FROM HEART CASTLE JUST TO PLAY WITH YOU STAINS.
SIDDOWN AND SHADDUP.
HEART CASTLE?
THAT MUST BE THE NAME OF THE PALACE I LIVED IN.

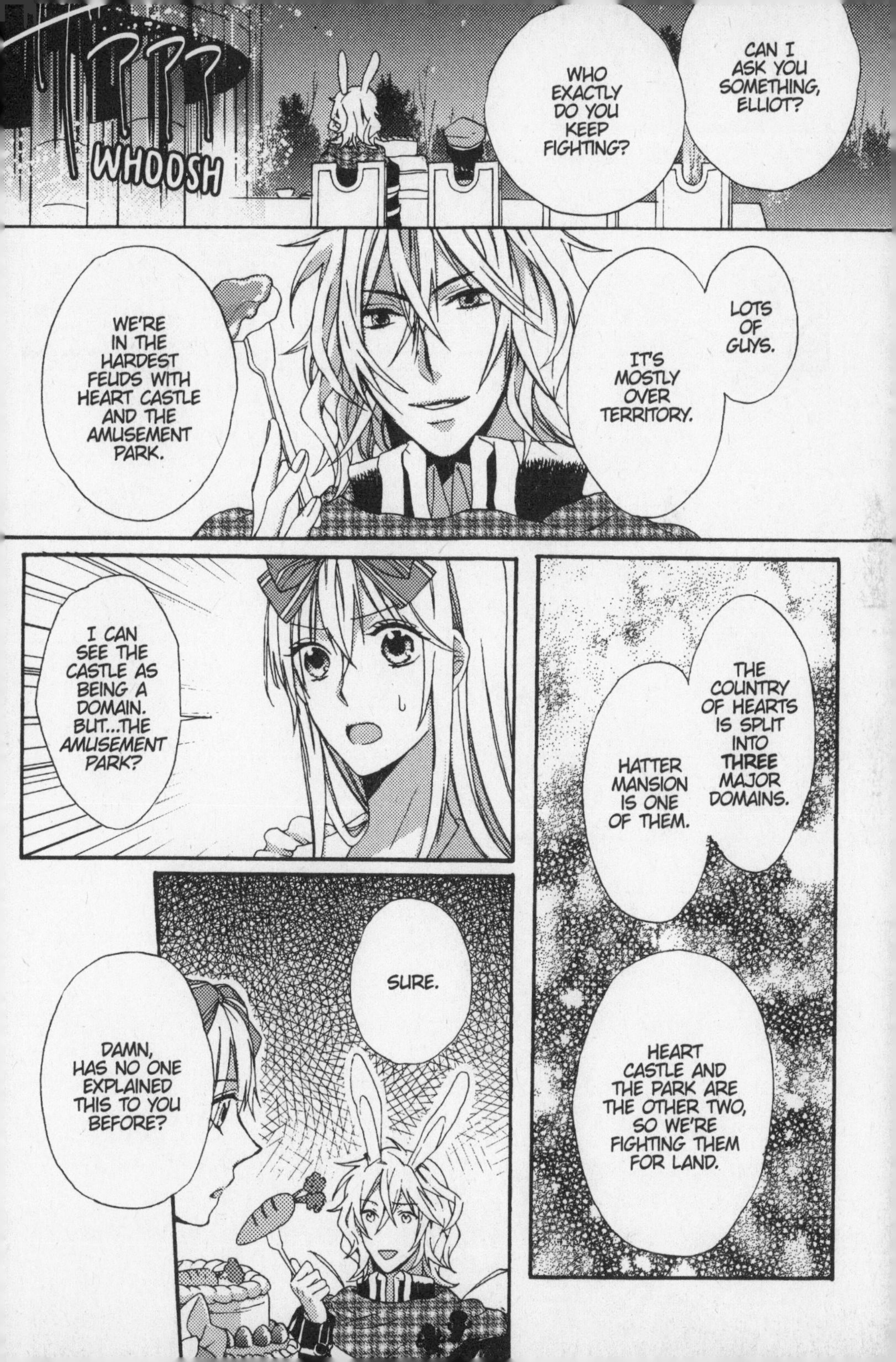

CAN I ASK YOU SOMETHING, ELLIOT?
WHO EXACTLY DO YOU KEEP FIGHTING?
???
WHOOSH
LOTS OF GUYS.
IT'S MOSTLY OVER TERRITORY.
WE'RE IN THE HARDEST FEUDS WITH HEART CASTLE AND THE AMUSEMENT PARK.
THE COUNTRY OF HEARTS IS SPLIT INTO THREE MAJOR DOMAINS.
HATTER MANSION IS ONE OF THEM.
HEART CASTLE AND THE PARK ARE THE OTHER TWO, SO WE'RE FIGHTING THEM FOR LAND.
I CAN SEE THE CASTLE AS BEING A DOMAIN. BUT...THE AMUSEMENT PARK?
SURE.
DAMN, HAS NO ONE EXPLAINED THIS TO YOU BEFORE?

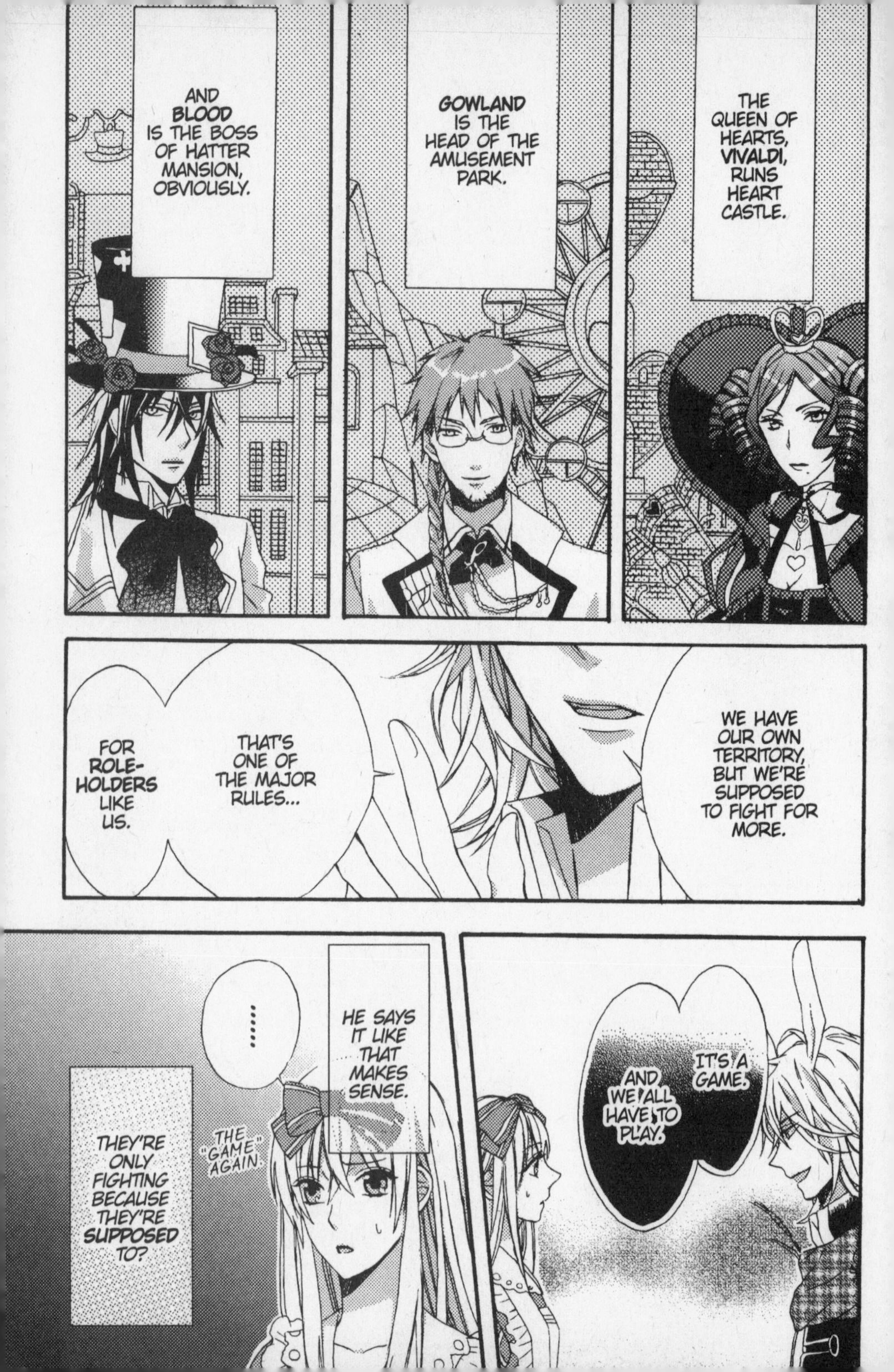
THE QUEEN OF HEARTS, VIVALDI, RUNS HEART CASTLE.
GOWLAND IS THE HEAD OF THE AMUSEMENT PARK.
AND BLOOD IS THE BOSS OF HATTER MANSION, OBVIOUSLY.
WE HAVE OUR OWN TERRITORY, BUT WE'RE SUPPOSED TO FIGHT FOR MORE.
THAT'S ONE OF THE MAJOR RULES...
FOR ROLE-HOLDERS LIKE US.
IT'S A GAME.
AND WE ALL HAVE TO PLAY.
HE SAYS IT LIKE THAT MAKES SENSE.
......
THE "GAME" AGAIN.
THEY'RE ONLY FIGHTING BECAUSE THEY'RE SUPPOSED TO?

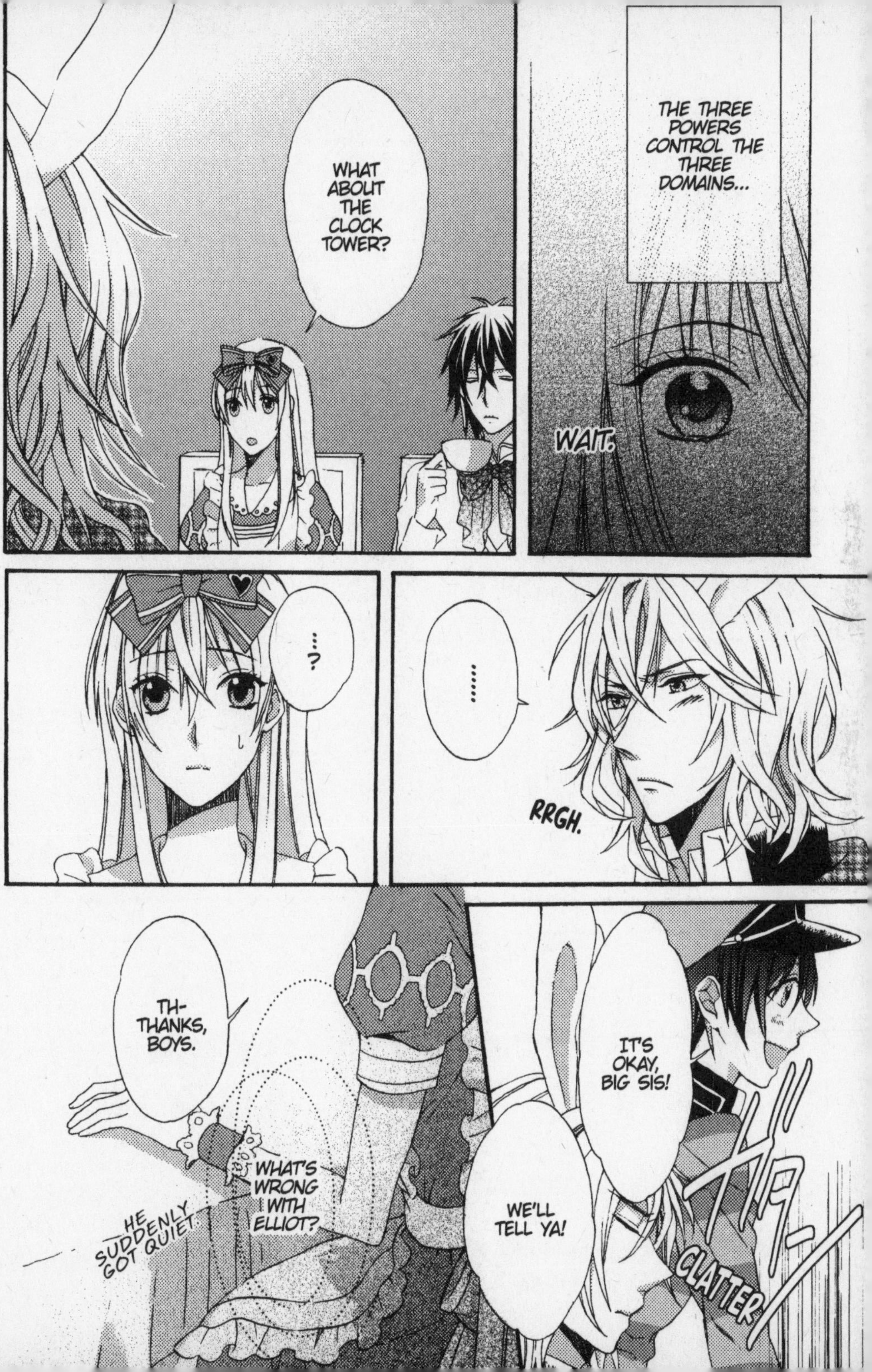
THE THREE POWERS CONTROL THE THREE DOMAINS...
WAIT.
WHAT ABOUT THE CLOCK TOWER?
......
RRGH.
...?
IT'S OKAY, BIG SIS!
WE'LL TELL YA!
CLATTER
TH-THANKS, BOYS.
WHAT'S WRONG WITH ELLIOT?
HE SUDDENLY GOT QUIET.

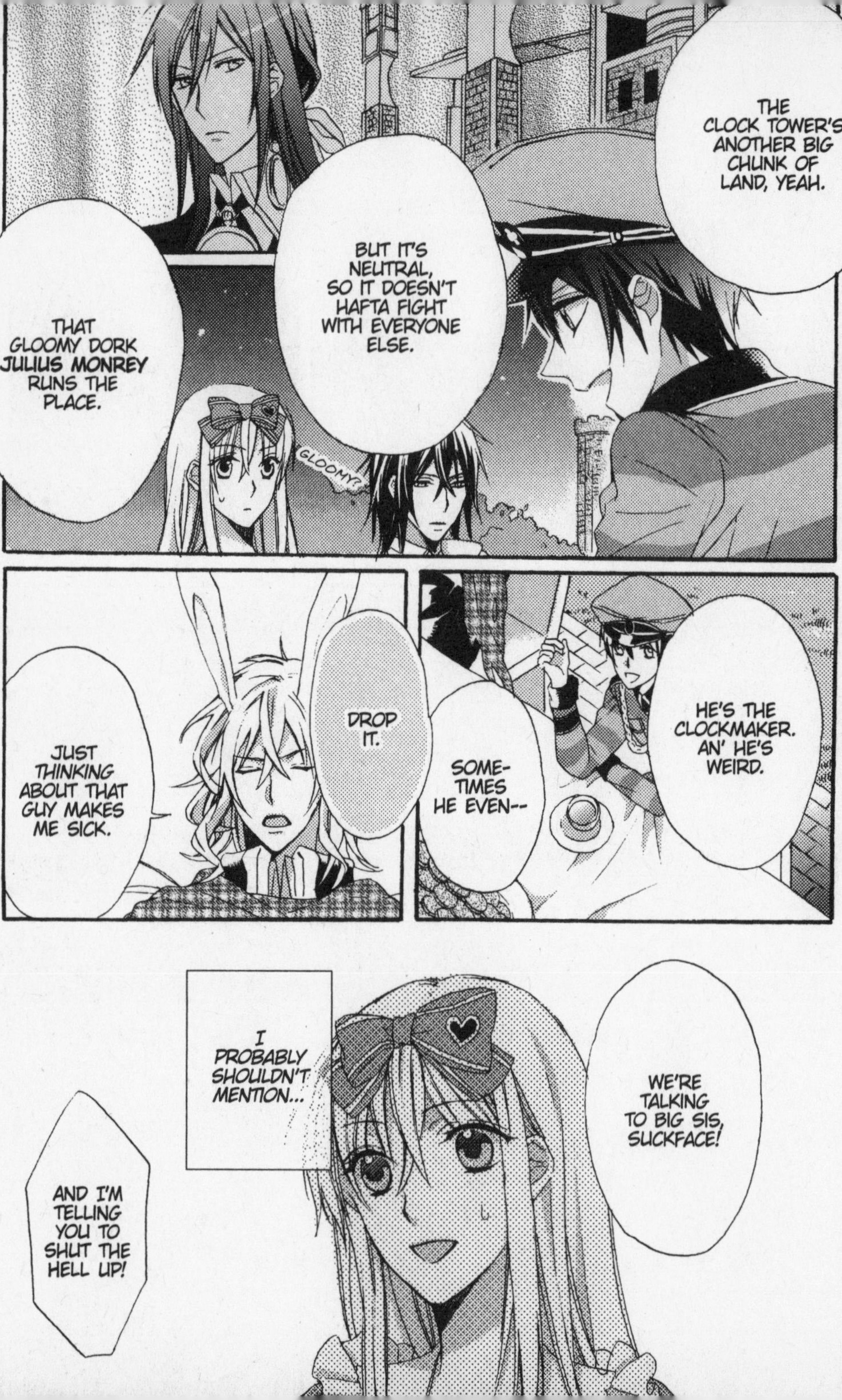
THE CLOCK TOWER'S ANOTHER BIG CHUNK OF LAND, YEAH.
BUT IT'S NEUTRAL, SO IT DOESN'T HAFTA FIGHT WITH EVERYONE ELSE.
THAT GLOOMY DORK JULIUS MONREY RUNS THE PLACE.
GLOOMY?
HE'S THE CLOCKMAKER. AN' HE'S WEIRD.
SOME-TIMES HE EVEN--
DROP IT.
JUST THINKING ABOUT THAT GUY MAKES ME SICK.
WE'RE TALKING TO BIG SIS, SUCKFACE!
I PROBABLY SHOULDN'T MENTION...
AND I'M TELLING YOU TO SHUT THE HELL UP!

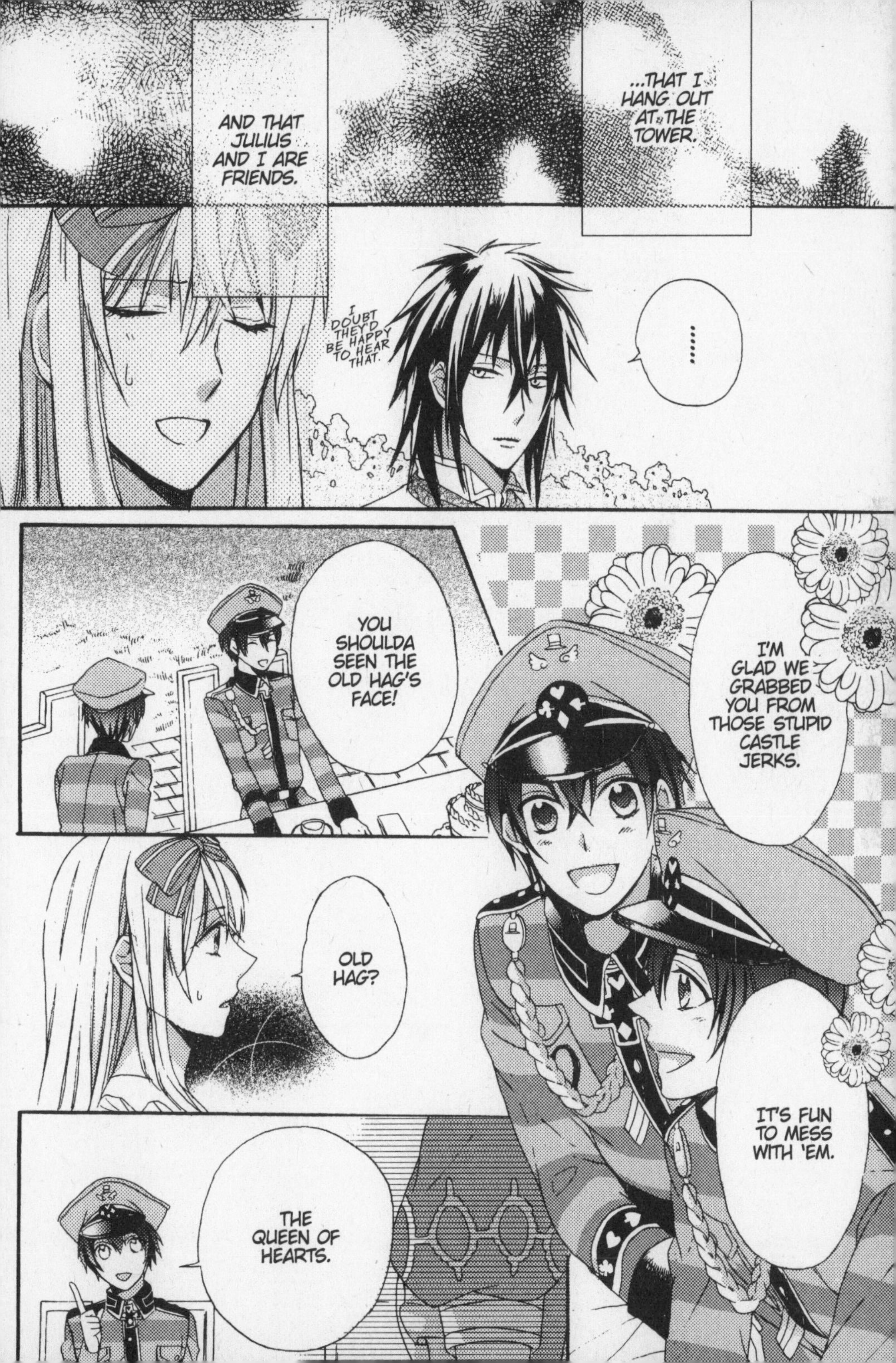
...THAT I HANG OUT AT THE TOWER.
AND THAT JULIUS AND I ARE FRIENDS.
……
I DOUBT THEY'D BE HAPPY TO HEAR THAT.
I'M GLAD WE GRABBED YOU FROM THOSE STUPID CASTLE JERKS.
IT'S FUN TO MESS WITH 'EM.
YOU SHOULDA SEEN THE OLD HAG'S FACE!
OLD HAG?
THE QUEEN OF HEARTS.

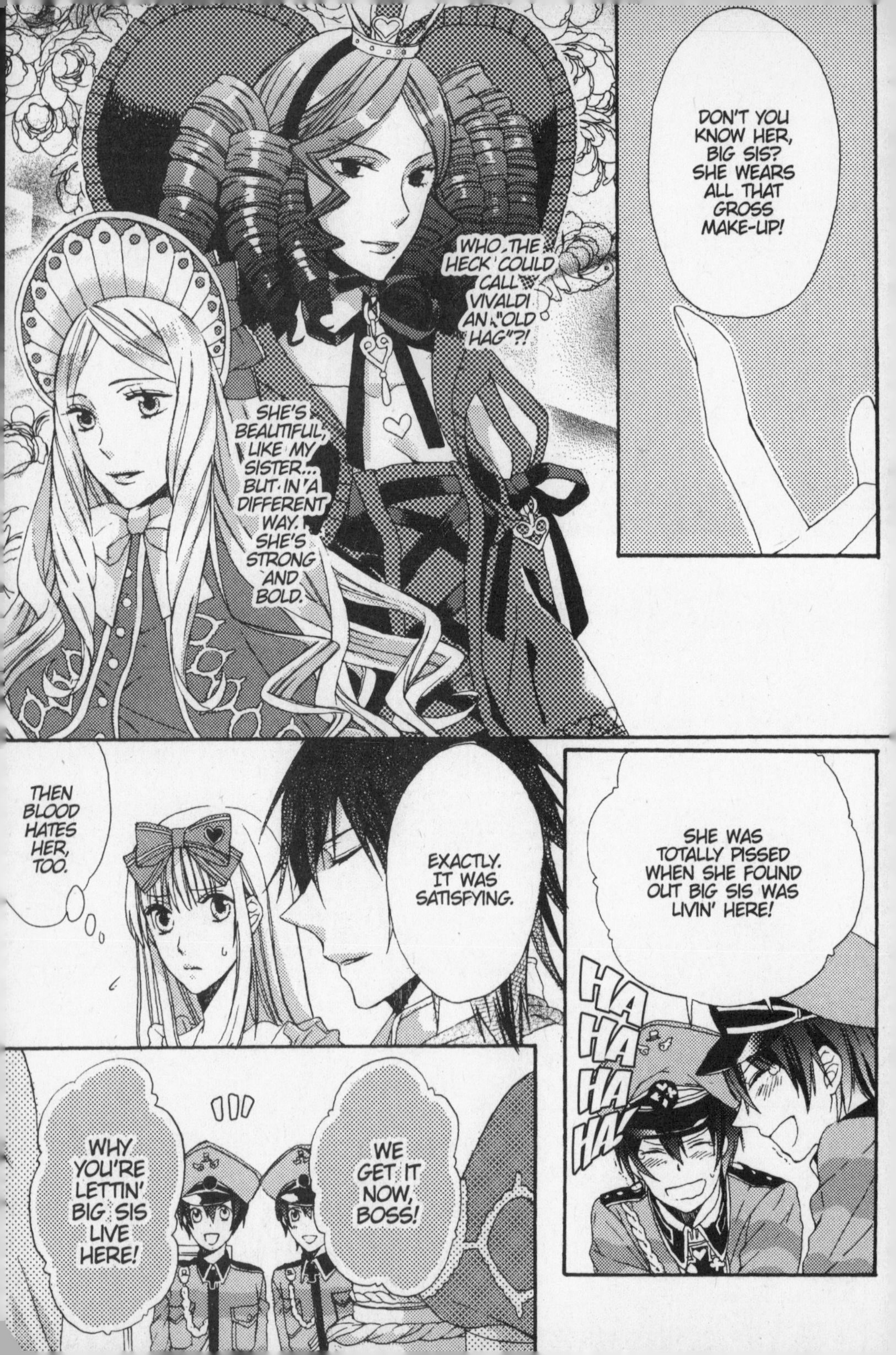
DON'T YOU KNOW HER, BIG SIS? SHE WEARS ALL THAT GROSS MAKE-UP!
WHO THE HECK COULD CALL VIVALDI AN "OLD HAG"?!
SHE'S BEAUTIFUL, LIKE MY SISTER... BUT IN A DIFFERENT WAY. SHE'S STRONG AND BOLD.
SHE WAS TOTALLY PISSED WHEN SHE FOUND OUT BIG SIS WAS LIVIN' HERE!
HA HA HA HA!
EXACTLY. IT WAS SATISFYING.
THEN BLOOD HATES HER, TOO.
WE GET IT NOW, BOSS!
WHY YOU'RE LETTIN' BIG SIS LIVE HERE!

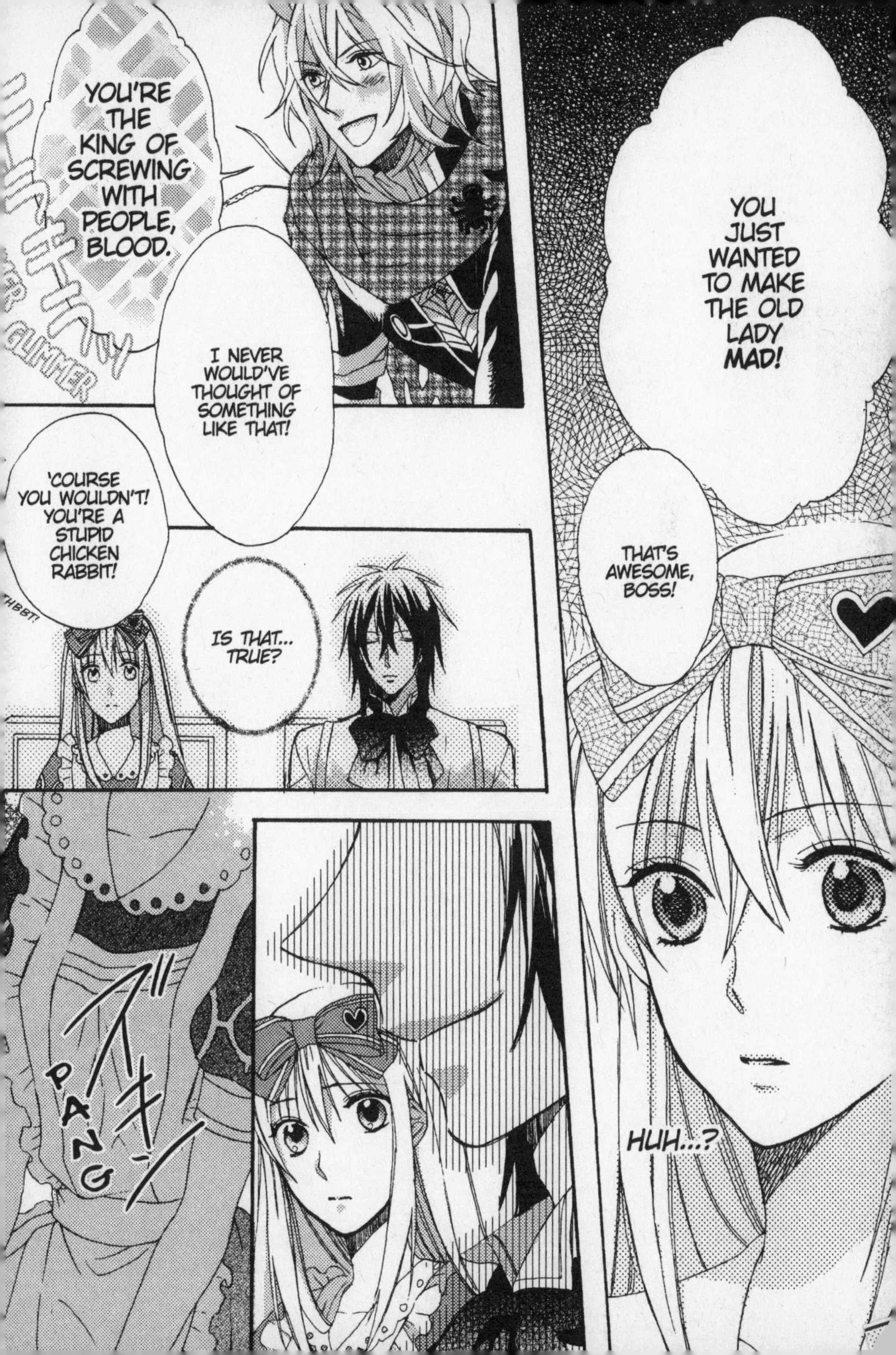
YOU JUST WANTED TO MAKE THE OLD LADY MAD!
THAT'S AWESOME, BOSS!
HUH...?
YOU'RE THE KING OF SCREWING WITH PEOPLE, BLOOD.
GLIMMER
I NEVER WOULD'VE THOUGHT OF SOMETHING LIKE THAT!
'COURSE YOU WOULDN'T! YOU'RE A STUPID CHICKEN RABBIT!
IS THAT... TRUE?
PANG

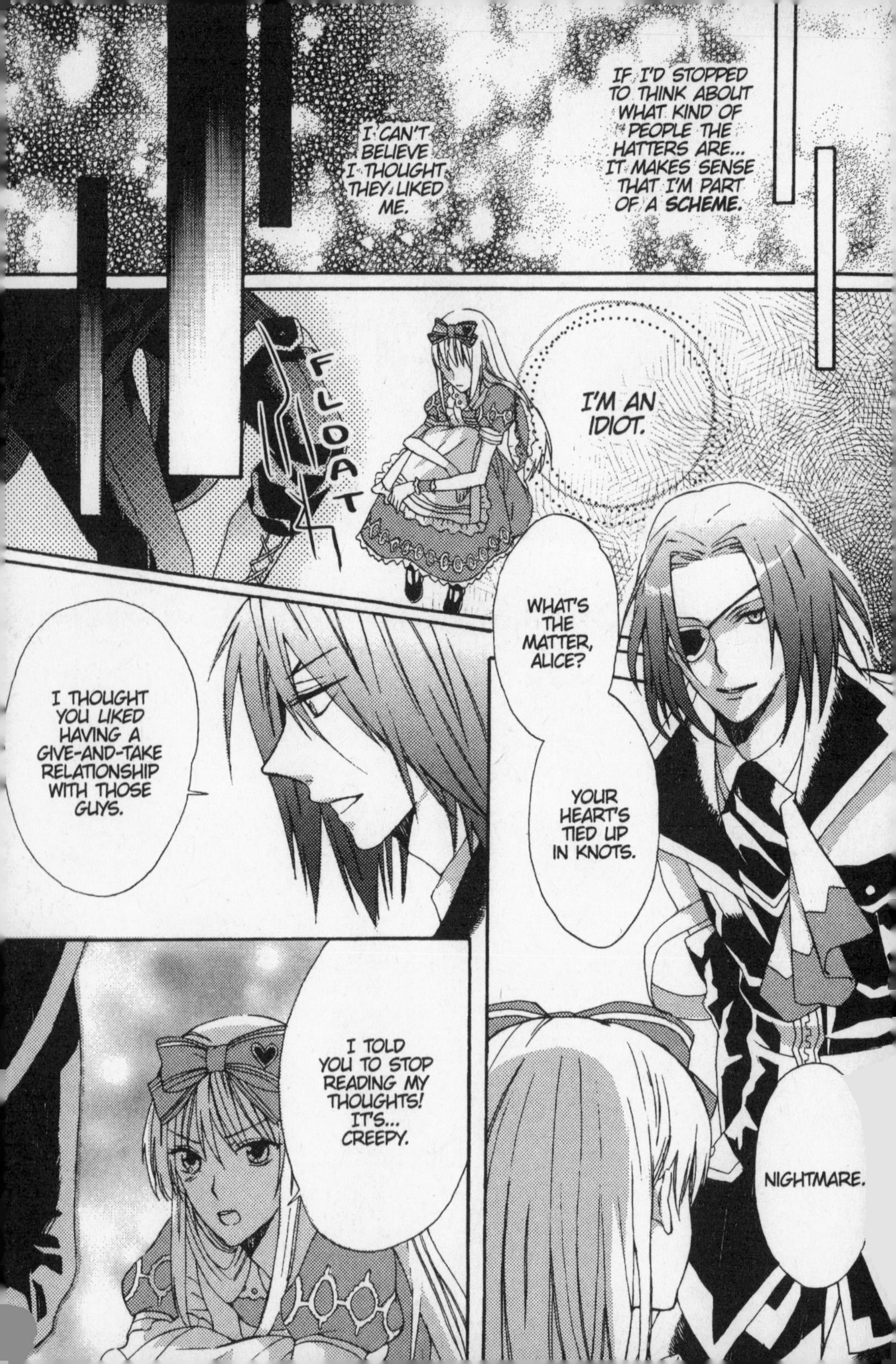
IF I'D STOPPED TO THINK ABOUT WHAT KIND OF PEOPLE THE HATTERS ARE... IT MAKES SENSE THAT I'M PART OF A SCHEME.
I CAN'T BELIEVE I THOUGHT THEY LIKED ME.
I'M AN IDIOT.
FLOAT
WHAT'S THE MATTER, ALICE?
YOUR HEART'S TIED UP IN KNOTS.
NIGHTMARE.
I THOUGHT YOU LIKED HAVING A GIVE-AND-TAKE RELATIONSHIP WITH THOSE GUYS.
I TOLD YOU TO STOP READING MY THOUGHTS! IT'S... CREEPY.

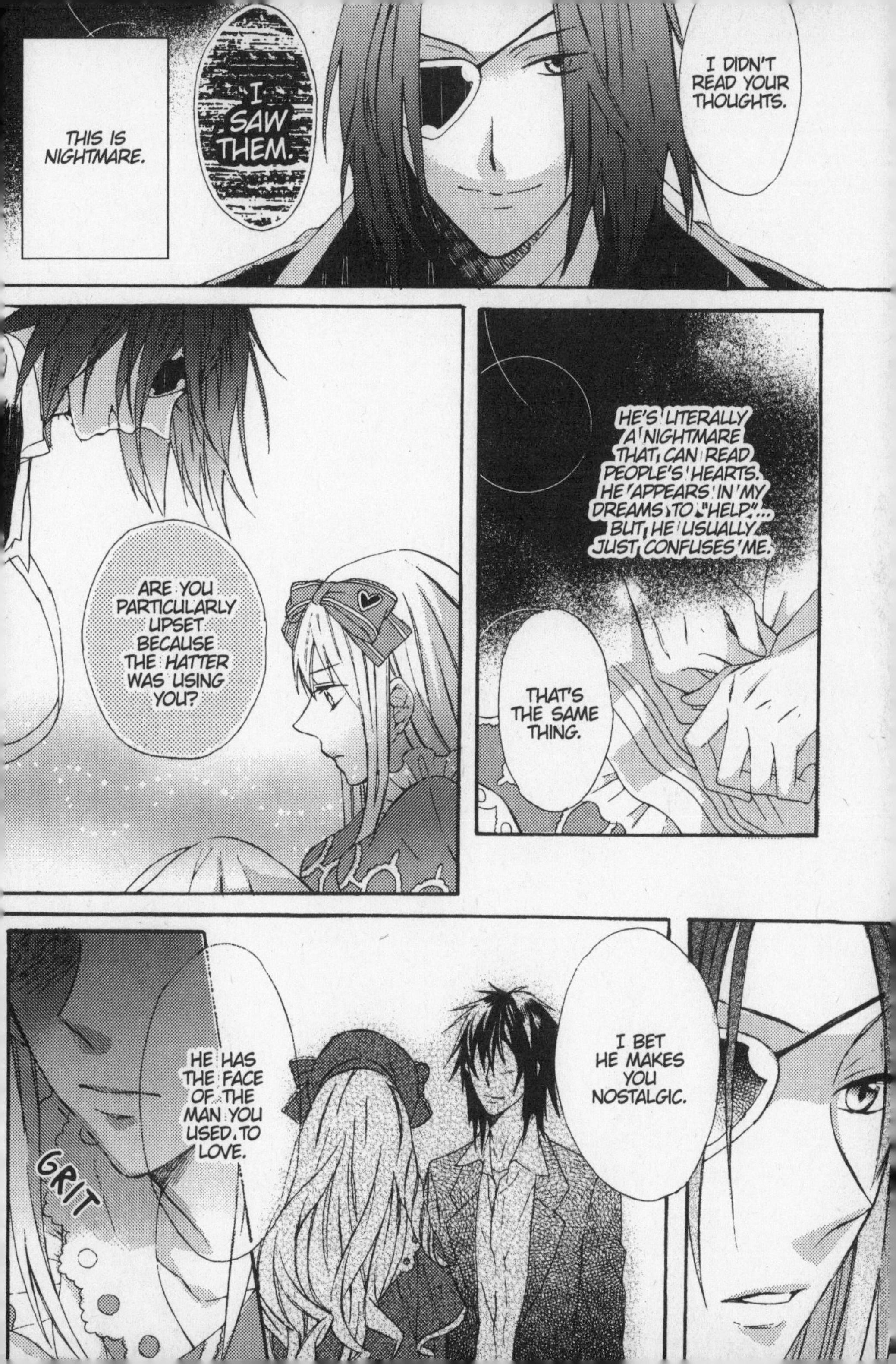
I DIDN'T READ YOUR THOUGHTS.
I SAW THEM.
THIS IS NIGHTMARE.
HE'S LITERALLY A NIGHTMARE THAT CAN READ PEOPLE'S HEARTS. HE APPEARS IN MY DREAMS TO "HELP"... BUT HE USUALLY JUST CONFUSES ME.
THAT'S THE SAME THING.
ARE YOU PARTICULARLY UPSET BECAUSE THE HATTER WAS USING YOU?
I BET HE MAKES YOU NOSTALGIC.
HE HAS THE FACE OF THE MAN YOU USED TO LOVE.
GRIT

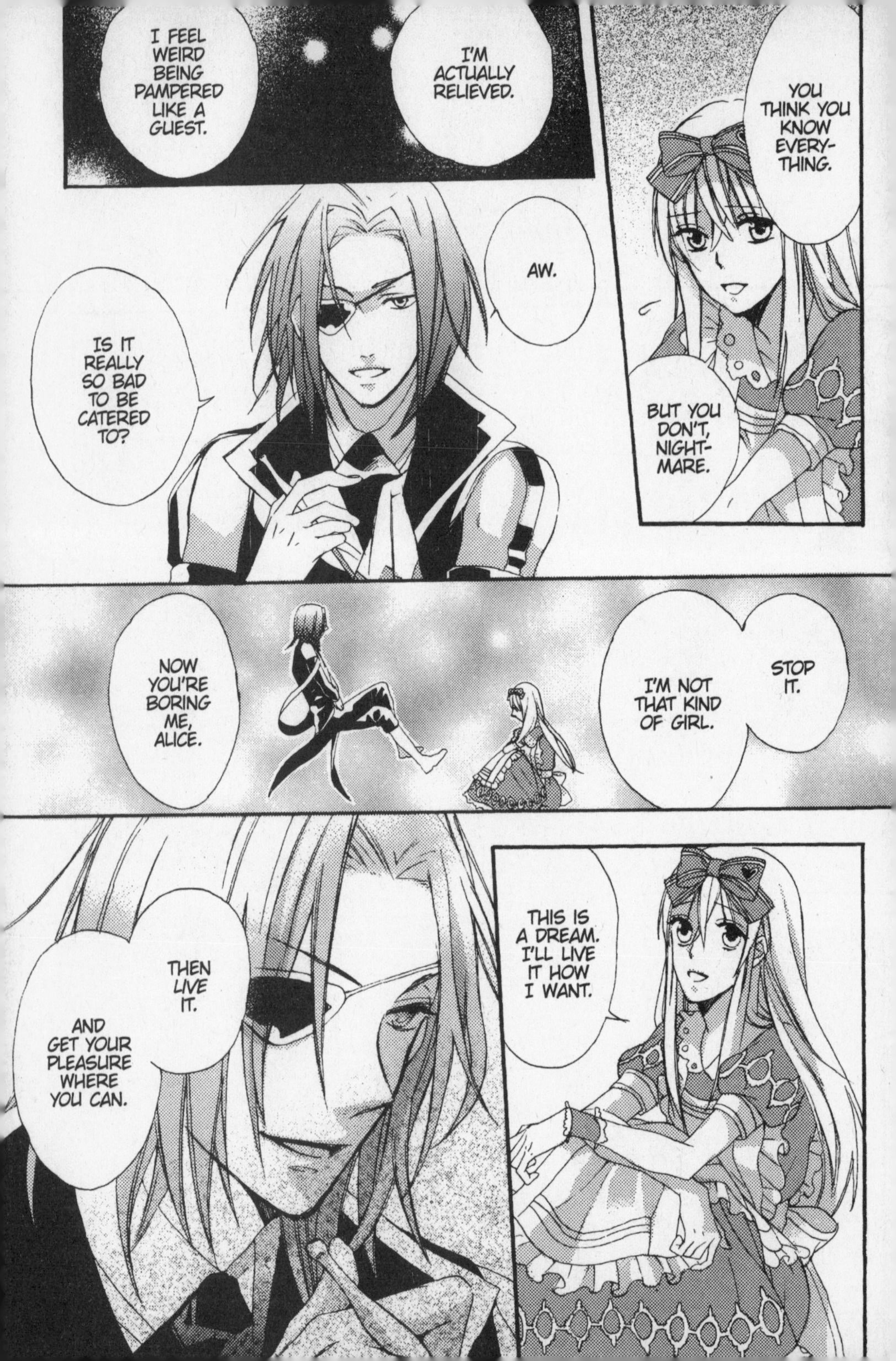
YOU THINK YOU KNOW EVERYTHING.
BUT YOU DON'T, NIGHTMARE.
I'M ACTUALLY RELIEVED.
I FEEL WEIRD BEING PAMPERED LIKE A GUEST.
AW.
IS IT REALLY SO BAD TO BE CATERED TO?
STOP IT.
I'M NOT THAT KIND OF GIRL.
NOW YOU'RE BORING ME, ALICE.
THIS IS A DREAM. I'LL LIVE IT HOW I WANT.
THEN LIVE IT.
AND GET YOUR PLEASURE WHERE YOU CAN.

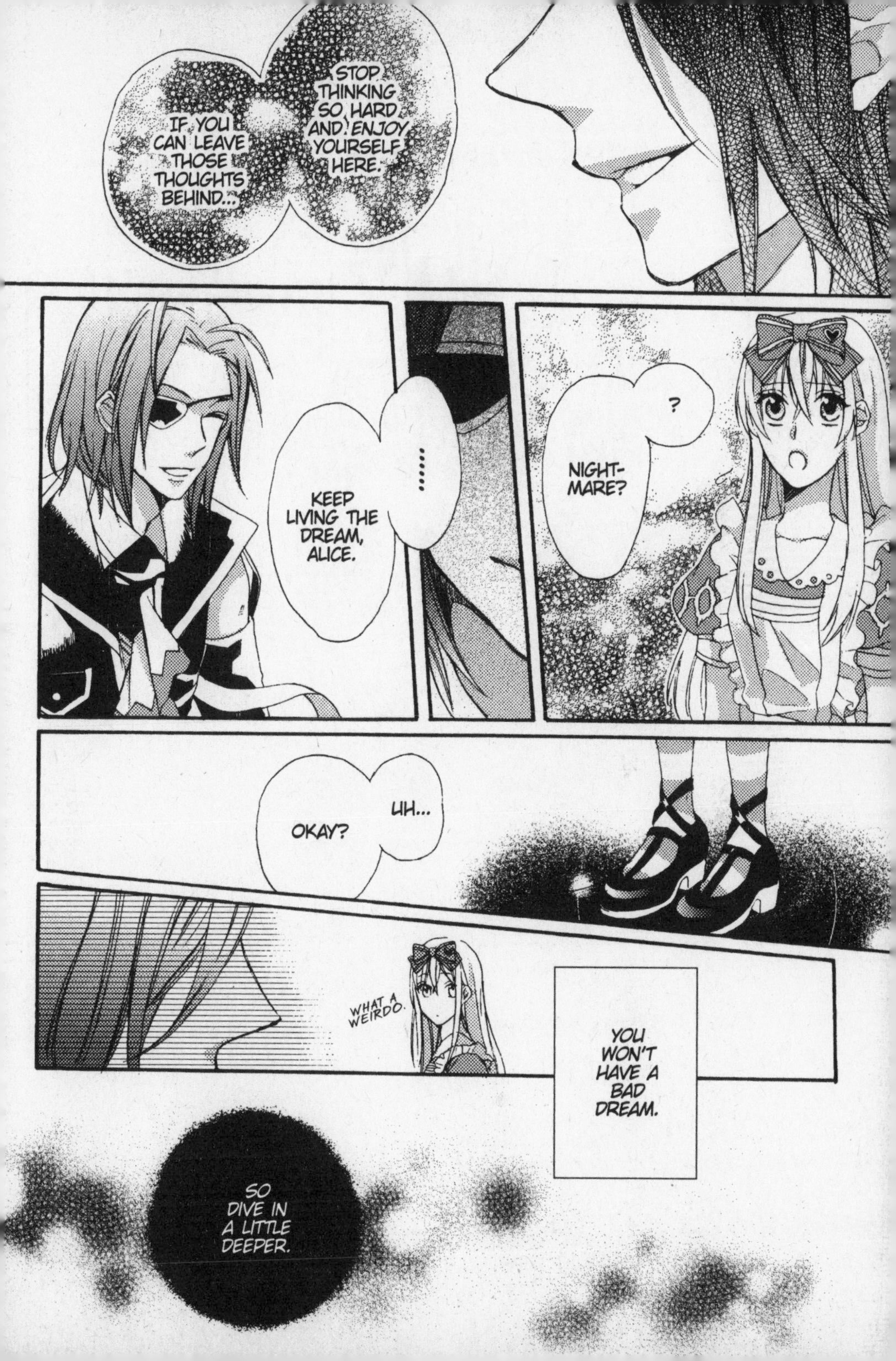
STOP THINKING SO HARD AND ENJOY YOURSELF HERE.
IF YOU CAN LEAVE THOSE THOUGHTS BEHIND...
?
NIGHT-MARE?
......
KEEP LIVING THE DREAM, ALICE.
UH...
OKAY?
YOU WON'T HAVE A BAD DREAM.
WHAT A WEIRDO.
SO DIVE IN A LITTLE DEEPER.

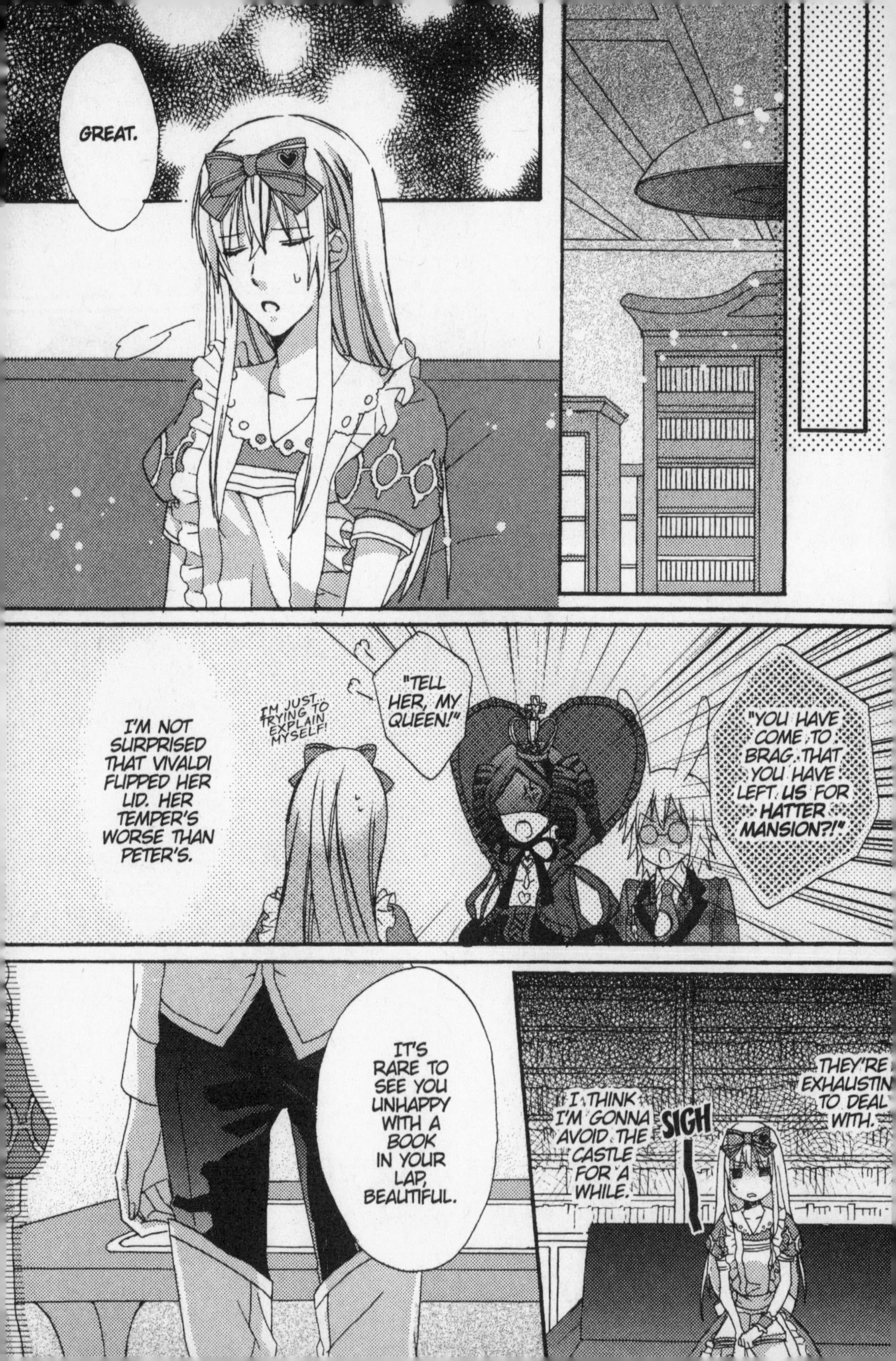
GREAT.
"YOU HAVE COME TO BRAG THAT YOU HAVE LEFT US FOR HATTER MANSION?!"
"TELL HER, MY QUEEN!"
I'M JUST TRYING TO EXPLAIN MYSELF!
I'M NOT SURPRISED THAT VIVALDI FLIPPED HER LID. HER TEMPER'S WORSE THAN PETER'S.
THEY'RE EXHAUSTIN TO DEAL WITH.
SIGH
I THINK I'M GONNA AVOID THE CASTLE FOR A WHILE.
IT'S RARE TO SEE YOU UNHAPPY WITH A BOOK IN YOUR LAP, BEAUTIFUL.

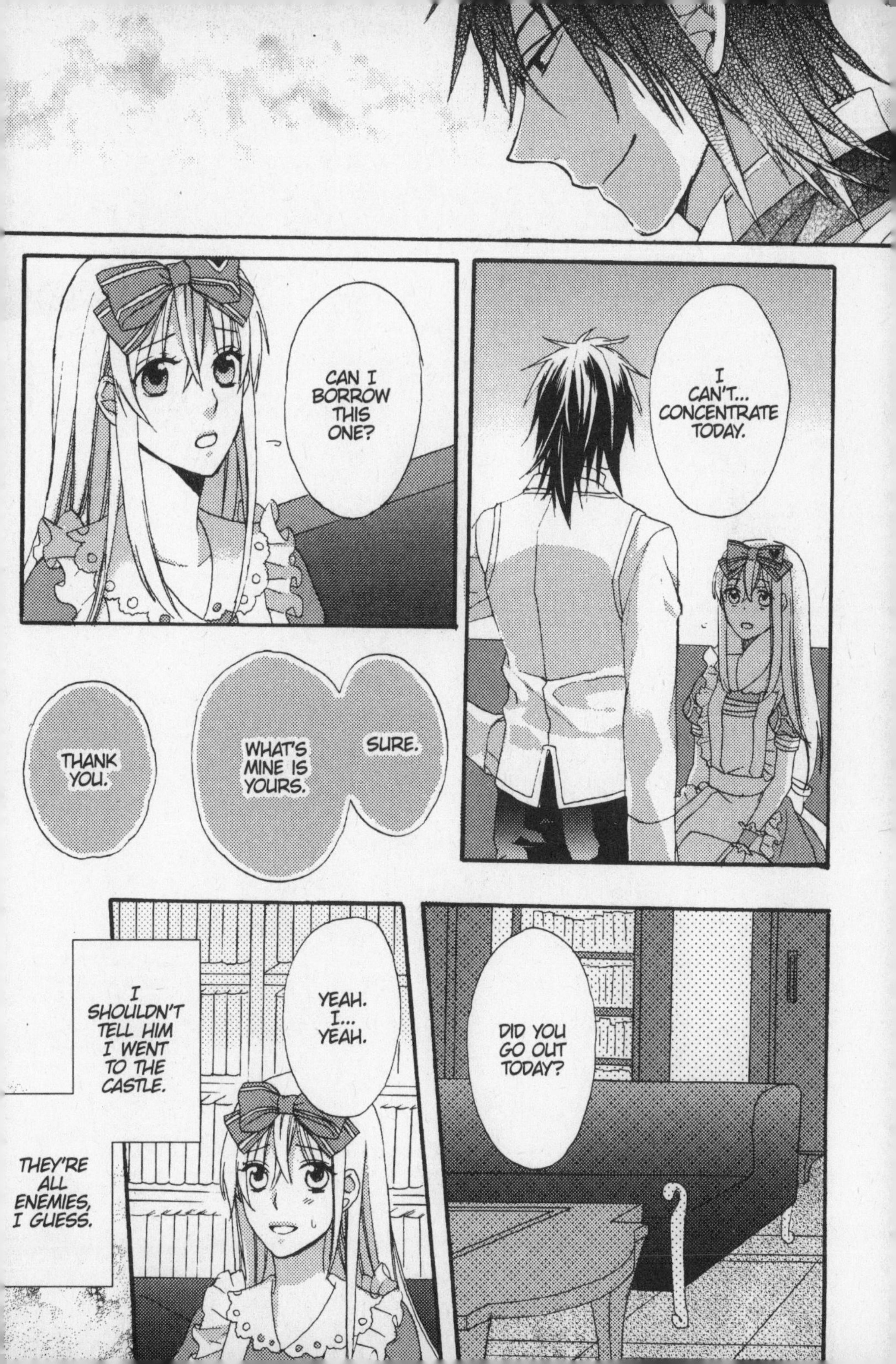

I CAN'T... CONCENTRATE TODAY.
CAN I BORROW THIS ONE?
SURE.
WHAT'S MINE IS YOURS.
THANK YOU.
DID YOU GO OUT TODAY?
YEAH. I... YEAH.
I SHOULDN'T TELL HIM I WENT TO THE CASTLE.
THEY'RE ALL ENEMIES, I GUESS.

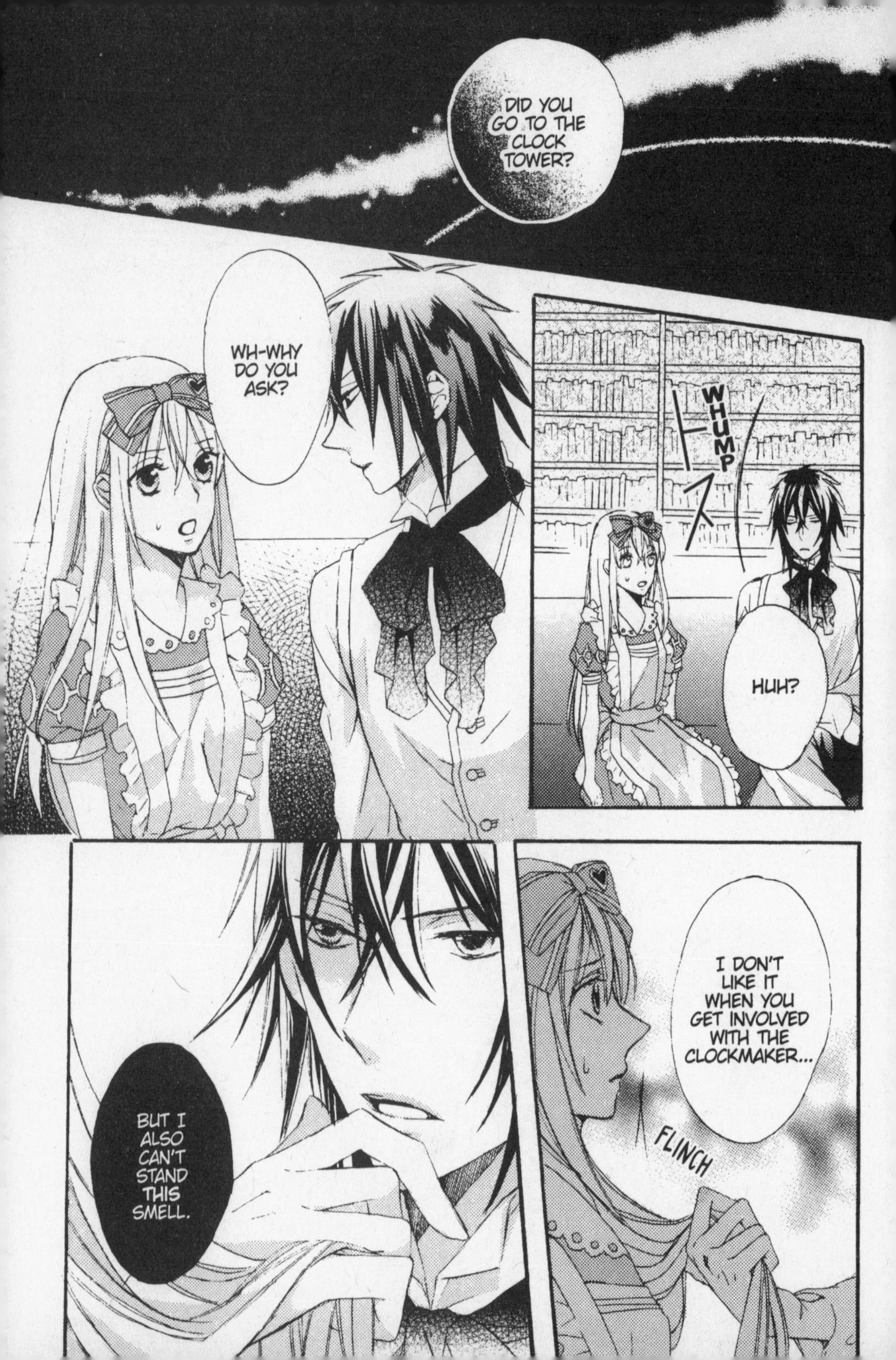
DID YOU GO TO THE CLOCK TOWER?
WHUMP
HUH?
WH-WHY DO YOU ASK?
I DON'T LIKE IT WHEN YOU GET INVOLVED WITH THE CLOCKMAKER...
FLINCH
BUT I ALSO CAN'T STAND THIS SMELL.

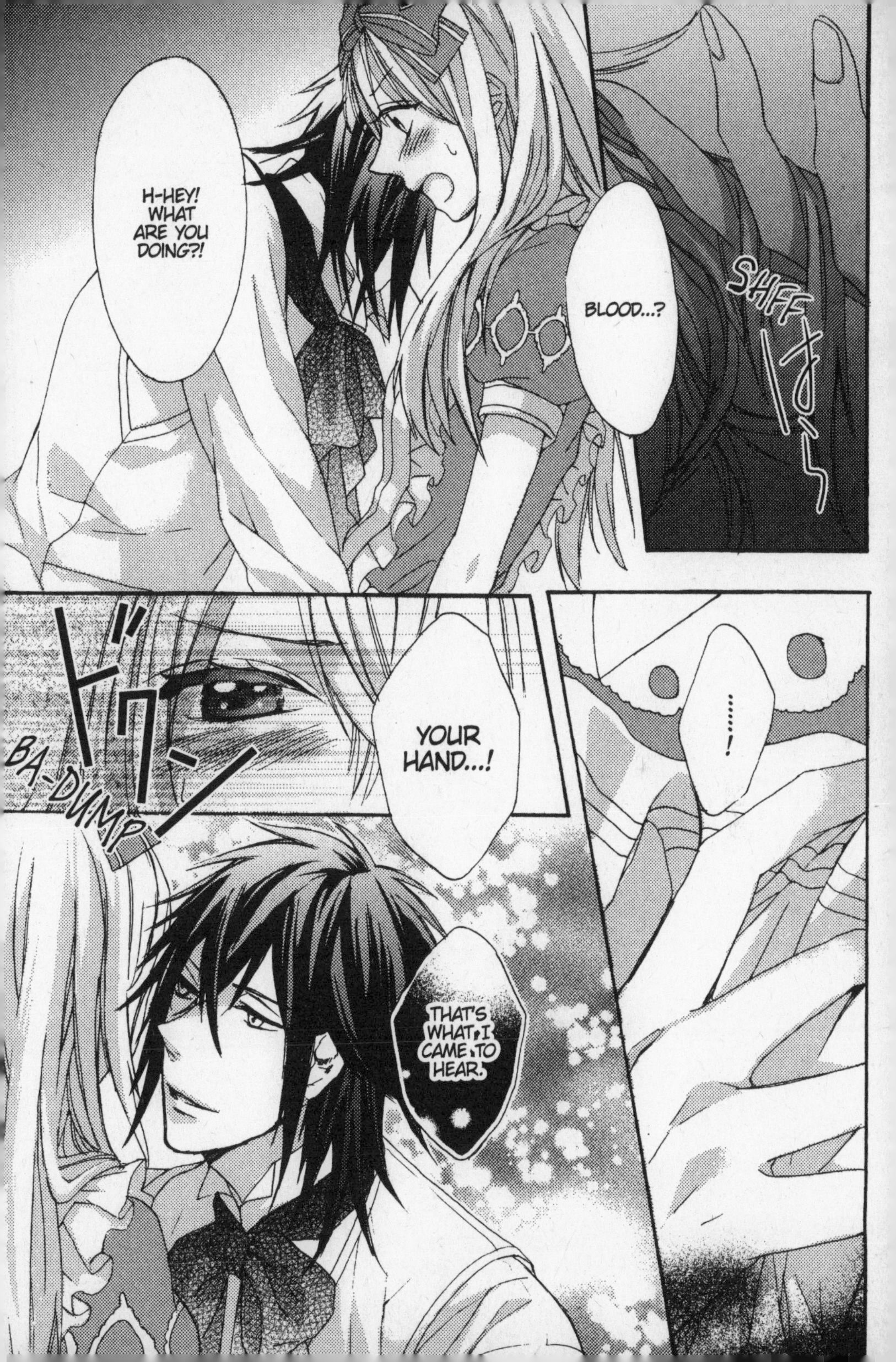
SHIFF
BLOOD...?
H-HEY! WHAT ARE YOU DOING?!
......!
YOUR HAND...!
BA-DUMP
THAT'S WHAT I CAME TO HEAR.

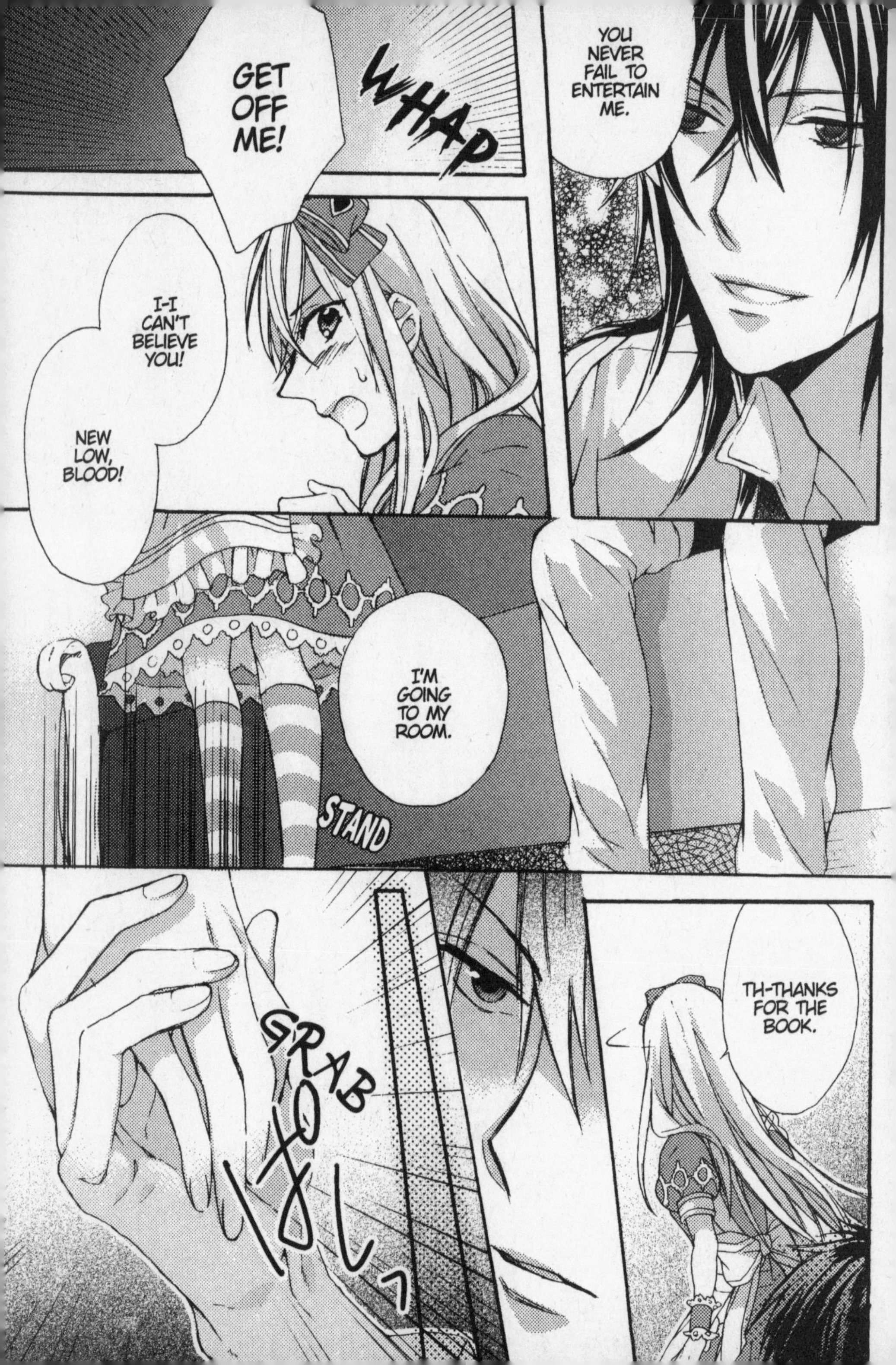
YOU NEVER FAIL TO ENTERTAIN ME.
GET OFF ME!
WHAP
I-I CAN'T BELIEVE YOU!
NEW LOW, BLOOD!
I'M GOING TO MY ROOM.
STAND
TH-THANKS FOR THE BOOK.
GRAB

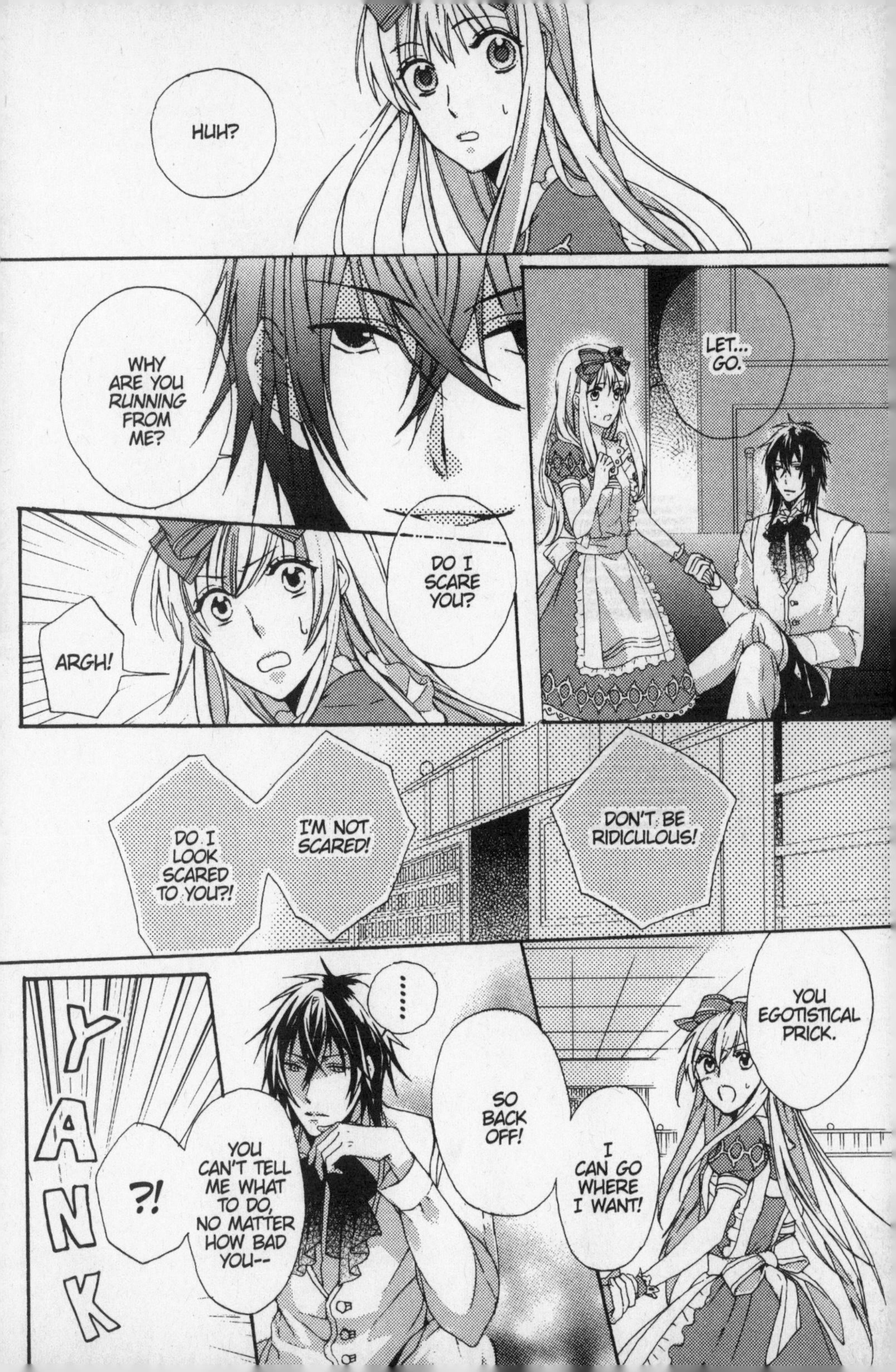
HUH?
LET... GO.
WHY ARE YOU RUNNING FROM ME?
DO I SCARE YOU?
ARGH!
DON'T BE RIDICULOUS!
I'M NOT SCARED!
DO I LOOK SCARED TO YOU?!
YOU EGOTISTICAL PRICK.
I CAN GO WHERE I WANT!
SO BACK OFF!
......
YOU CAN'T TELL ME WHAT TO DO, NO MATTER HOW BAD YOU--
?!
YANK

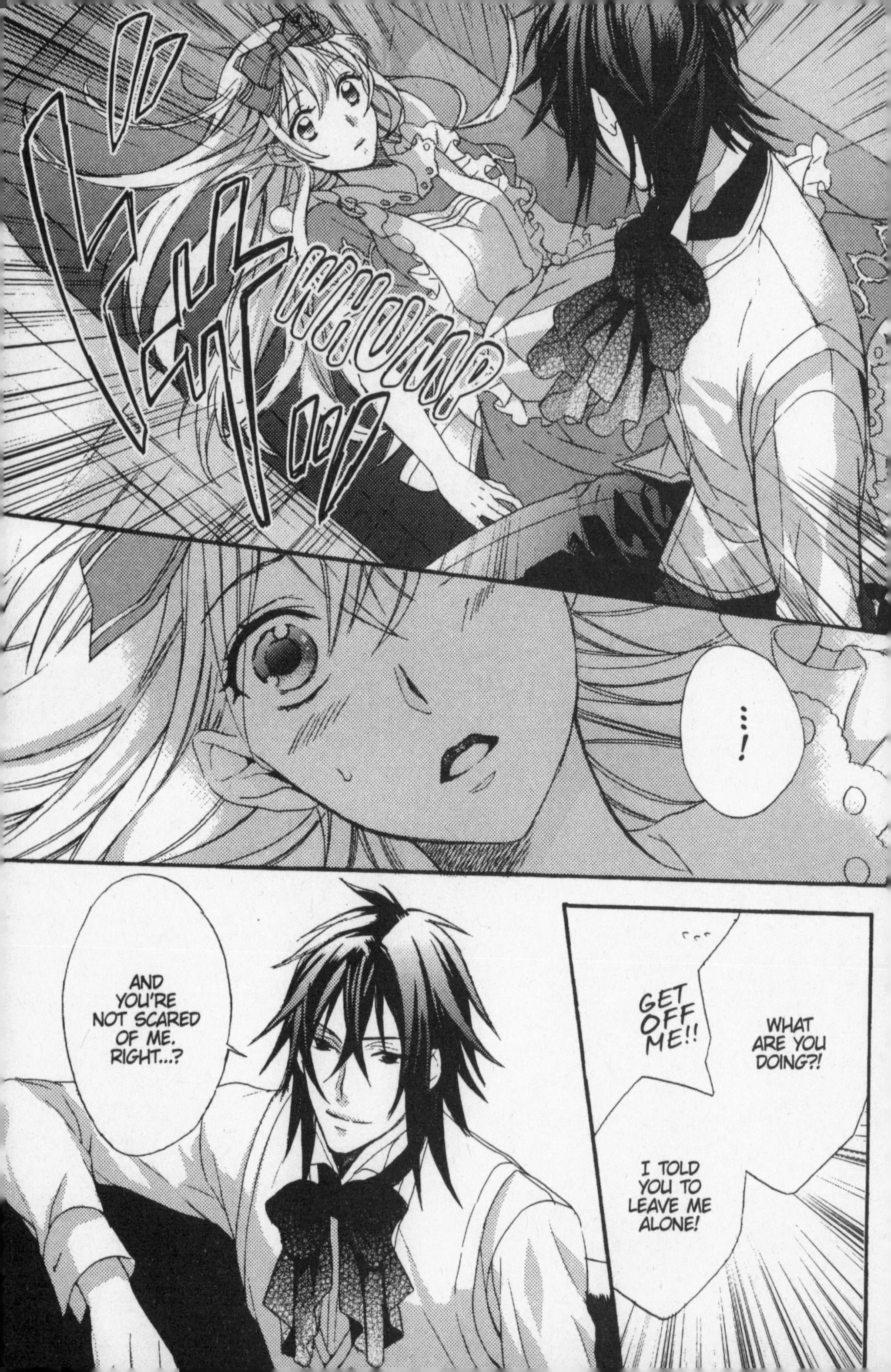
WHUMP
...!
WHAT ARE YOU DOING?!
GET OFF ME!!
I TOLD YOU TO LEAVE ME ALONE!
AND YOU'RE NOT SCARED OF ME. RIGHT...?

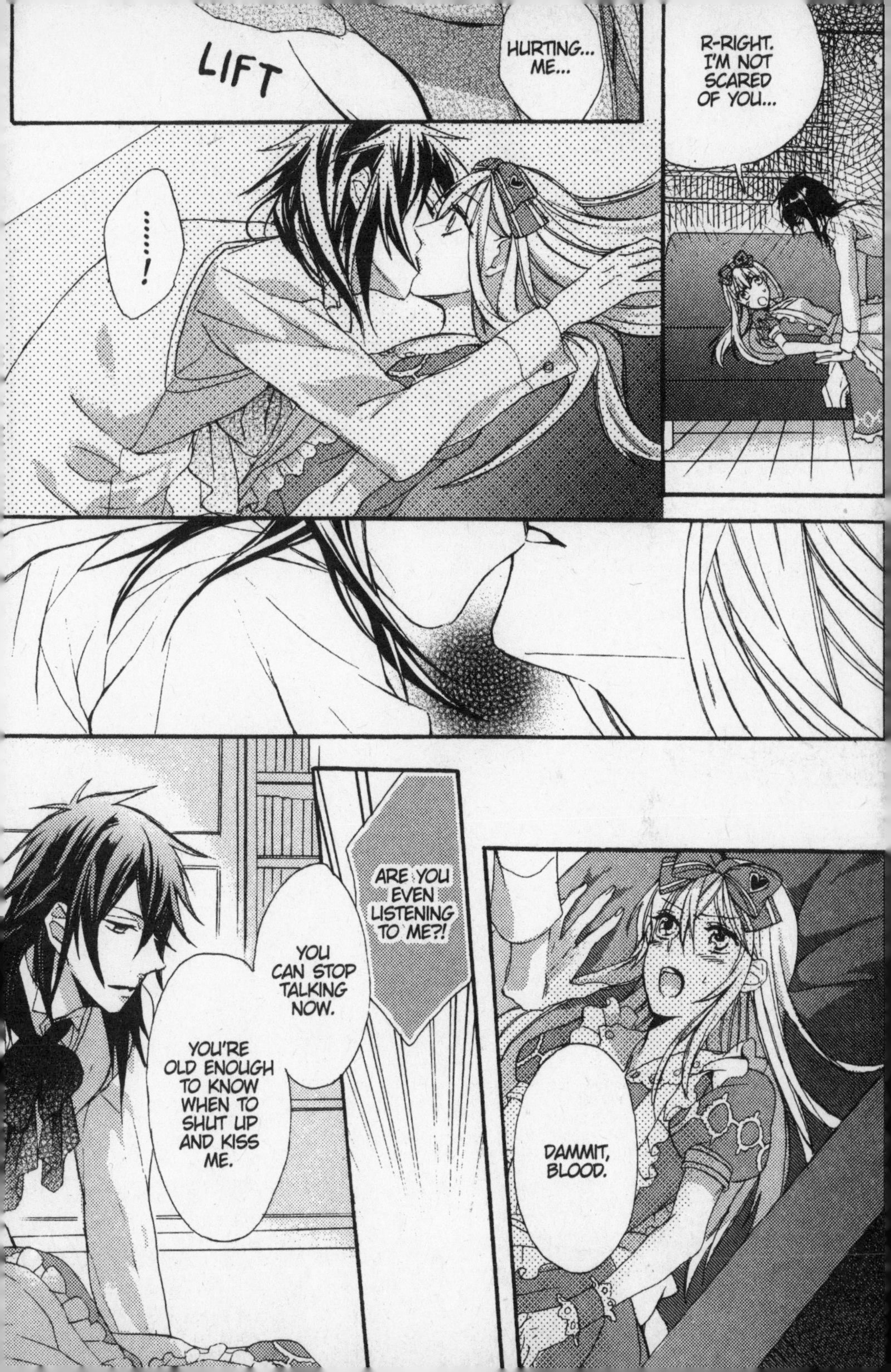
R-RIGHT. I'M NOT SCARED OF YOU...
HURTING... ME...
LIFT
......!
DAMMIT, BLOOD.
ARE YOU EVEN LISTENING TO ME?!
YOU CAN STOP TALKING NOW.
YOU'RE OLD ENOUGH TO KNOW WHEN TO SHUT UP AND KISS ME.

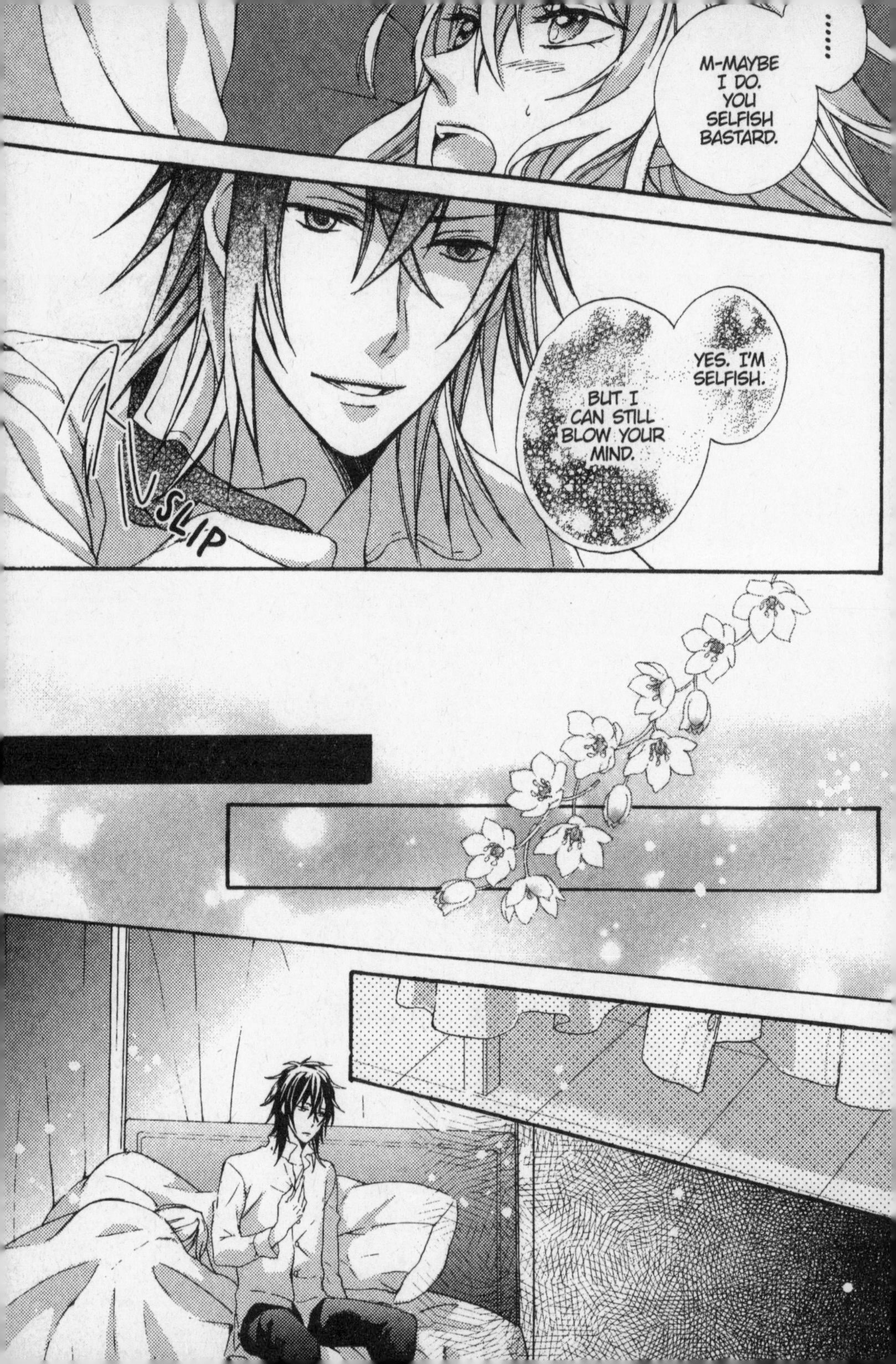
......
M-MAYBE I DO. YOU SELFISH BASTARD.
YES. I'M SELFISH.
BUT I CAN STILL BLOW YOUR MIND.
SLIP

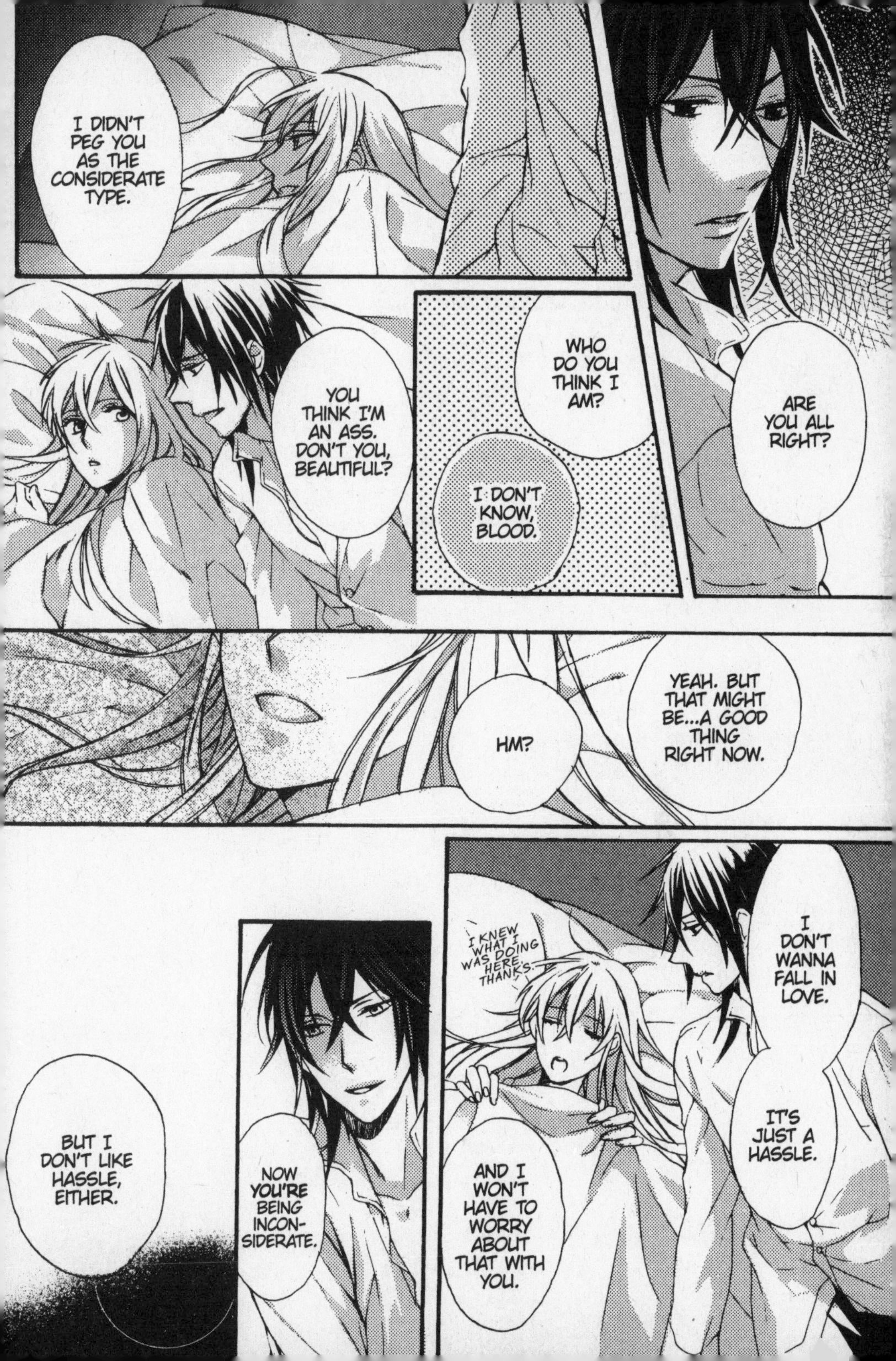

ARE YOU ALL RIGHT?
I DIDN'T PEG YOU AS THE CONSIDERATE TYPE.
WHO DO YOU THINK I AM?
I DON'T KNOW, BLOOD.
YOU THINK I'M AN ASS. DON'T YOU, BEAUTIFUL?
YEAH. BUT THAT MIGHT BE...A GOOD THING RIGHT NOW.
HM?
I DON'T WANNA FALL IN LOVE.
I KNEW WHAT I WAS DOING HERE THANKS.
IT'S JUST A HASSLE.
AND I WON'T HAVE TO WORRY ABOUT THAT WITH YOU.
NOW YOU'RE BEING INCON-SIDERATE.
BUT I DON'T LIKE HASSLE, EITHER.

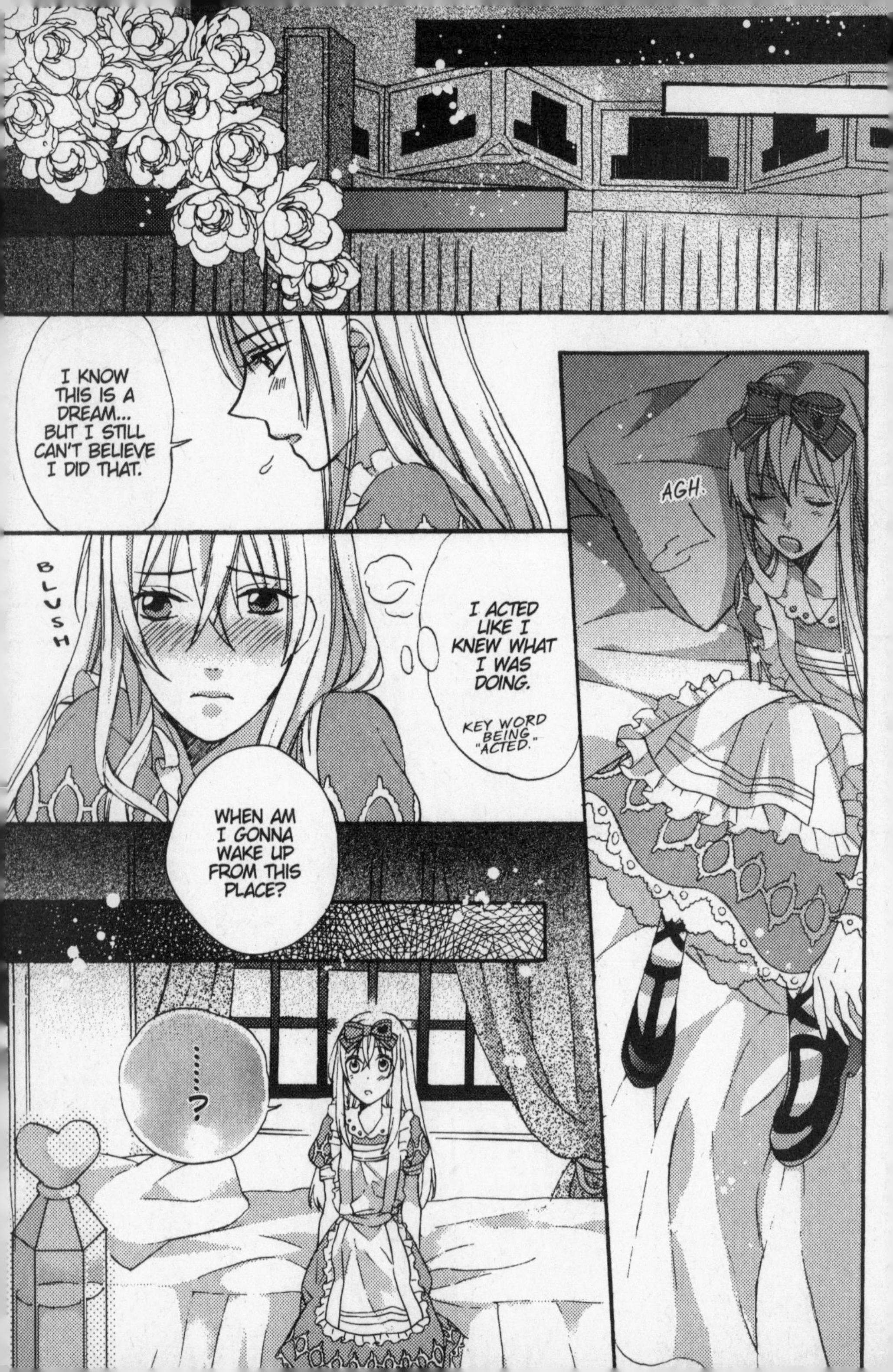
AGH.
I KNOW THIS IS A DREAM... BUT I STILL CAN'T BELIEVE I DID THAT.
BLUSH
I ACTED LIKE I KNEW WHAT I WAS DOING.
KEY WORD BEING "ACTED."
WHEN AM I GONNA WAKE UP FROM THIS PLACE?
......?

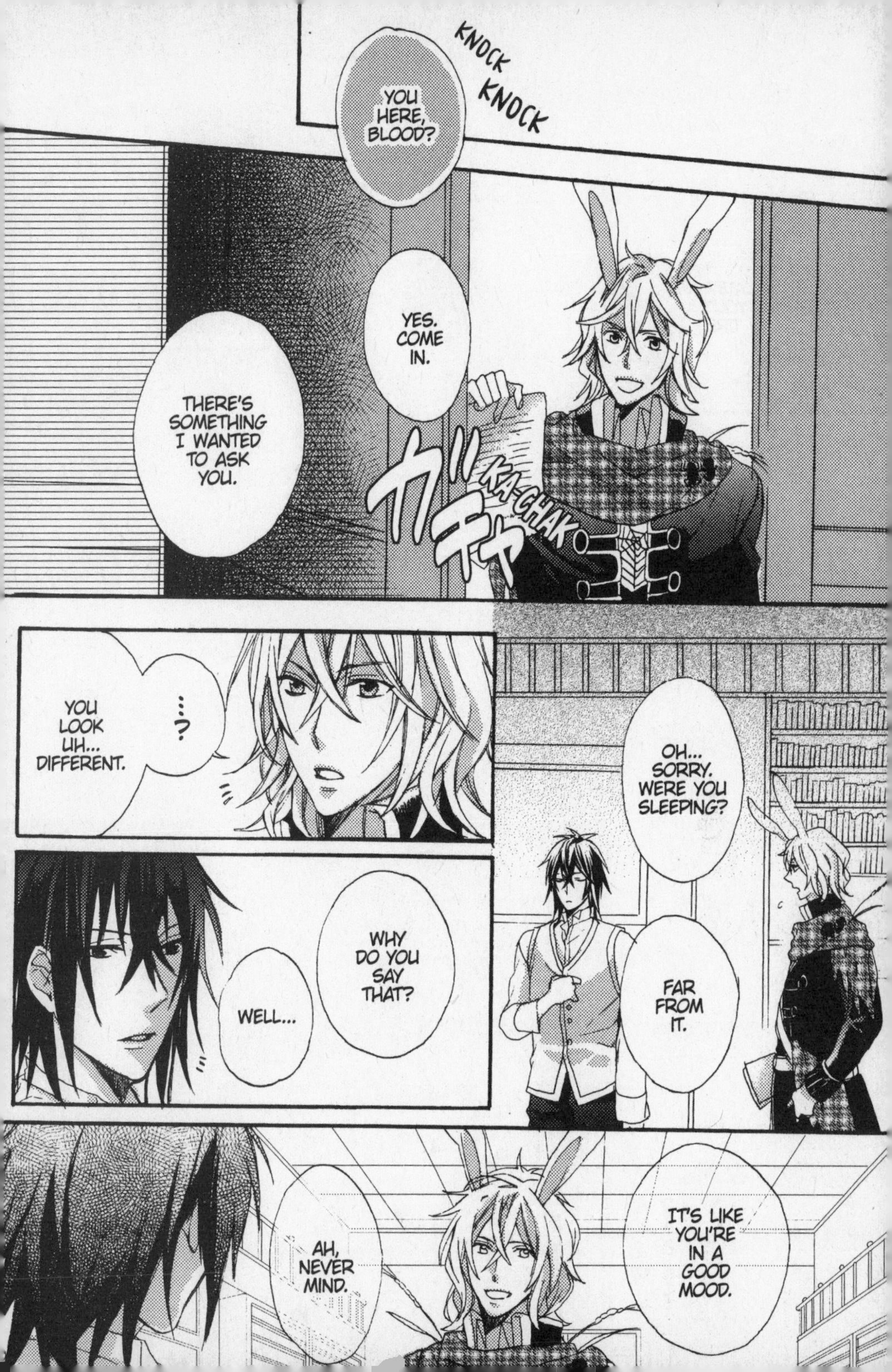
KNOCK KNOCK
YOU HERE, BLOOD?
YES. COME IN.
THERE'S SOMETHING I WANTED TO ASK YOU.
KA-CHAK
OH... SORRY. WERE YOU SLEEPING?
FAR FROM IT.
...?
YOU LOOK UH... DIFFERENT.
WHY DO YOU SAY THAT?
WELL...
IT'S LIKE YOU'RE IN A GOOD MOOD.
AH, NEVER MIND.

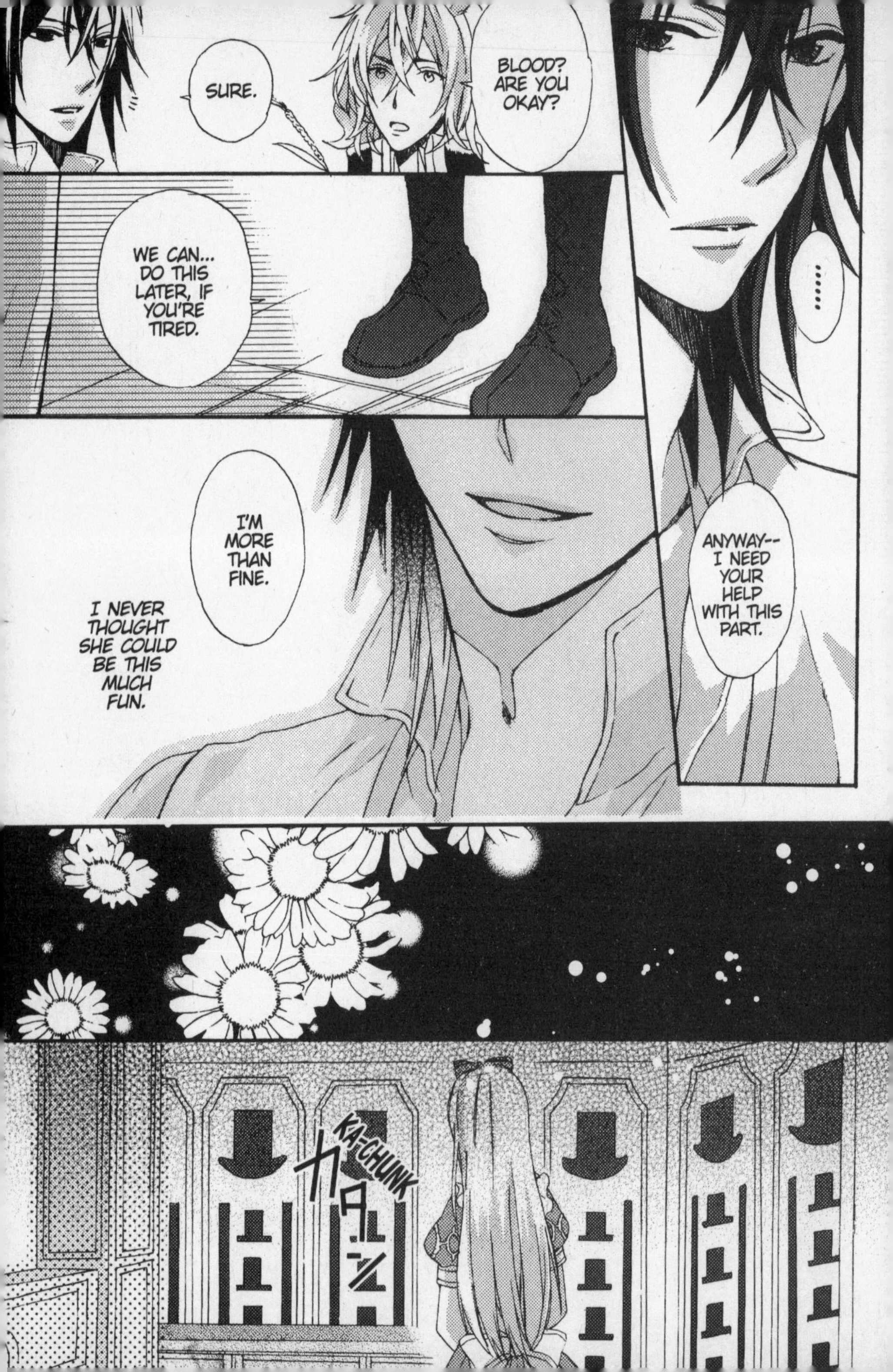
......
ANYWAY-- I NEED YOUR HELP WITH THIS PART.
BLOOD? ARE YOU OKAY?
SURE.
WE CAN... DO THIS LATER, IF YOU'RE TIRED.
I'M MORE THAN FINE.
I NEVER THOUGHT SHE COULD BE THIS MUCH FUN.
KA-CHUNK

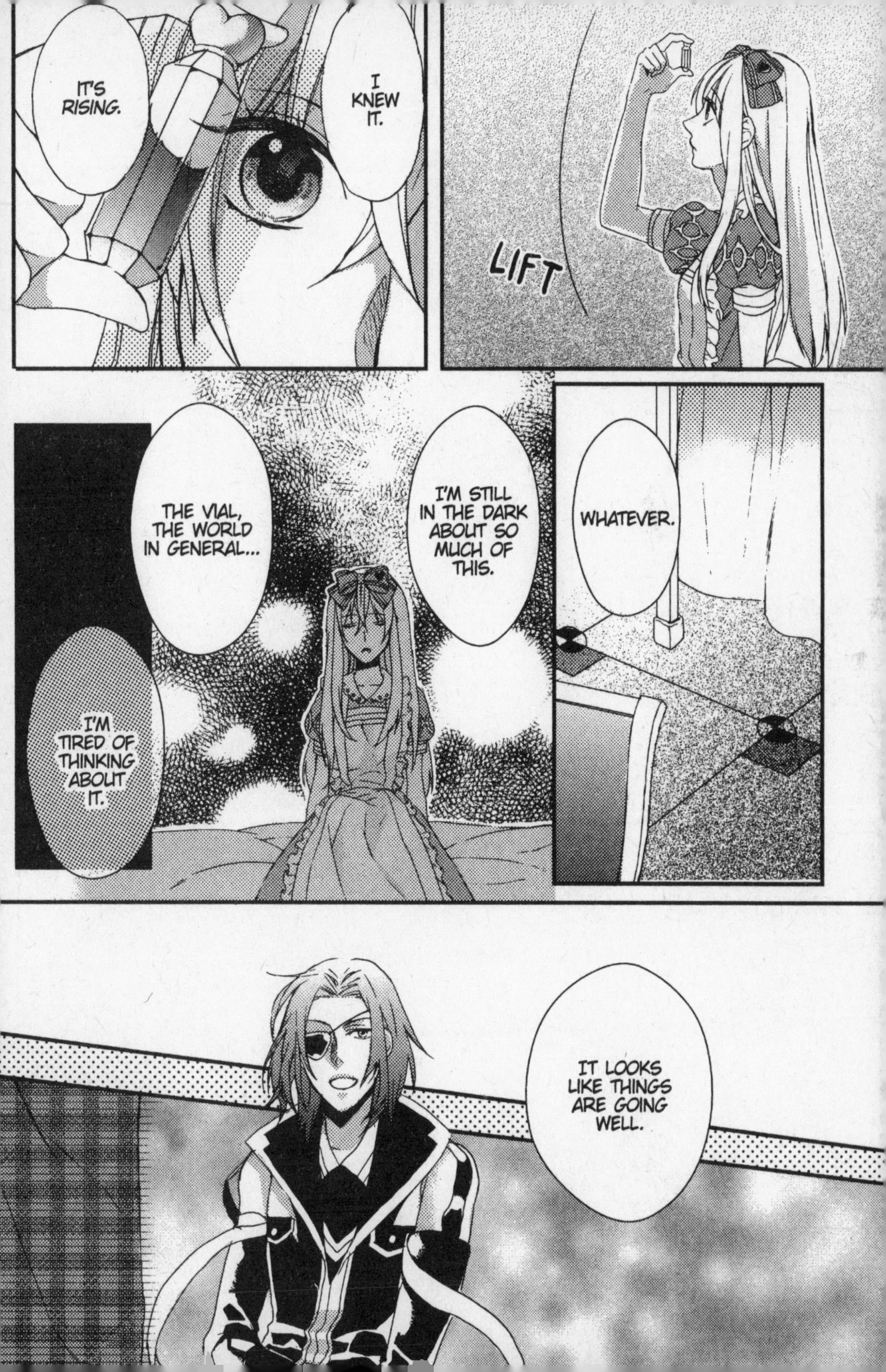
LIFT
I KNEW IT.
IT'S RISING.
WHATEVER.
I'M STILL IN THE DARK ABOUT SO MUCH OF THIS.
THE VIAL, THE WORLD IN GENERAL...
I'M TIRED OF THINKING ABOUT IT.
IT LOOKS LIKE THINGS ARE GOING WELL.

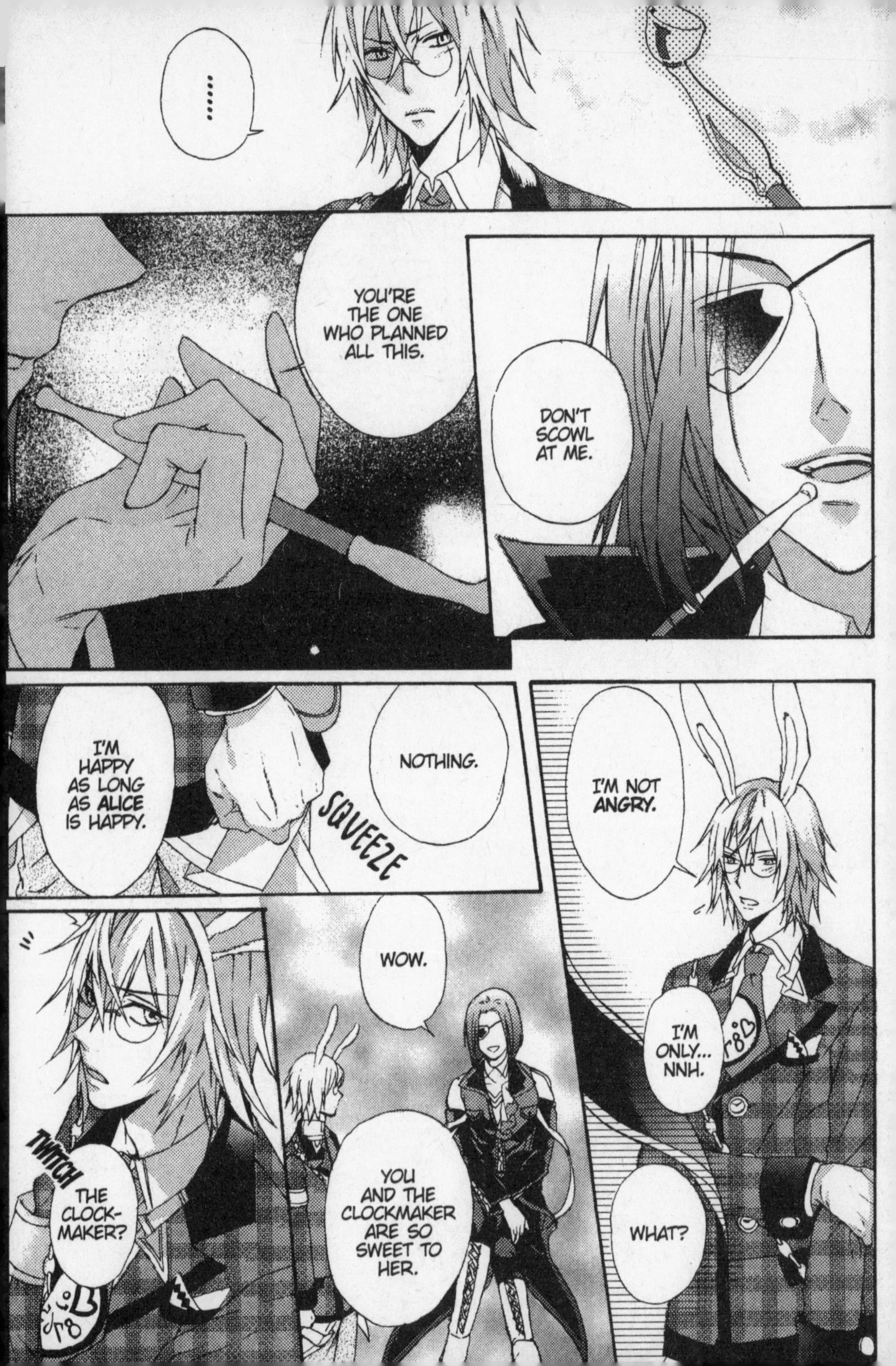
......
DON'T SCOWL AT ME.
YOU'RE THE ONE WHO PLANNED ALL THIS.
I'M NOT ANGRY.
I'M ONLY... NNH.
WHAT?
NOTHING.
SQUEEZE
I'M HAPPY AS LONG AS ALICE IS HAPPY.
WOW.
YOU AND THE CLOCKMAKER ARE SO SWEET TO HER.
TWITCH
THE CLOCK-MAKER?

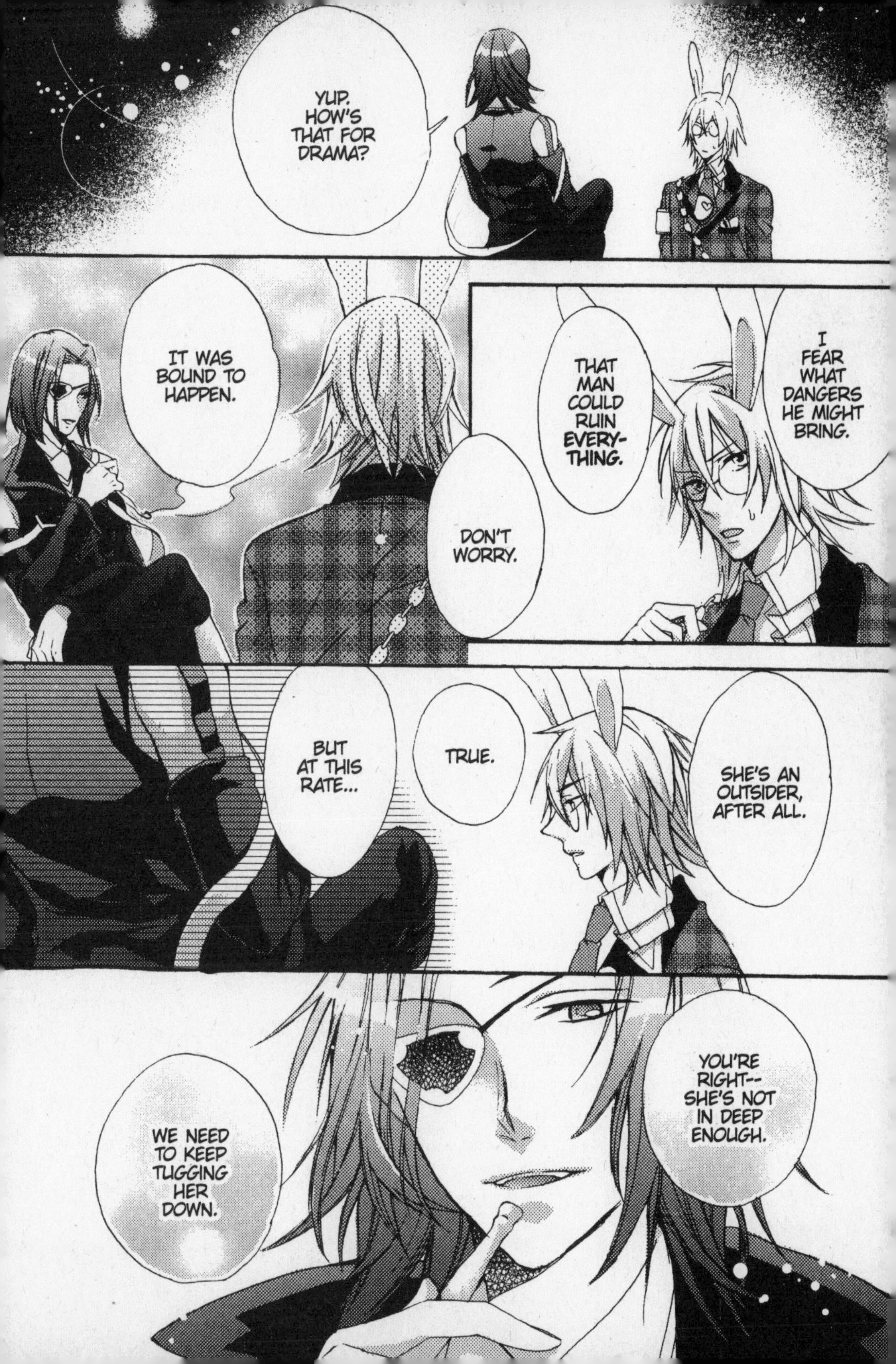
YUP. HOW'S THAT FOR DRAMA?
I FEAR WHAT DANGERS HE MIGHT BRING.
THAT MAN COULD RUIN EVERY-THING.
DON'T WORRY.
IT WAS BOUND TO HAPPEN.
SHE'S AN OUTSIDER, AFTER ALL.
TRUE.
BUT AT THIS RATE...
YOU'RE RIGHT-- SHE'S NOT IN DEEP ENOUGH.
WE NEED TO KEEP TUGGING HER DOWN.

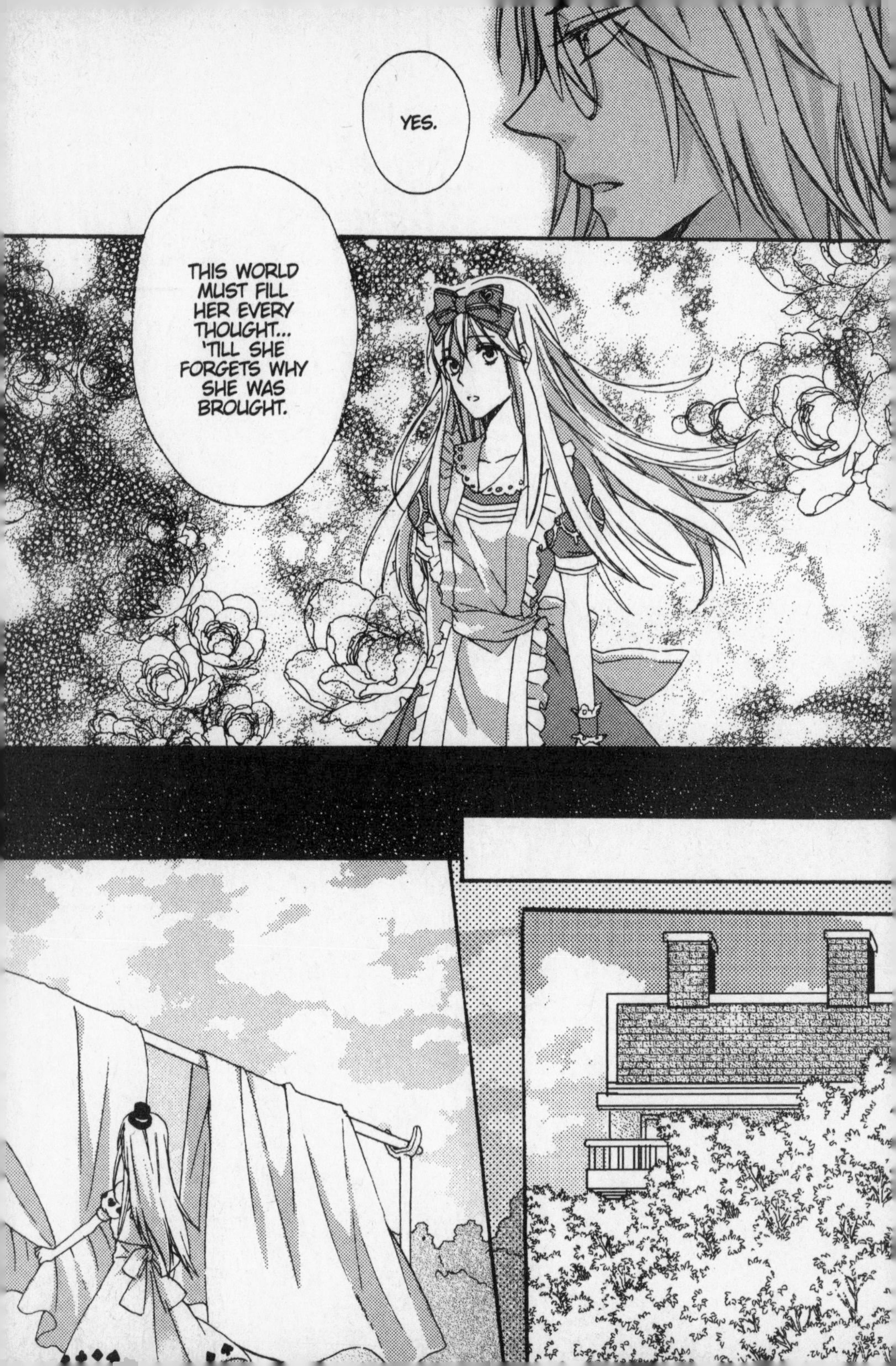
YES.
THIS WORLD MUST FILL HER EVERY THOUGHT... 'TILL SHE FORGETS WHY SHE WAS BROUGHT.

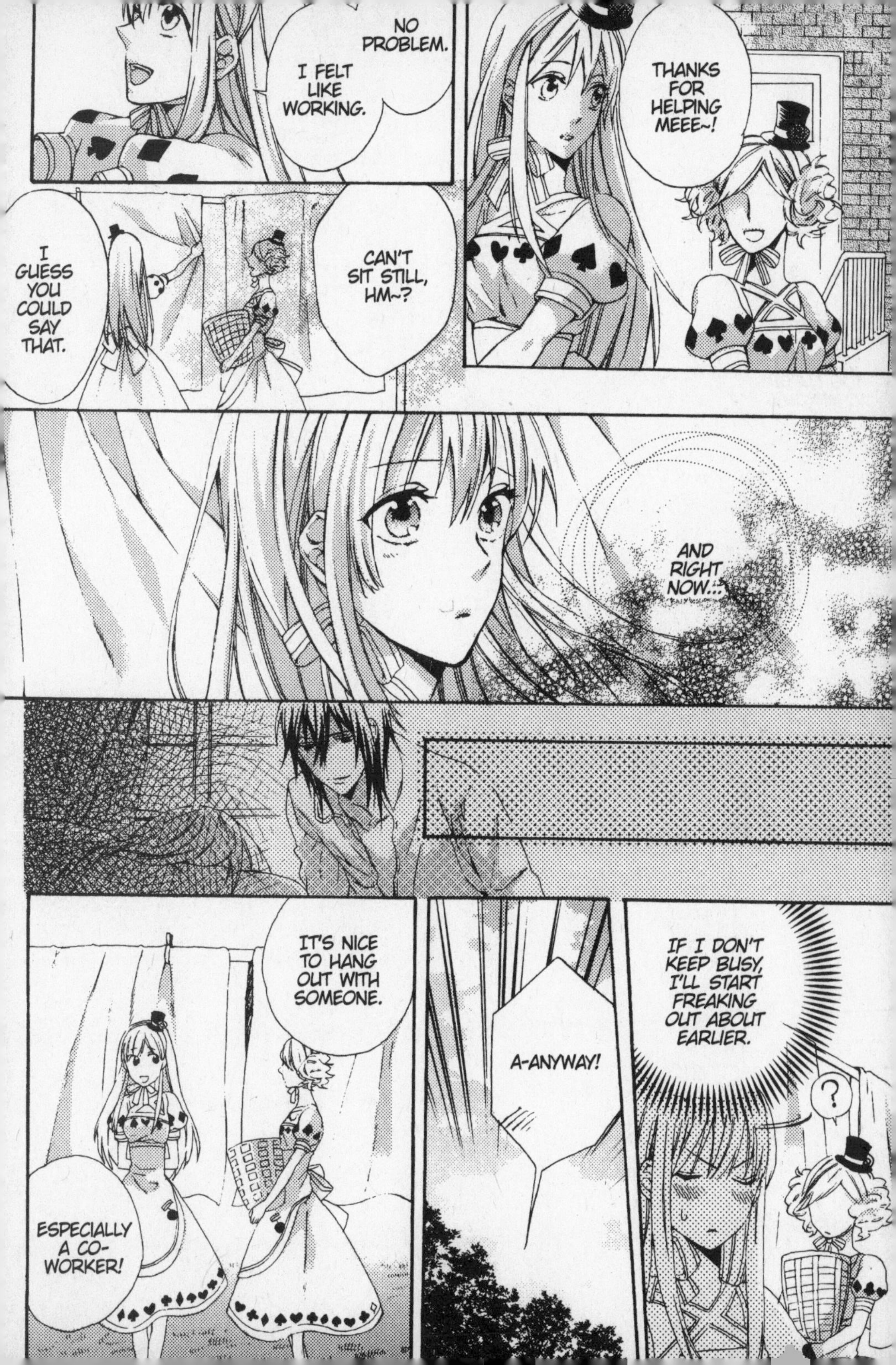
THANKS FOR HELPING MEEE~!
NO PROBLEM.
I FELT LIKE WORKING.
CAN'T SIT STILL, HM~?
I GUESS YOU COULD SAY THAT.
AND RIGHT NOW...
IF I DON'T KEEP BUSY, I'LL START FREAKING OUT ABOUT EARLIER.
?
A-ANYWAY!
IT'S NICE TO HANG OUT WITH SOMEONE.
ESPECIALLY A CO-WORKER!

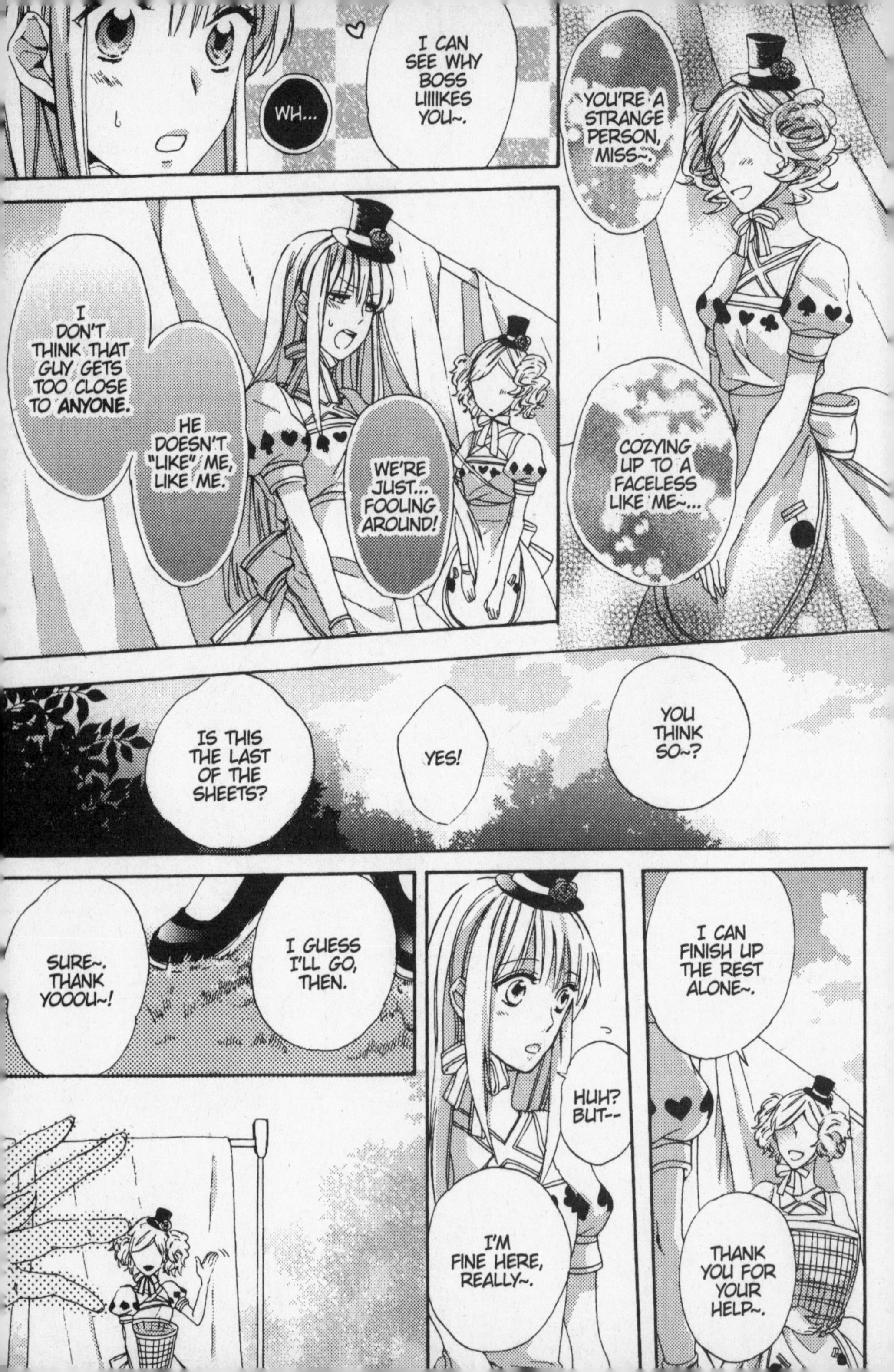

YOU'RE A STRANGE PERSON, MISS~.
COZYING UP TO A FACELESS LIKE ME~...
I CAN SEE WHY BOSS LIIIIKES YOU~.
WH...
WE'RE JUST... FOOLING AROUND!
HE DOESN'T "LIKE" ME, LIKE ME.
I DON'T THINK THAT GUY GETS TOO CLOSE TO **ANYONE**.
YOU THINK SO~?
YES!
IS THIS THE LAST OF THE SHEETS?
I CAN FINISH UP THE REST ALONE~.
THANK YOU FOR YOUR HELP~.
HUH? BUT--
I'M FINE HERE, REALLY~.
I GUESS I'LL GO, THEN.
SURE~. THANK YOOOU~!

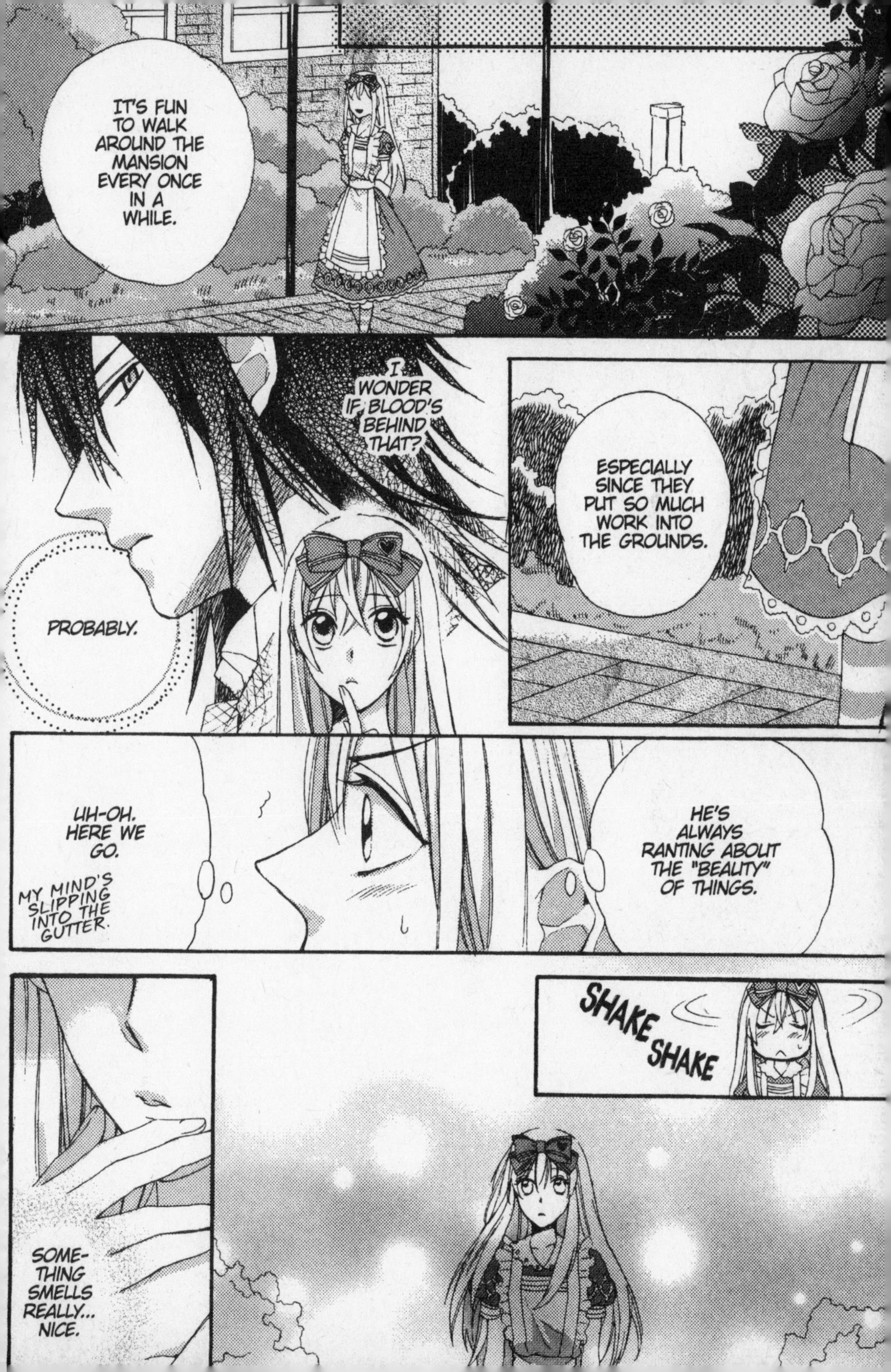

IT'S FUN TO WALK AROUND THE MANSION EVERY ONCE IN A WHILE.
ESPECIALLY SINCE THEY PUT SO MUCH WORK INTO THE GROUNDS.
I WONDER IF BLOOD'S BEHIND THAT?
PROBABLY.
HE'S ALWAYS RANTING ABOUT THE "BEAUTY" OF THINGS.
UH-OH. HERE WE GO.
MY MIND'S SLIPPING INTO THE GUTTER.
SHAKE SHAKE
SOME-THING SMELLS REALLY... NICE.

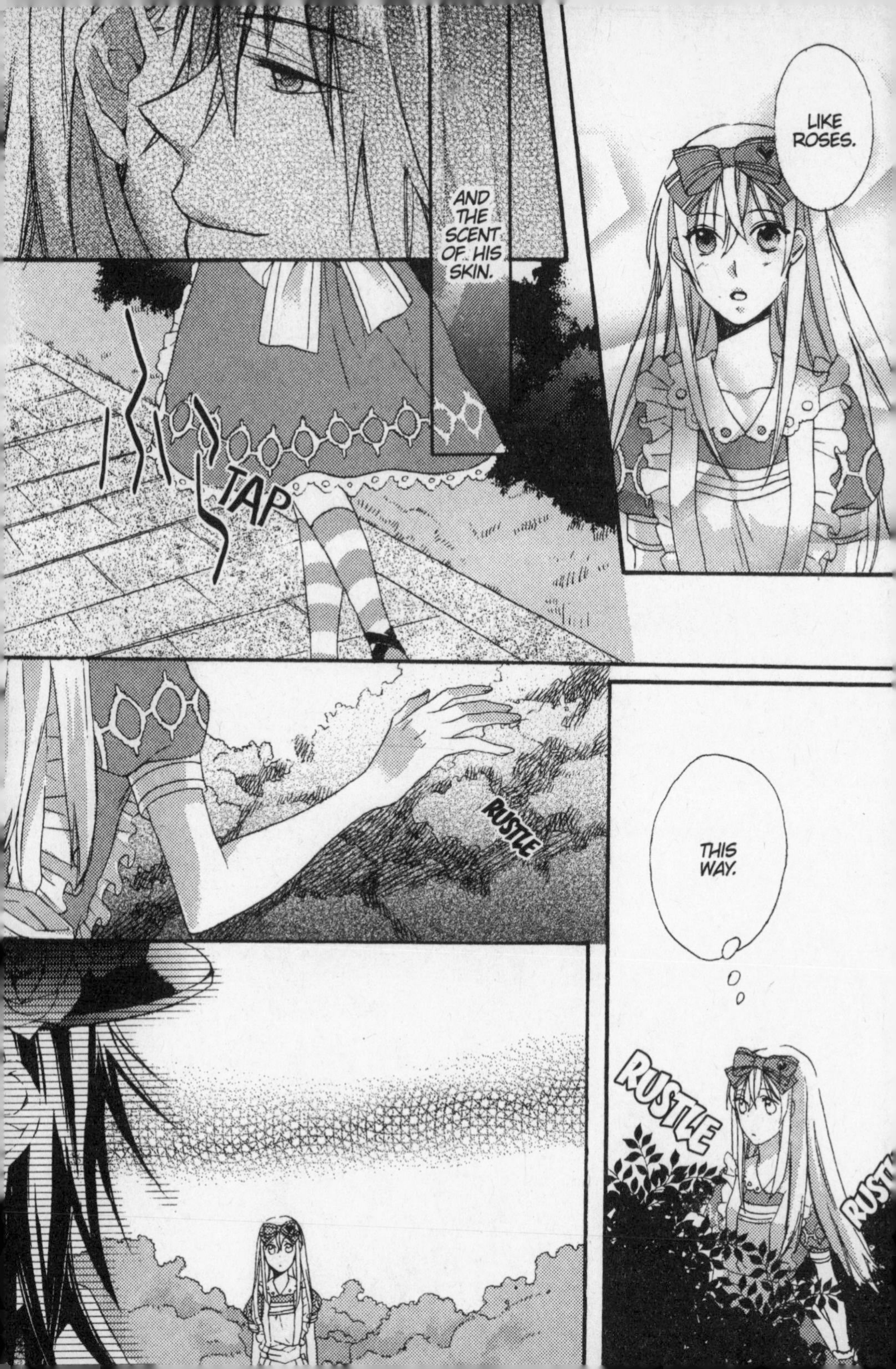
LIKE ROSES.
AND THE SCENT OF HIS SKIN.
TAP
THIS WAY.
RUSTLE
RUSTLE

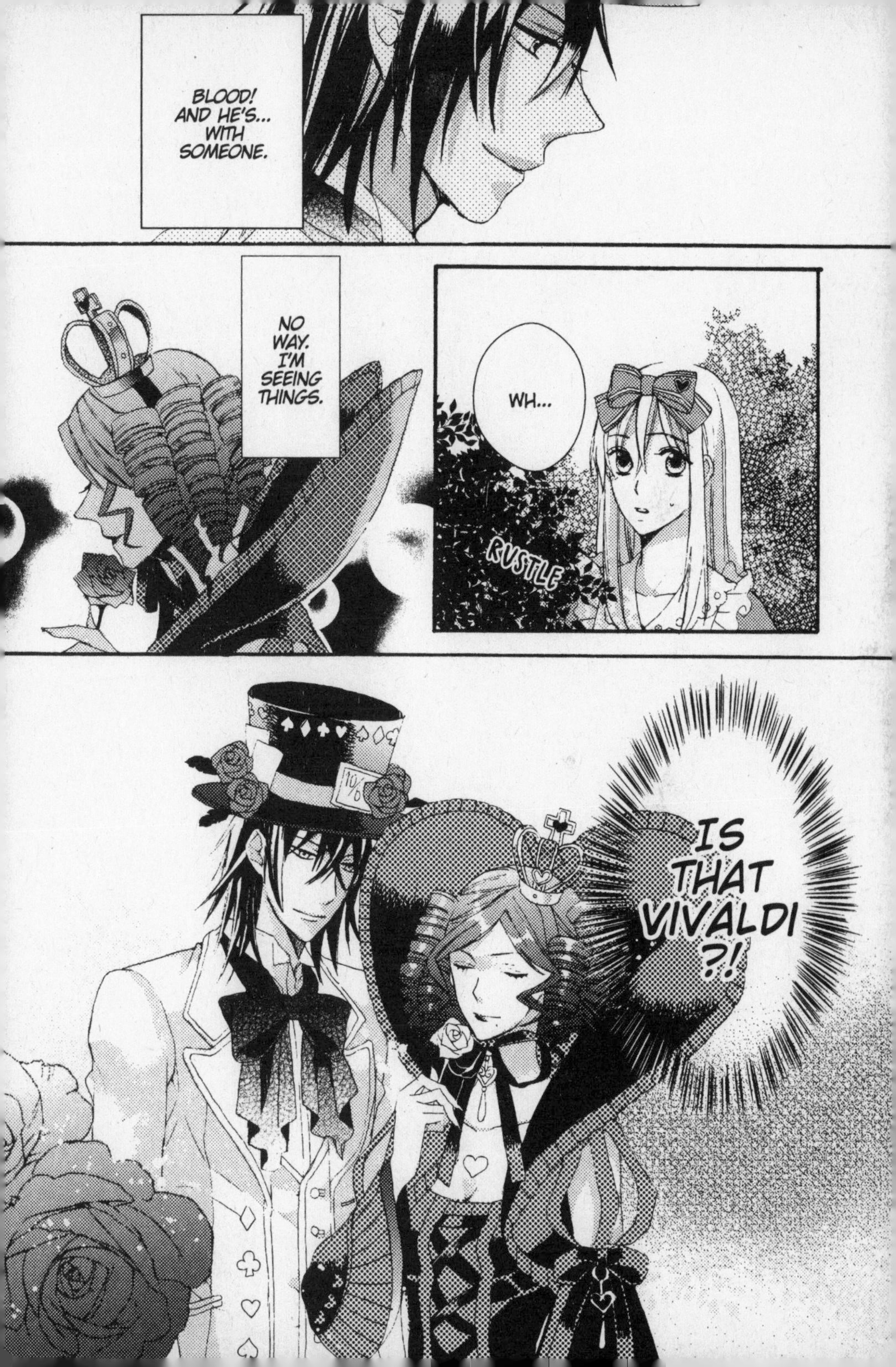
BLOOD! AND HE'S... WITH SOMEONE.
WH...
RUSTLE
NO WAY. I'M SEEING THINGS.
IS THAT VIVALDI ?!

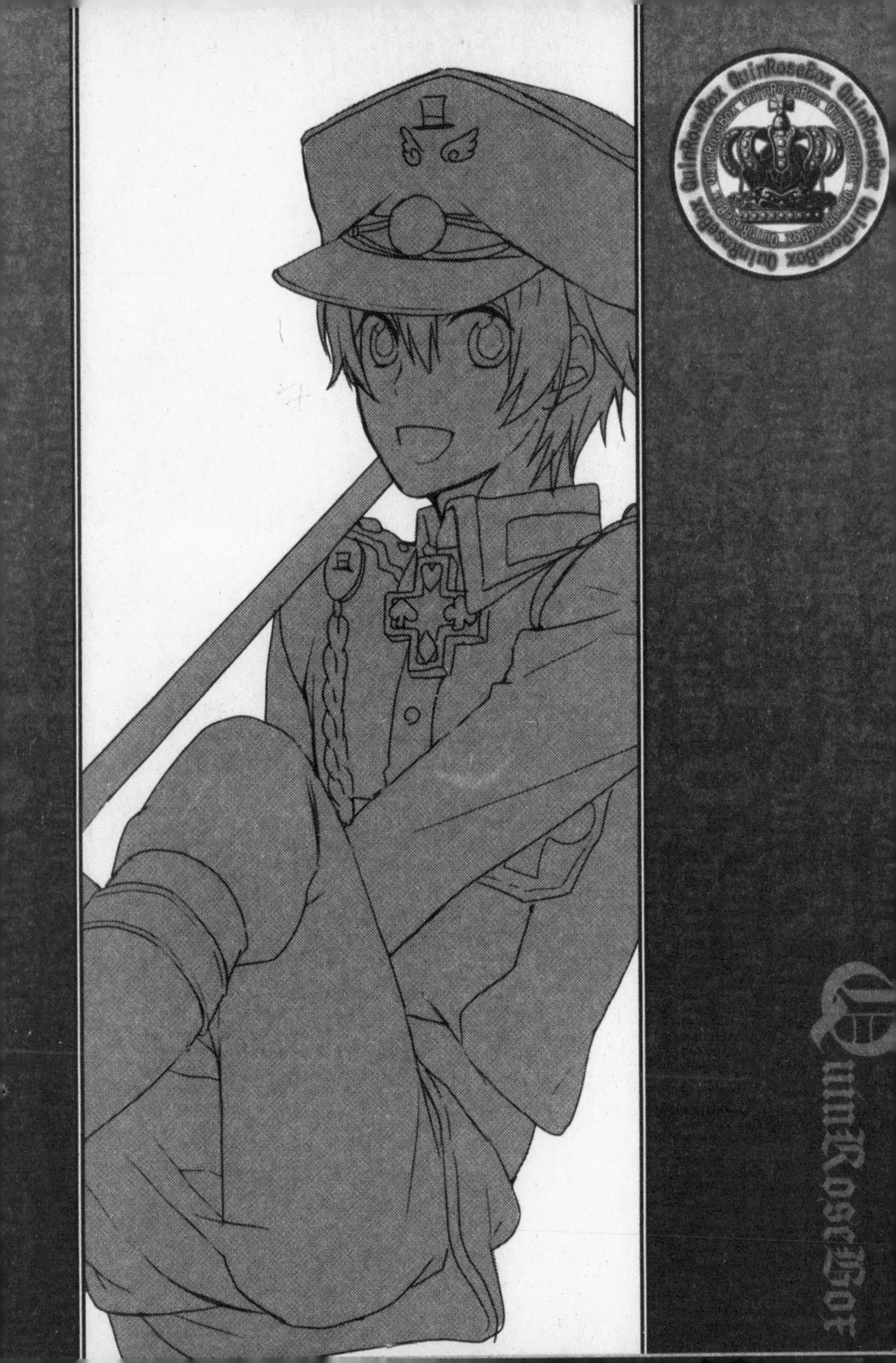
QuinRoseBox
QuinRoseBox

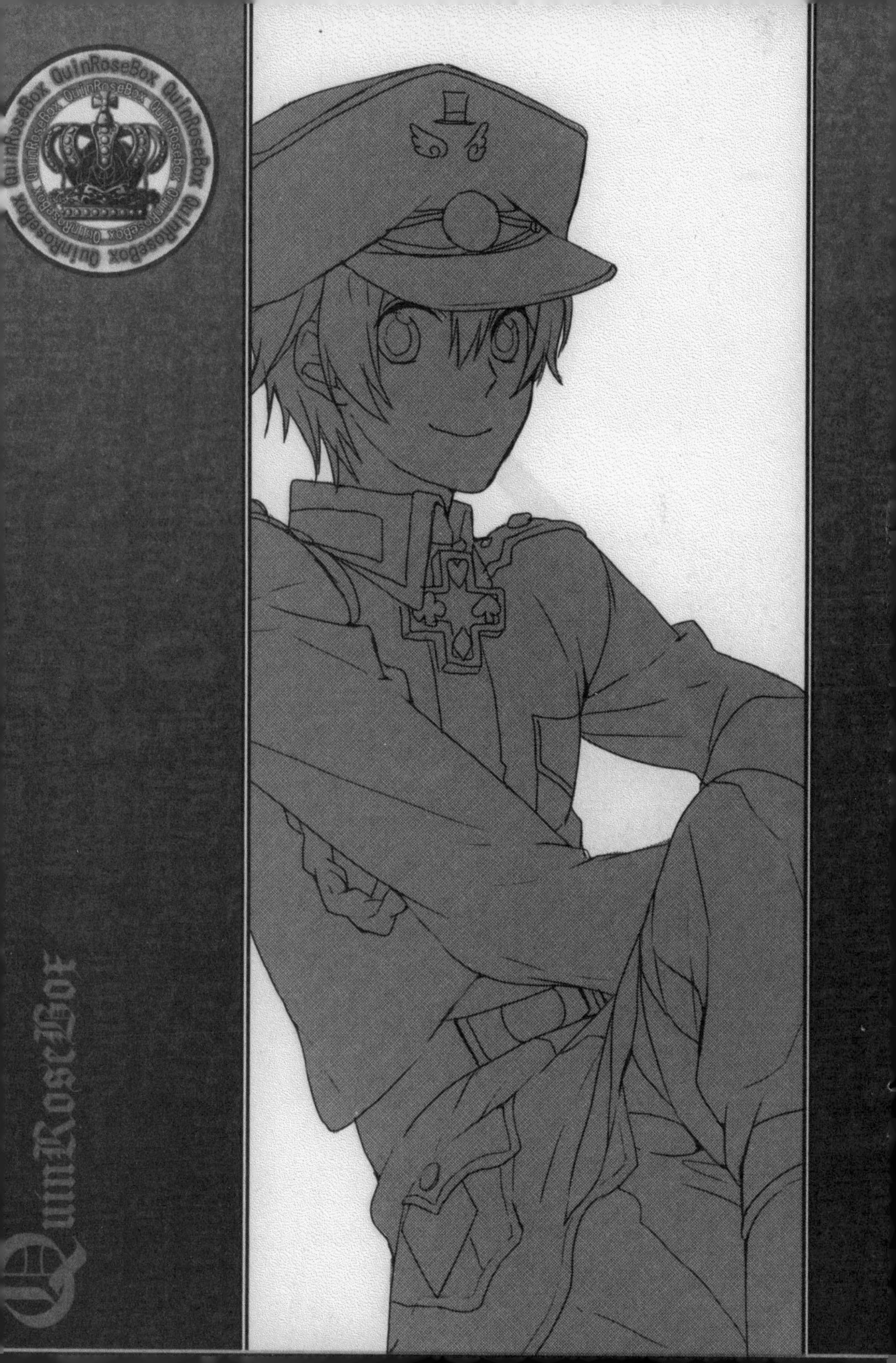
QuinRoseBox

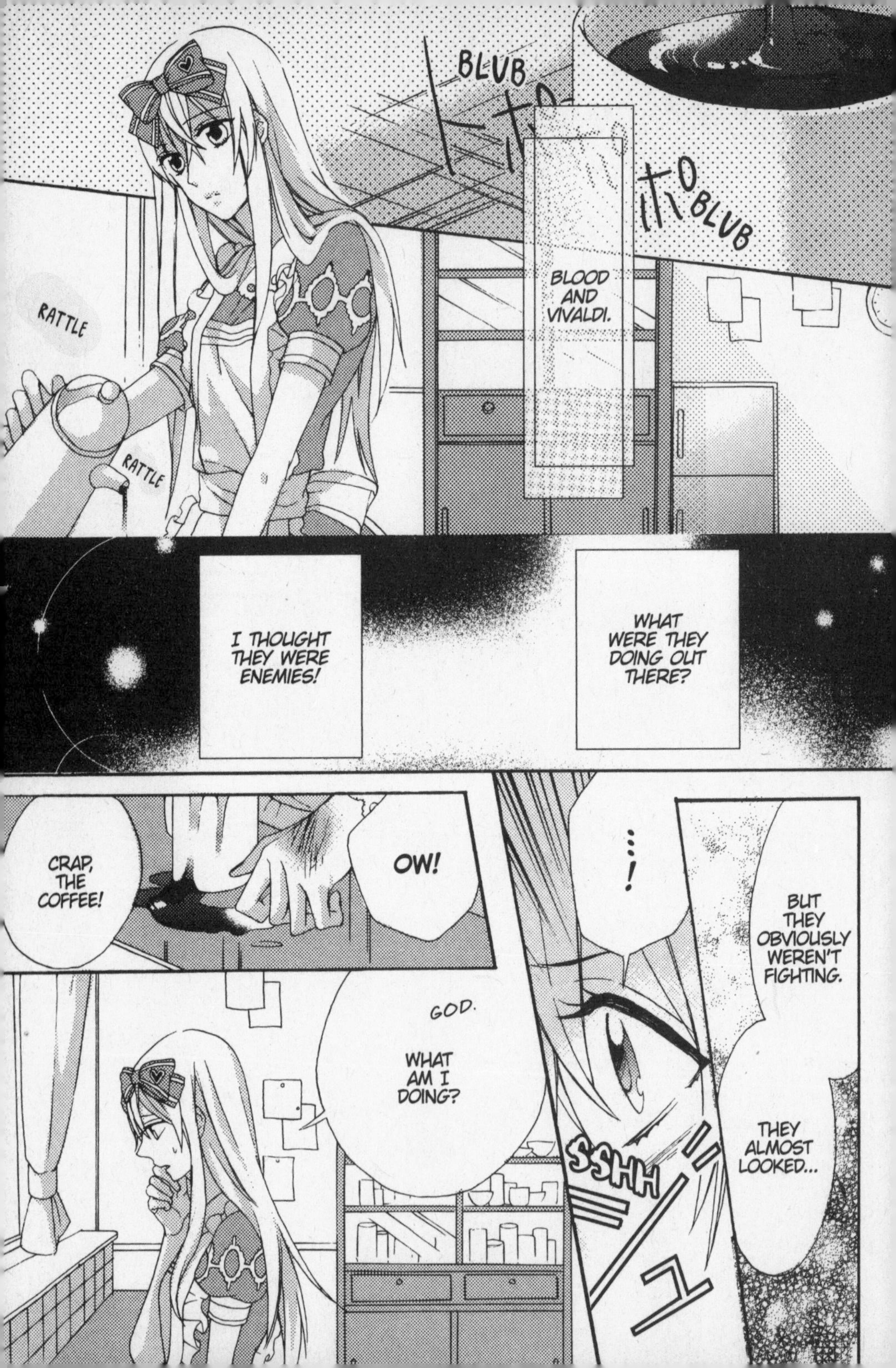
BLUB
BLUB
BLOOD AND VIVALDI.
RATTLE
RATTLE
WHAT WERE THEY DOING OUT THERE?
I THOUGHT THEY WERE ENEMIES!
...!
BUT THEY OBVIOUSLY WEREN'T FIGHTING.
THEY ALMOST LOOKED...
SSHH
OW!
CRAP, THE COFFEE!
GOD.
WHAT AM I DOING?

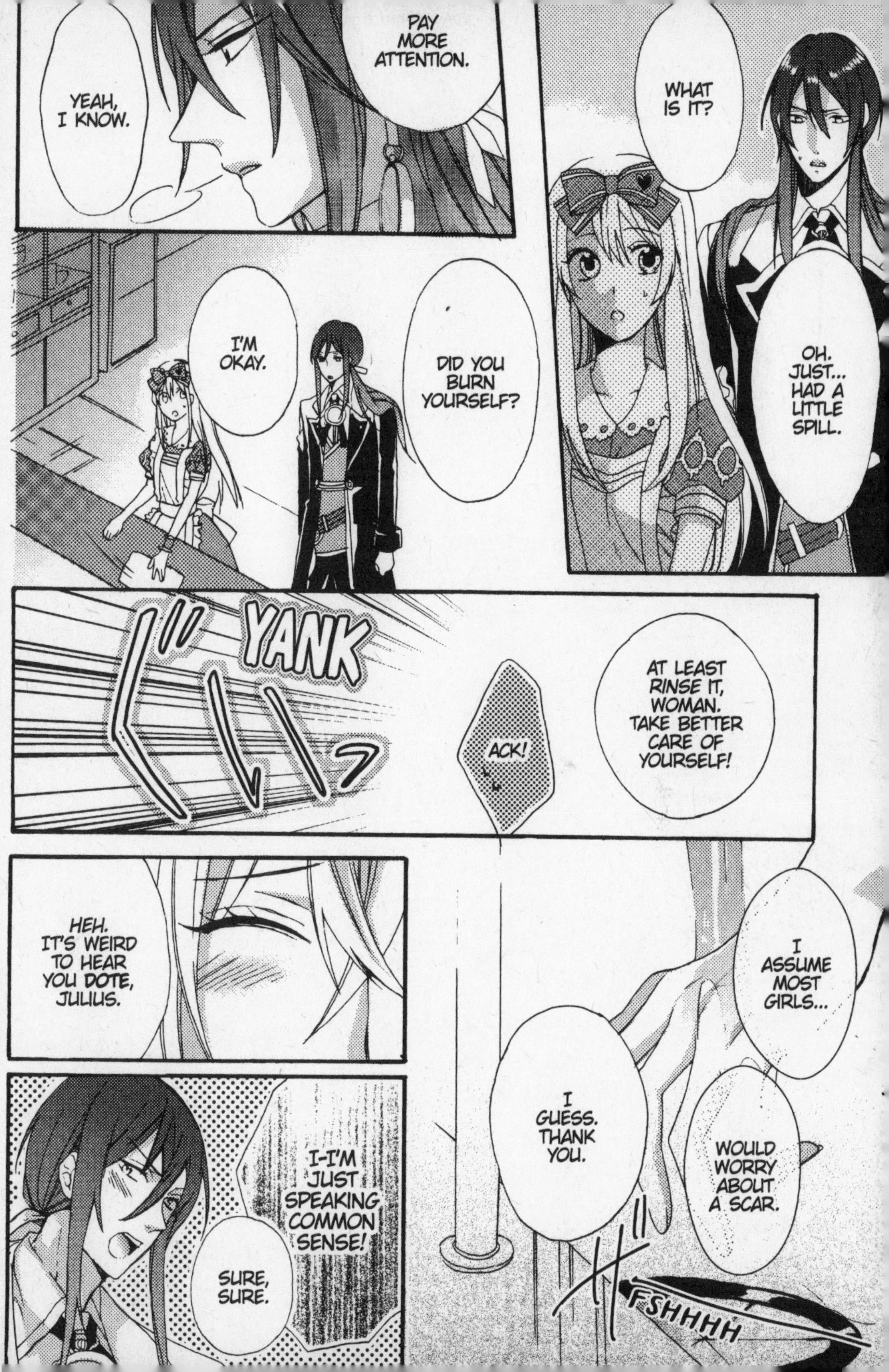
WHAT IS IT?
OH. JUST... HAD A LITTLE SPILL.
PAY MORE ATTENTION.
YEAH, I KNOW.
DID YOU BURN YOURSELF?
I'M OKAY.
AT LEAST RINSE IT, WOMAN. TAKE BETTER CARE OF YOURSELF!
ACK!
YANK
I ASSUME MOST GIRLS...
WOULD WORRY ABOUT A SCAR.
I GUESS. THANK YOU.
FSHHHH
HEH. IT'S WEIRD TO HEAR YOU DOTE, JULIUS.
I-I'M JUST SPEAKING COMMON SENSE!
SURE, SURE.

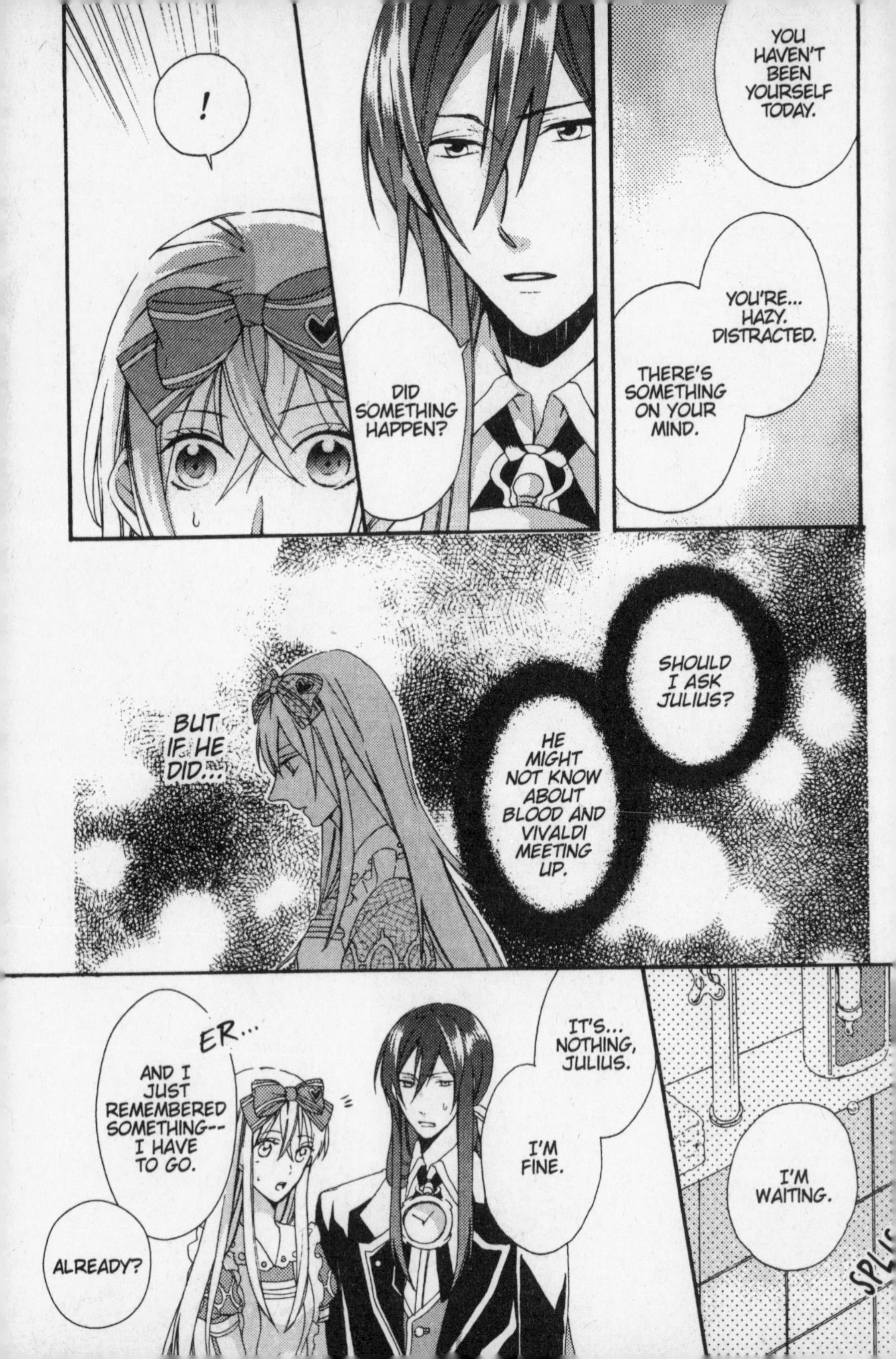
YOU HAVEN'T BEEN YOURSELF TODAY.
YOU'RE... HAZY. DISTRACTED.
THERE'S SOMETHING ON YOUR MIND.
DID SOMETHING HAPPEN?
!
SHOULD I ASK JULIUS?
HE MIGHT NOT KNOW ABOUT BLOOD AND VIVALDI MEETING UP.
BUT IF HE DID...
I'M WAITING.
IT'S... NOTHING, JULIUS.
I'M FINE.
ER...
AND I JUST REMEMBERED SOMETHING-- I HAVE TO GO.
ALREADY?

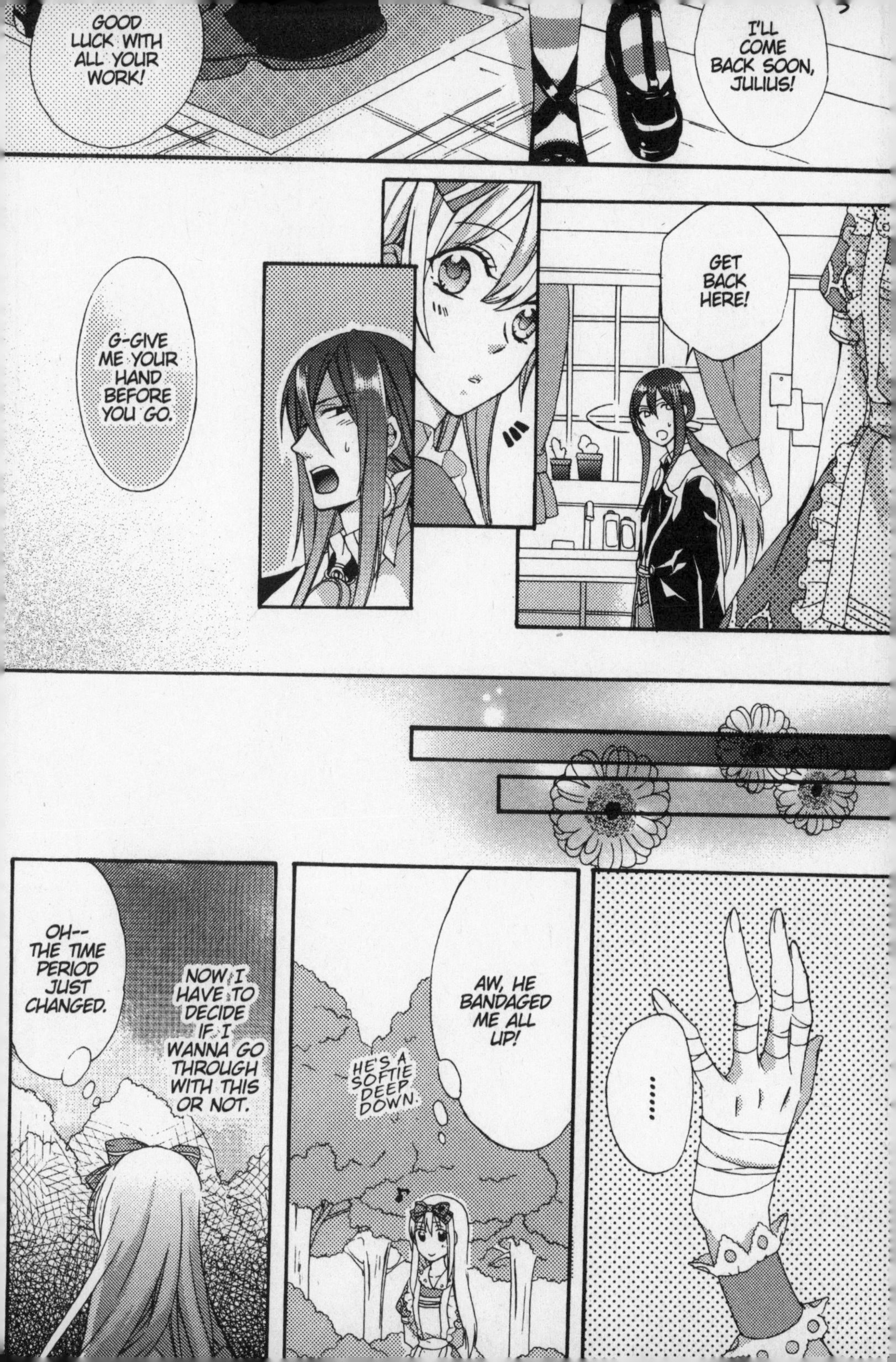
I'LL COME BACK SOON, JULIUS!
GOOD LUCK WITH ALL YOUR WORK!
GET BACK HERE!
G-GIVE ME YOUR HAND BEFORE YOU GO.
......
AW, HE BANDAGED ME ALL UP!
HE'S A SOFTIE DEEP DOWN.
OH-- THE TIME PERIOD JUST CHANGED.
NOW I HAVE TO DECIDE IF I WANNA GO THROUGH WITH THIS OR NOT.

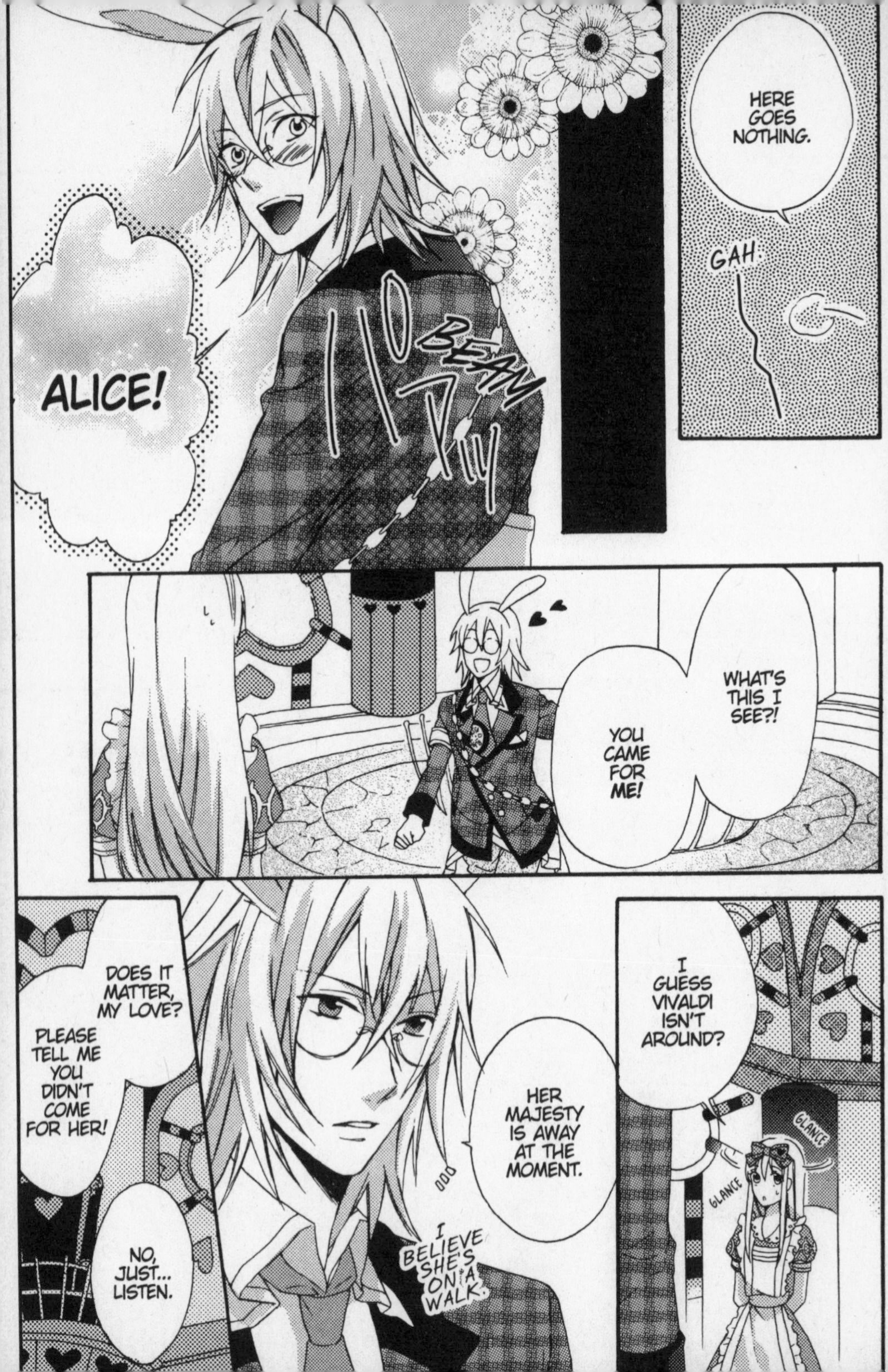
HERE GOES NOTHING.
GAH.
BEAM
ALICE!
WHAT'S THIS I SEE?!
YOU CAME FOR ME!
I GUESS VIVALDI ISN'T AROUND?
GLANCE
GLANCE
HER MAJESTY IS AWAY AT THE MOMENT.
I BELIEVE SHE'S ON A WALK.
DOES IT MATTER, MY LOVE?
PLEASE TELL ME YOU DIDN'T COME FOR HER!
NO, JUST... LISTEN.

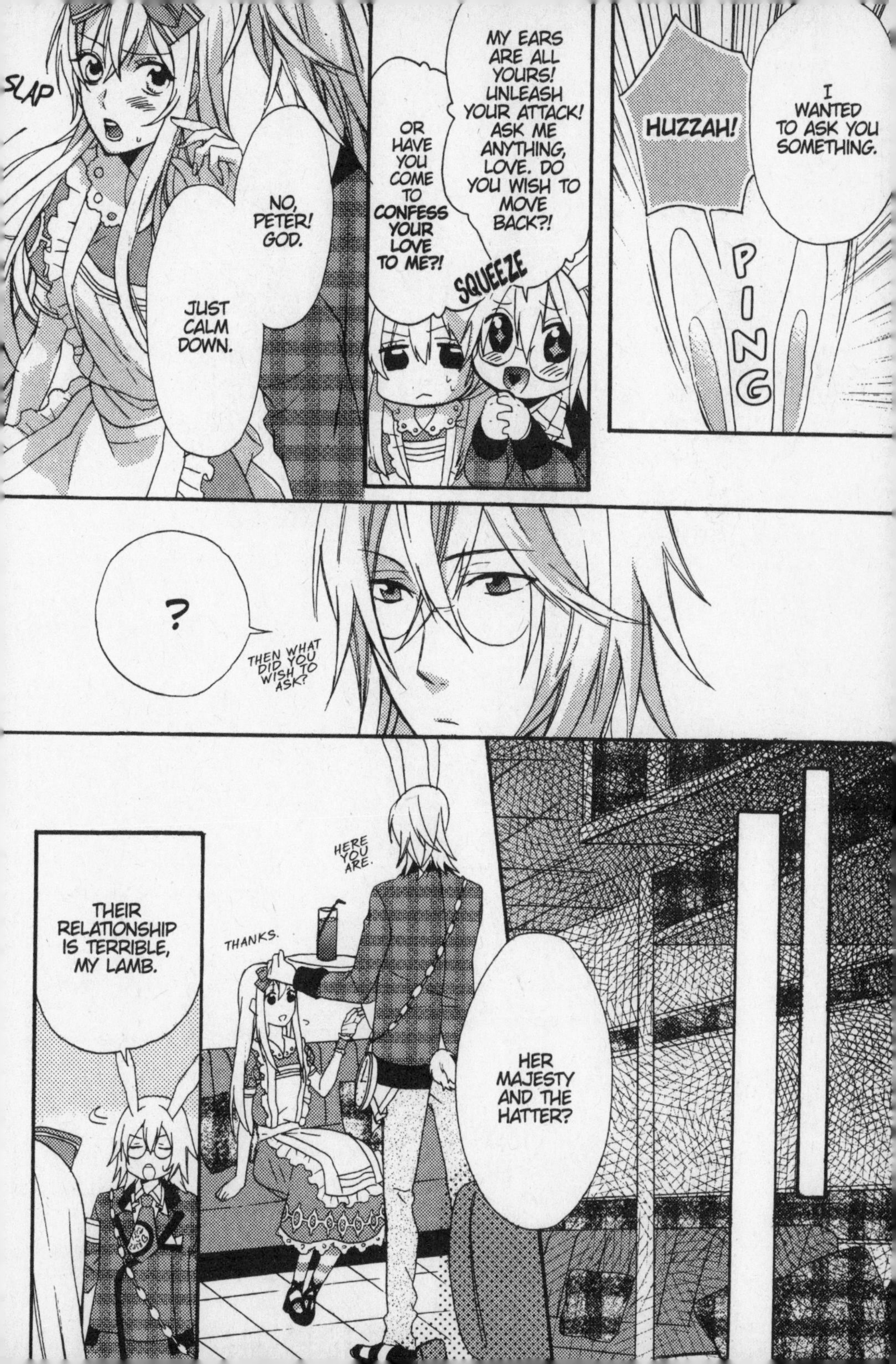

I WANTED TO ASK YOU SOMETHING.
HUZZAH!
PING
MY EARS ARE ALL YOURS! UNLEASH YOUR ATTACK! ASK ME ANYTHING, LOVE. DO YOU WISH TO MOVE BACK?!
OR HAVE YOU COME TO CONFESS YOUR LOVE TO ME?!
SQUEEZE
SLAP
NO, PETER! GOD.
JUST CALM DOWN.
THEN WHAT DID YOU WISH TO ASK?
?
HER MAJESTY AND THE HATTER?
HERE YOU ARE.
THANKS.
THEIR RELATIONSHIP IS TERRIBLE, MY LAMB.

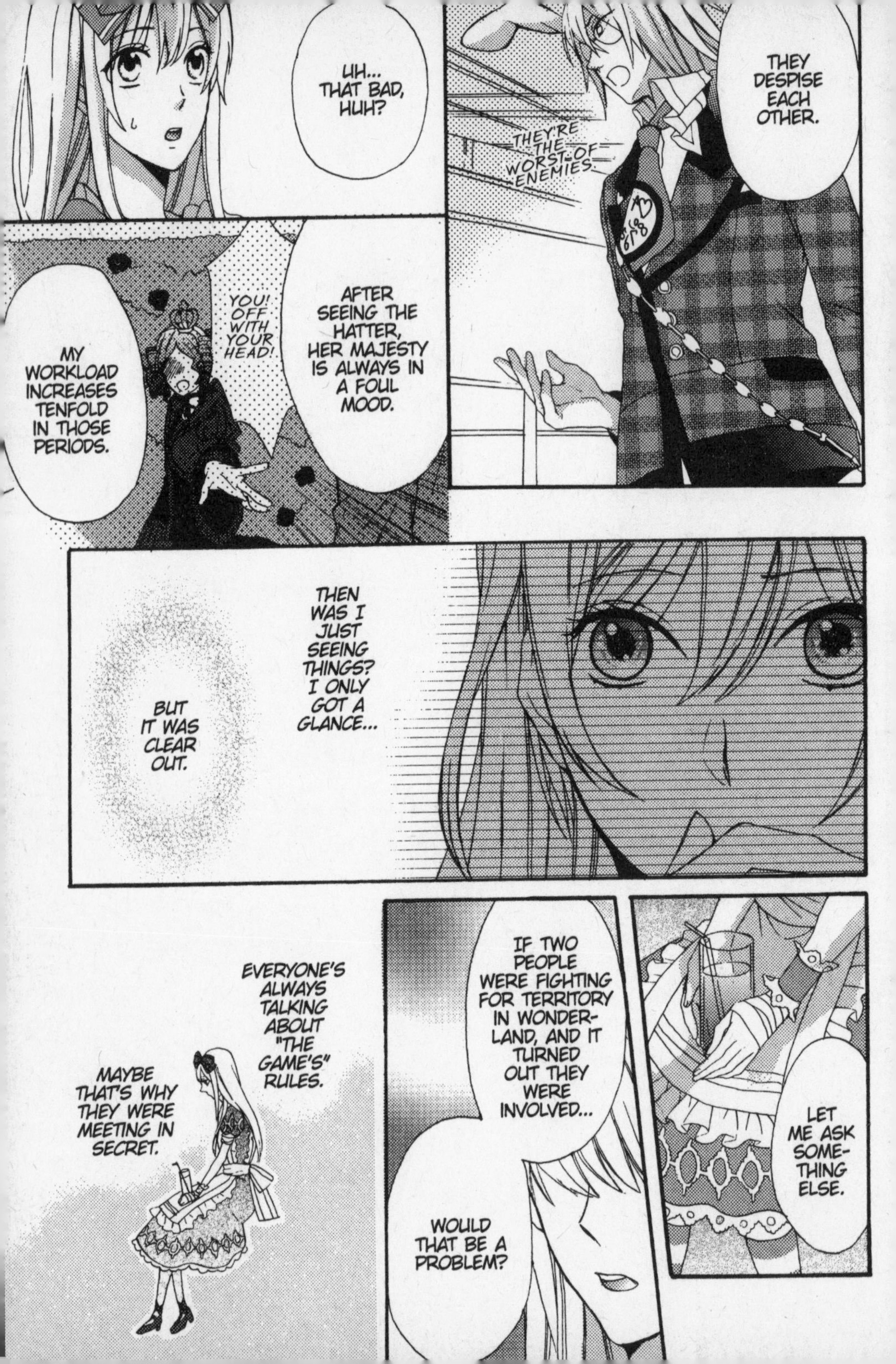
THEY DESPISE EACH OTHER.
THEY'RE THE WORST OF ENEMIES.
UH... THAT BAD, HUH?
AFTER SEEING THE HATTER, HER MAJESTY IS ALWAYS IN A FOUL MOOD.
YOU! OFF WITH YOUR HEAD!
MY WORKLOAD INCREASES TENFOLD IN THOSE PERIODS.
THEN WAS I JUST SEEING THINGS? I ONLY GOT A GLANCE...
BUT IT WAS CLEAR OUT.
LET ME ASK SOME-THING ELSE.
IF TWO PEOPLE WERE FIGHTING FOR TERRITORY IN WONDER-LAND, AND IT TURNED OUT THEY WERE INVOLVED...
WOULD THAT BE A PROBLEM?
EVERYONE'S ALWAYS TALKING ABOUT "THE GAME'S" RULES.
MAYBE THAT'S WHY THEY WERE MEETING IN SECRET.

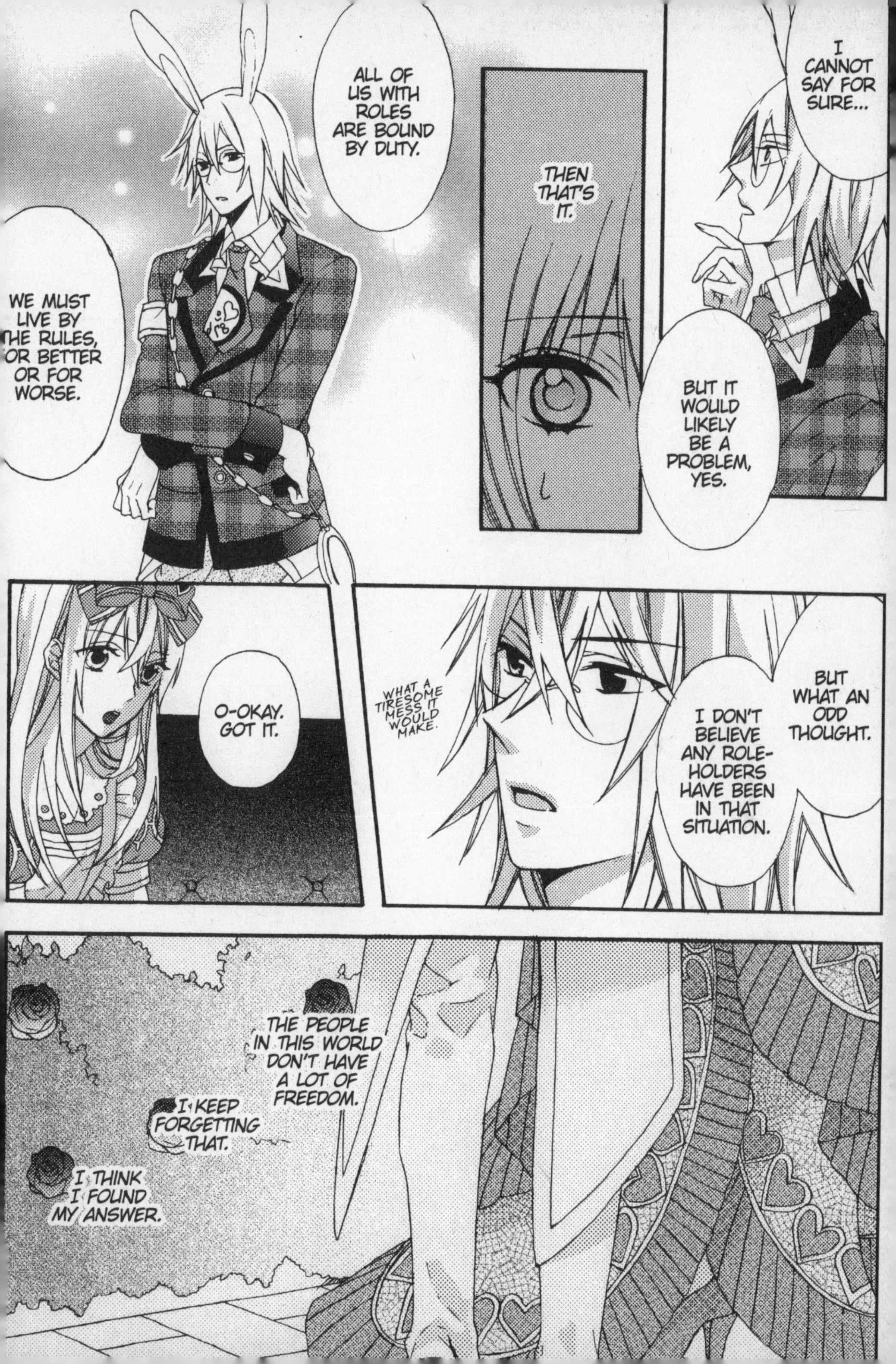
I CANNOT SAY FOR SURE...
BUT IT WOULD LIKELY BE A PROBLEM, YES.
THEN THAT'S IT.
ALL OF US WITH ROLES ARE BOUND BY DUTY.
WE MUST LIVE BY THE RULES, OR BETTER OR FOR WORSE.
BUT WHAT AN ODD THOUGHT.
I DON'T BELIEVE ANY ROLE-HOLDERS HAVE BEEN IN THAT SITUATION.
WHAT A TIRESOME MESS IT WOULD MAKE.
O-OKAY. GOT IT.
THE PEOPLE IN THIS WORLD DON'T HAVE A LOT OF FREEDOM.
I KEEP FORGETTING THAT.
I THINK I FOUND MY ANSWER.

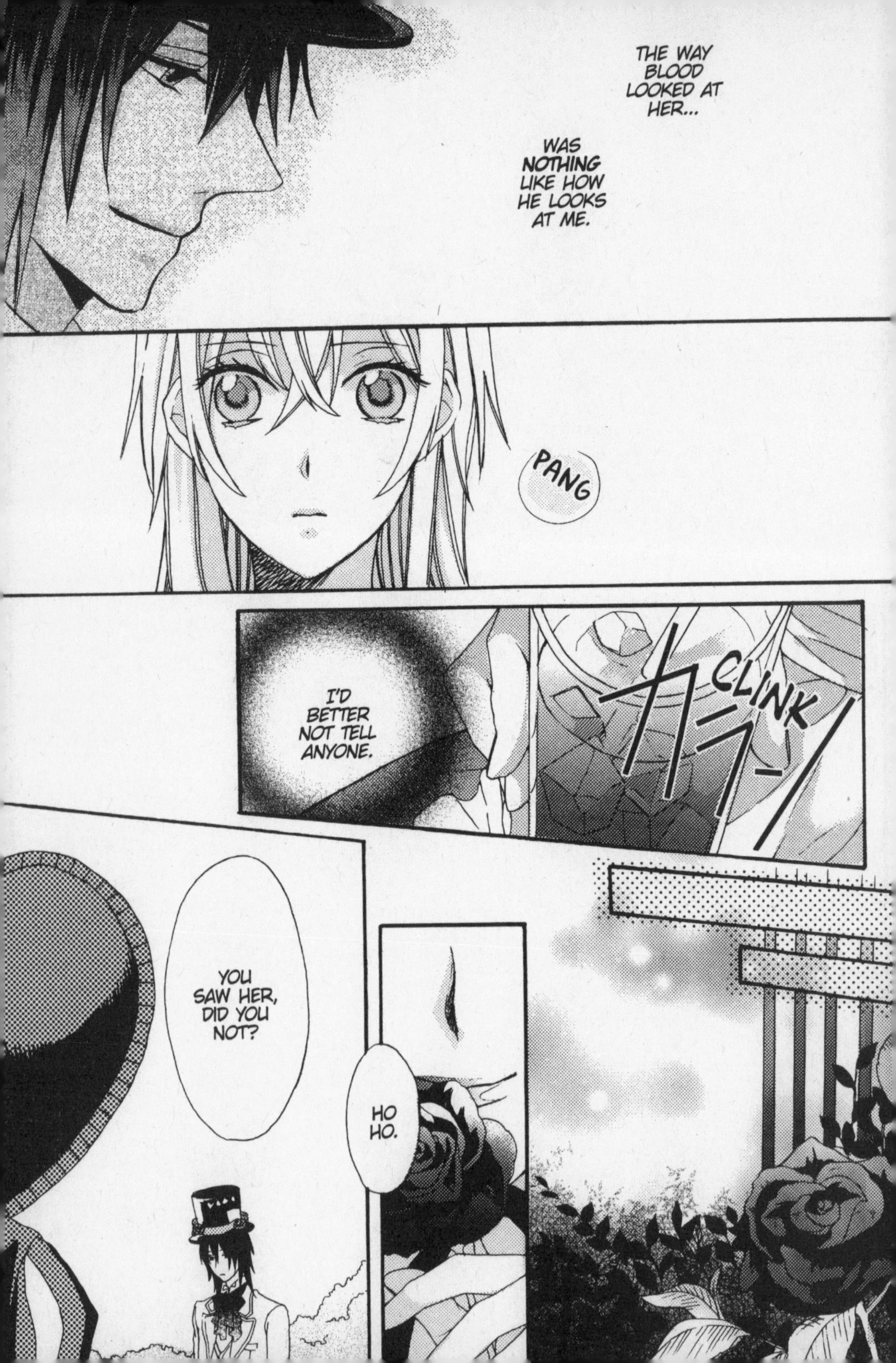
THE WAY BLOOD LOOKED AT HER...
WAS NOTHING LIKE HOW HE LOOKS AT ME.
PANG
CLINK
I'D BETTER NOT TELL ANYONE.
HO HO.
YOU SAW HER, DID YOU NOT?

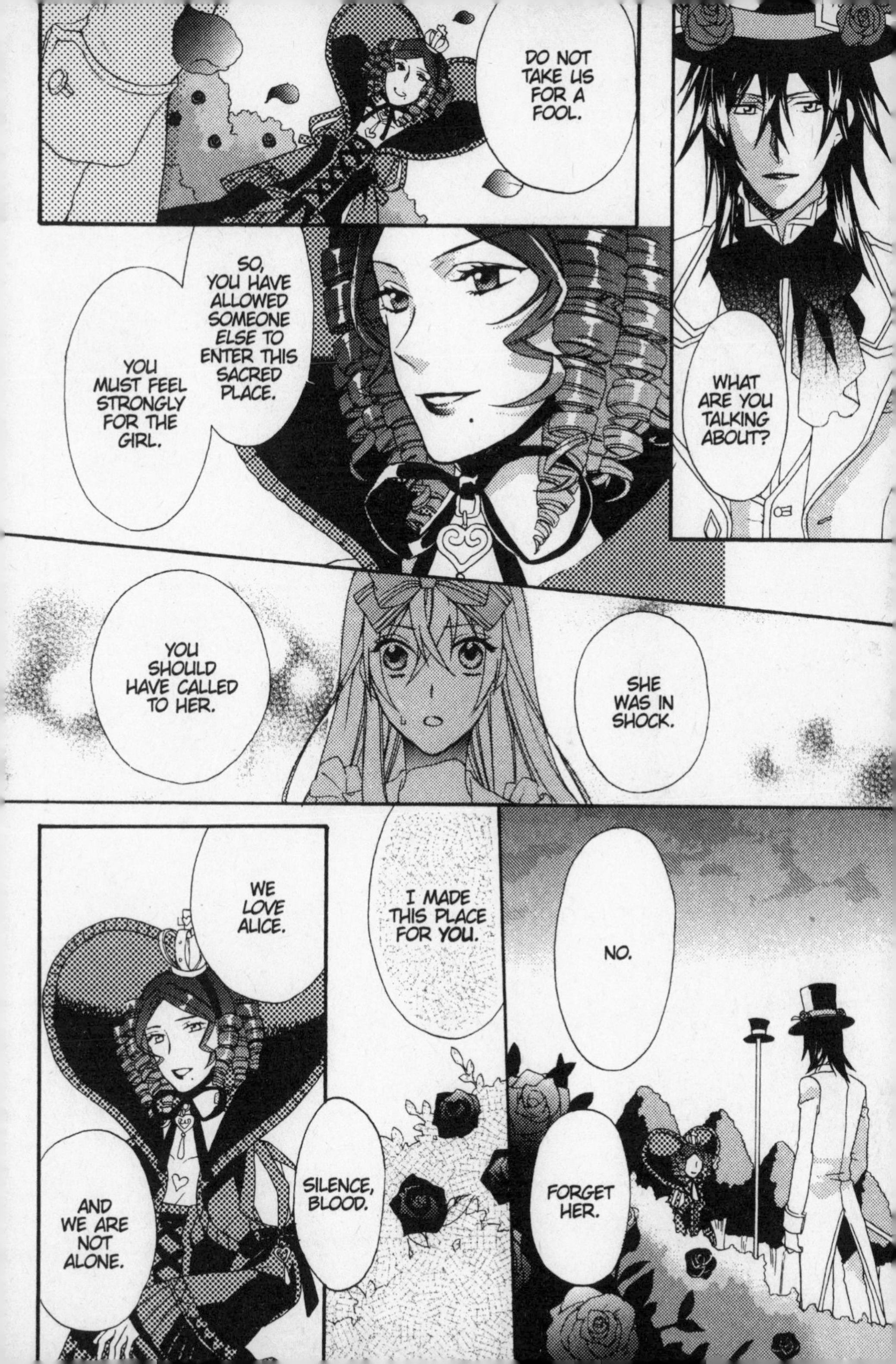
DO NOT TAKE US FOR A FOOL.
WHAT ARE YOU TALKING ABOUT?
SO, YOU HAVE ALLOWED SOMEONE ELSE TO ENTER THIS SACRED PLACE.
YOU MUST FEEL STRONGLY FOR THE GIRL.
SHE WAS IN SHOCK.
YOU SHOULD HAVE CALLED TO HER.
NO.
FORGET HER.
I MADE THIS PLACE FOR YOU.
SILENCE, BLOOD.
WE LOVE ALICE.
AND WE ARE NOT ALONE.

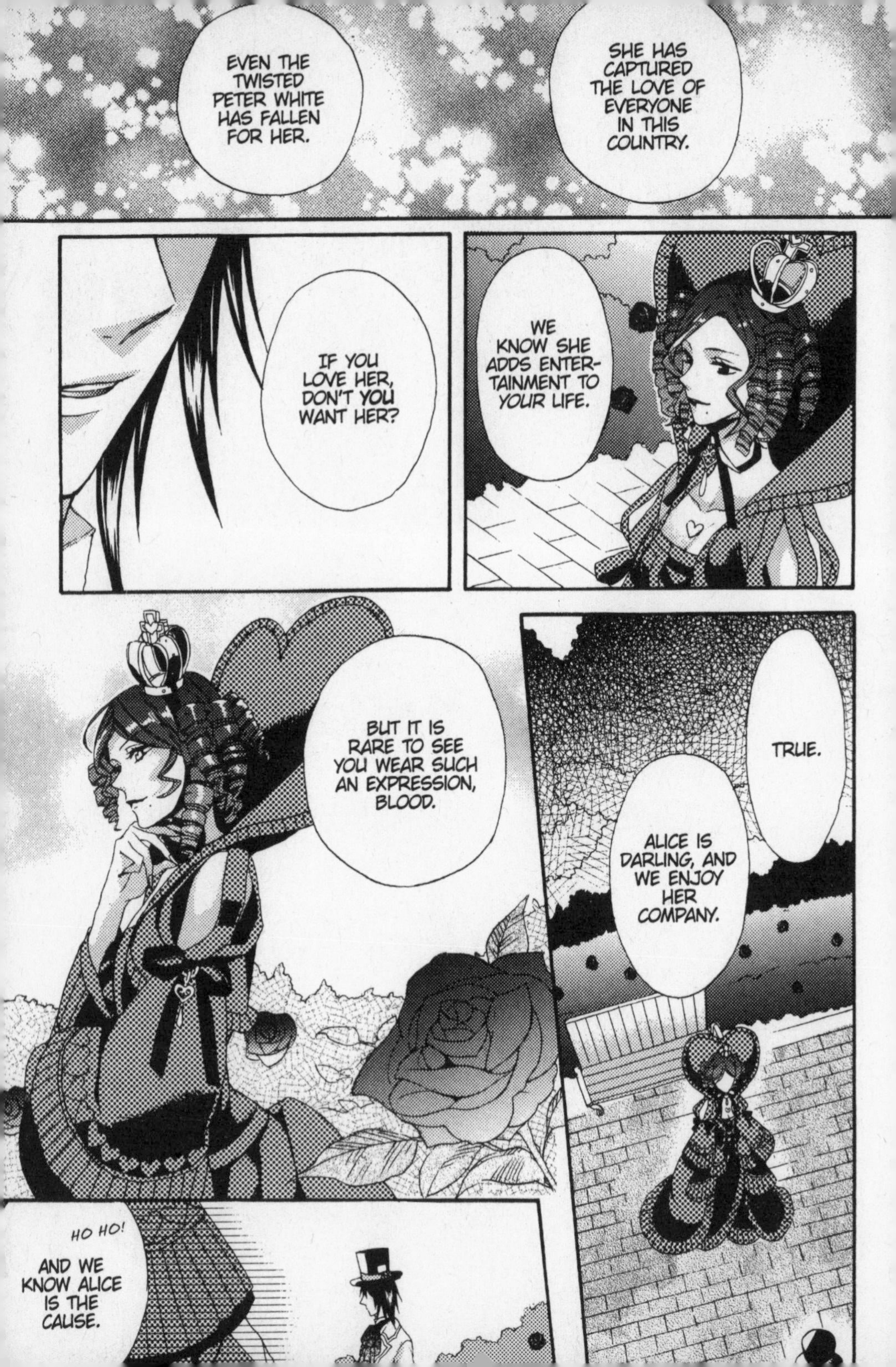
SHE HAS CAPTURED THE LOVE OF EVERYONE IN THIS COUNTRY.
EVEN THE TWISTED PETER WHITE HAS FALLEN FOR HER.
WE KNOW SHE ADDS ENTERTAINMENT TO *YOUR* LIFE.
IF YOU LOVE HER, DON'T *YOU* WANT HER?
TRUE.
ALICE IS DARLING, AND WE ENJOY HER COMPANY.
BUT IT IS RARE TO SEE YOU WEAR SUCH AN EXPRESSION, BLOOD.
HO HO!
AND WE KNOW ALICE IS THE CAUSE.

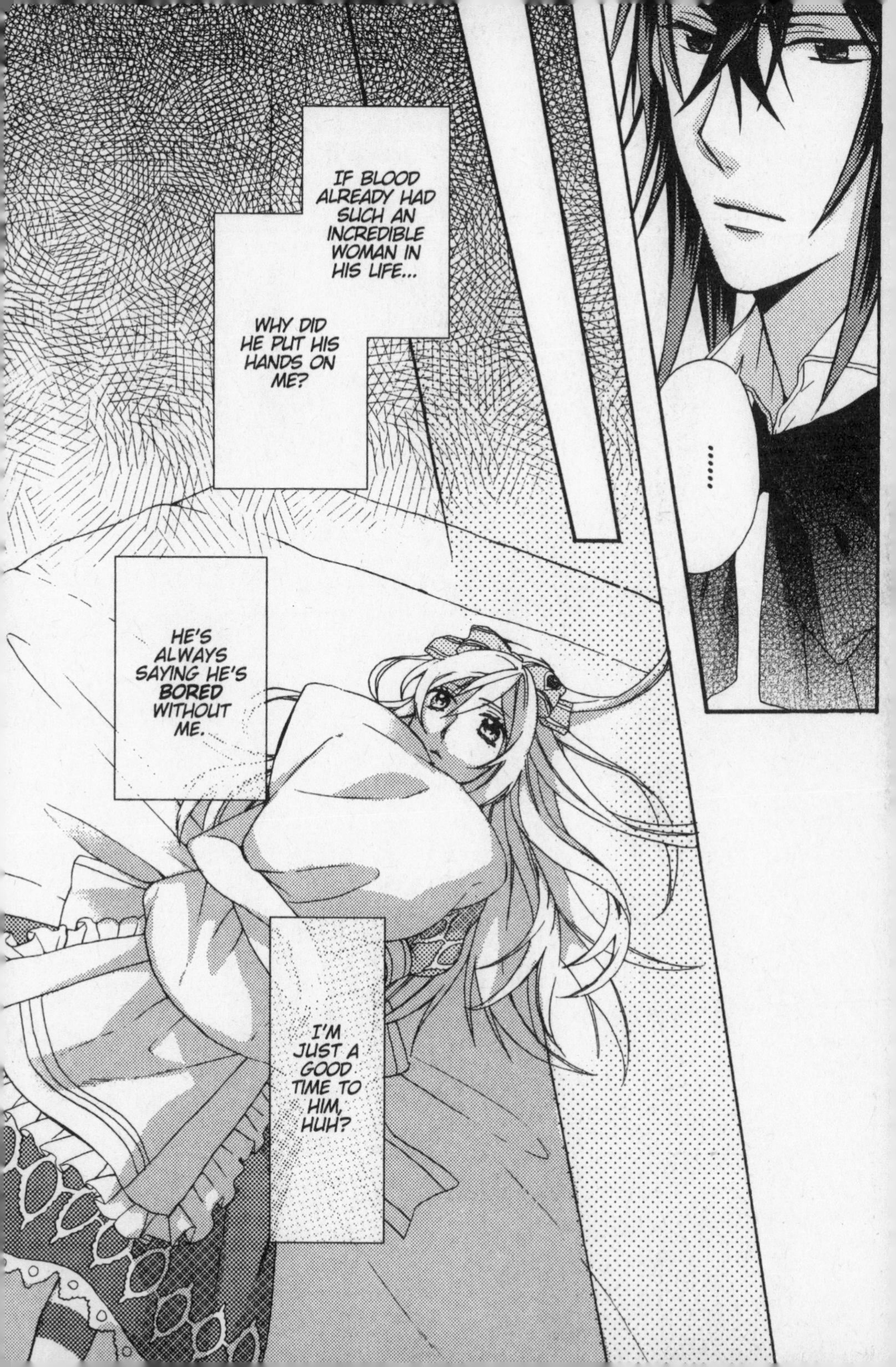
......
IF BLOOD ALREADY HAD SUCH AN INCREDIBLE WOMAN IN HIS LIFE...
WHY DID HE PUT HIS HANDS ON ME?
HE'S ALWAYS SAYING HE'S BORED WITHOUT ME.
I'M JUST A GOOD TIME TO HIM, HUH?

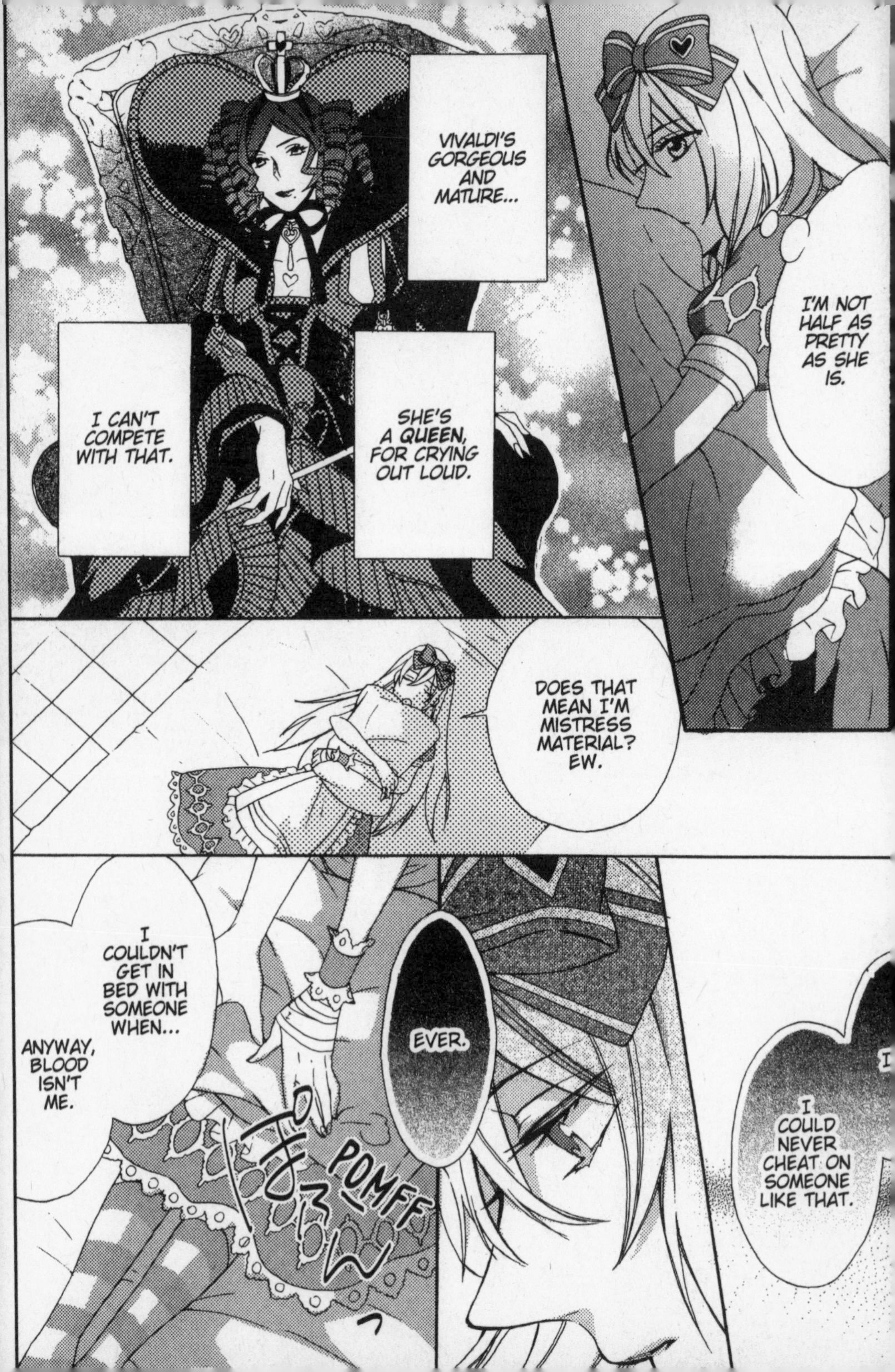
I'M NOT HALF AS PRETTY AS SHE IS.
VIVALDI'S GORGEOUS AND MATURE...
SHE'S A QUEEN, FOR CRYING OUT LOUD.
I CAN'T COMPETE WITH THAT.
DOES THAT MEAN I'M MISTRESS MATERIAL? EW.
I
I COULD NEVER CHEAT ON SOMEONE LIKE THAT.
EVER.
I COULDN'T GET IN BED WITH SOMEONE WHEN...
ANYWAY, BLOOD ISN'T ME.
POMFF

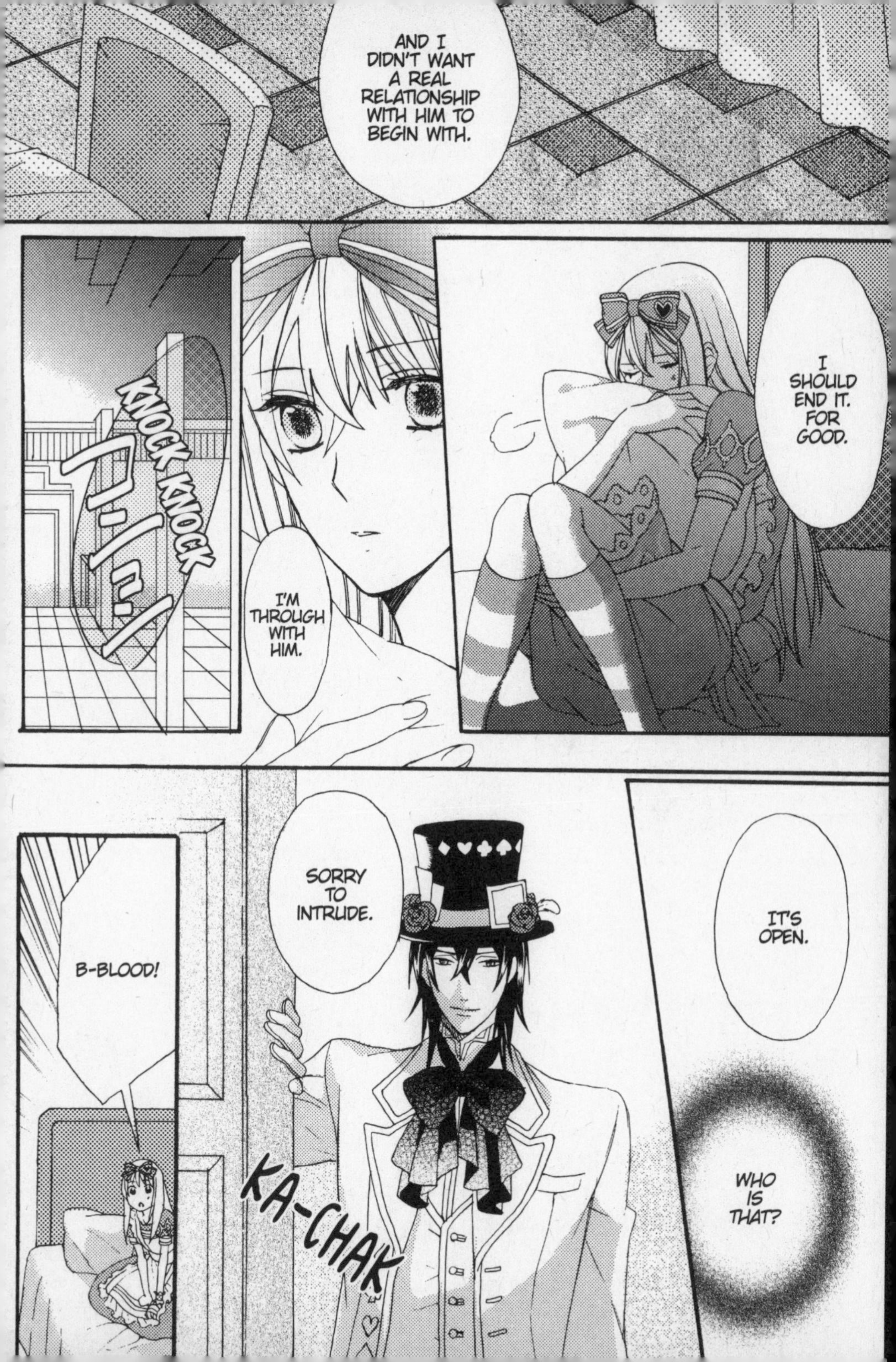
AND I DIDN'T WANT A REAL RELATIONSHIP WITH HIM TO BEGIN WITH.
I SHOULD END IT. FOR GOOD.
I'M THROUGH WITH HIM.
KNOCK KNOCK
IT'S OPEN.
WHO IS THAT?
SORRY TO INTRUDE.
KA-CHAK
B-BLOOD!

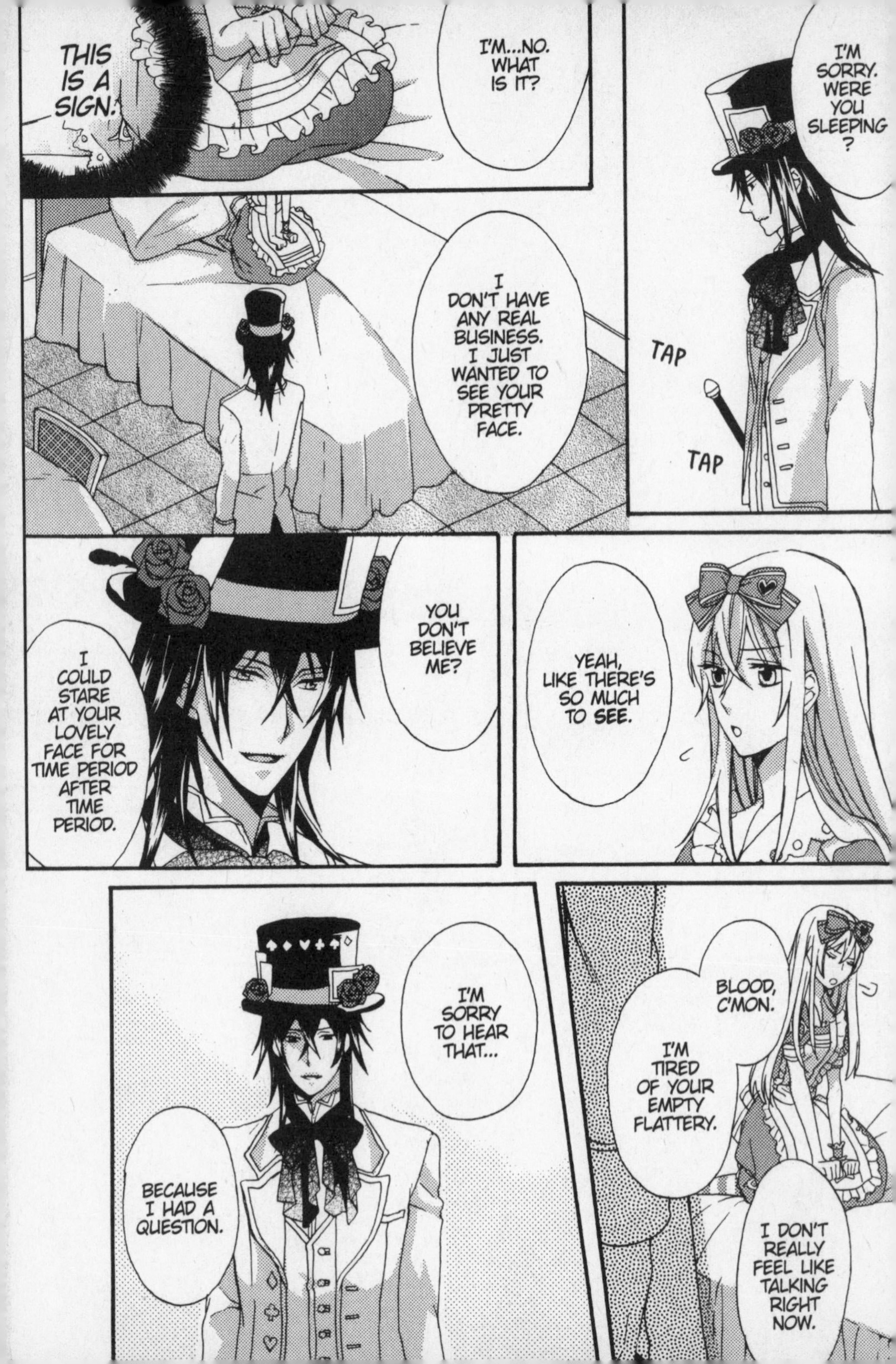

I'M SORRY. WERE YOU SLEEPING?
TAP
TAP
I'M...NO. WHAT IS IT?
THIS IS A SIGN.
I DON'T HAVE ANY REAL BUSINESS. I JUST WANTED TO SEE YOUR PRETTY FACE.
YEAH, LIKE THERE'S SO MUCH TO SEE.
YOU DON'T BELIEVE ME?
I COULD STARE AT YOUR LOVELY FACE FOR TIME PERIOD AFTER TIME PERIOD.
BLOOD, C'MON.
I'M TIRED OF YOUR EMPTY FLATTERY.
I DON'T REALLY FEEL LIKE TALKING RIGHT NOW.
I'M SORRY TO HEAR THAT...
BECAUSE I HAD A QUESTION.

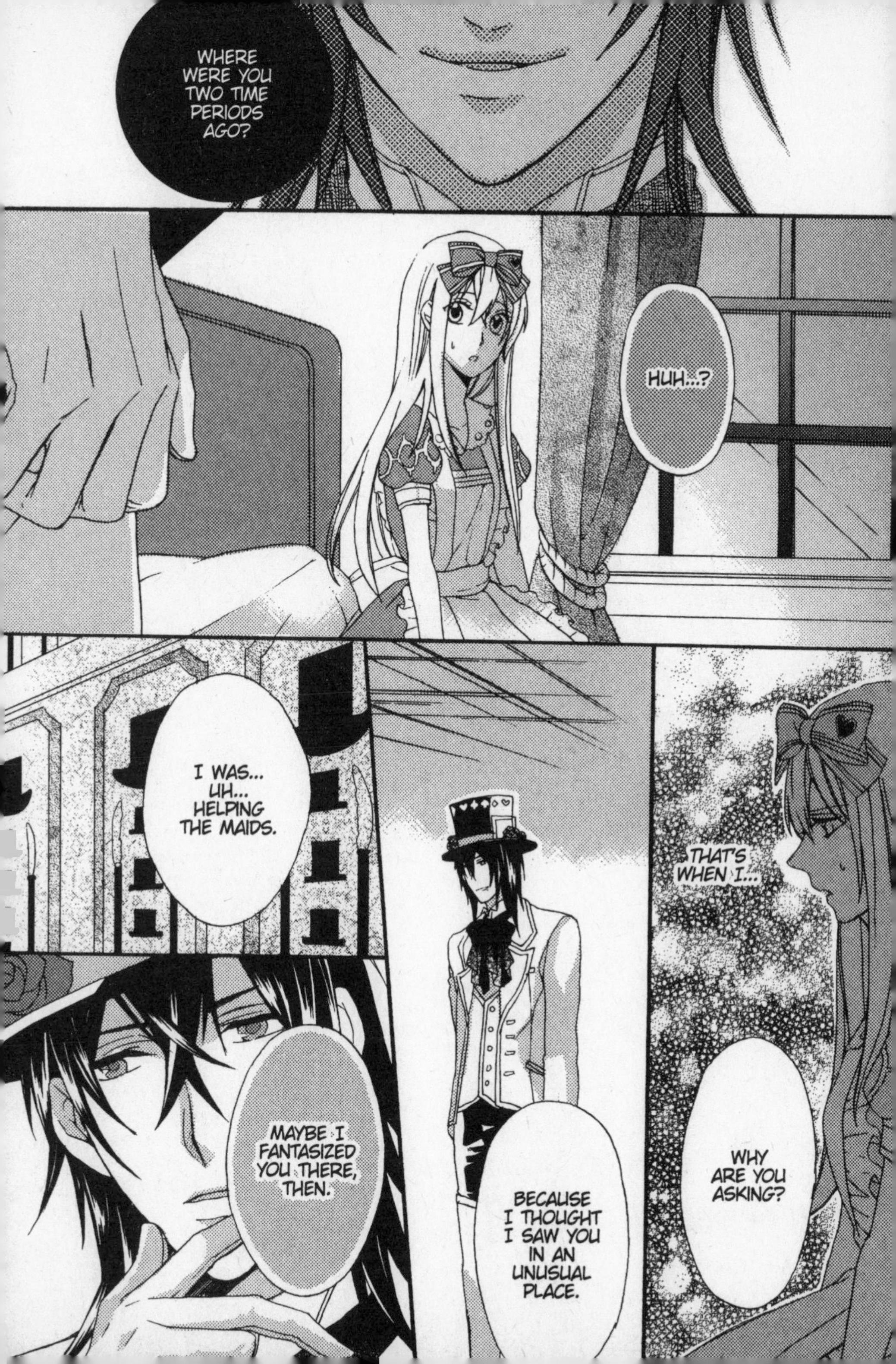
WHERE WERE YOU TWO TIME PERIODS AGO?
HUH...?
THAT'S WHEN I...
WHY ARE YOU ASKING?
BECAUSE I THOUGHT I SAW YOU IN AN UNUSUAL PLACE.
I WAS... UH... HELPING THE MAIDS.
MAYBE I FANTASIZED YOU THERE, THEN.

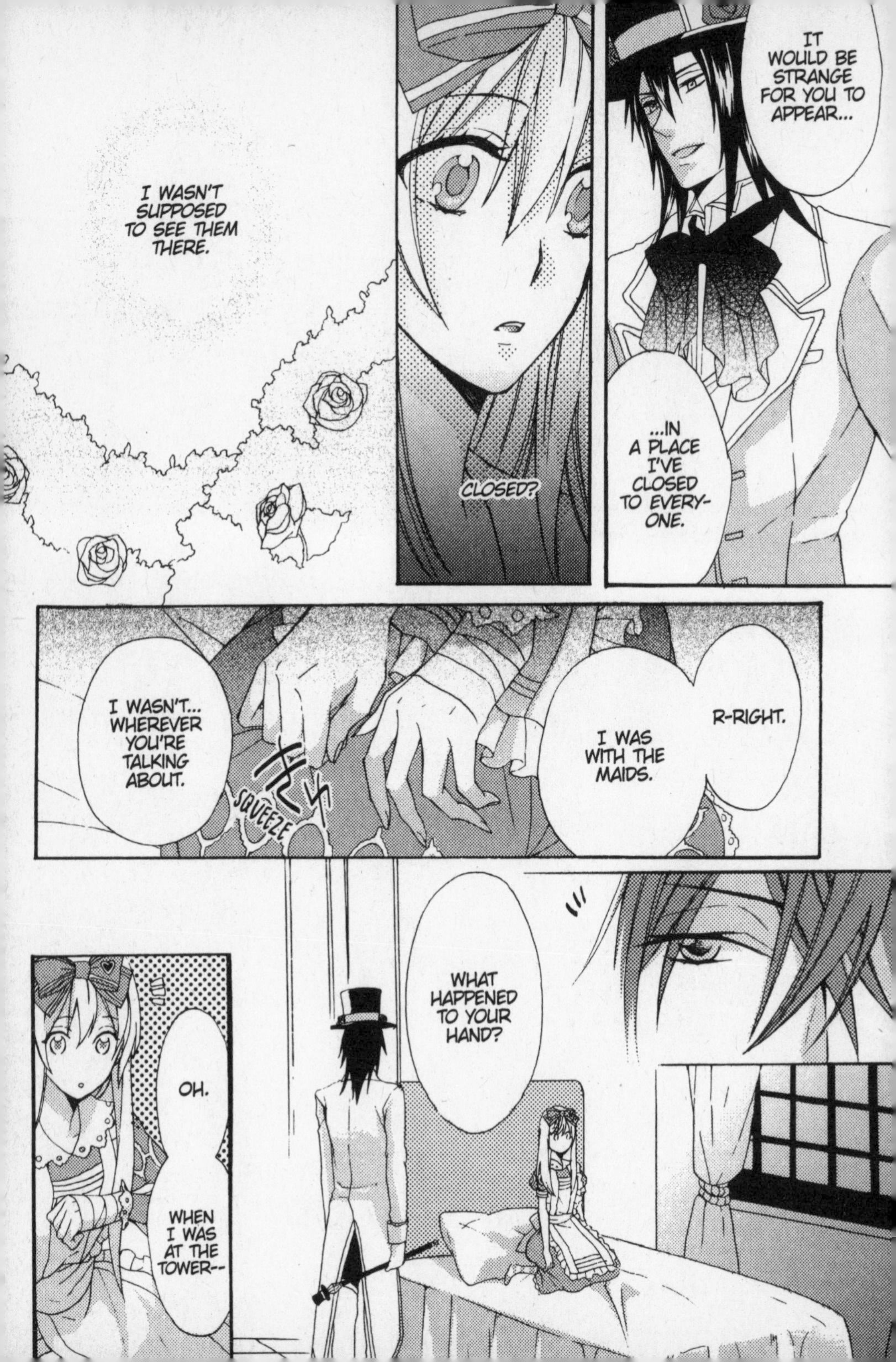
IT WOULD BE STRANGE FOR YOU TO APPEAR...
...IN A PLACE I'VE CLOSED TO EVERY-ONE.
CLOSED?
I WASN'T SUPPOSED TO SEE THEM THERE.
R-RIGHT.
I WAS WITH THE MAIDS.
I WASN'T... WHEREVER YOU'RE TALKING ABOUT.
SQUEEZE
WHAT HAPPENED TO YOUR HAND?
OH.
WHEN I WAS AT THE TOWER--

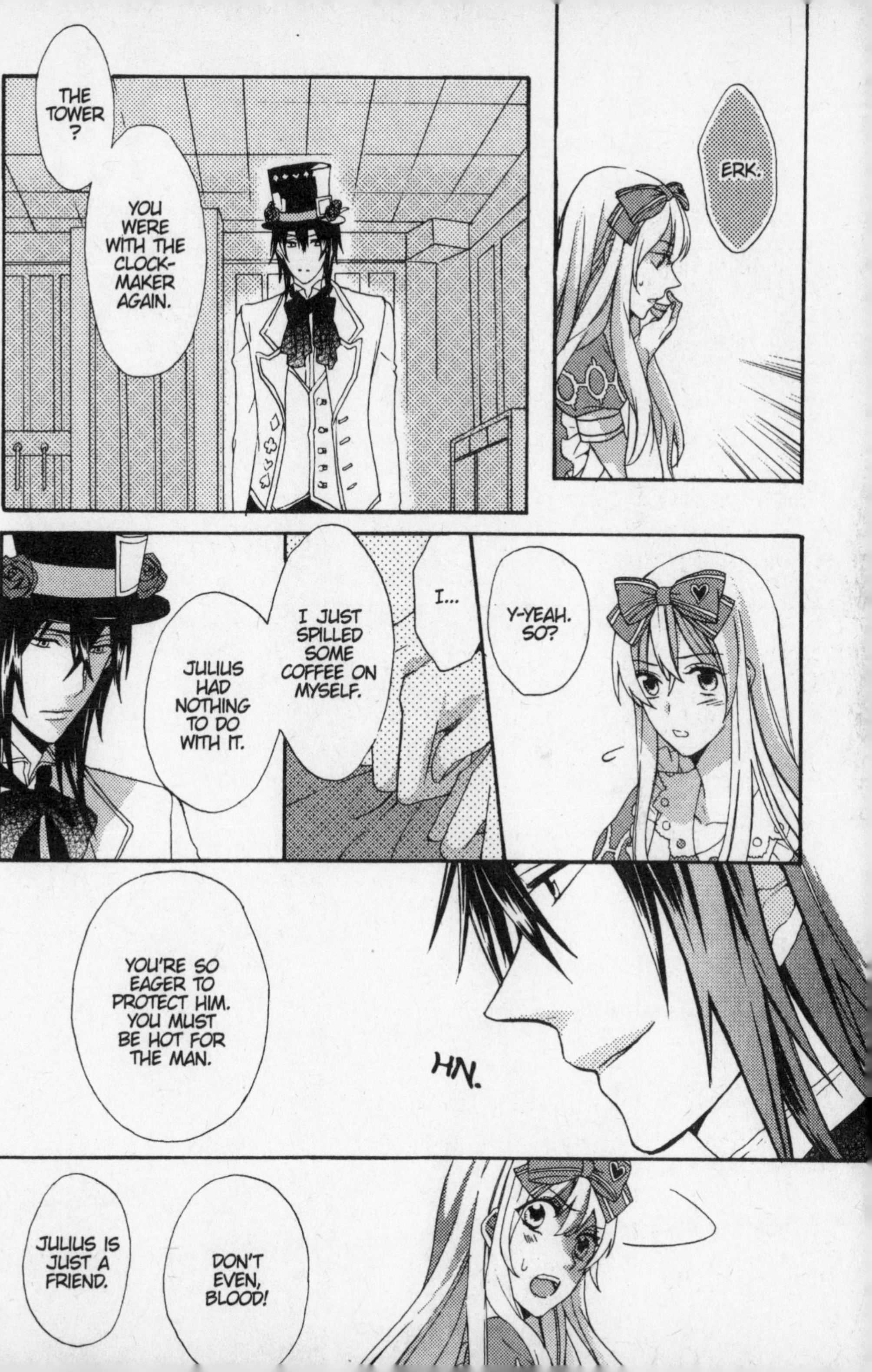
ERK.
THE TOWER?
YOU WERE WITH THE CLOCK-MAKER AGAIN.
Y-YEAH. SO?
I...
I JUST SPILLED SOME COFFEE ON MYSELF.
JULIUS HAD NOTHING TO DO WITH IT.
HN.
YOU'RE SO EAGER TO PROTECT HIM. YOU MUST BE HOT FOR THE MAN.
DON'T EVEN, BLOOD!
JULIUS IS JUST A FRIEND.

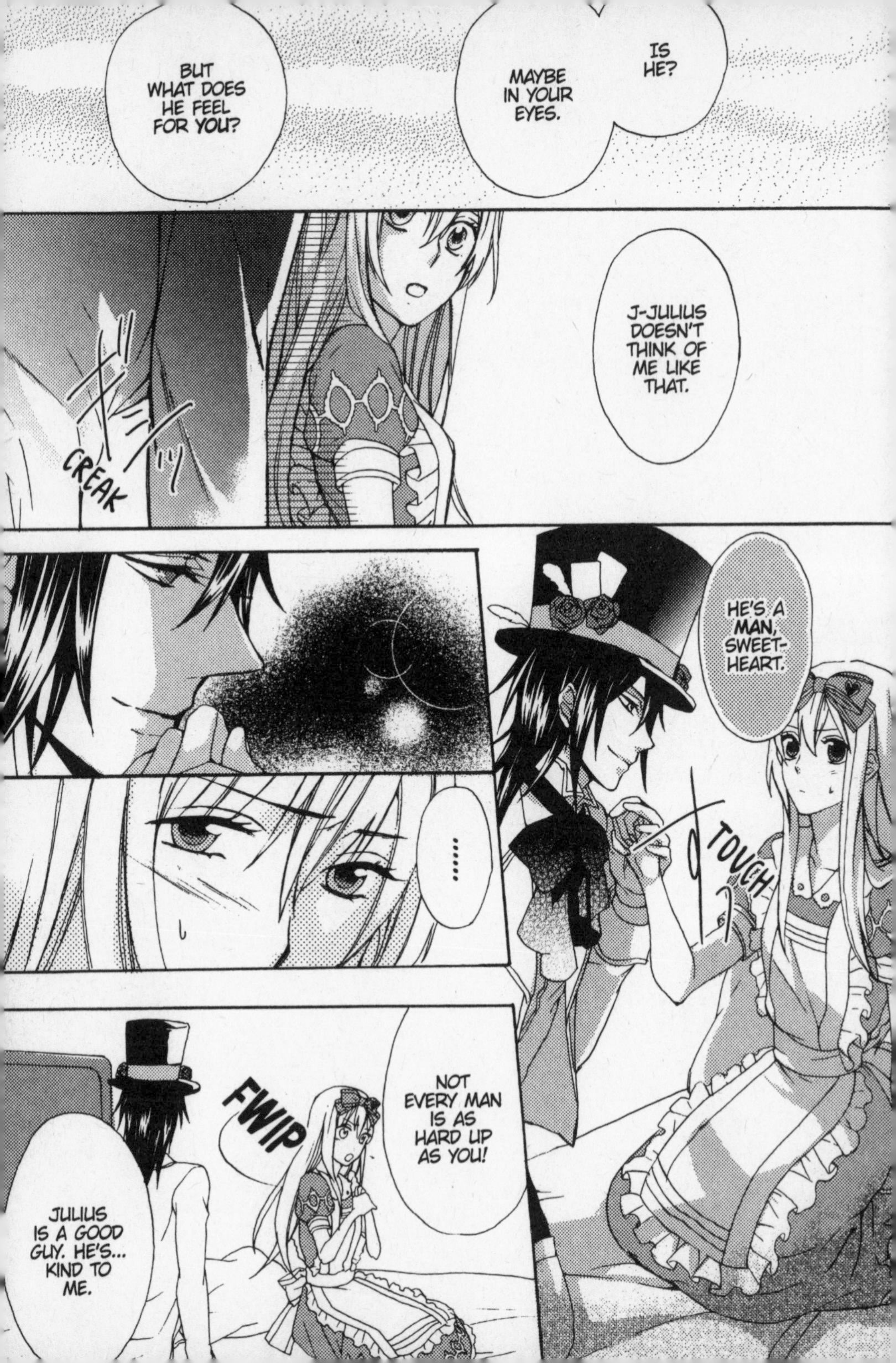
IS HE?
MAYBE IN YOUR EYES.
BUT WHAT DOES HE FEEL FOR YOU?
J-JULIUS DOESN'T THINK OF ME LIKE THAT.
CREAK
HE'S A MAN, SWEET-HEART.
TOUCH
......
NOT EVERY MAN IS AS HARD UP AS YOU!
FWIP
JULIUS IS A GOOD GUY. HE'S... KIND TO ME.

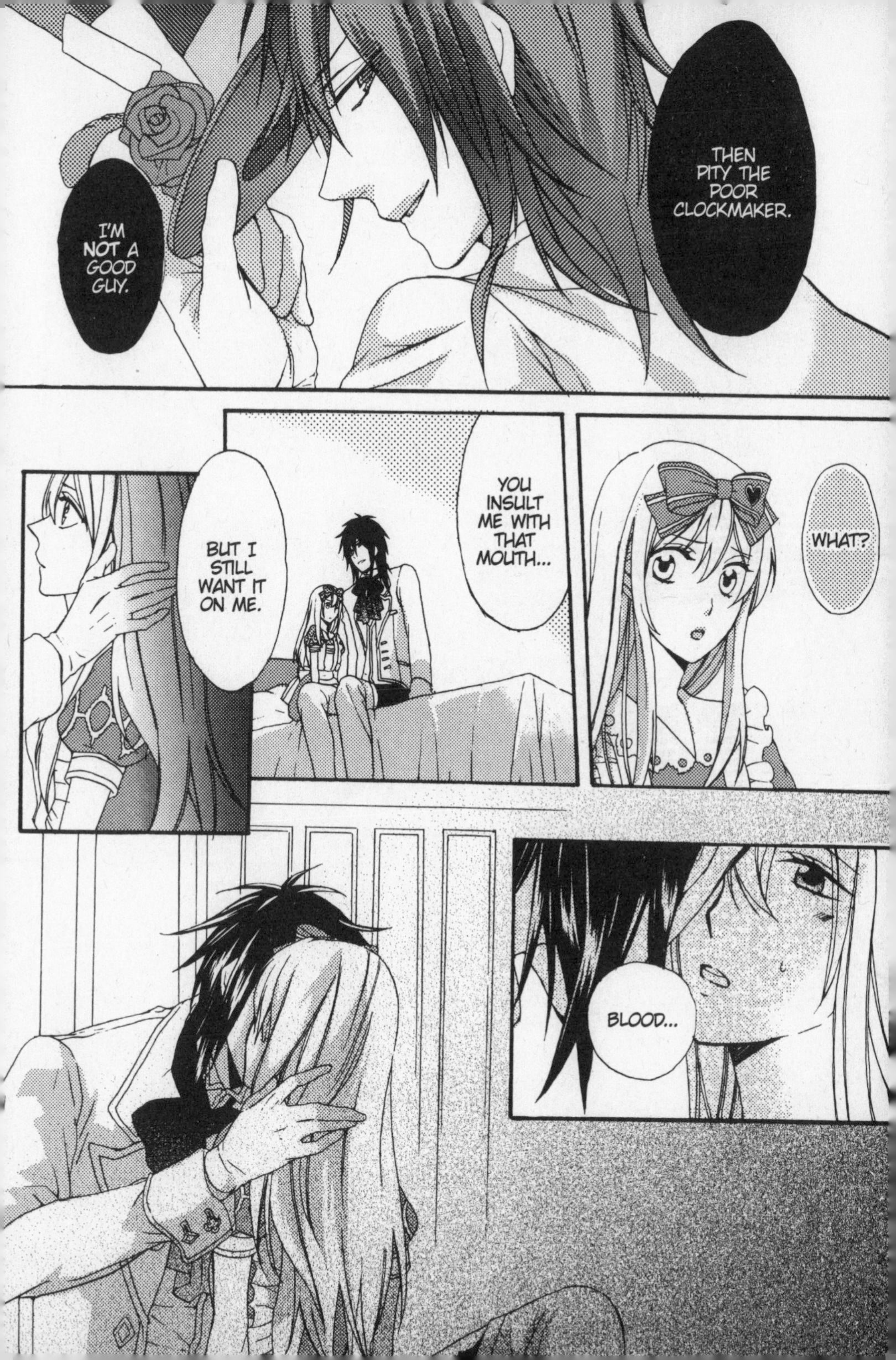
THEN PITY THE POOR CLOCKMAKER.
I'M NOT A GOOD GUY.
WHAT?
YOU INSULT ME WITH THAT MOUTH...
BUT I STILL WANT IT ON ME.
BLOOD...

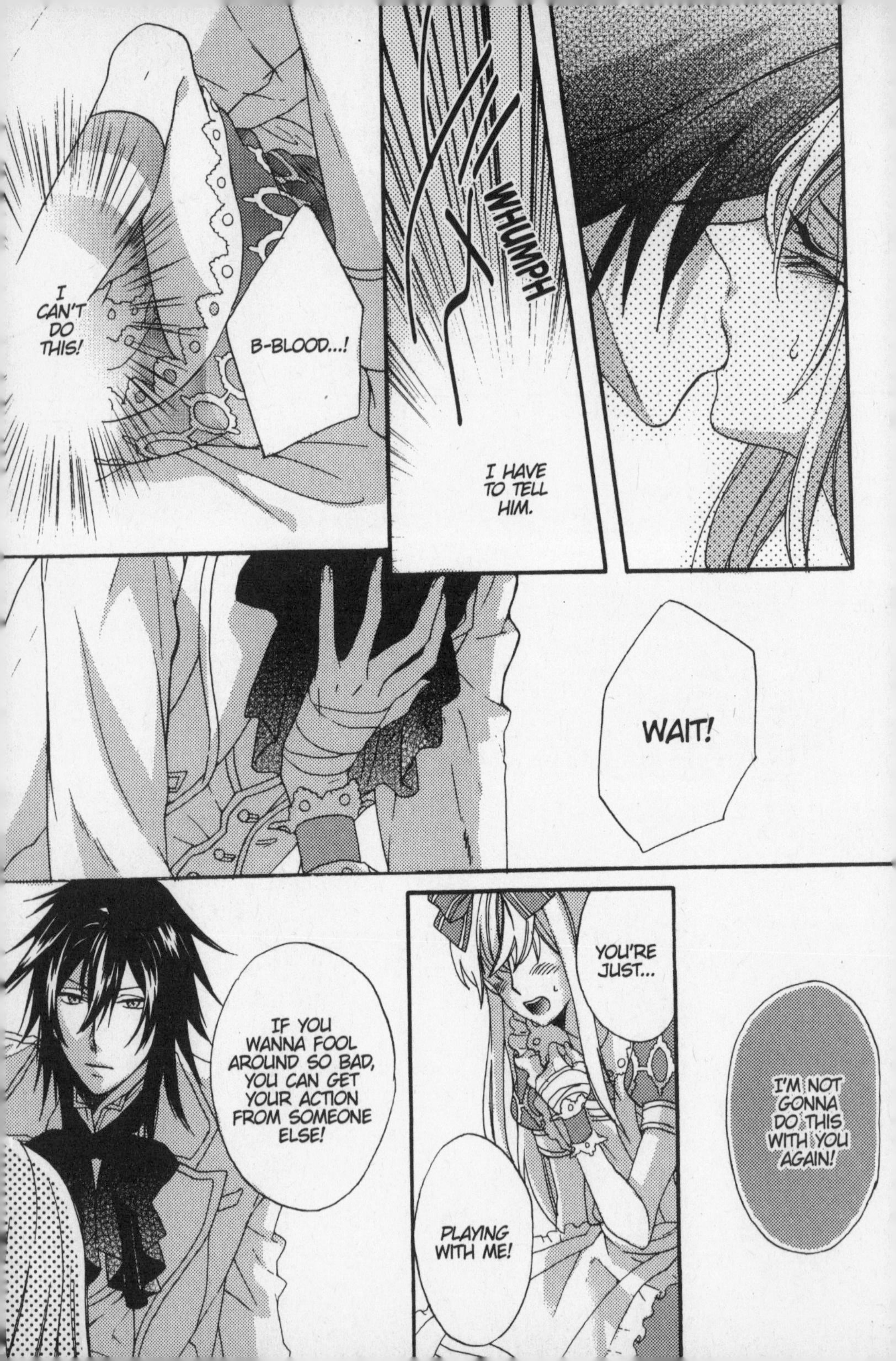
WHUMPH
I HAVE TO TELL HIM.
B-BLOOD...!
I CAN'T DO THIS!
WAIT!
I'M NOT GONNA DO THIS WITH YOU AGAIN!
YOU'RE JUST...
PLAYING WITH ME!
IF YOU WANNA FOOL AROUND SO BAD, YOU CAN GET YOUR ACTION FROM SOMEONE ELSE!

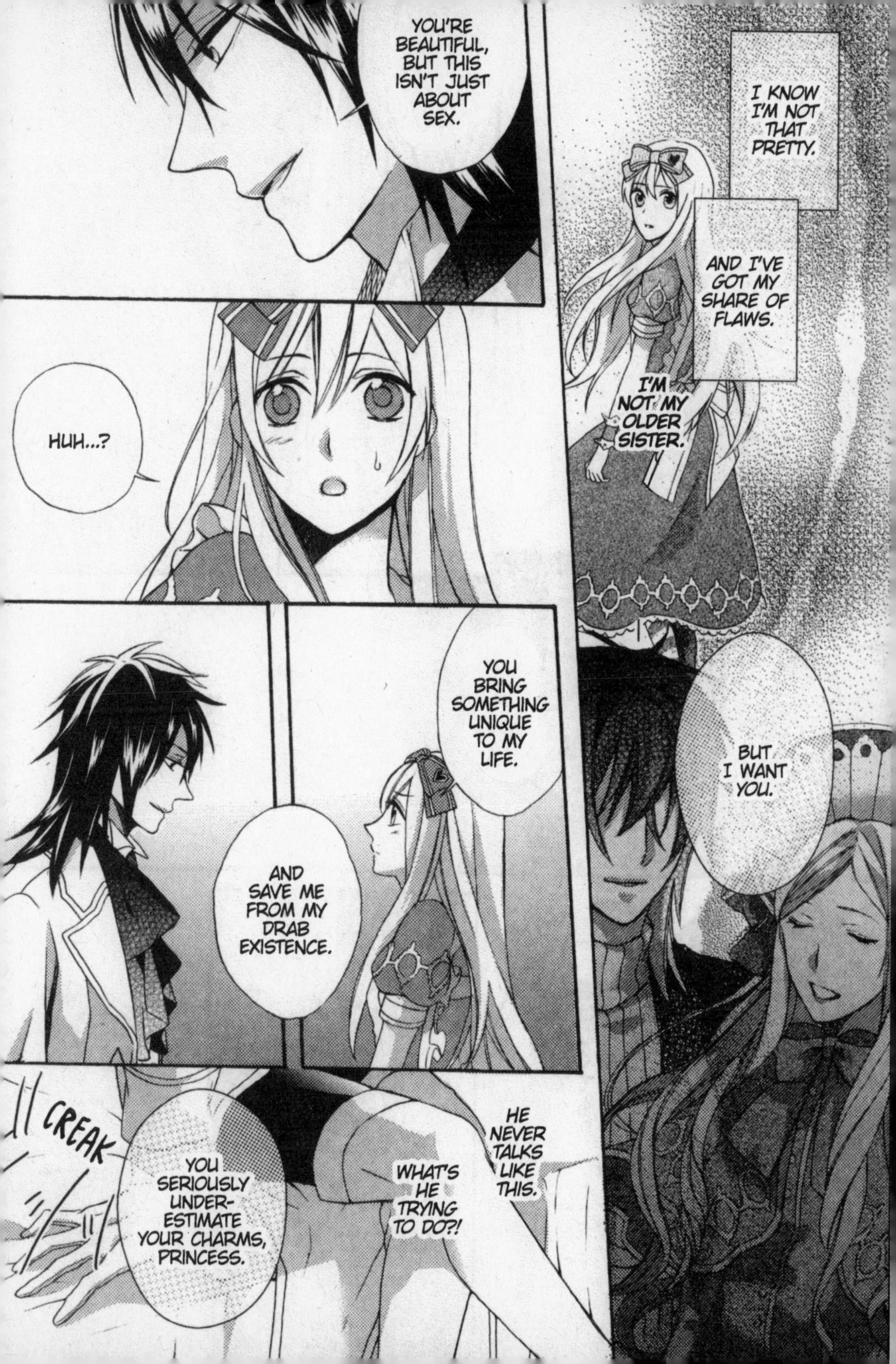
I KNOW I'M NOT THAT PRETTY.
AND I'VE GOT MY SHARE OF FLAWS.
I'M NOT MY OLDER SISTER.
BUT I WANT YOU.
YOU'RE BEAUTIFUL, BUT THIS ISN'T JUST ABOUT SEX.
HUH...?
YOU BRING SOMETHING UNIQUE TO MY LIFE.
AND SAVE ME FROM MY DRAB EXISTENCE.
HE NEVER TALKS LIKE THIS.
WHAT'S HE TRYING TO DO?!
CREAK
YOU SERIOUSLY UNDER-ESTIMATE YOUR CHARMS, PRINCESS.

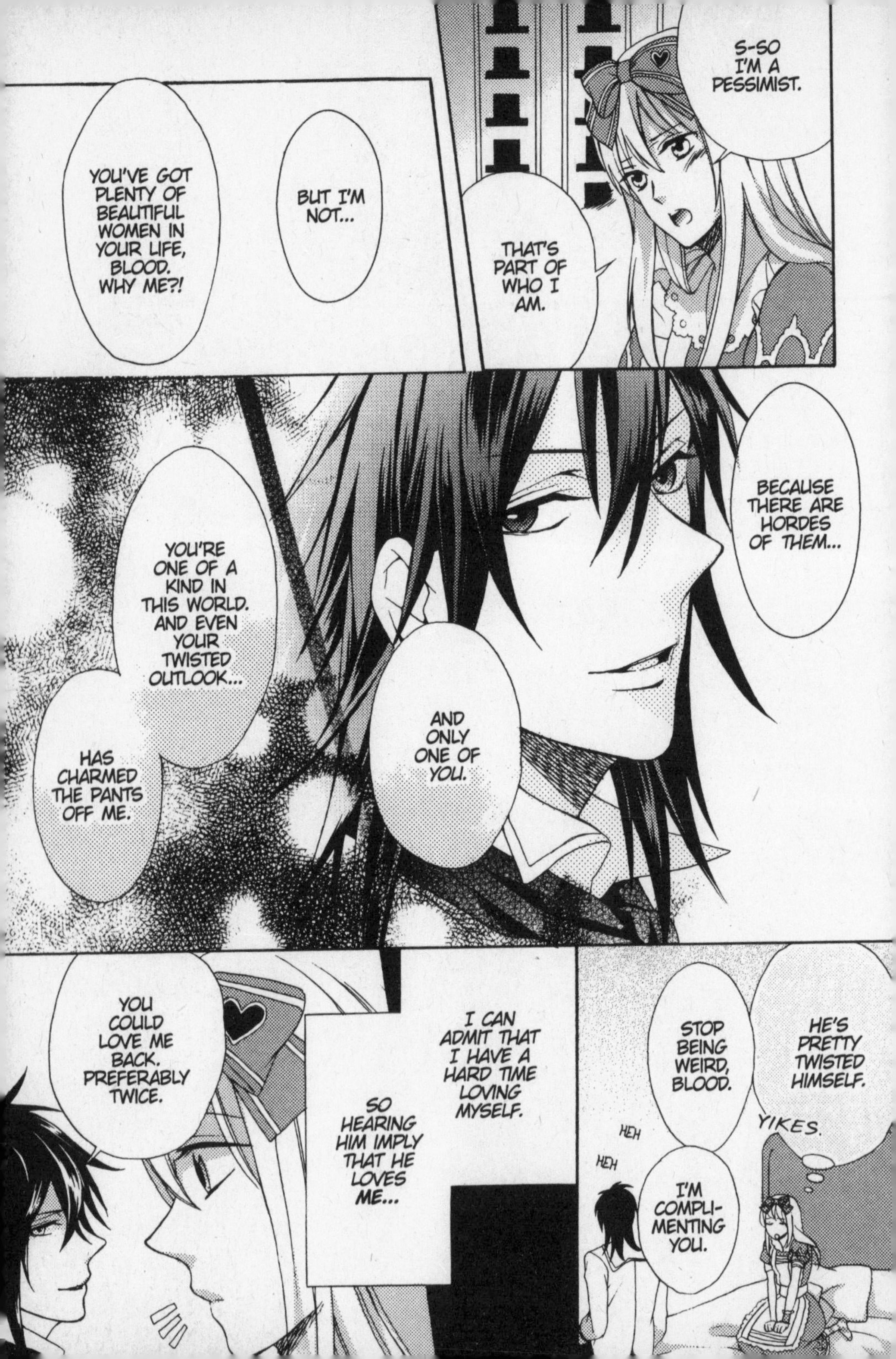
S-SO I'M A PESSIMIST.
THAT'S PART OF WHO I AM.
BUT I'M NOT...
YOU'VE GOT PLENTY OF BEAUTIFUL WOMEN IN YOUR LIFE, BLOOD. WHY ME?!
BECAUSE THERE ARE HORDES OF THEM...
AND ONLY ONE OF YOU.
YOU'RE ONE OF A KIND IN THIS WORLD. AND EVEN YOUR TWISTED OUTLOOK...
HAS CHARMED THE PANTS OFF ME.
HE'S PRETTY TWISTED HIMSELF.
YIKES.
STOP BEING WEIRD, BLOOD.
HEH
HEH
I'M COMPLI-MENTING YOU.
I CAN ADMIT THAT I HAVE A HARD TIME LOVING MYSELF.
SO HEARING HIM IMPLY THAT HE LOVES ME...
YOU COULD LOVE ME BACK. PREFERABLY TWICE.

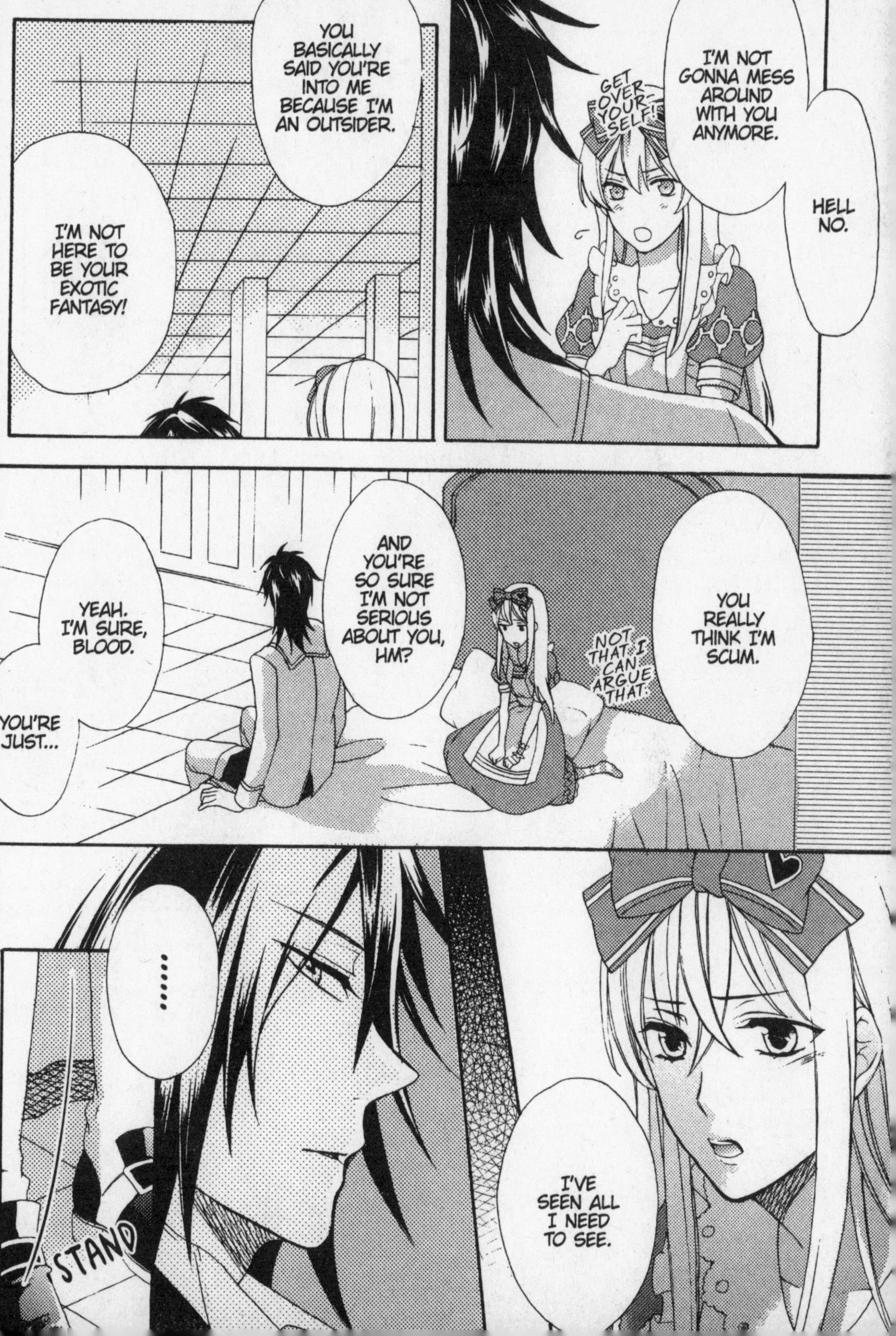
I'M NOT GONNA MESS AROUND WITH YOU ANYMORE.
GET OVER-YOUR-SELF!
HELL NO.
YOU BASICALLY SAID YOU'RE INTO ME BECAUSE I'M AN OUTSIDER.
I'M NOT HERE TO BE YOUR EXOTIC FANTASY!
YOU REALLY THINK I'M SCUM.
NOT THAT I CAN ARGUE THAT.
AND YOU'RE SO SURE I'M NOT SERIOUS ABOUT YOU, HM?
YEAH. I'M SURE, BLOOD.
YOU'RE JUST...
I'VE SEEN ALL I NEED TO SEE.
......
STAND

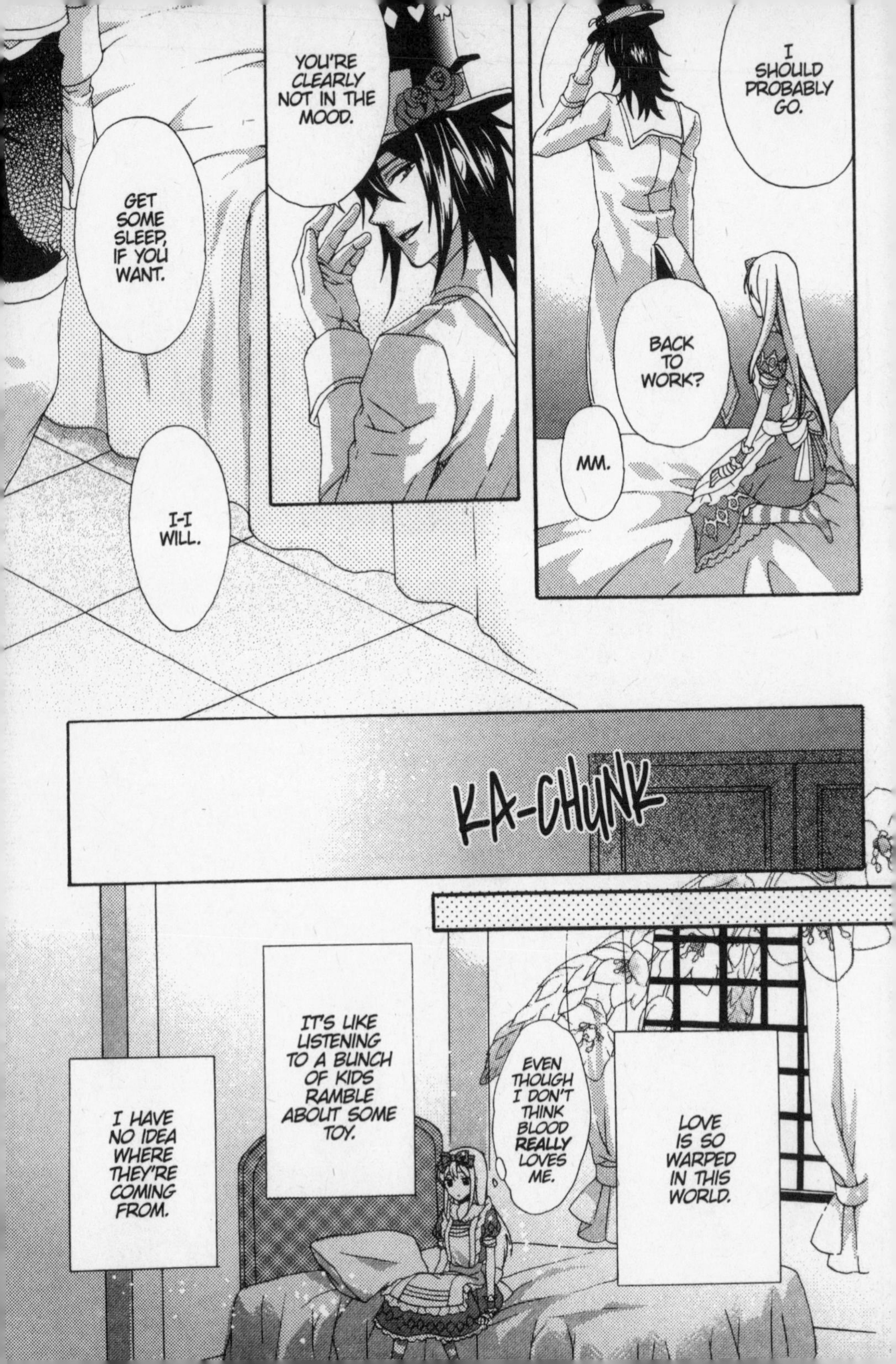
I SHOULD PROBABLY GO.
BACK TO WORK?
MM.
YOU'RE CLEARLY NOT IN THE MOOD.
GET SOME SLEEP, IF YOU WANT.
I-I WILL.
KA-CHUNK
LOVE IS SO WARPED IN THIS WORLD.
EVEN THOUGH I DON'T THINK BLOOD REALLY LOVES ME.
IT'S LIKE LISTENING TO A BUNCH OF KIDS RAMBLE ABOUT SOME TOY.
I HAVE NO IDEA WHERE THEY'RE COMING FROM.

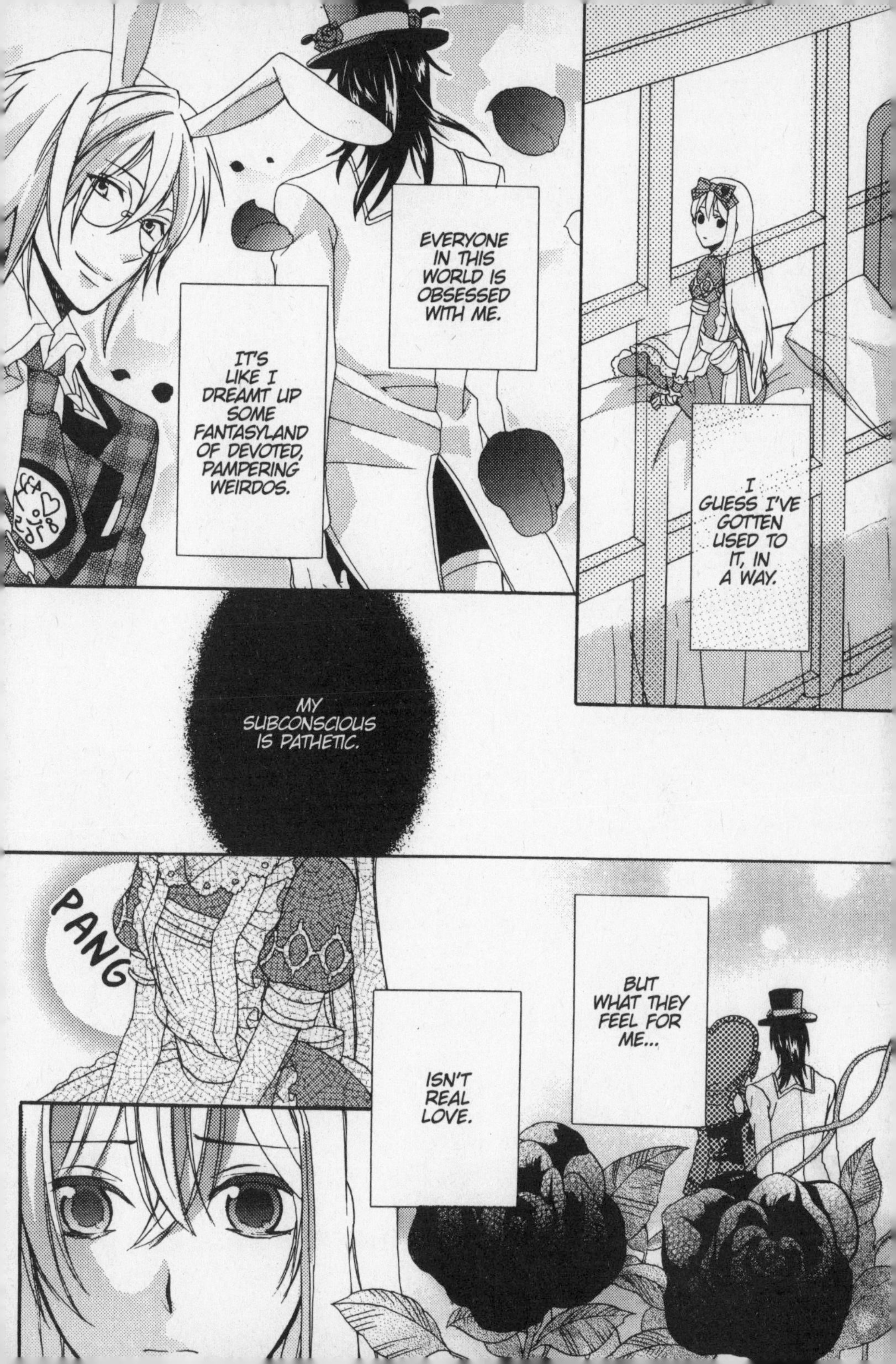
I GUESS I'VE GOTTEN USED TO IT, IN A WAY.
EVERYONE IN THIS WORLD IS OBSESSED WITH ME.
IT'S LIKE I DREAMT UP SOME FANTASYLAND OF DEVOTED, PAMPERING WEIRDOS.
MY SUBCONSCIOUS IS PATHETIC.
BUT WHAT THEY FEEL FOR ME...
ISN'T REAL LOVE.
PANG

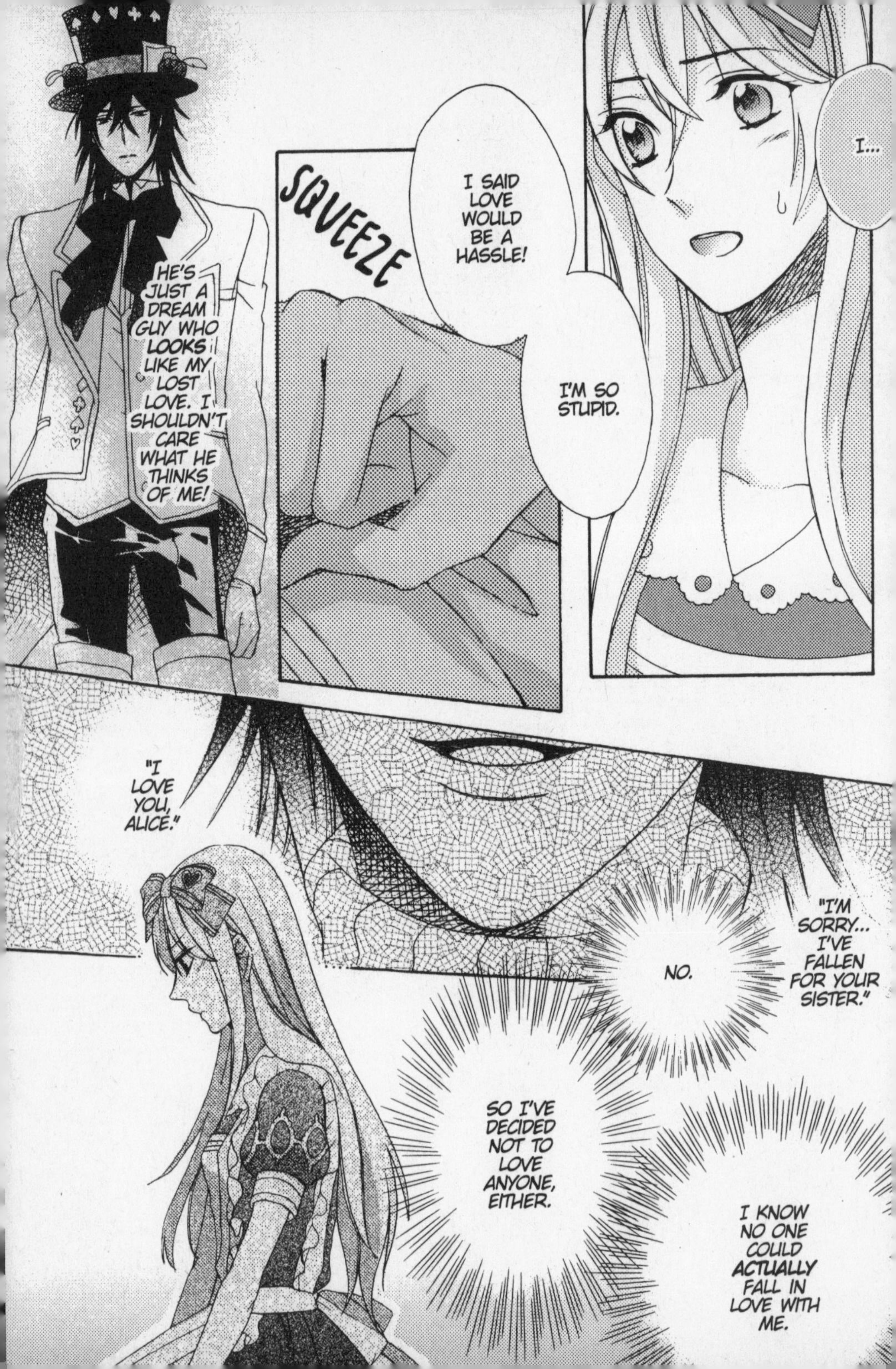
I...
I SAID LOVE WOULD BE A HASSLE!
SQUEEZE
I'M SO STUPID.
HE'S JUST A DREAM GUY WHO LOOKS LIKE MY LOST LOVE. I SHOULDN'T CARE WHAT HE THINKS OF ME!
"I LOVE YOU, ALICE."
"I'M SORRY... I'VE FALLEN FOR YOUR SISTER."
NO.
I KNOW NO ONE COULD ACTUALLY FALL IN LOVE WITH ME.
SO I'VE DECIDED NOT TO LOVE ANYONE, EITHER.

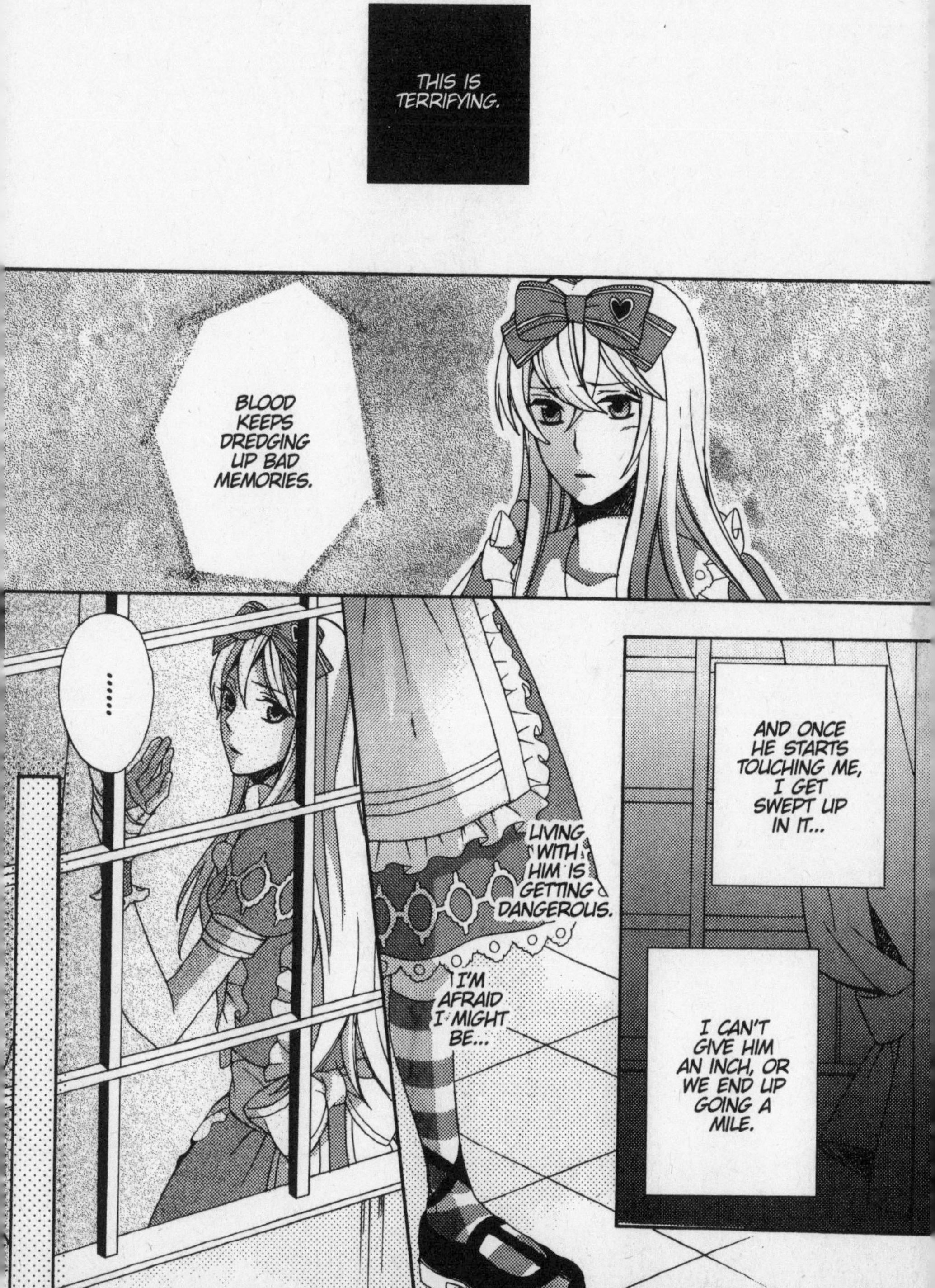
THIS IS TERRIFYING.
BLOOD KEEPS DREDGING UP BAD MEMORIES.
AND ONCE HE STARTS TOUCHING ME, I GET SWEPT UP IN IT...
I CAN'T GIVE HIM AN INCH, OR WE END UP GOING A MILE.
LIVING WITH HIM IS GETTING DANGEROUS.
I'M AFRAID I MIGHT BE...
......

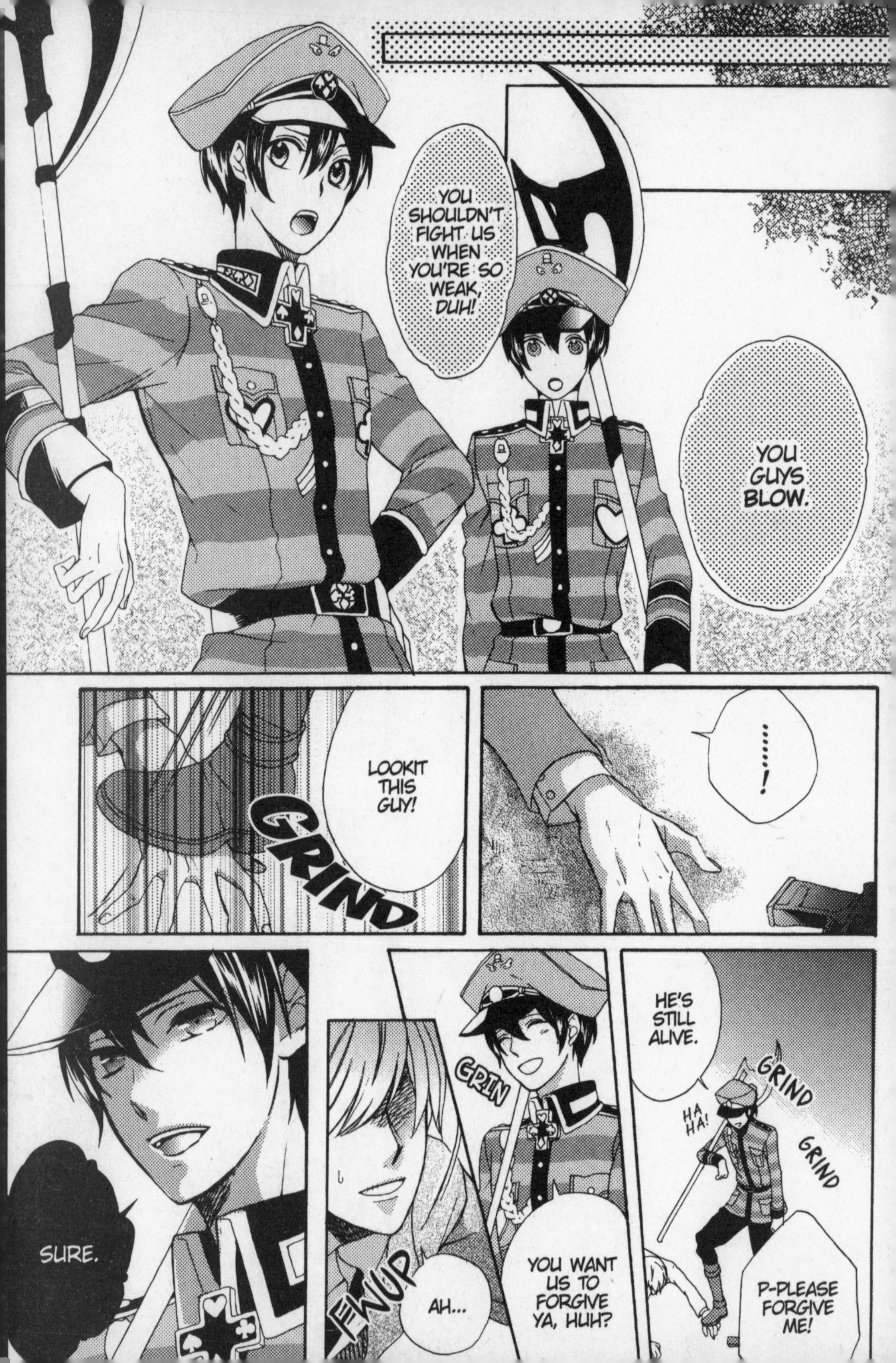
YOU SHOULDN'T FIGHT US WHEN YOU'RE SO WEAK, DUH!
YOU GUYS BLOW.
......!
LOOKIT THIS GUY!
GRIND
HE'S STILL ALIVE.
GRIND
HA HA!
GRIND
P-PLEASE FORGIVE ME!
GRIN
YOU WANT US TO FORGIVE YA, HUH?
AH...
FWUP
SURE.

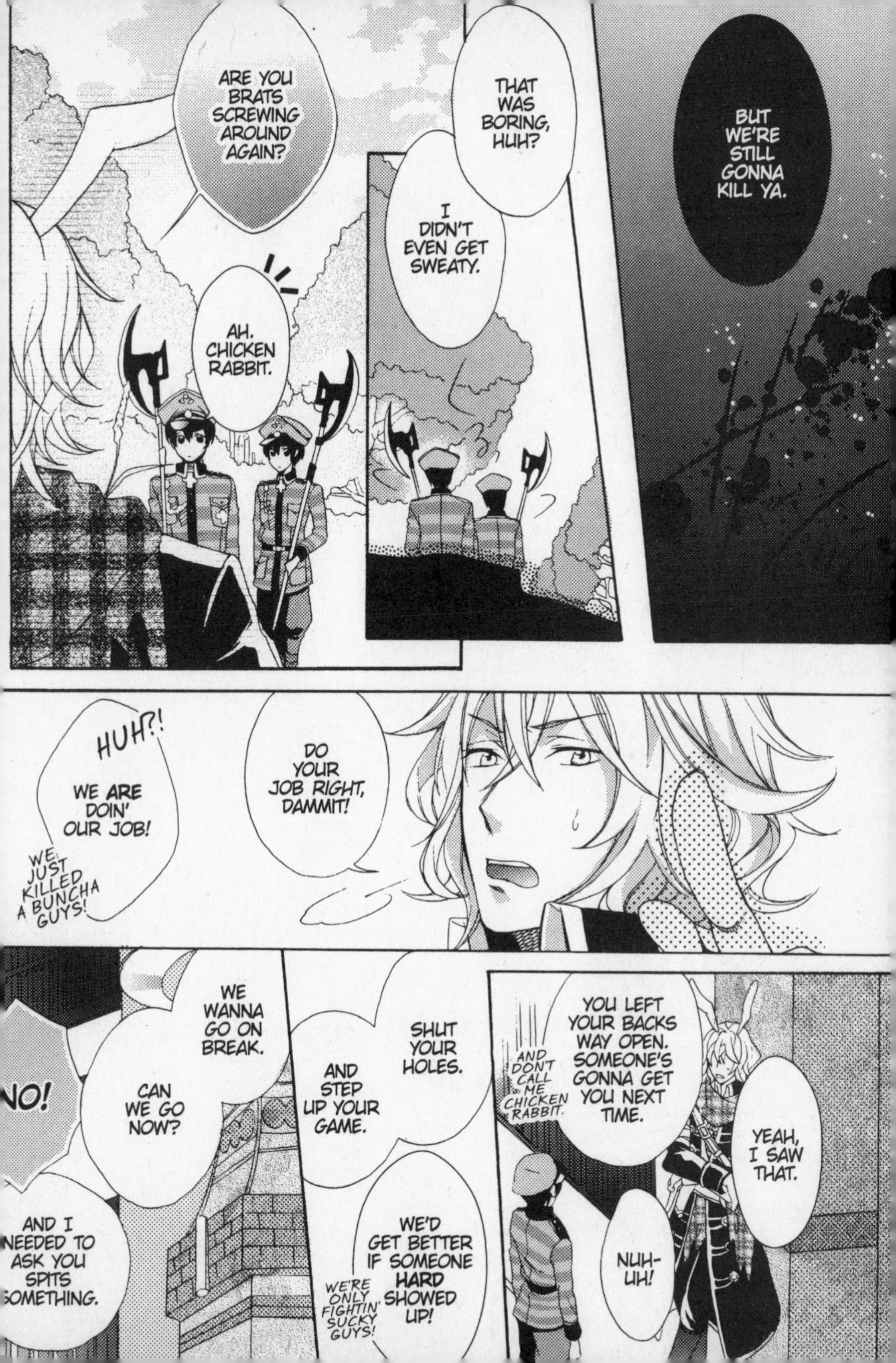
BUT WE'RE STILL GONNA KILL YA.
THAT WAS BORING, HUH?
I DIDN'T EVEN GET SWEATY.
ARE YOU BRATS SCREWING AROUND AGAIN?
AH. CHICKEN RABBIT.
DO YOUR JOB RIGHT, DAMMIT!
HUH?!
WE ARE DOIN' OUR JOB!
WE JUST KILLED A BUNCHA GUYS!
YOU LEFT YOUR BACKS WAY OPEN. SOMEONE'S GONNA GET YOU NEXT TIME.
AND DON'T CALL ME CHICKEN RABBIT.
YEAH, I SAW THAT.
NUH-UH!
SHUT YOUR HOLES.
AND STEP UP YOUR GAME.
WE'D GET BETTER IF SOMEONE HARD SHOWED UP!
WE'RE ONLY FIGHTIN' SUCKY GUYS!
WE WANNA GO ON BREAK.
CAN WE GO NOW?
NO!
AND I NEEDED TO ASK YOU SPITS SOMETHING.

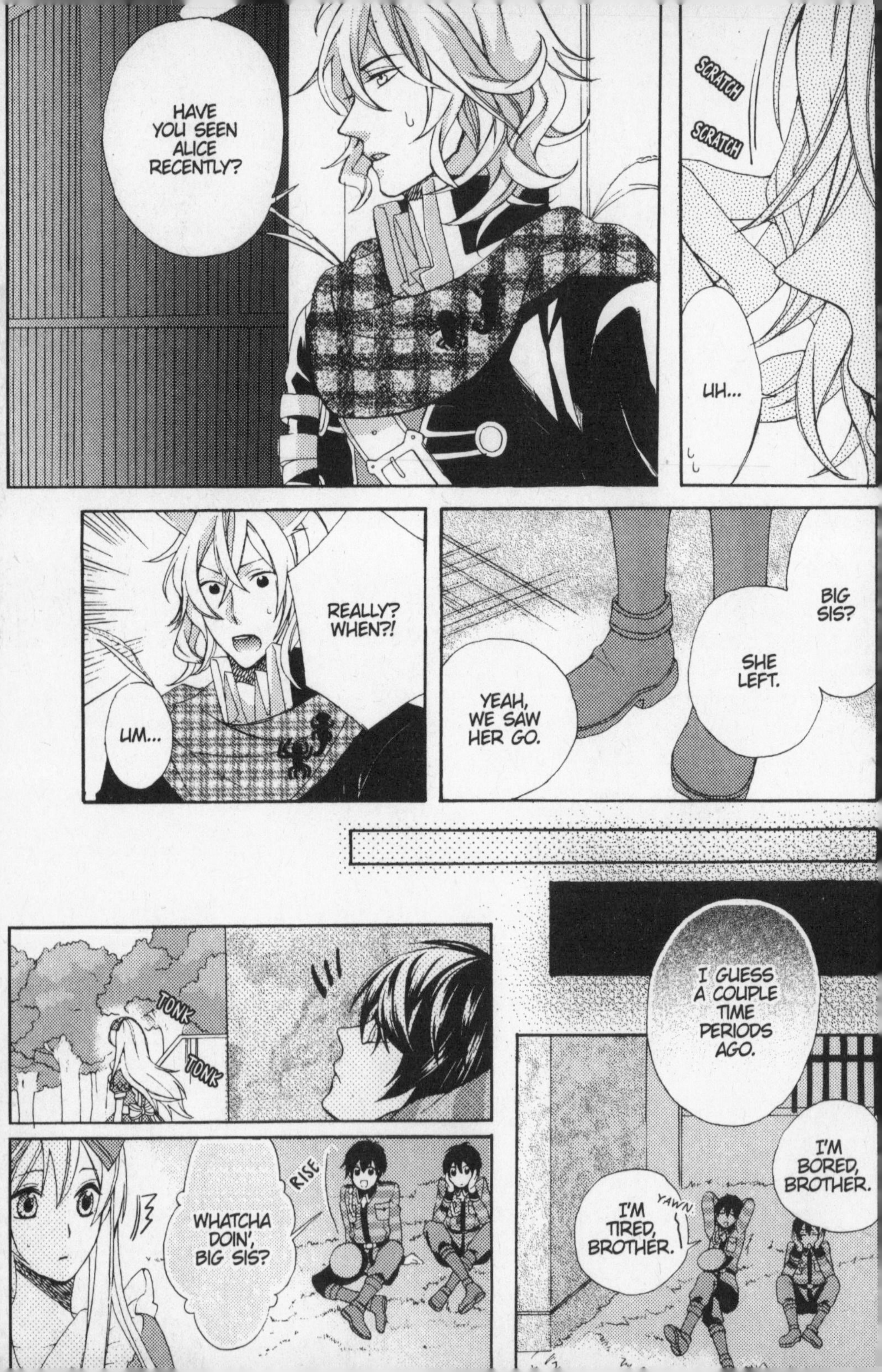
SCRATCH
SCRATCH
UH...
HAVE YOU SEEN ALICE RECENTLY?
BIG SIS?
SHE LEFT.
YEAH, WE SAW HER GO.
REALLY? WHEN?!
UM...
I GUESS A COUPLE TIME PERIODS AGO.
I'M BORED, BROTHER.
YAWN
I'M TIRED, BROTHER.
TONK
TONK
RISE
WHATCHA DOIN', BIG SIS?

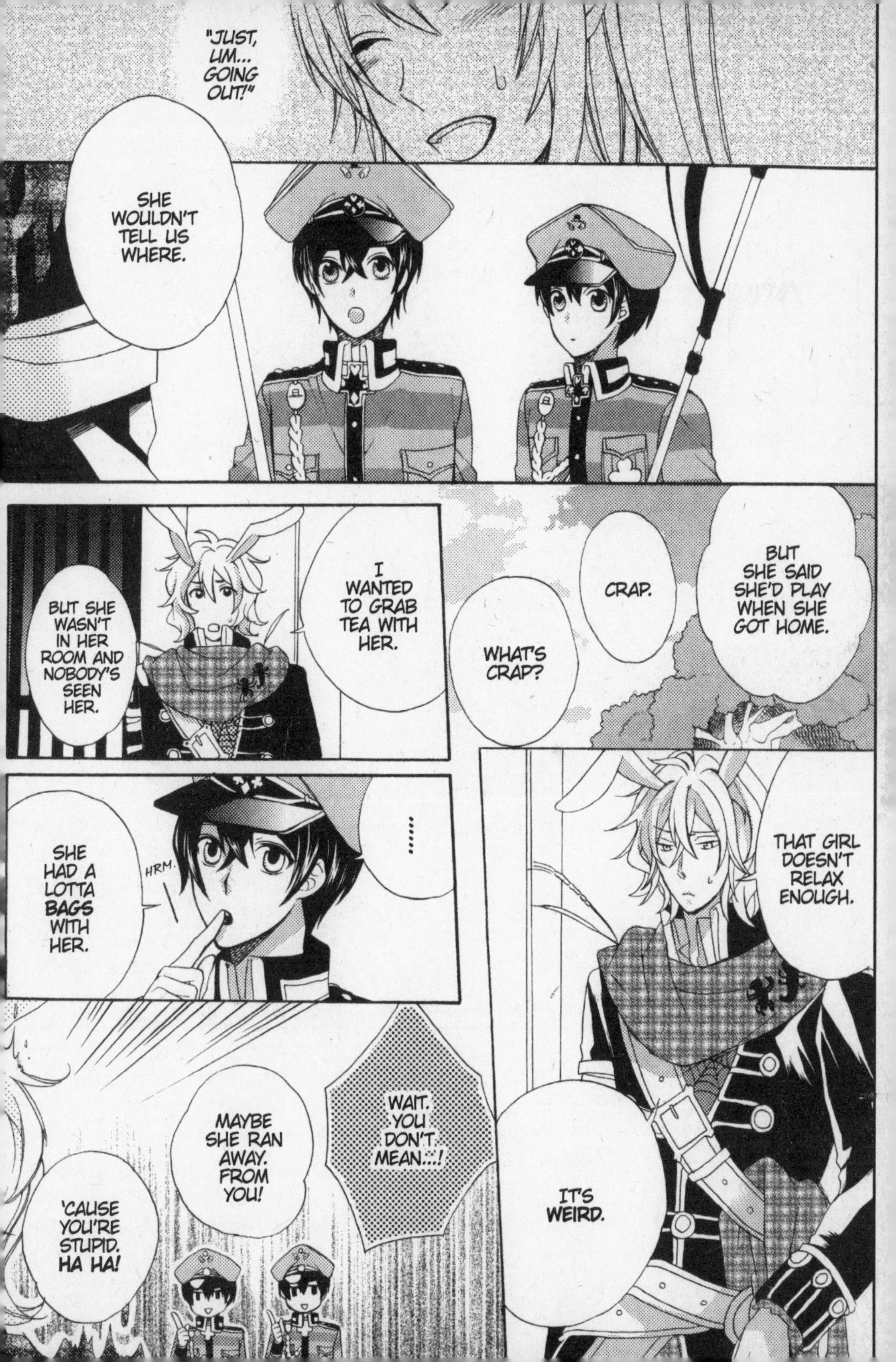
"JUST, UM... GOING OUT!"
SHE WOULDN'T TELL US WHERE.
BUT SHE SAID SHE'D PLAY WHEN SHE GOT HOME.
CRAP.
WHAT'S CRAP?
I WANTED TO GRAB TEA WITH HER.
BUT SHE WASN'T IN HER ROOM AND NOBODY'S SEEN HER.
THAT GIRL DOESN'T RELAX ENOUGH.
IT'S WEIRD.
......
HRM.
SHE HAD A LOTTA BAGS WITH HER.
WAIT. YOU DON'T MEAN...!
MAYBE SHE RAN AWAY. FROM YOU!
'CAUSE YOU'RE STUPID. HA HA!

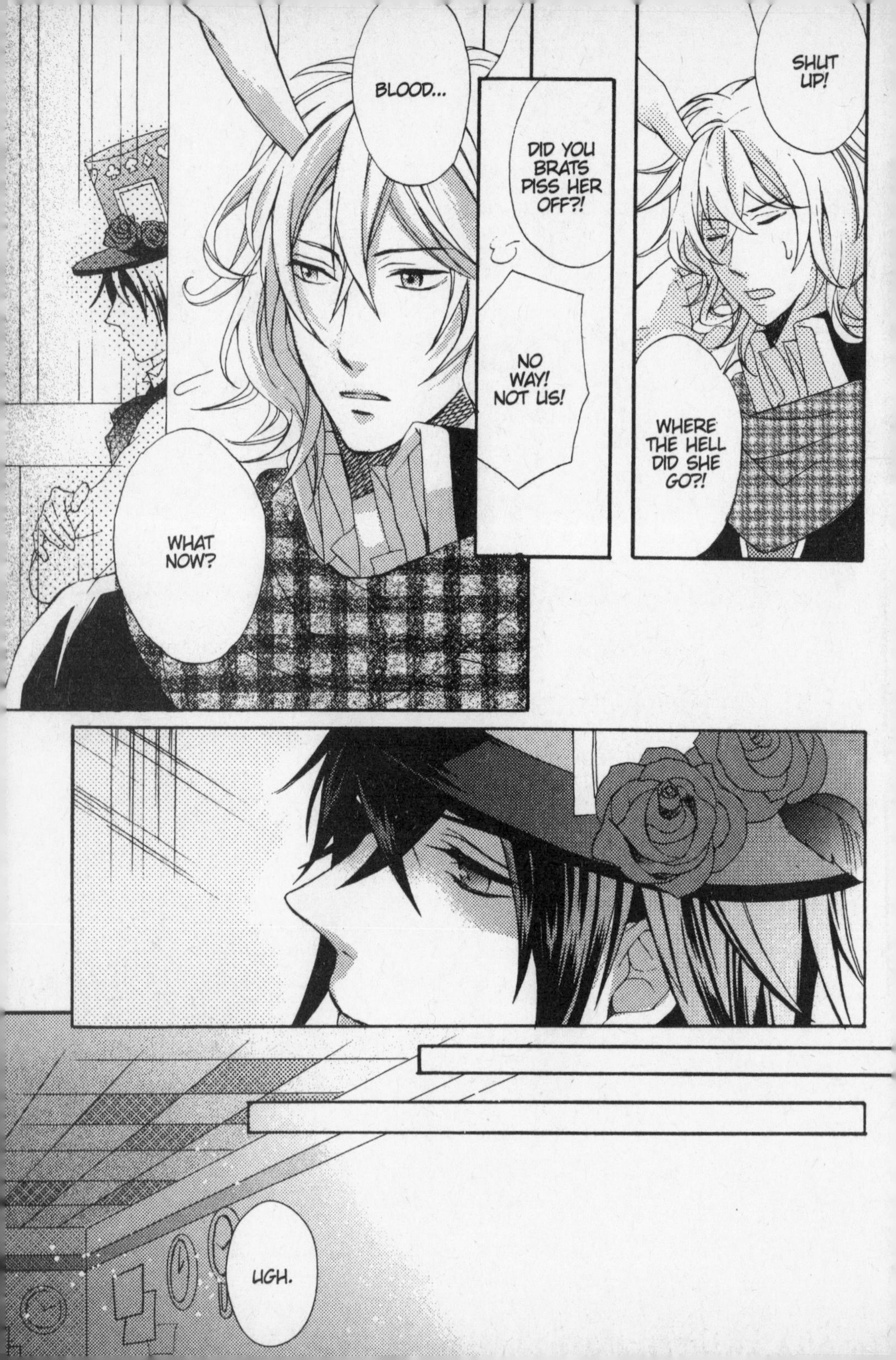
SHUT UP!
WHERE THE HELL DID SHE GO?!
DID YOU BRATS PISS HER OFF?!
NO WAY! NOT US!
BLOOD...
WHAT NOW?
UGH.

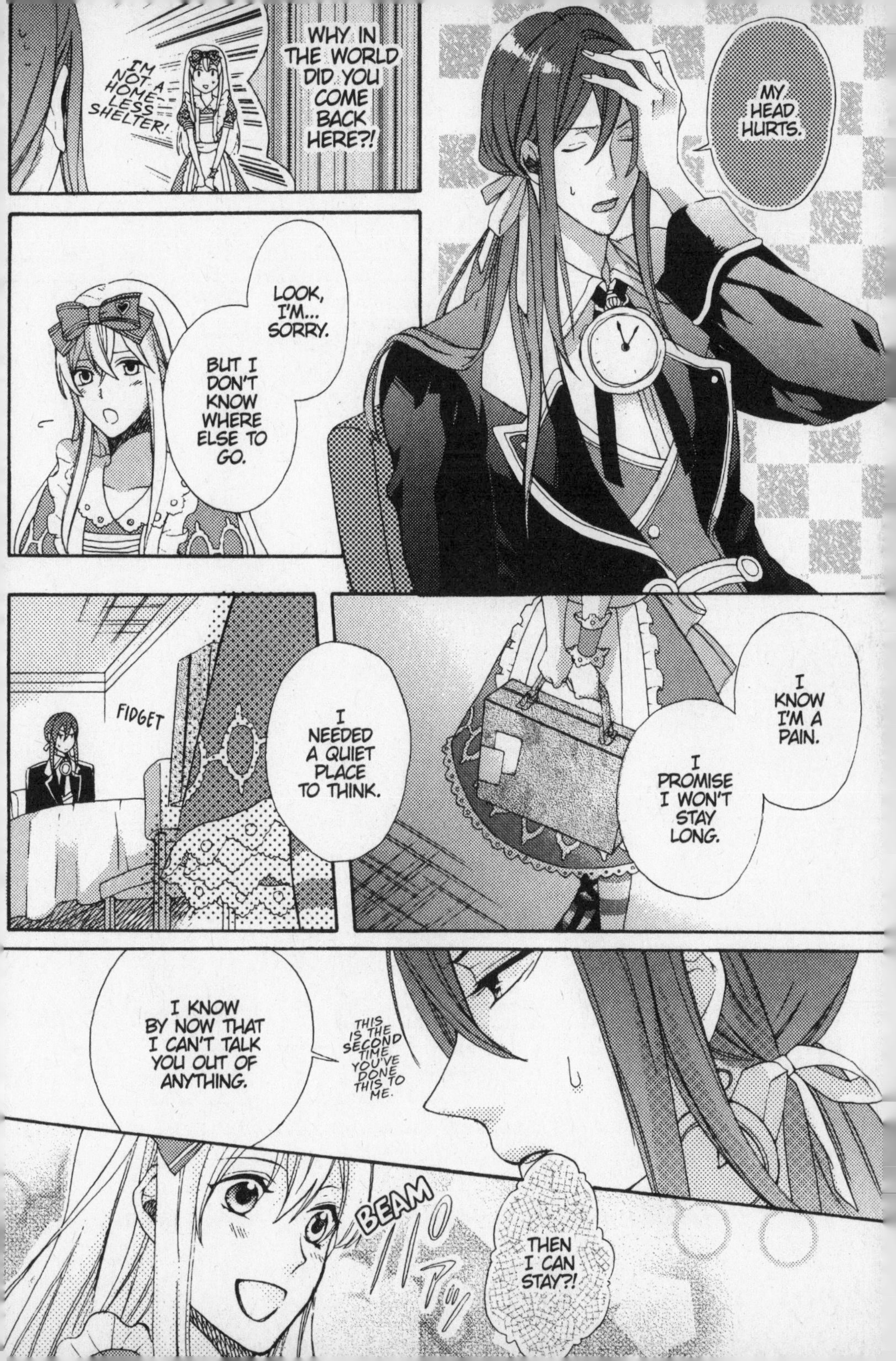
MY HEAD HURTS.
WHY IN THE WORLD DID YOU COME BACK HERE?!
I'M NOT A HOMELESS SHELTER!
LOOK, I'M... SORRY.
BUT I DON'T KNOW WHERE ELSE TO GO.
I KNOW I'M A PAIN.
I PROMISE I WON'T STAY LONG.
I NEEDED A QUIET PLACE TO THINK.
FIDGET
I KNOW BY NOW THAT I CAN'T TALK YOU OUT OF ANYTHING.
THIS IS THE SECOND TIME YOU'VE DONE THIS TO ME.
BEAM
THEN I CAN STAY?!

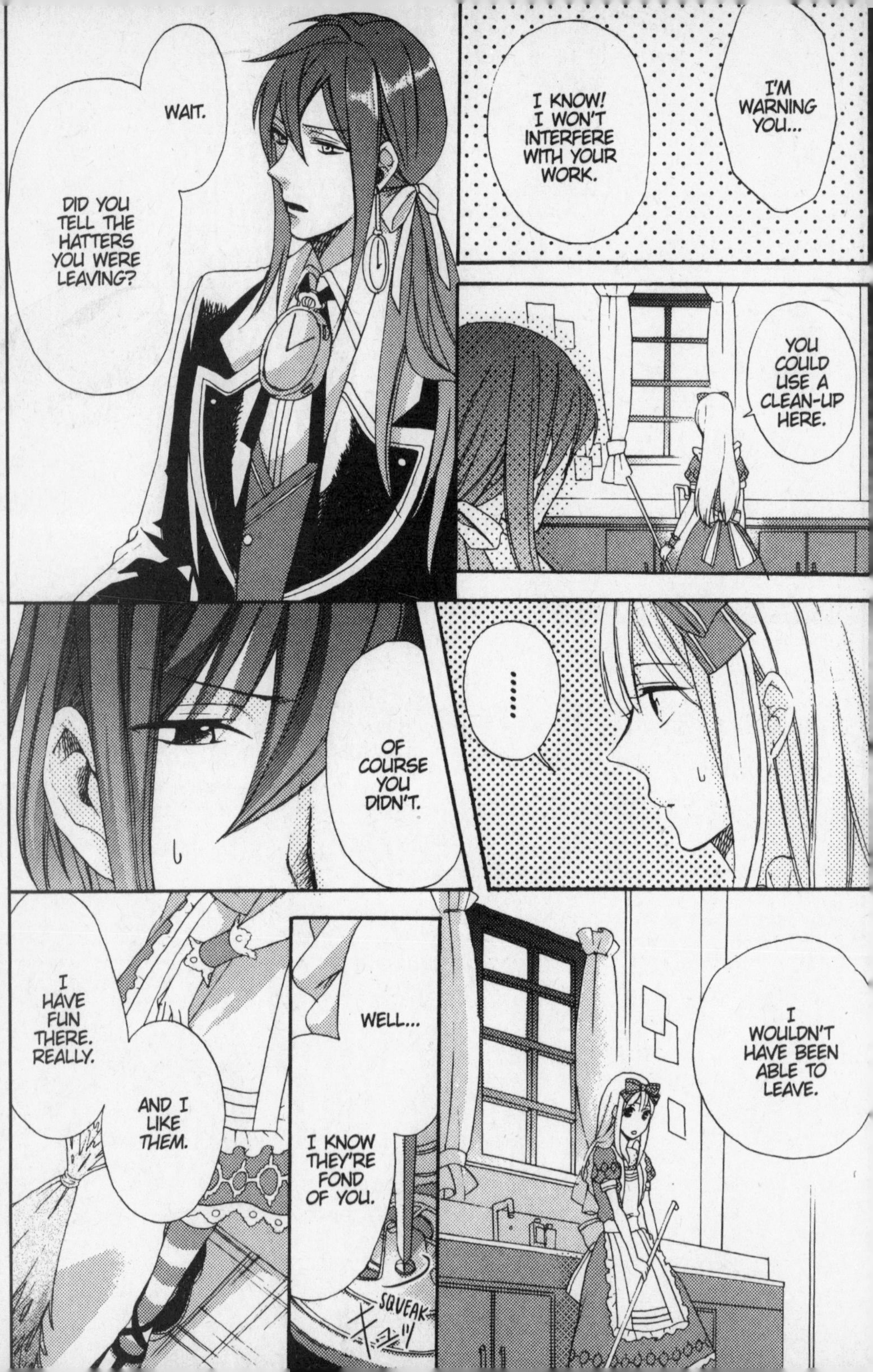
I'M WARNING YOU...
I KNOW! I WON'T INTERFERE WITH YOUR WORK.
YOU COULD USE A CLEAN-UP HERE.
WAIT.
DID YOU TELL THE HATTERS YOU WERE LEAVING?
......
OF COURSE YOU DIDN'T.
I WOULDN'T HAVE BEEN ABLE TO LEAVE.
WELL...
I KNOW THEY'RE FOND OF YOU.
SQUEAK
I HAVE FUN THERE. REALLY.
AND I LIKE THEM.

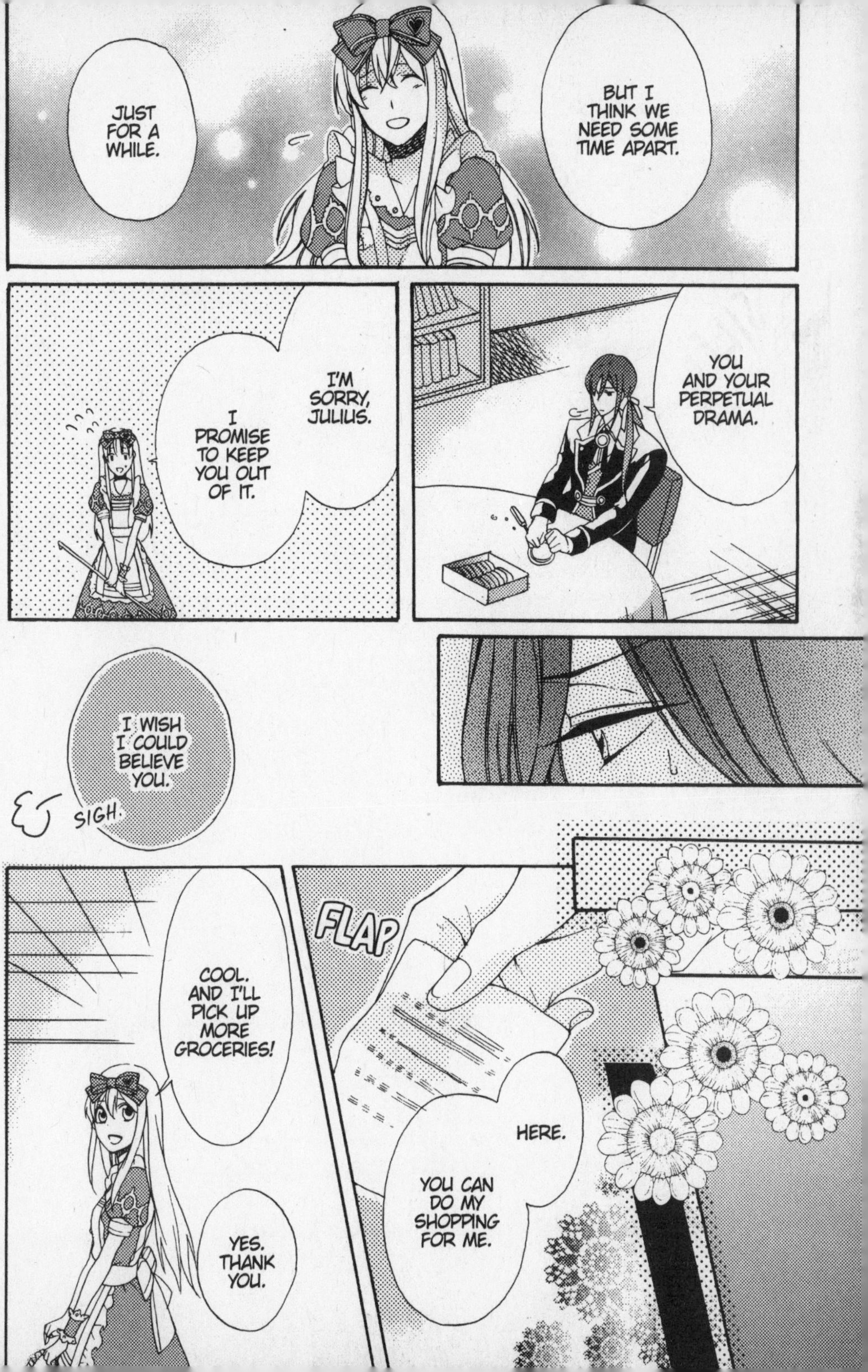
BUT I THINK WE NEED SOME TIME APART.
JUST FOR A WHILE.
YOU AND YOUR PERPETUAL DRAMA.
I'M SORRY, JULIUS.
I PROMISE TO KEEP YOU OUT OF IT.
I WISH I COULD BELIEVE YOU.
SIGH.
FLAP
HERE.
YOU CAN DO MY SHOPPING FOR ME.
YES. THANK YOU.
COOL. AND I'LL PICK UP MORE GROCERIES!

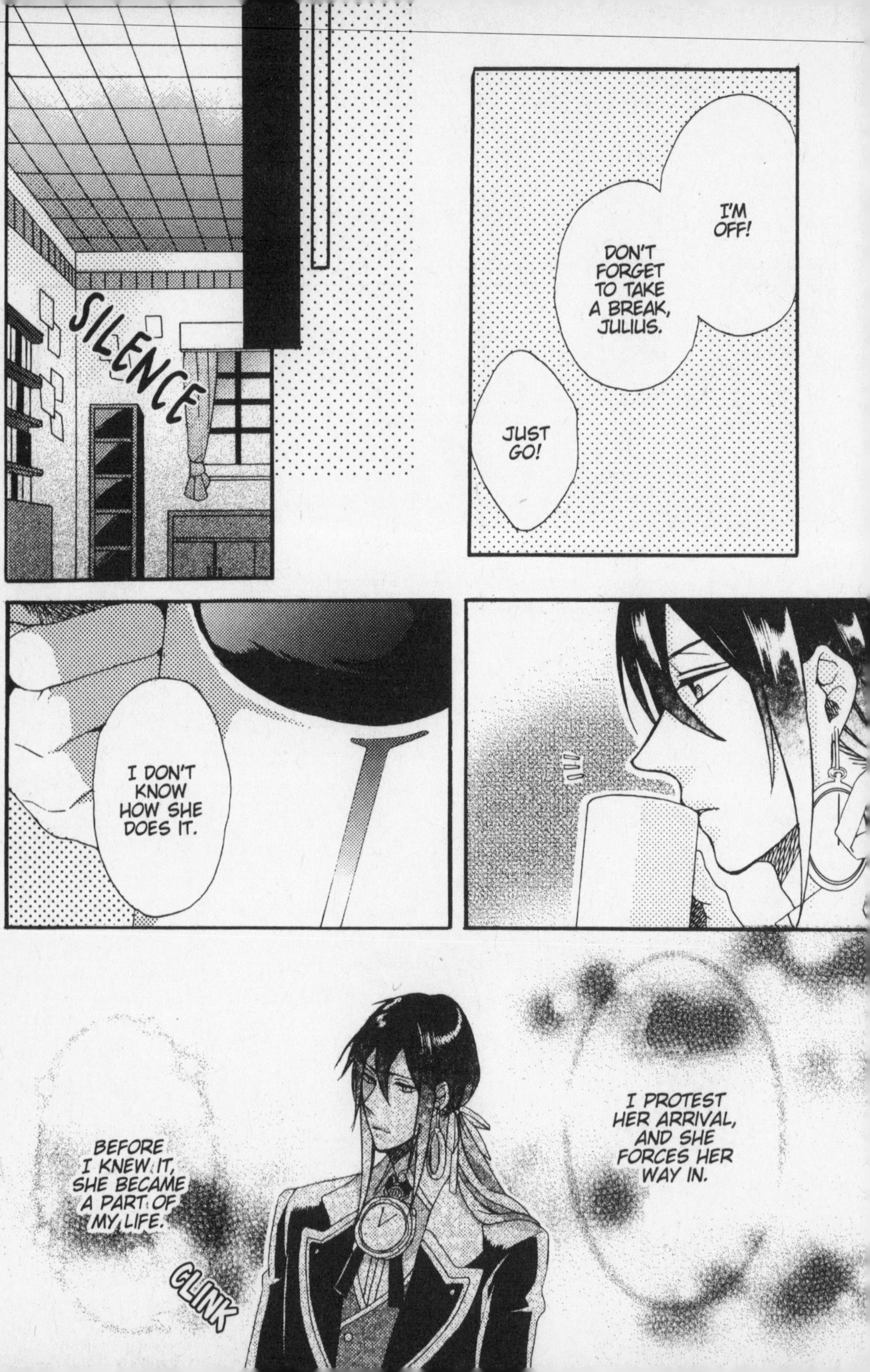
I'M OFF!
DON'T FORGET TO TAKE A BREAK, JULIUS.
JUST GO!
SILENCE
I DON'T KNOW HOW SHE DOES IT.
I PROTEST HER ARRIVAL, AND SHE FORCES HER WAY IN.
BEFORE I KNEW IT, SHE BECAME A PART OF MY LIFE.
CLINK

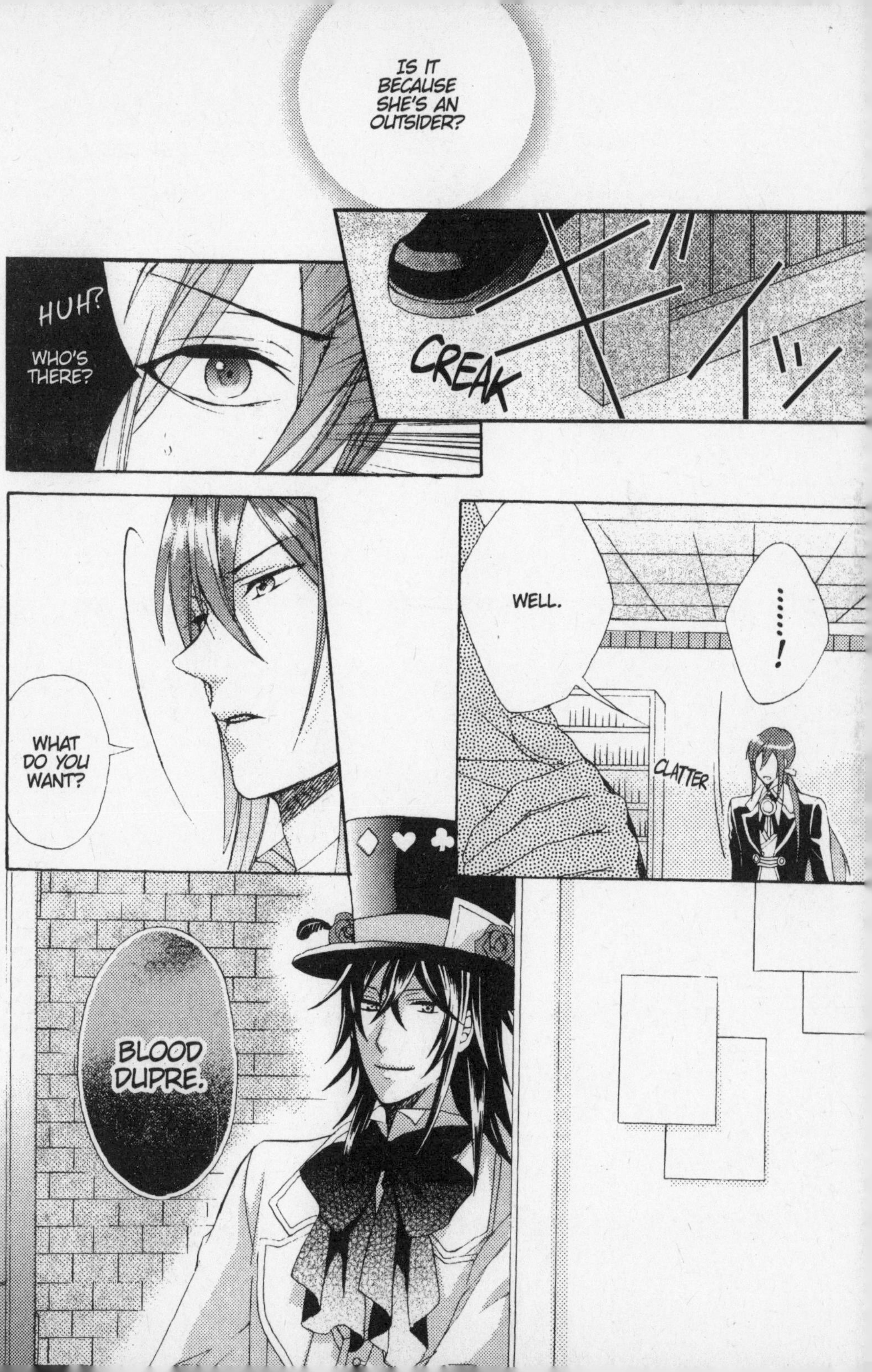
IS IT BECAUSE SHE'S AN OUTSIDER?
CREAK
HUH?
WHO'S THERE?
......!
WELL.
CLATTER
WHAT DO YOU WANT?
BLOOD DUPRE.

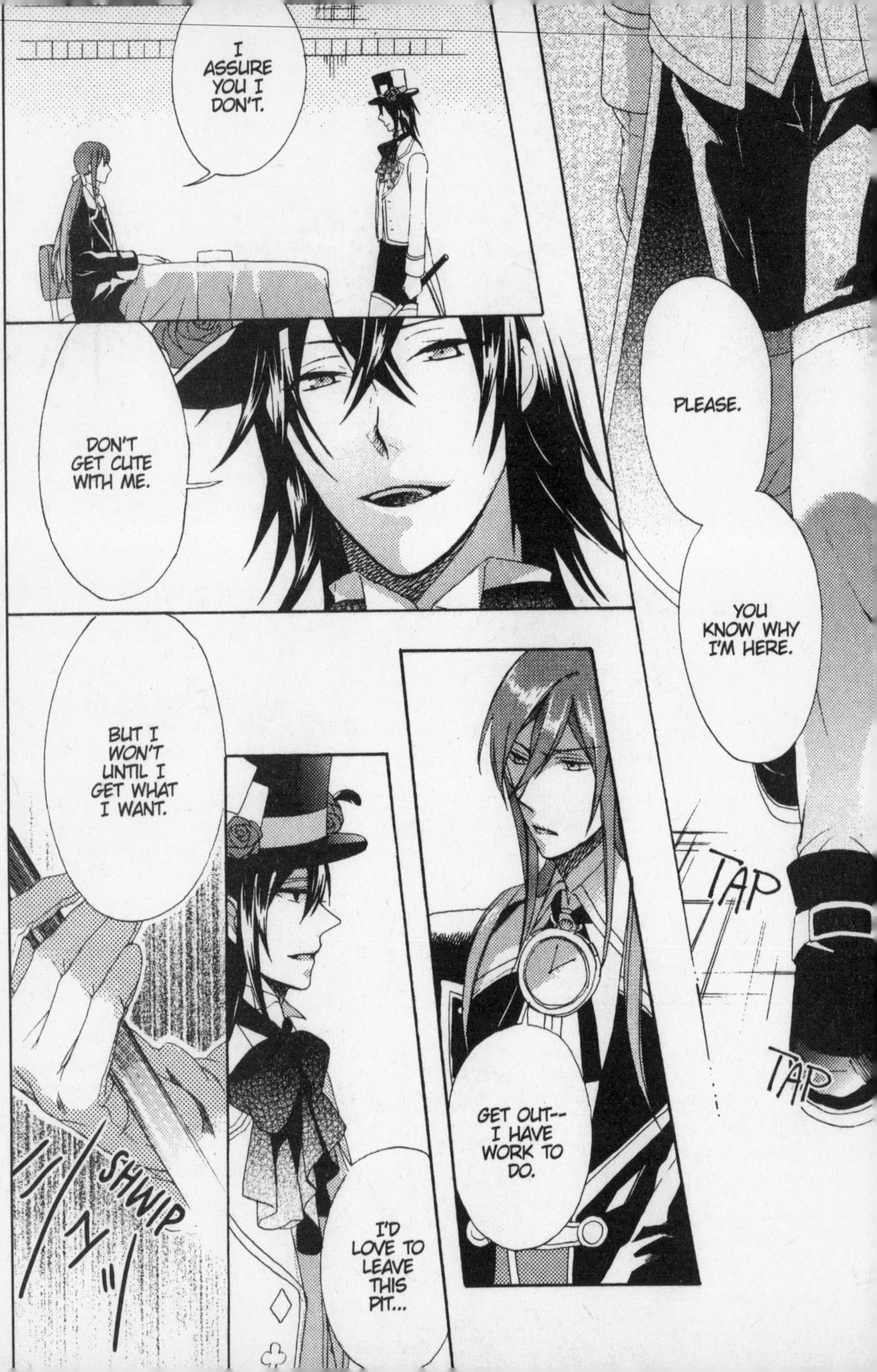
PLEASE.
YOU KNOW WHY I'M HERE.
TAP
TAP
I ASSURE YOU I DON'T.
DON'T GET CUTE WITH ME.
GET OUT-- I HAVE WORK TO DO.
I'D LOVE TO LEAVE THIS PIT...
BUT I WON'T UNTIL I GET WHAT I WANT.
SHWIP

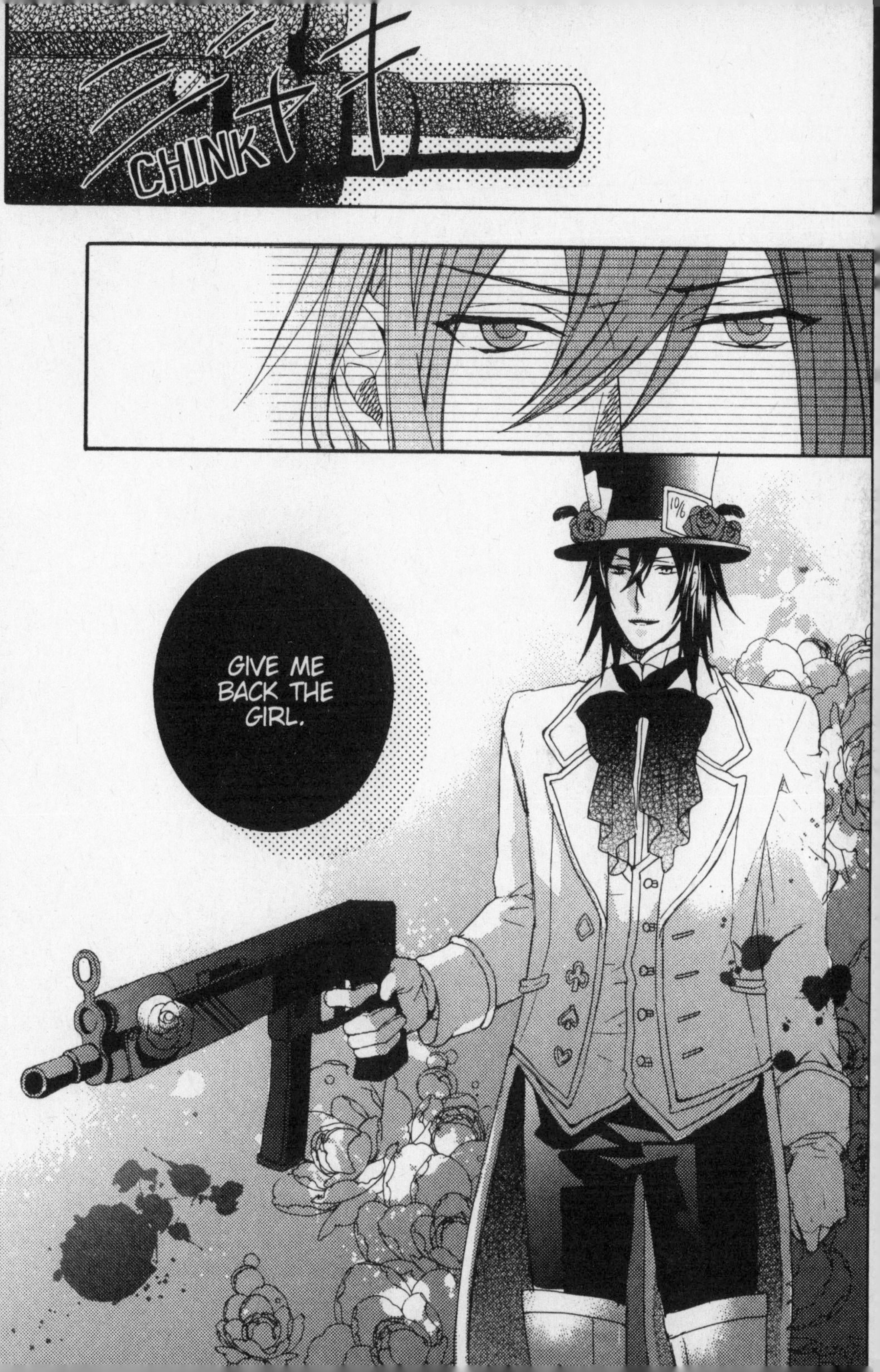
CHINK
GIVE ME BACK THE GIRL.

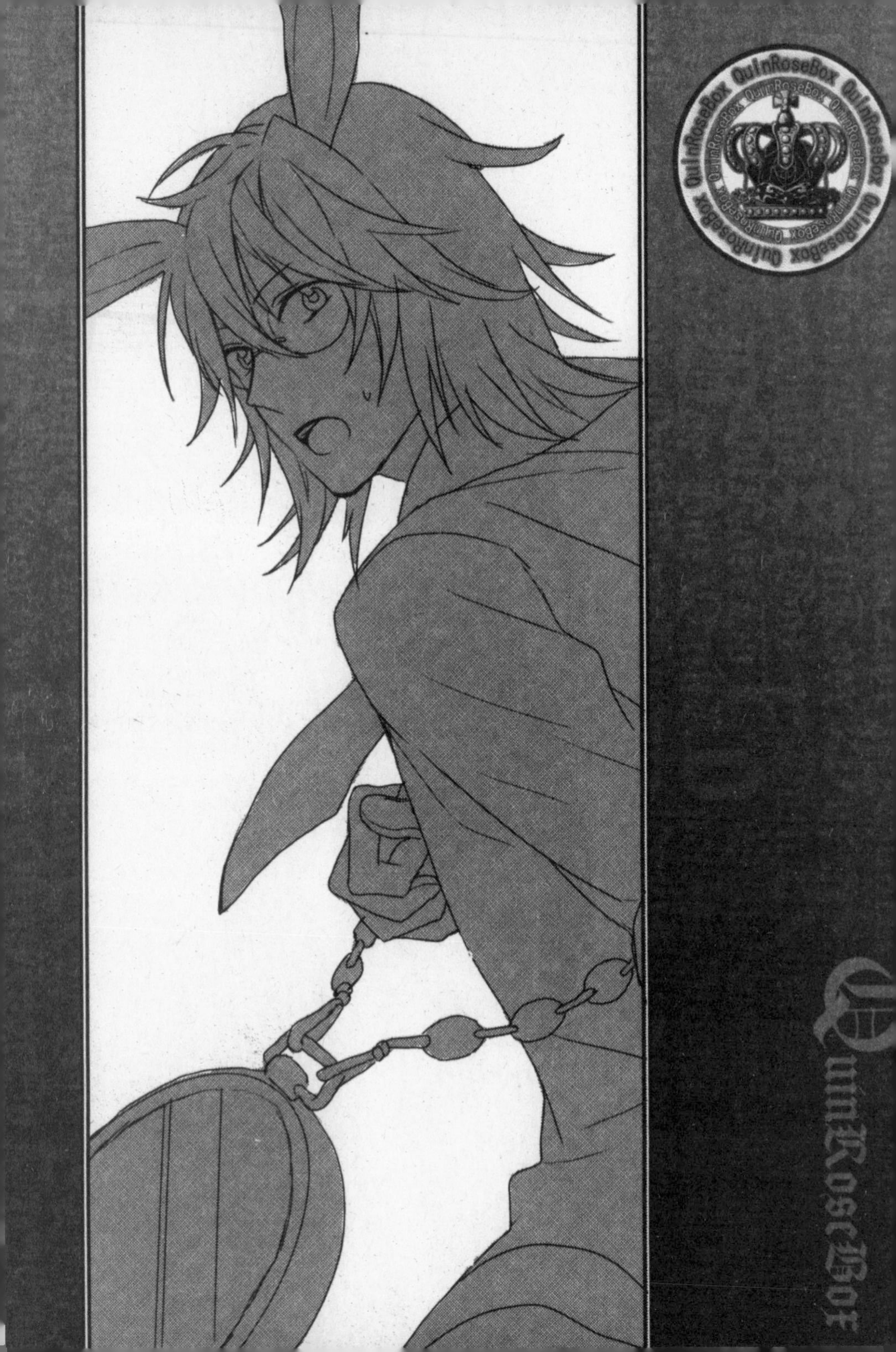
QuinRoseBox

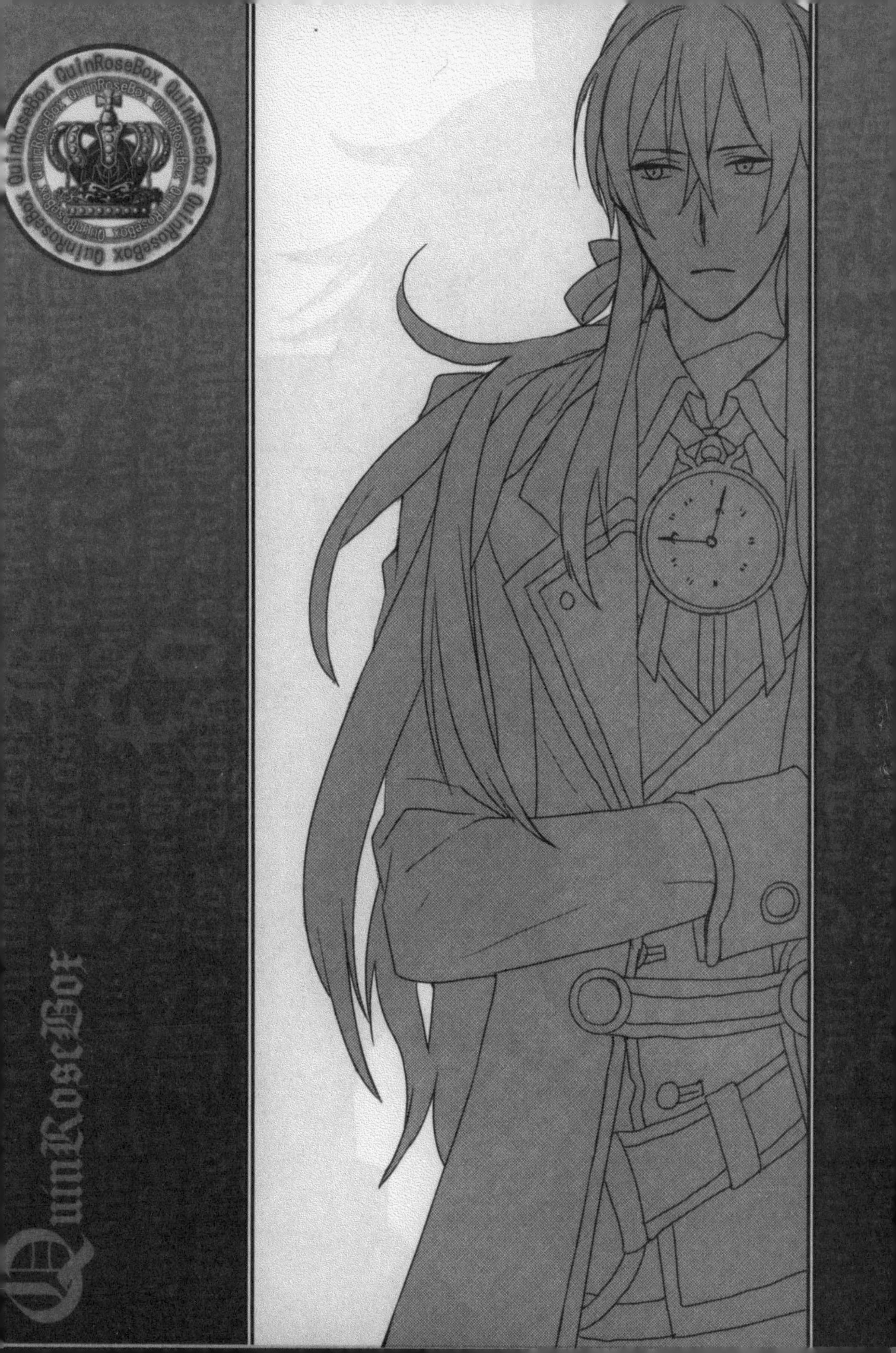
QuinRoseBox

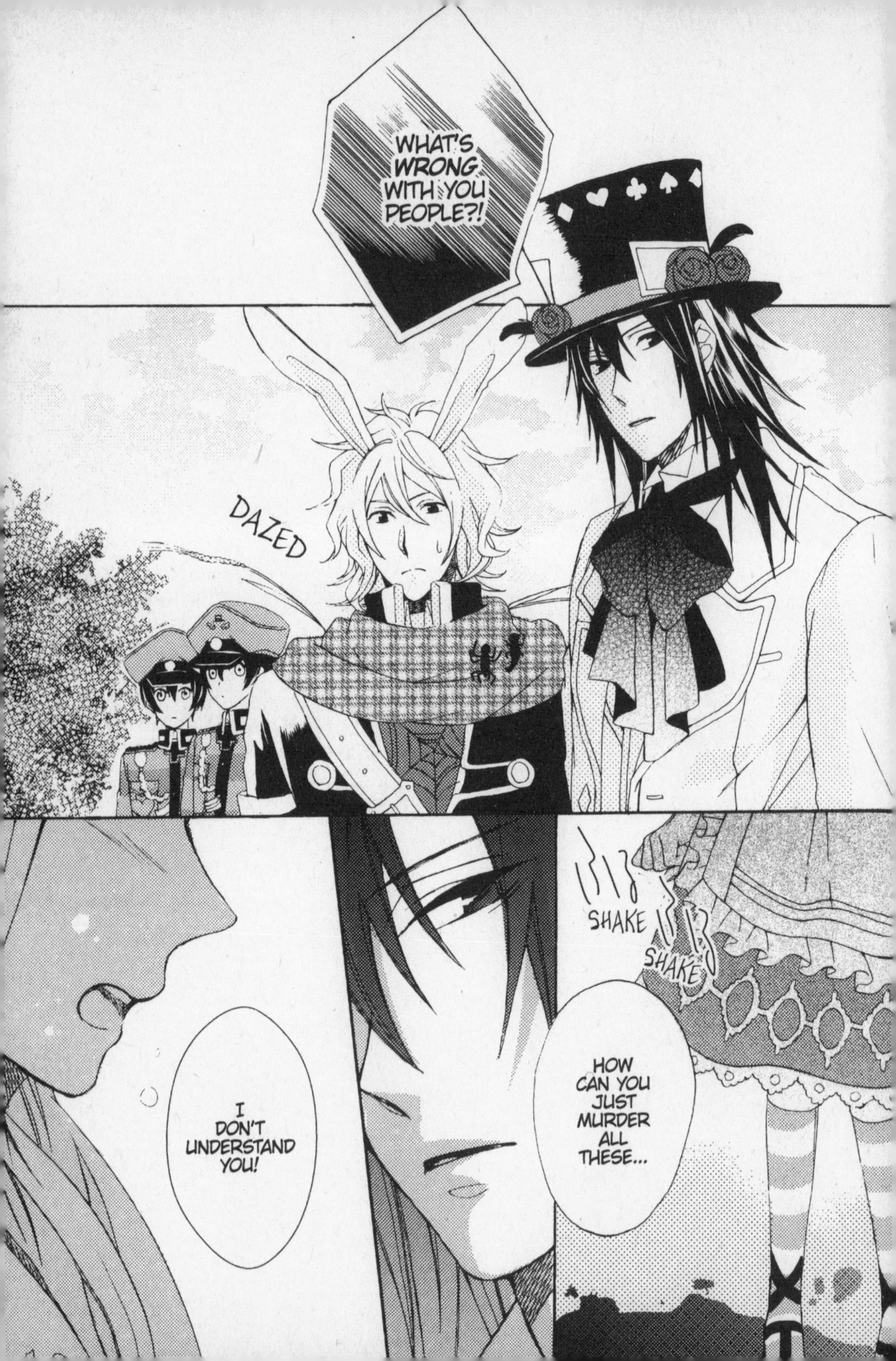
WHAT'S WRONG WITH YOU PEOPLE?!
DAZED
SHAKE SHAKE
HOW CAN YOU JUST MURDER ALL THESE...
I DON'T UNDERSTAND YOU!

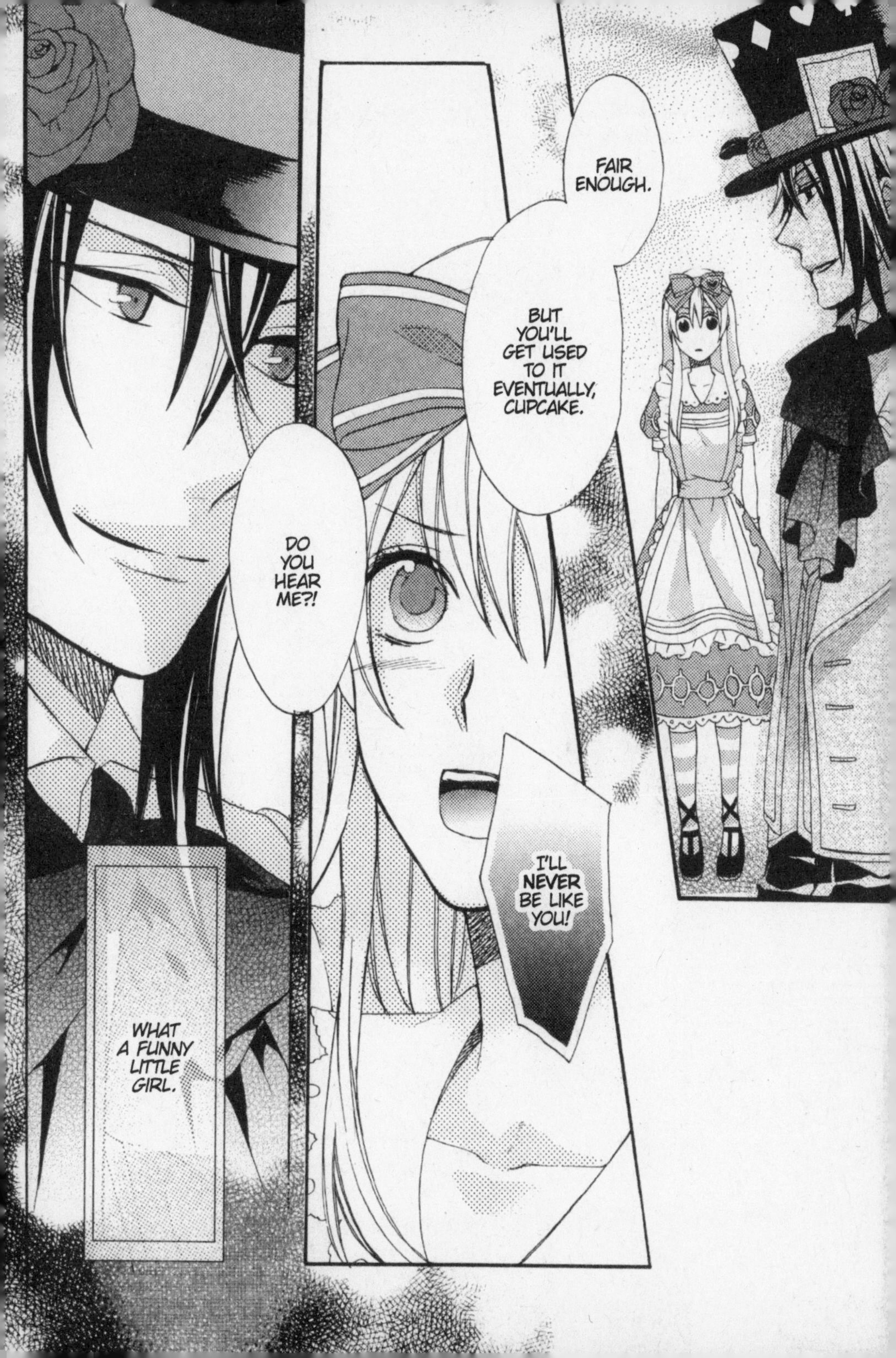
FAIR ENOUGH.
BUT YOU'LL GET USED TO IT EVENTUALLY, CUPCAKE.
DO YOU HEAR ME?!
I'LL NEVER BE LIKE YOU!
WHAT A FUNNY LITTLE GIRL.

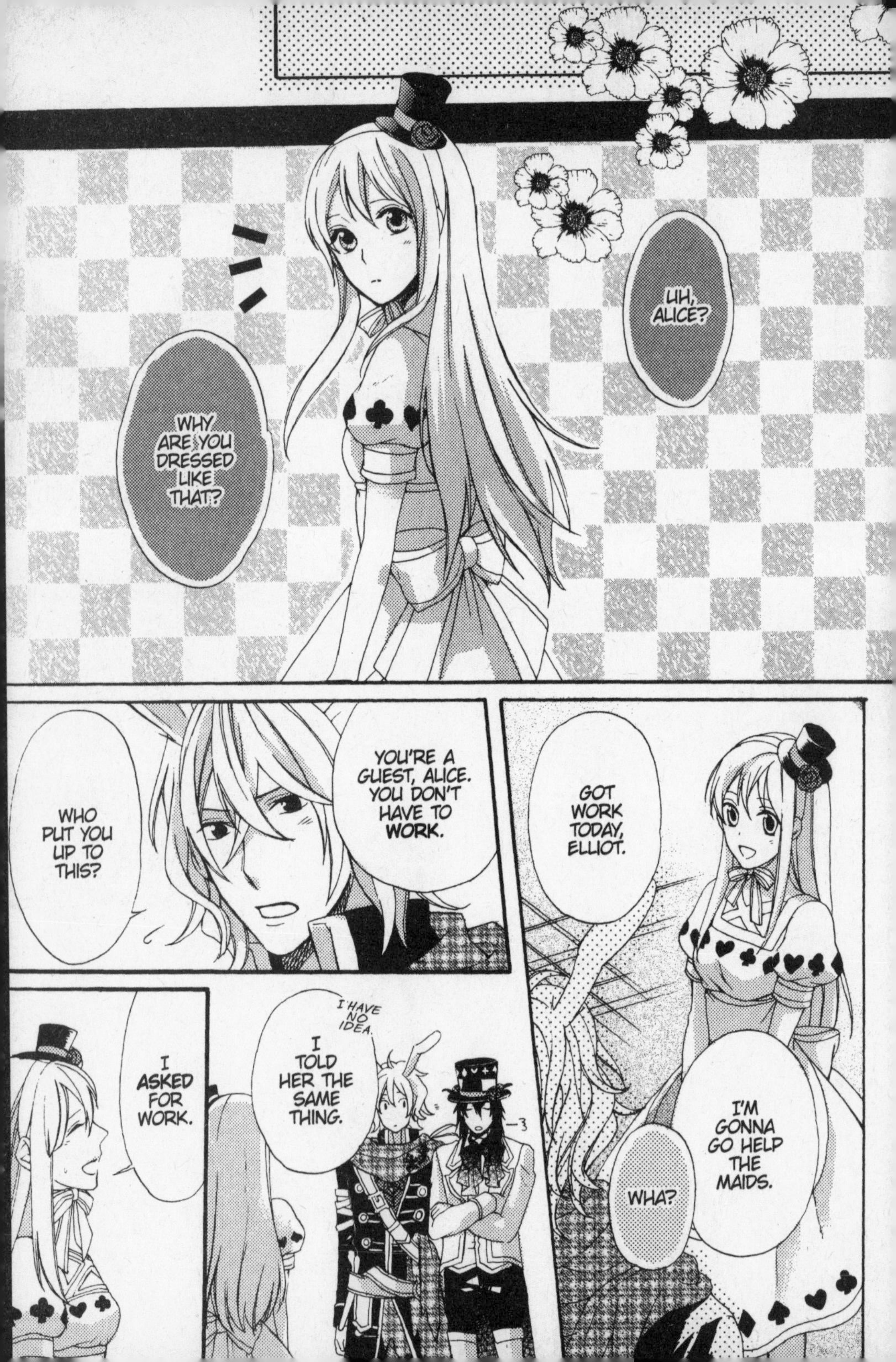
UH, ALICE?
WHY ARE YOU DRESSED LIKE THAT?
GOT WORK TODAY, ELLIOT.
I'M GONNA GO HELP THE MAIDS.
WHA?
YOU'RE A GUEST, ALICE. YOU DON'T HAVE TO WORK.
WHO PUT YOU UP TO THIS?
I HAVE NO IDEA.
I TOLD HER THE SAME THING.
I ASKED FOR WORK.

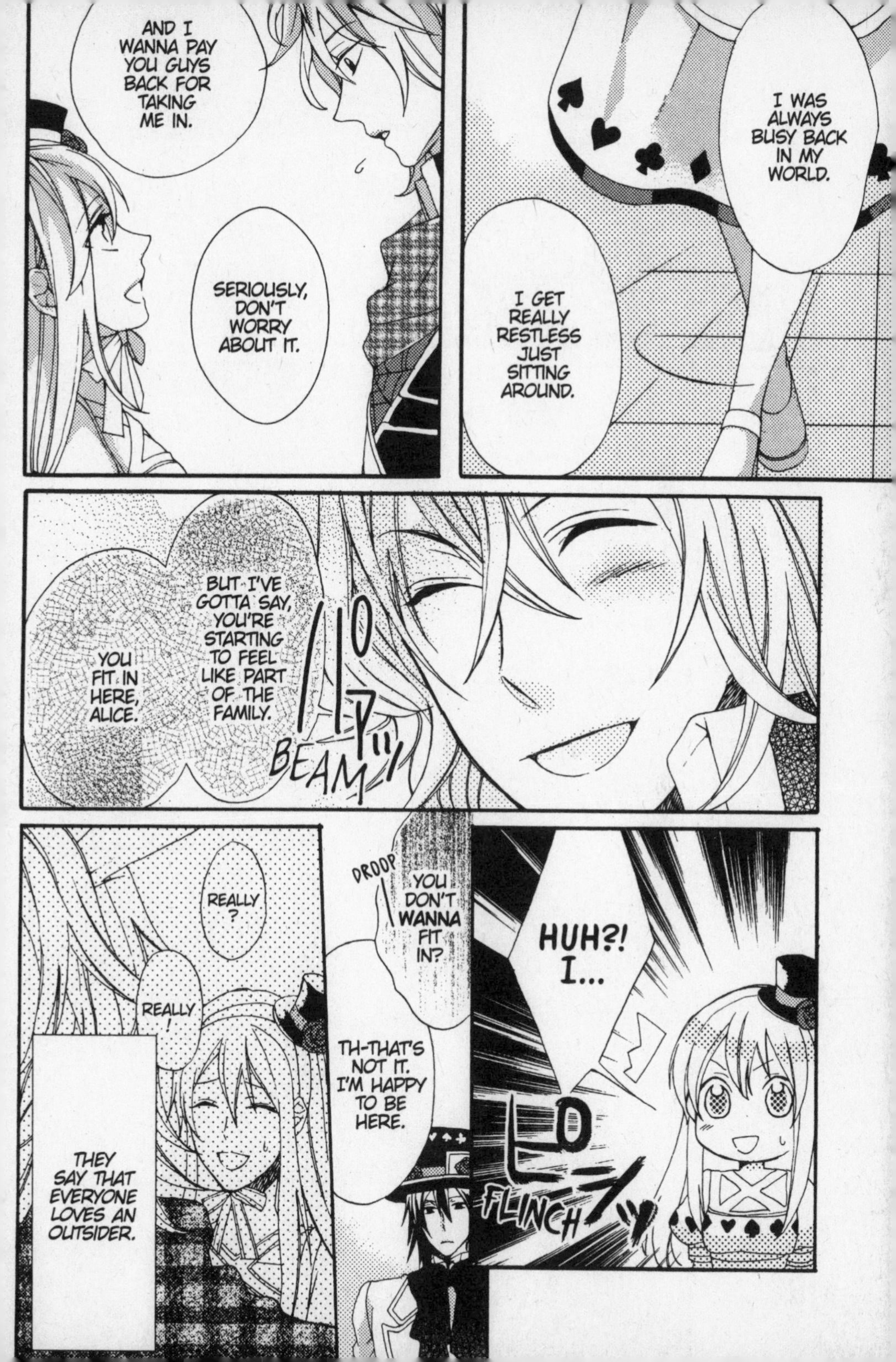
I WAS ALWAYS BUSY BACK IN MY WORLD.
I GET REALLY RESTLESS JUST SITTING AROUND.
AND I WANNA PAY YOU GUYS BACK FOR TAKING ME IN.
SERIOUSLY, DON'T WORRY ABOUT IT.
BUT I'VE GOTTA SAY, YOU'RE STARTING TO FEEL LIKE PART OF THE FAMILY.
BEAM
YOU FIT IN HERE, ALICE.
HUH?! I...
FLINCH
YOU DON'T WANNA FIT IN?
DROOP
TH-THAT'S NOT IT. I'M HAPPY TO BE HERE.
REALLY?
REALLY!
THEY SAY THAT EVERYONE LOVES AN OUTSIDER.

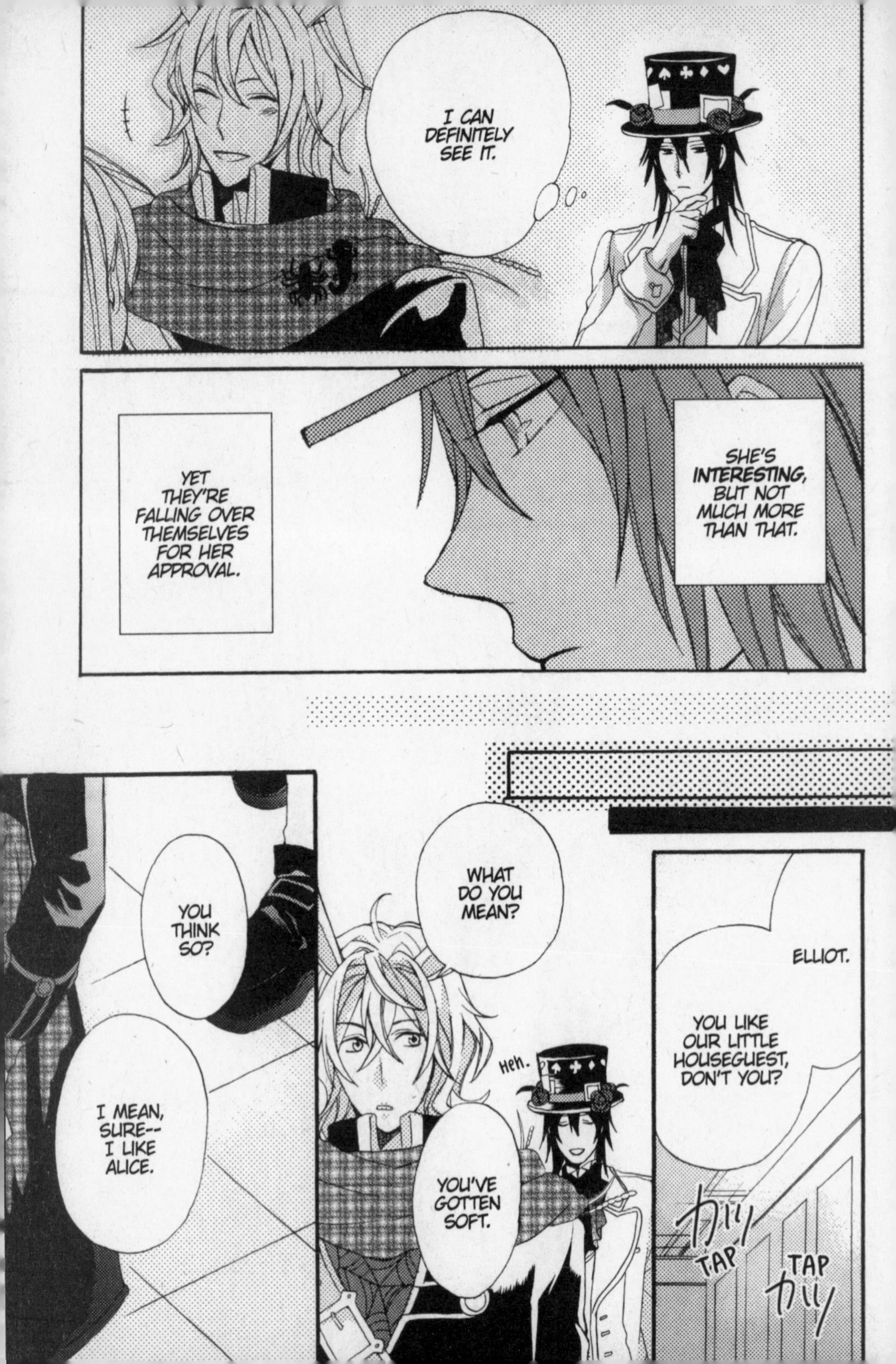
I CAN DEFINITELY SEE IT.
SHE'S INTERESTING, BUT NOT MUCH MORE THAN THAT.
YET THEY'RE FALLING OVER THEMSELVES FOR HER APPROVAL.
ELLIOT.
YOU LIKE OUR LITTLE HOUSEGUEST, DON'T YOU?
TAP
TAP
WHAT DO YOU MEAN?
Heh.
YOU'VE GOTTEN SOFT.
YOU THINK SO?
I MEAN, SURE-- I LIKE ALICE.

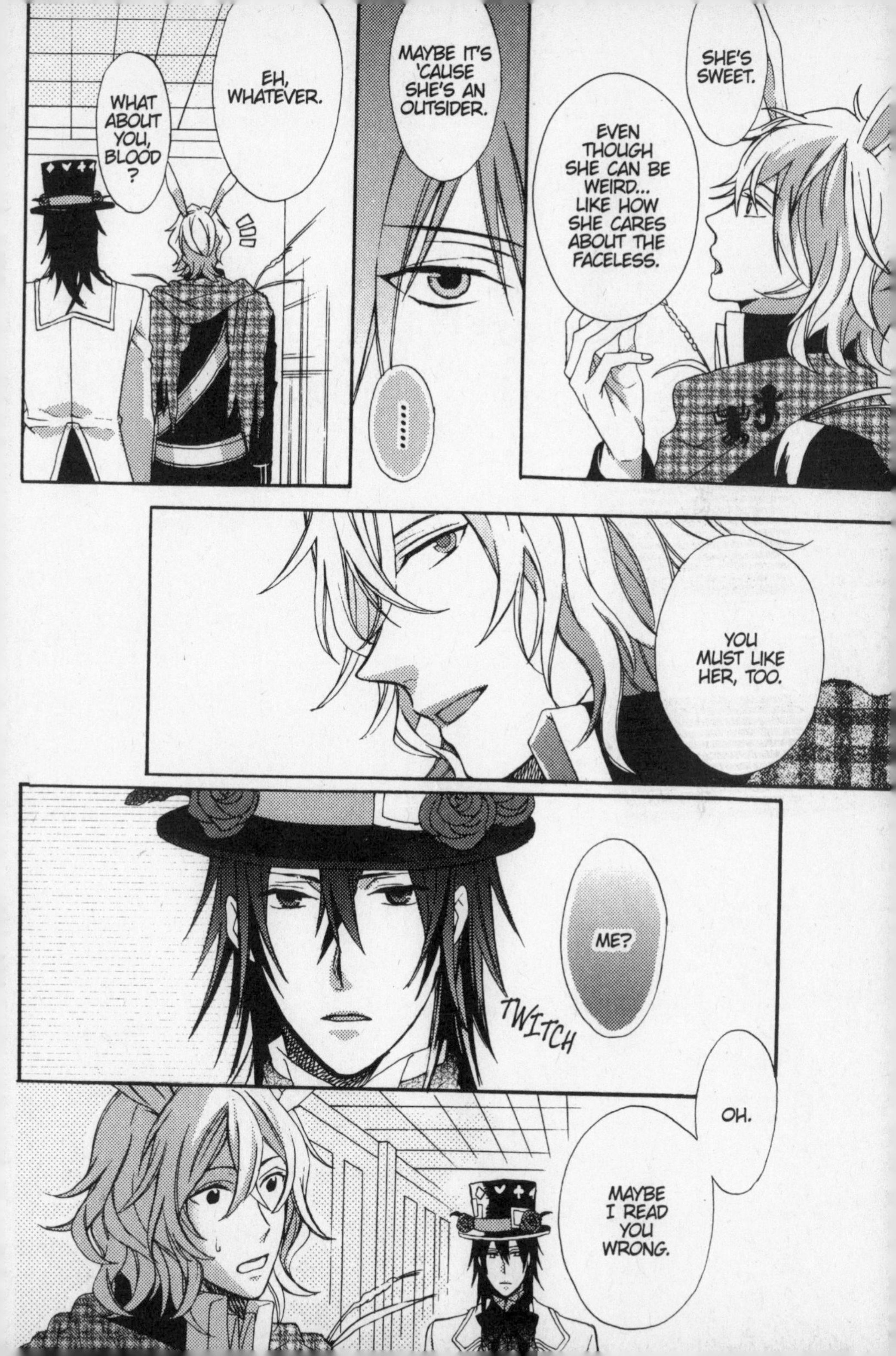
SHE'S SWEET.
EVEN THOUGH SHE CAN BE WEIRD... LIKE HOW SHE CARES ABOUT THE FACELESS.
MAYBE IT'S 'CAUSE SHE'S AN OUTSIDER.
......
EH, WHATEVER.
WHAT ABOUT YOU, BLOOD?
YOU MUST LIKE HER, TOO.
ME?
TWITCH
OH.
MAYBE I READ YOU WRONG.

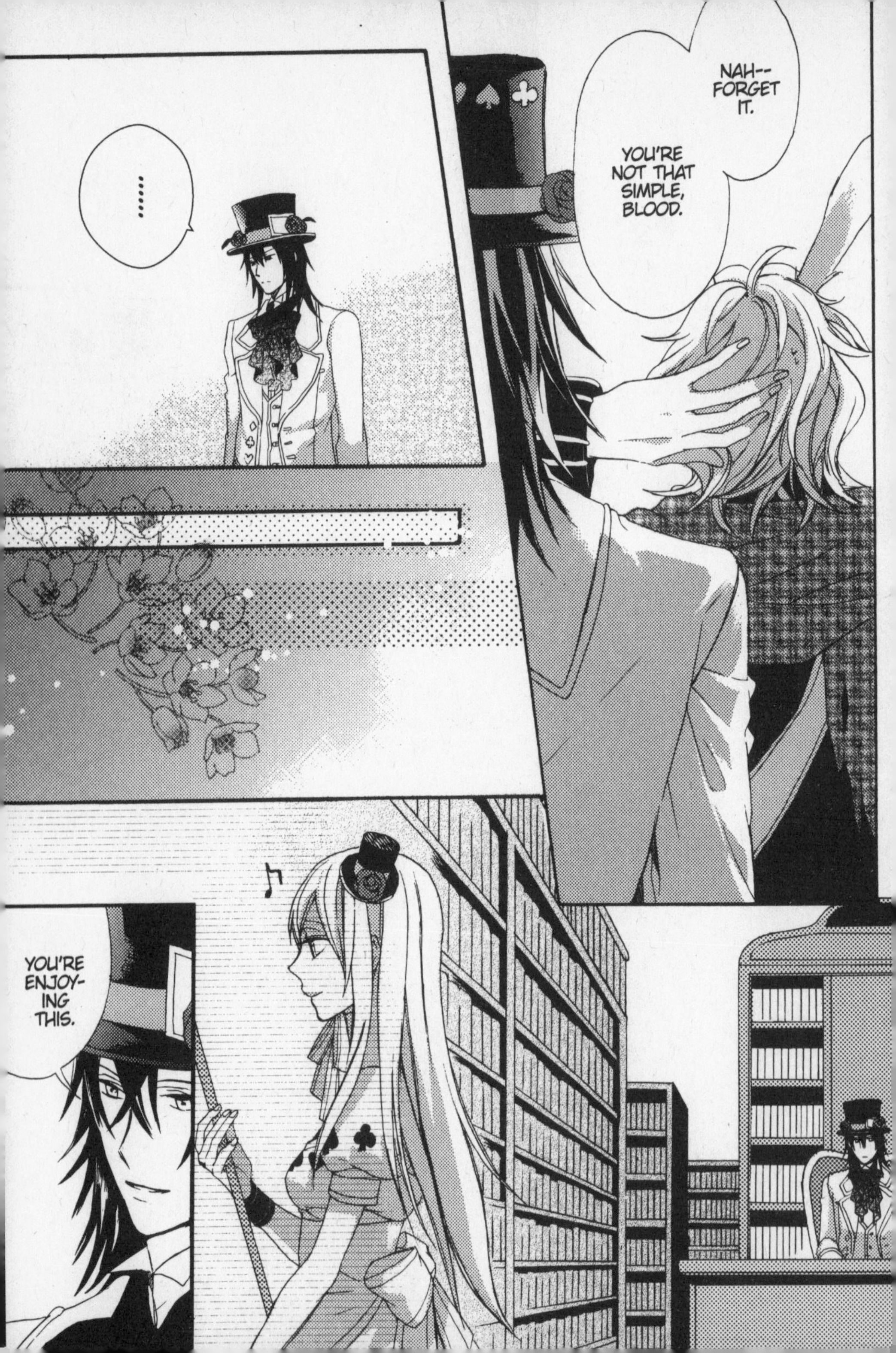
NAH-- FORGET IT.
YOU'RE NOT THAT SIMPLE, BLOOD.
......
YOU'RE ENJOY-ING THIS.

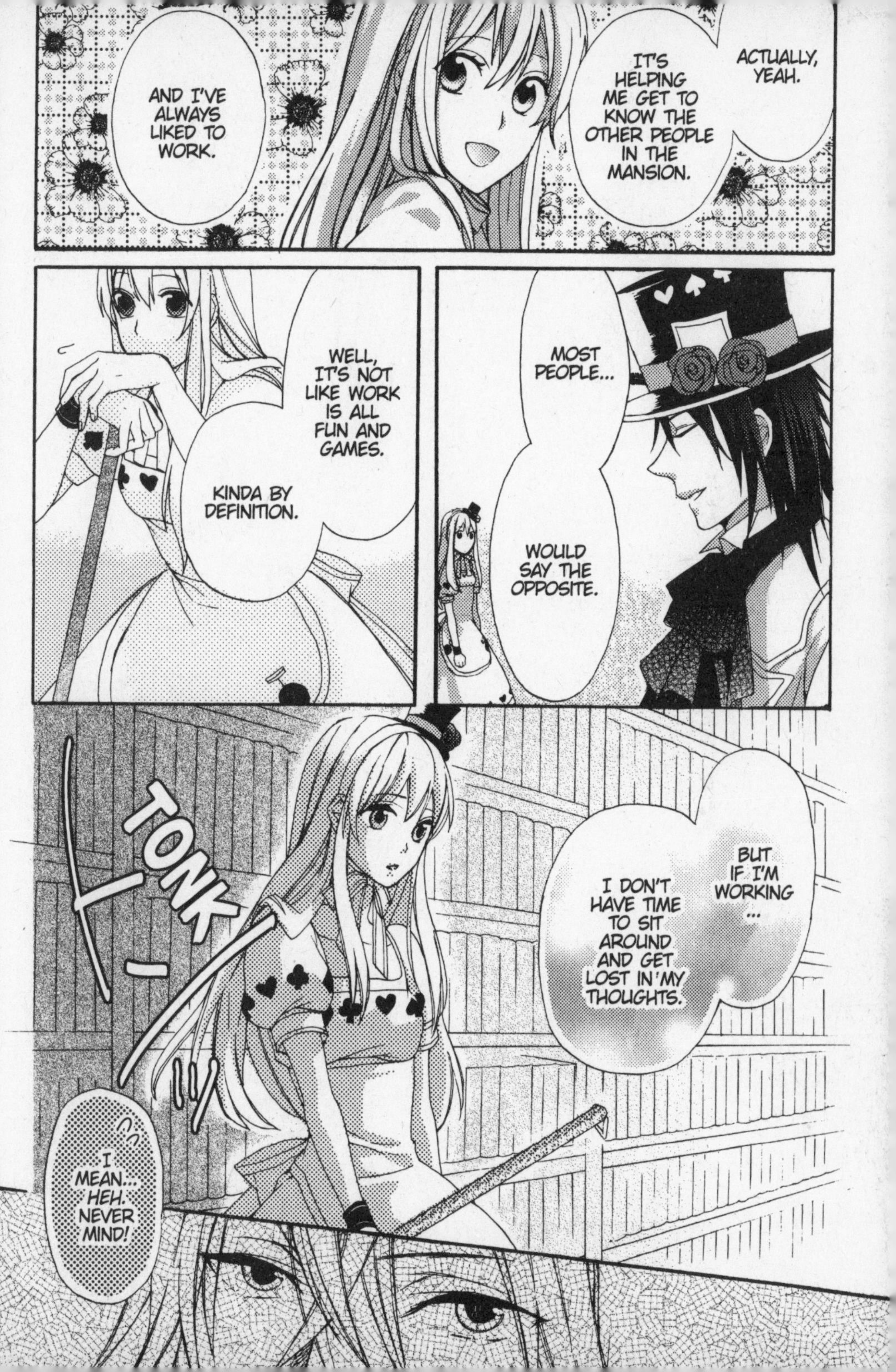
ACTUALLY, YEAH.
IT'S HELPING ME GET TO KNOW THE OTHER PEOPLE IN THE MANSION.
AND I'VE ALWAYS LIKED TO WORK.
MOST PEOPLE...
WOULD SAY THE OPPOSITE.
WELL, IT'S NOT LIKE WORK IS ALL FUN AND GAMES.
KINDA BY DEFINITION.
BUT IF I'M WORKING...
I DON'T HAVE TIME TO SIT AROUND AND GET LOST IN MY THOUGHTS.
TONK
I MEAN... HEH. NEVER MIND!

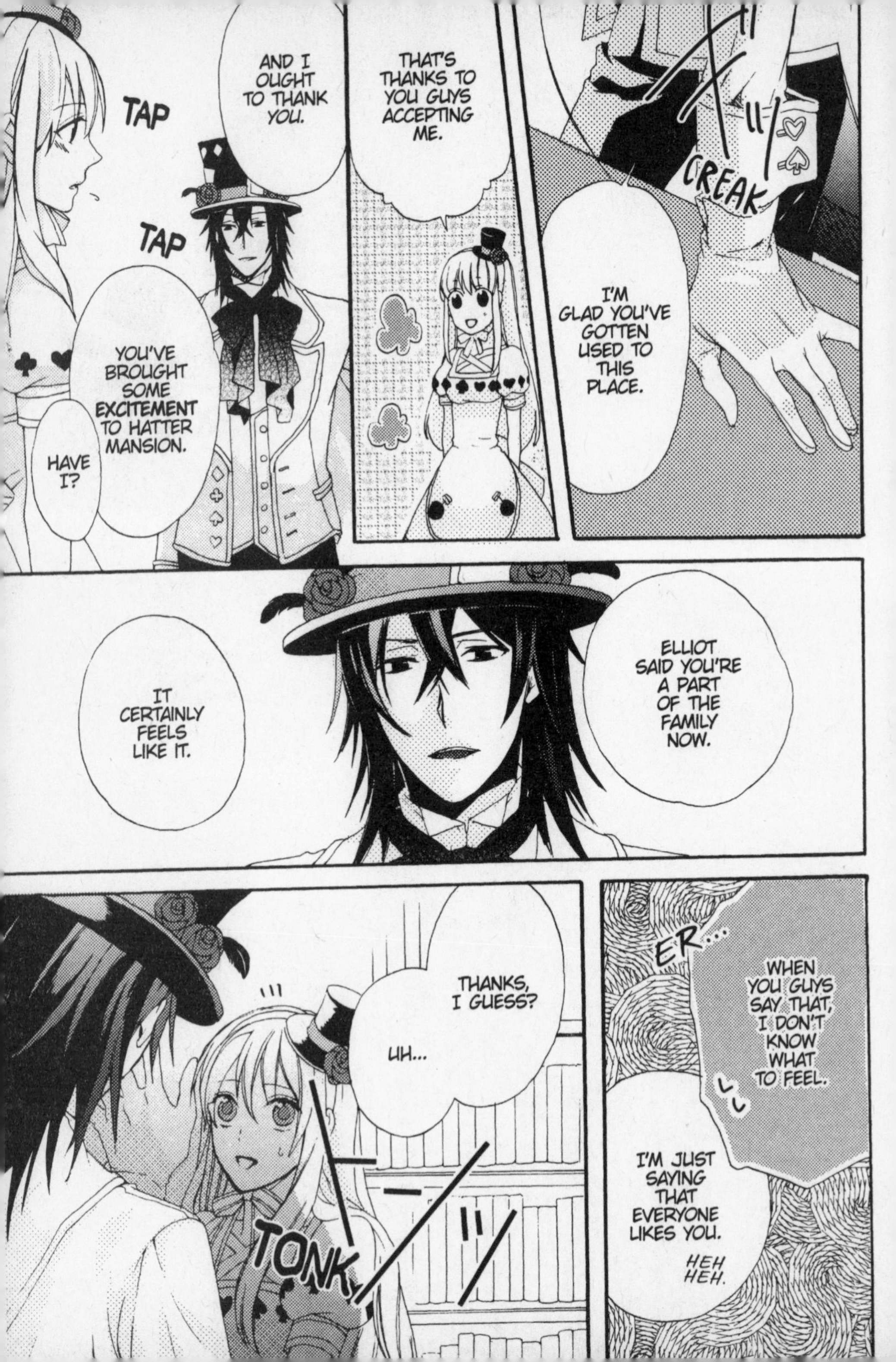
CREAK
I'M GLAD YOU'VE GOTTEN USED TO THIS PLACE.
THAT'S THANKS TO YOU GUYS ACCEPTING ME.
AND I OUGHT TO THANK YOU.
TAP
TAP
YOU'VE BROUGHT SOME EXCITEMENT TO HATTER MANSION.
HAVE I?
ELLIOT SAID YOU'RE A PART OF THE FAMILY NOW.
IT CERTAINLY FEELS LIKE IT.
ER...
WHEN YOU GUYS SAY THAT, I DON'T KNOW WHAT TO FEEL.
I'M JUST SAYING THAT EVERYONE LIKES YOU.
HEH HEH.
THANKS, I GUESS?
UH...
TONK

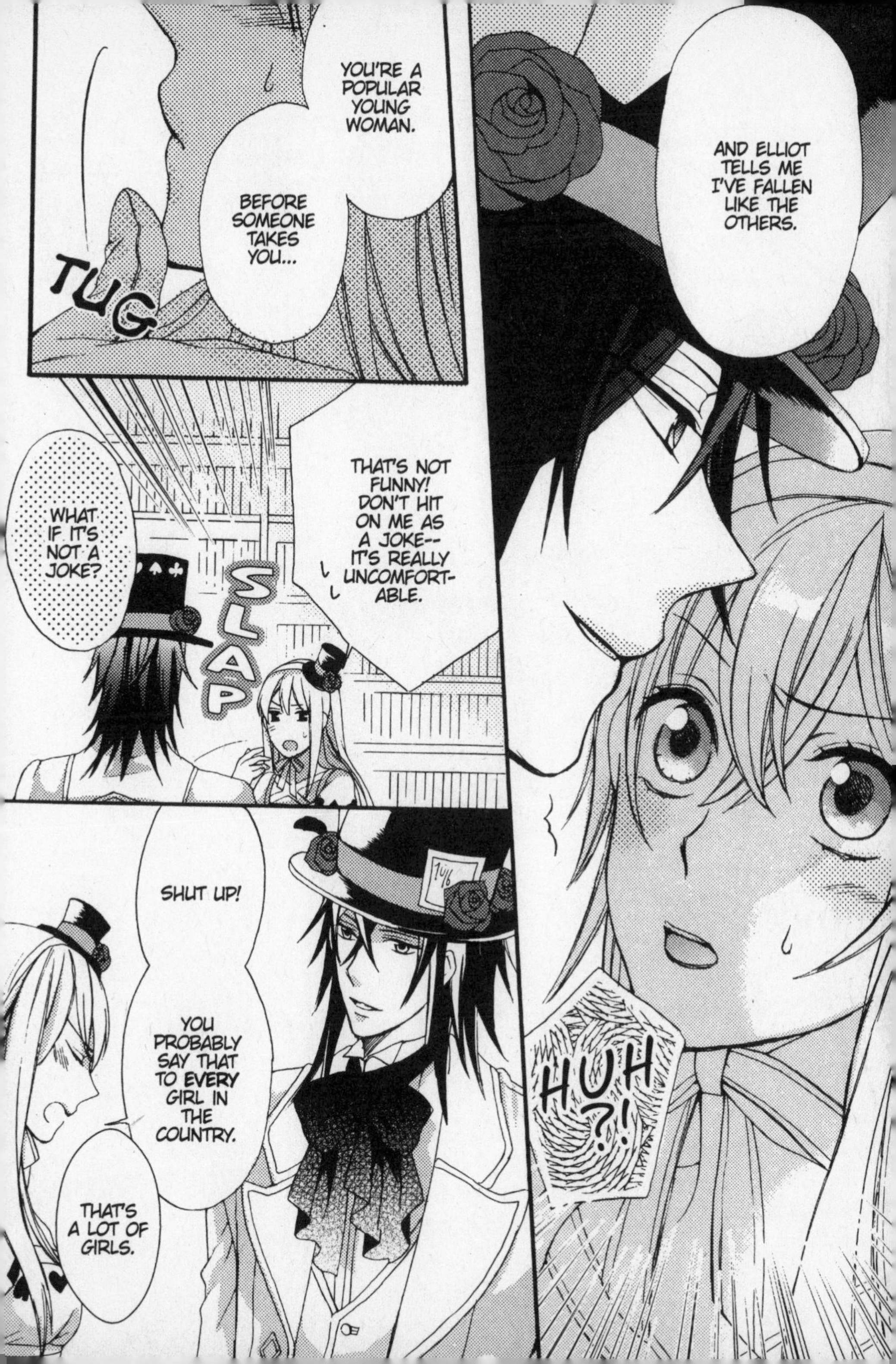
AND ELLIOT TELLS ME I'VE FALLEN LIKE THE OTHERS.
HUH?!
YOU'RE A POPULAR YOUNG WOMAN.
BEFORE SOMEONE TAKES YOU...
TUG
THAT'S NOT FUNNY! DON'T HIT ON ME AS A JOKE-- IT'S REALLY UNCOMFORTABLE.
SLAP
WHAT IF IT'S NOT A JOKE?
SHUT UP!
YOU PROBABLY SAY THAT TO EVERY GIRL IN THE COUNTRY.
THAT'S A LOT OF GIRLS.

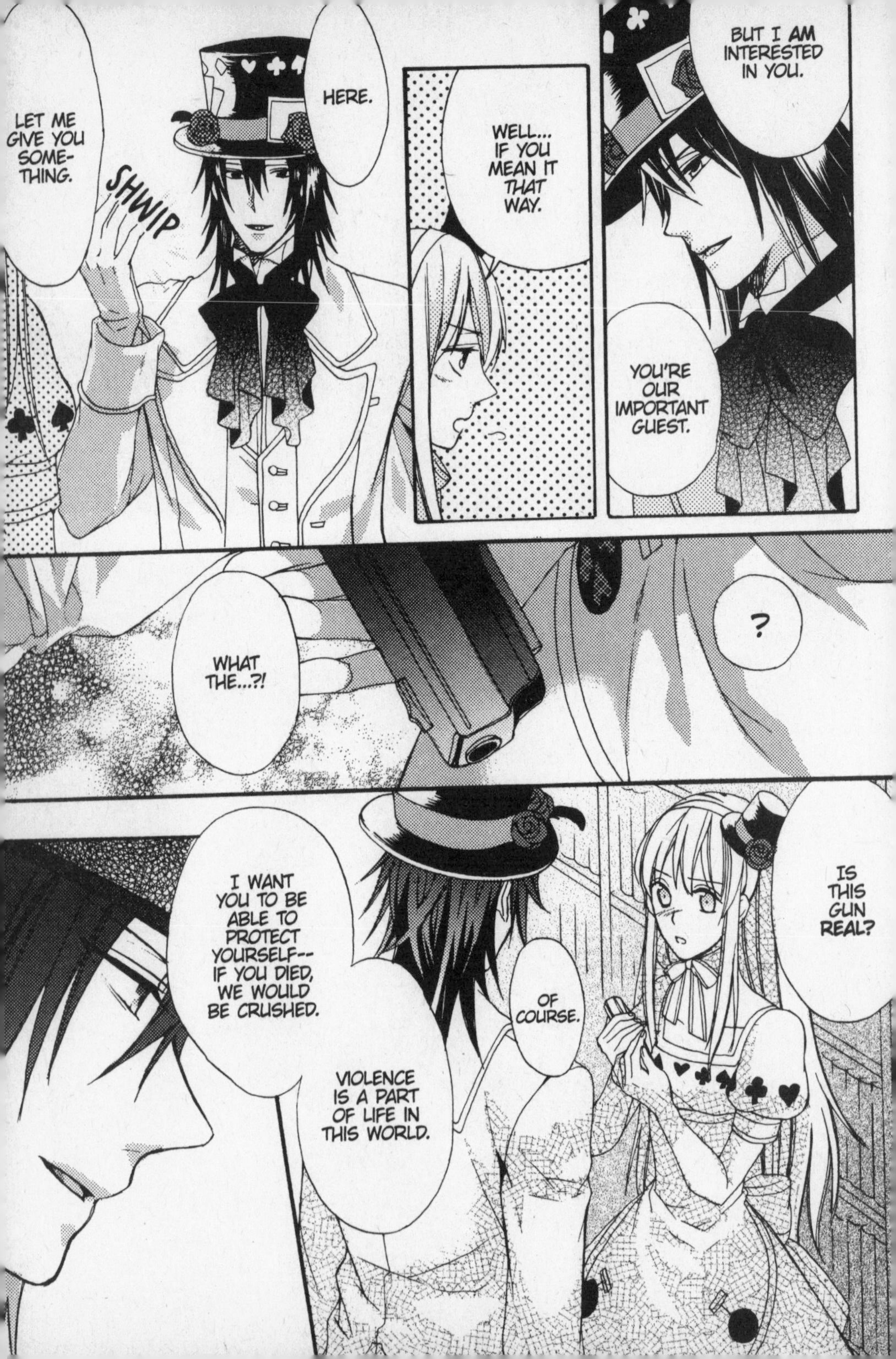
BUT I AM INTERESTED IN YOU.
YOU'RE OUR IMPORTANT GUEST.
WELL... IF YOU MEAN IT THAT WAY.
HERE.
LET ME GIVE YOU SOME-THING.
SHWIP
?
WHAT THE...?!
IS THIS GUN REAL?
OF COURSE.
I WANT YOU TO BE ABLE TO PROTECT YOURSELF-- IF YOU DIED, WE WOULD BE CRUSHED.
VIOLENCE IS A PART OF LIFE IN THIS WORLD.

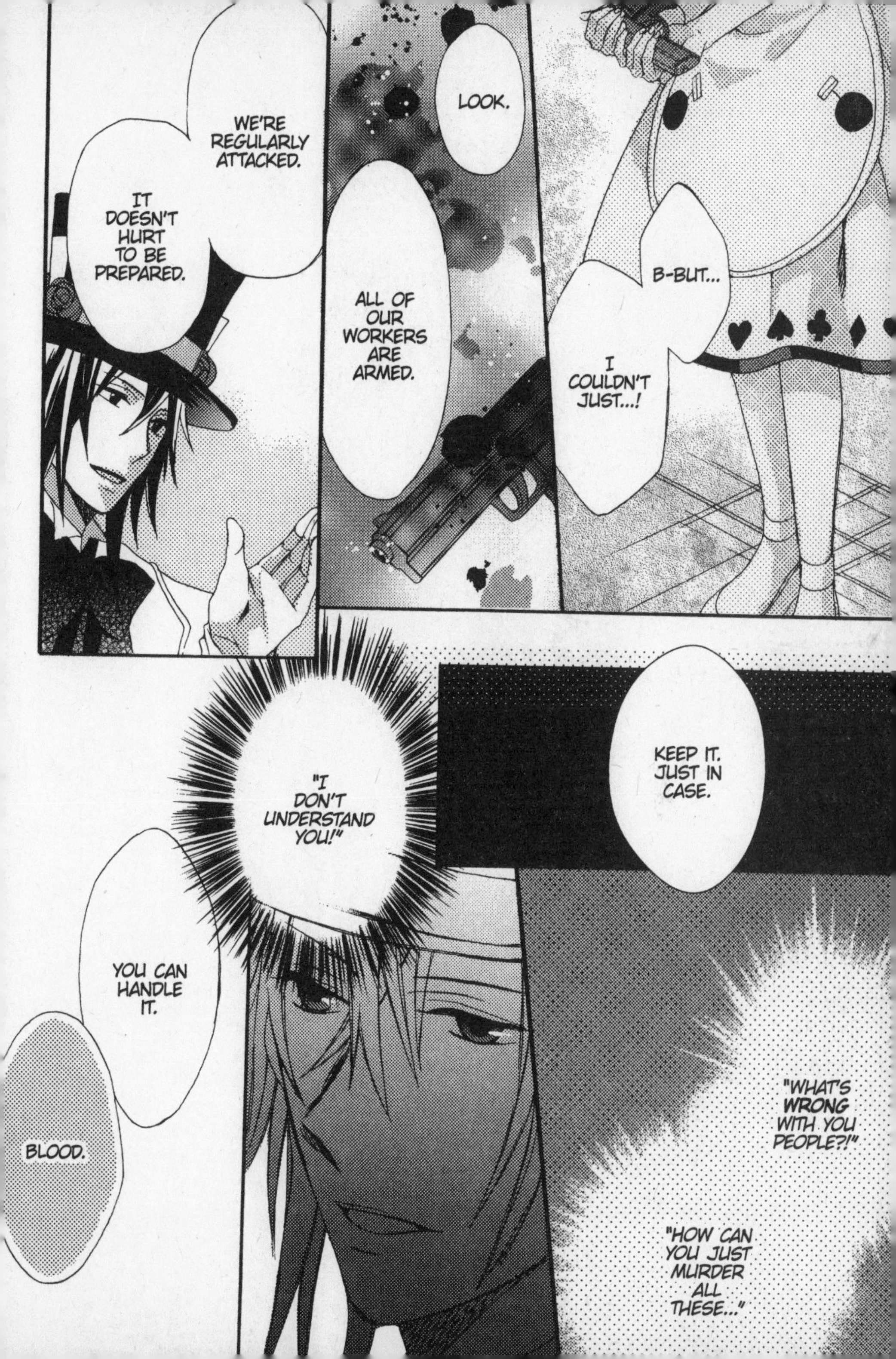
B-BUT...
I COULDN'T JUST...!
LOOK.
ALL OF OUR WORKERS ARE ARMED.
WE'RE REGULARLY ATTACKED.
IT DOESN'T HURT TO BE PREPARED.
KEEP IT. JUST IN CASE.
"I DON'T UNDERSTAND YOU!"
"WHAT'S WRONG WITH YOU PEOPLE?!"
"HOW CAN YOU JUST MURDER ALL THESE..."
YOU CAN HANDLE IT.
BLOOD.

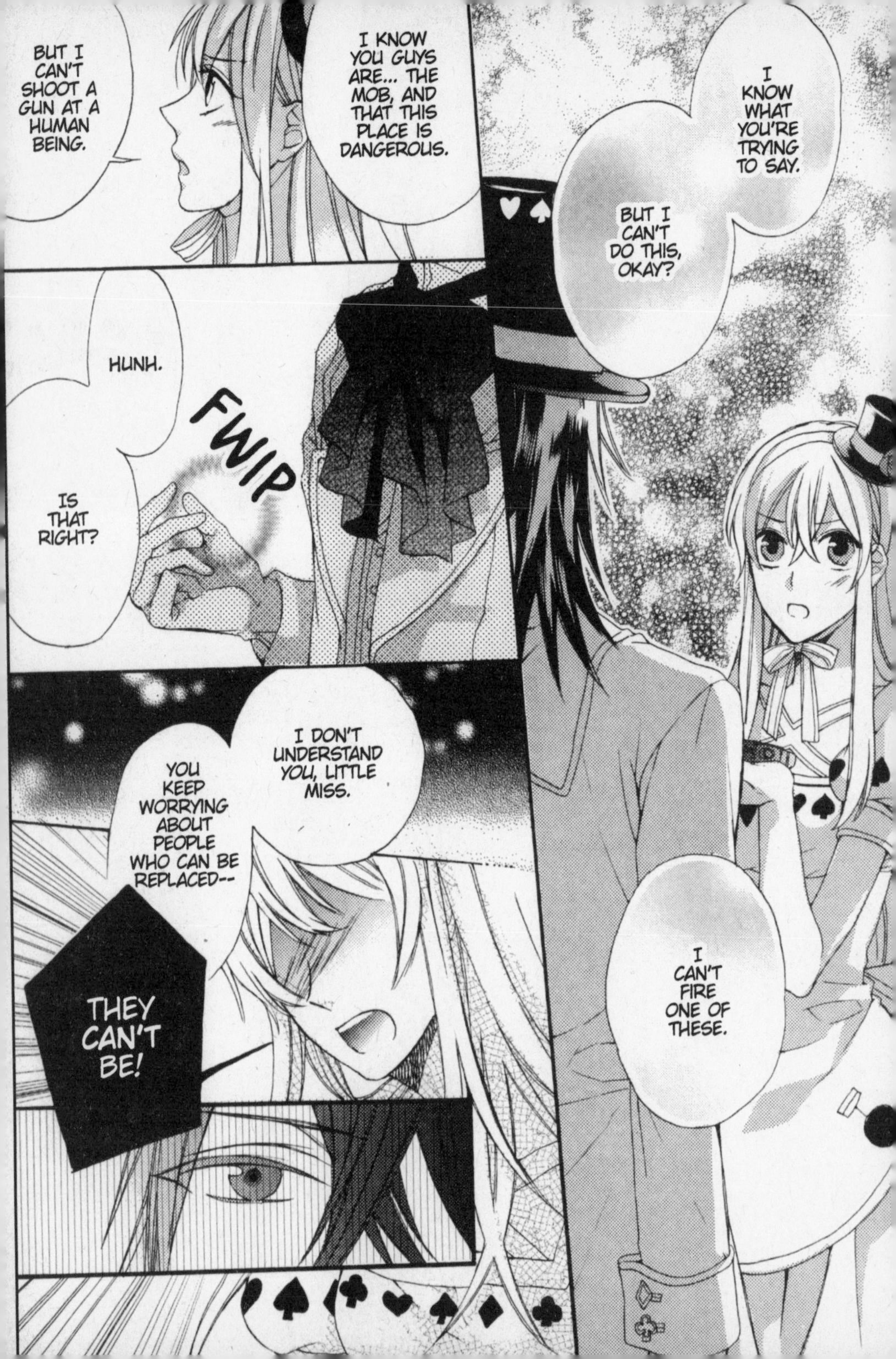
I KNOW WHAT YOU'RE TRYING TO SAY.
BUT I CAN'T DO THIS, OKAY?
I CAN'T FIRE ONE OF THESE.
I KNOW YOU GUYS ARE... THE MOB, AND THAT THIS PLACE IS DANGEROUS.
BUT I CAN'T SHOOT A GUN AT A HUMAN BEING.
HUNH.
FWIP
IS THAT RIGHT?
I DON'T UNDERSTAND YOU, LITTLE MISS.
YOU KEEP WORRYING ABOUT PEOPLE WHO CAN BE REPLACED--
THEY CAN'T BE!

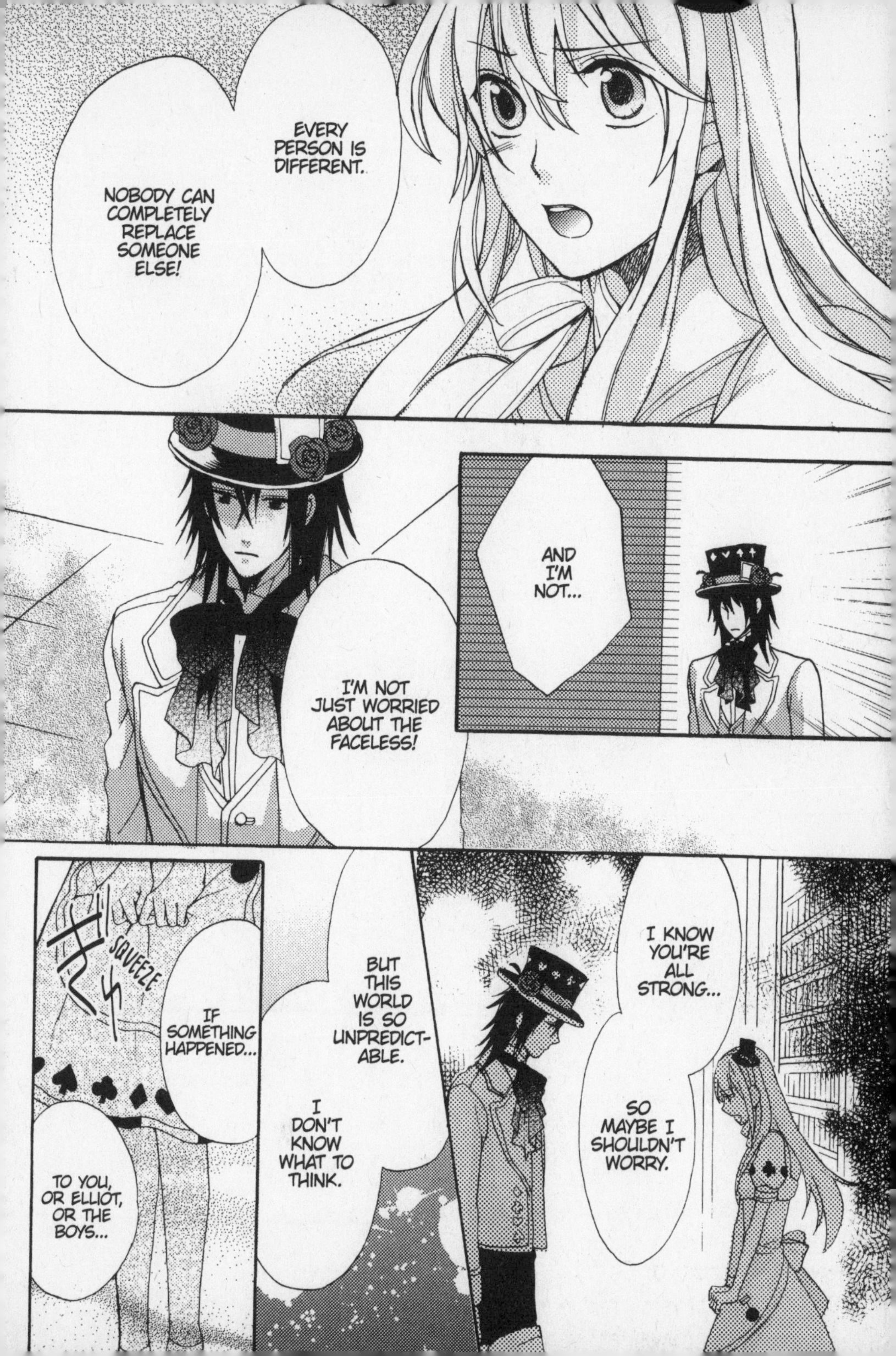
EVERY PERSON IS DIFFERENT.
NOBODY CAN COMPLETELY REPLACE SOMEONE ELSE!
AND I'M NOT...
I'M NOT JUST WORRIED ABOUT THE FACELESS!
I KNOW YOU'RE ALL STRONG...
SO MAYBE I SHOULDN'T WORRY.
BUT THIS WORLD IS SO UNPREDICT-ABLE.
I DON'T KNOW WHAT TO THINK.
SQUEEZE
IF SOMETHING HAPPENED...
TO YOU, OR ELLIOT, OR THE BOYS...

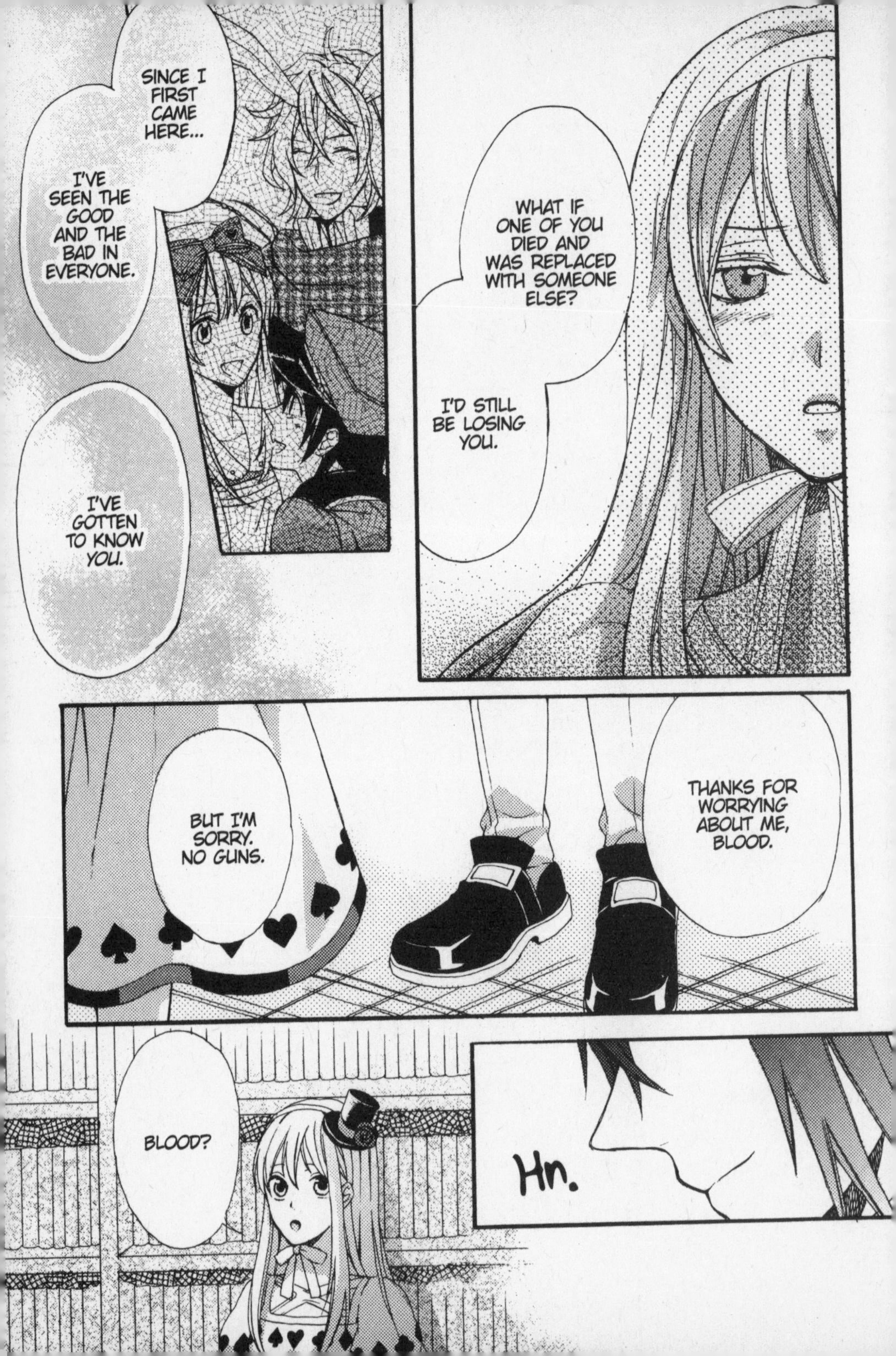
WHAT IF ONE OF YOU DIED AND WAS REPLACED WITH SOMEONE ELSE?
I'D STILL BE LOSING YOU.
SINCE I FIRST CAME HERE...
I'VE SEEN THE GOOD AND THE BAD IN EVERYONE.
I'VE GOTTEN TO KNOW YOU.
THANKS FOR WORRYING ABOUT ME, BLOOD.
BUT I'M SORRY. NO GUNS.
Hn.
BLOOD?

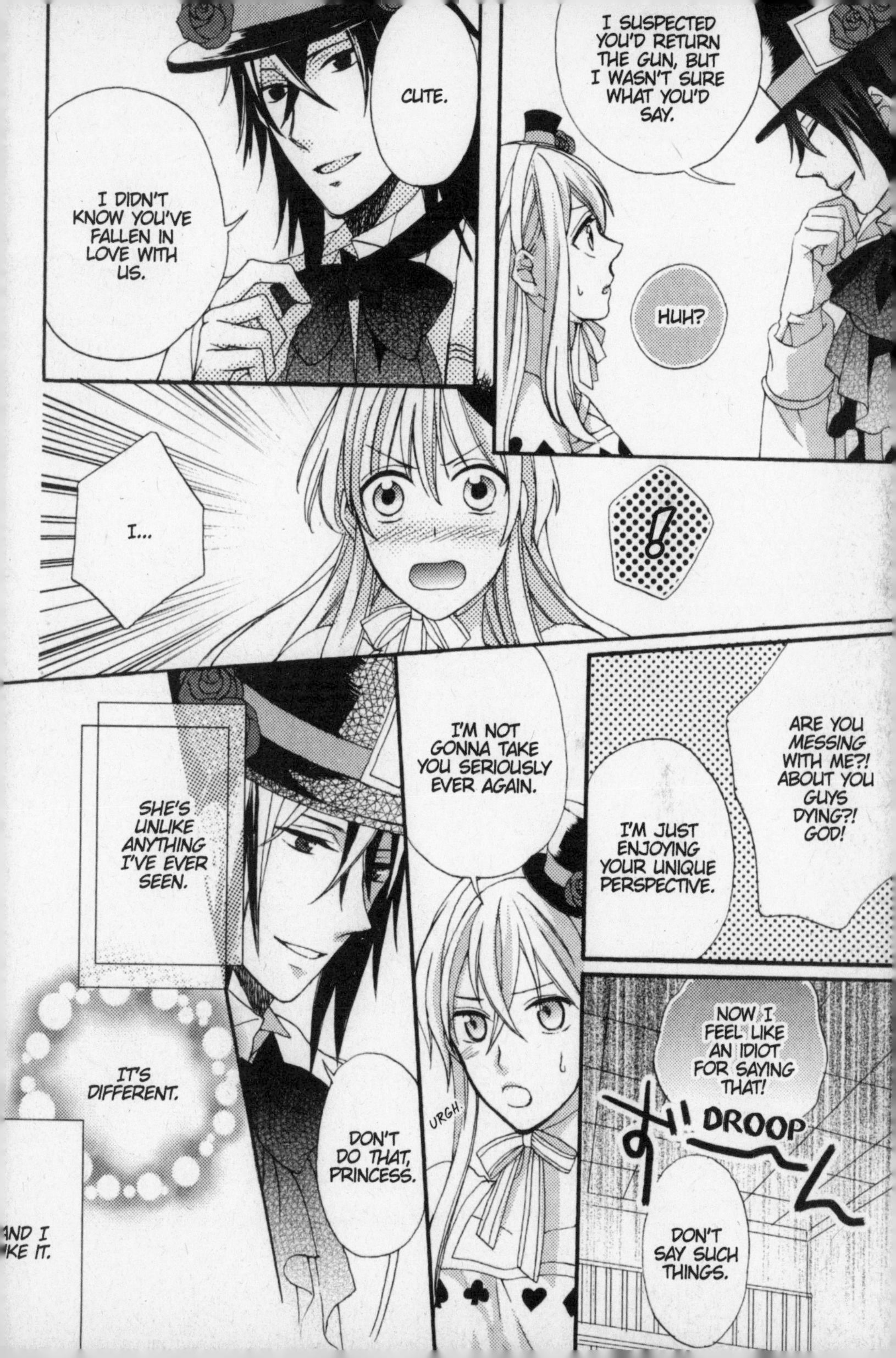
I SUSPECTED YOU'D RETURN THE GUN, BUT I WASN'T SURE WHAT YOU'D SAY.
HUH?
CUTE.
I DIDN'T KNOW YOU'VE FALLEN IN LOVE WITH US.
!
I...
ARE YOU MESSING WITH ME?! ABOUT YOU GUYS DYING?! GOD!
I'M JUST ENJOYING YOUR UNIQUE PERSPECTIVE.
NOW I FEEL LIKE AN IDIOT FOR SAYING THAT!
DROOP
DON'T SAY SUCH THINGS.
I'M NOT GONNA TAKE YOU SERIOUSLY EVER AGAIN.
URGH.
DON'T DO THAT, PRINCESS.
SHE'S UNLIKE ANYTHING I'VE EVER SEEN.
IT'S DIFFERENT.
AND I IKE IT.

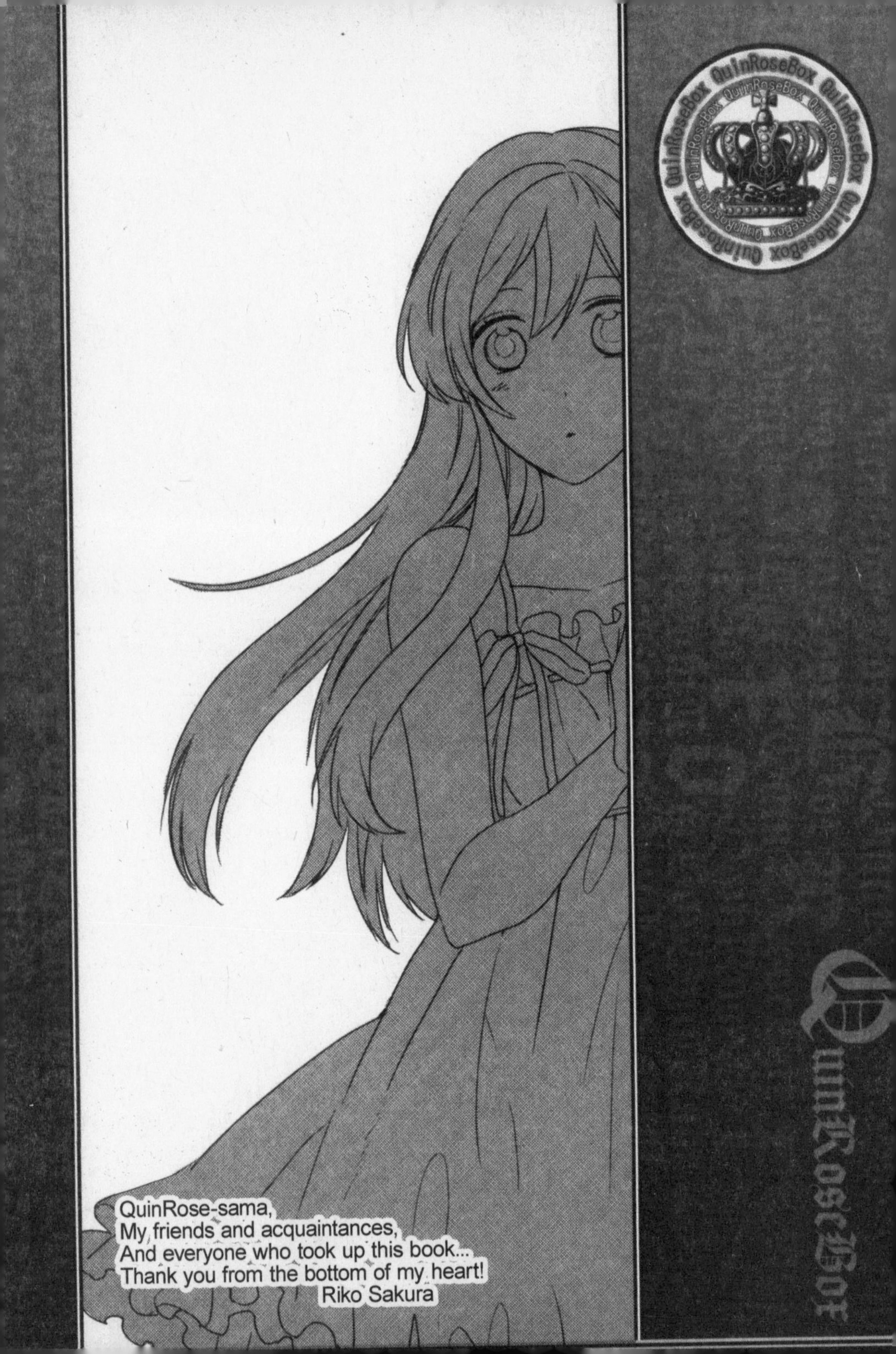
QuinRose-sama,
My friends and acquaintances,
And everyone who took up this book...
Thank you from the bottom of my heart!
Riko Sakura
QuinRoseBox

NOD
NOD
BLOOD LOOKS REALLY SLEEPY DURING ANY TIME PERIOD THAT'S NOT DAYTIME.
BUT...
MAYBE I'M AWAKE BECAUSE I DRANK TEA.
WAIT, THAT WAS COFFEE.
TWITCH
IT WAS GOOD, BUT...
I THINK I LIKE TEA BETTER.
TWITCH
GULP
HE'S GOT THE EARS OF THE OB-SESSED.
I HEARD THE WORD "TEA," MISSY.

IT MUST BE HARD HAVING BLOOD FOR A BOSS, ELLIOT.
ARE YOU KIDDING? HE'S THE BEST BOSS A GUY COULD HOPE FOR!
GLARE
IF I HAVE TO TALK TO HIM, NO MATTER HOW TIRED HE IS...
LISTEN TO THIS, BLOOD!
DROP
SLEEPING
HE ALWAYS LISTENS! I CAN TELL 'CAUSE HE NODS.
HE CARES ABOUT MY OPINION!
ELLIOT...!
SOB

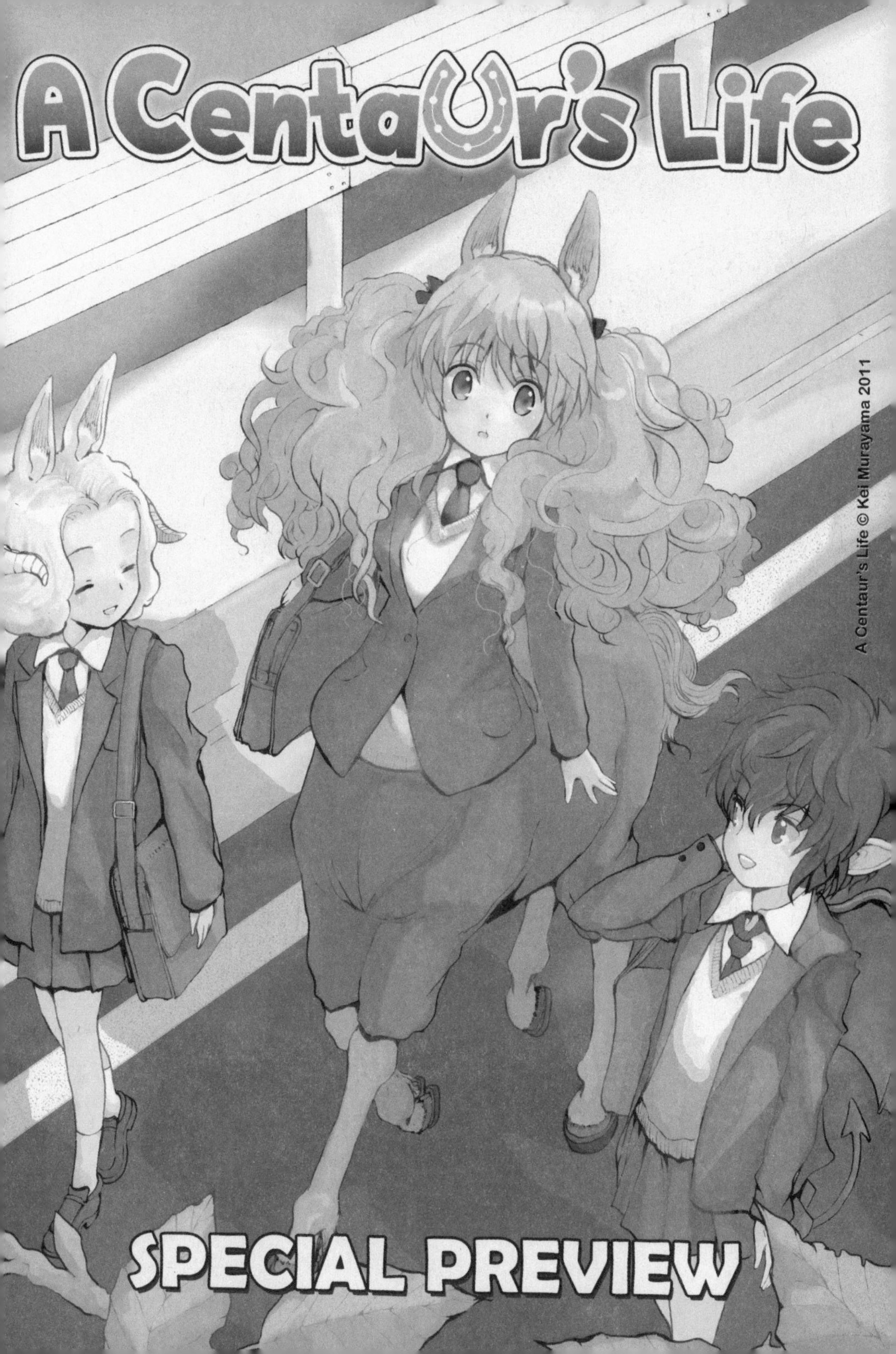
A Centaur's Life
SPECIAL PREVIEW
A Centaur's Life © Kei Murayama 2011

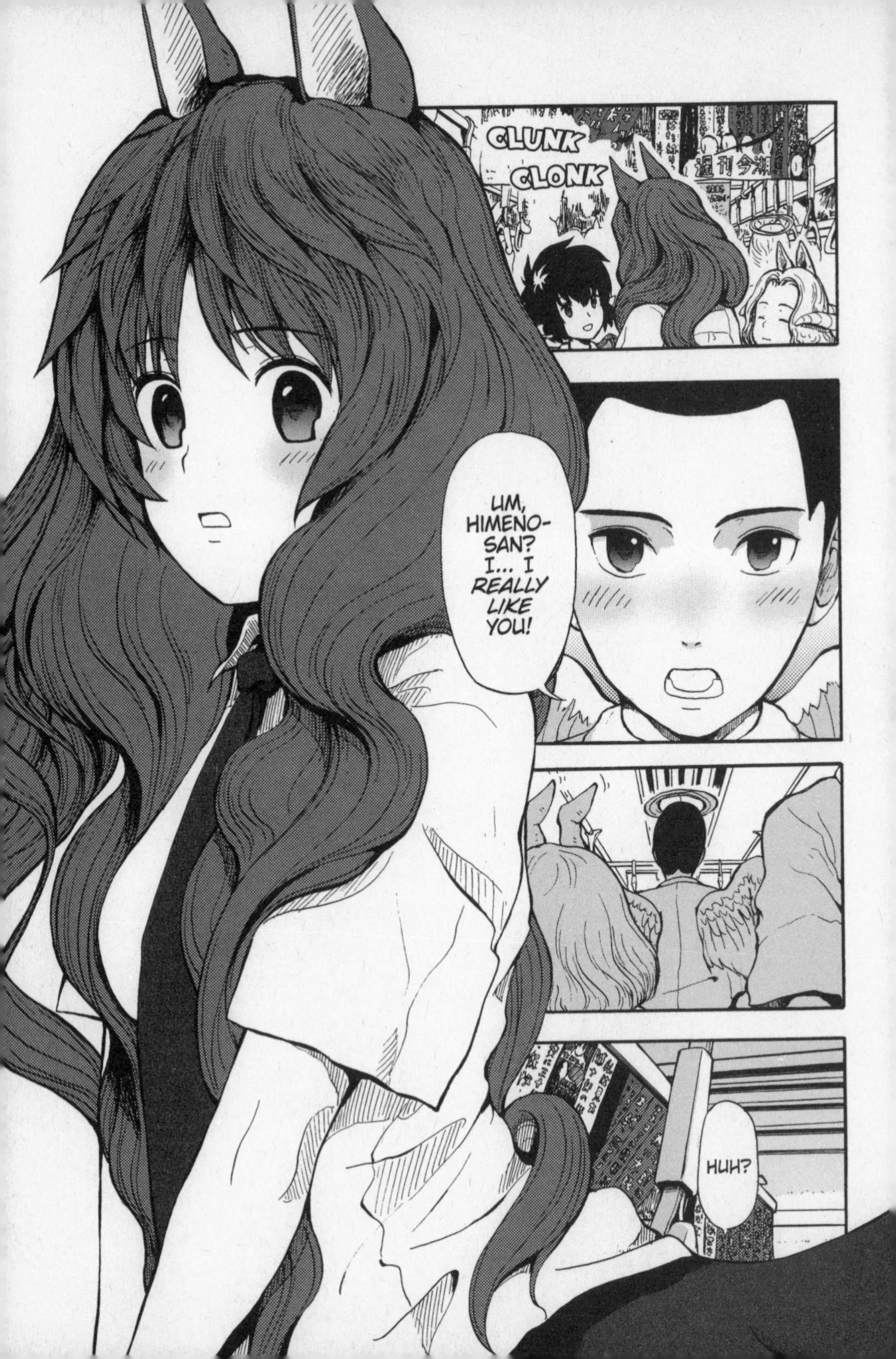
CLUNK
CLONK
UM, HIMENO-SAN? I... I REALLY LIKE YOU!
HUH?

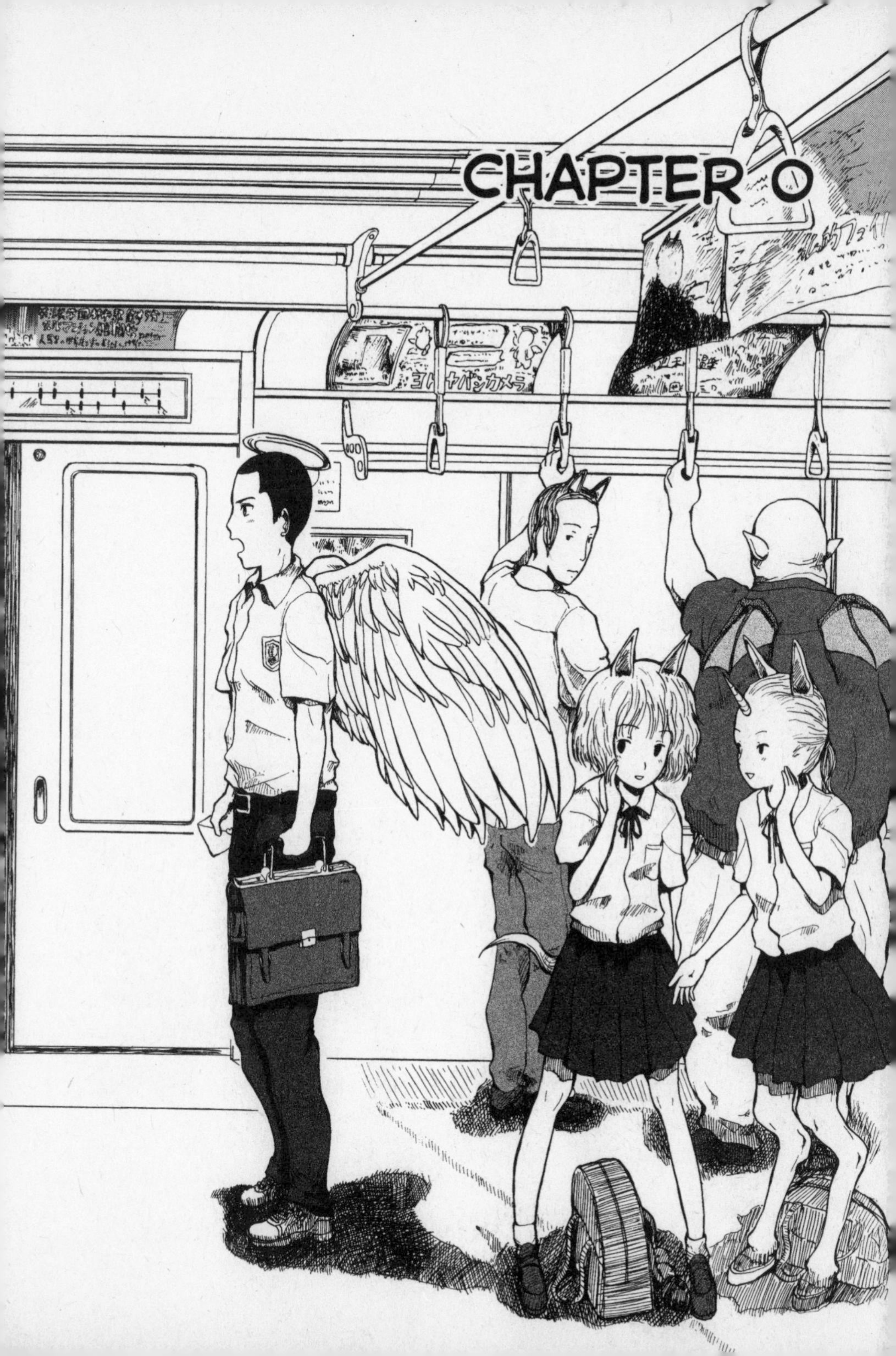
CHAPTER 0

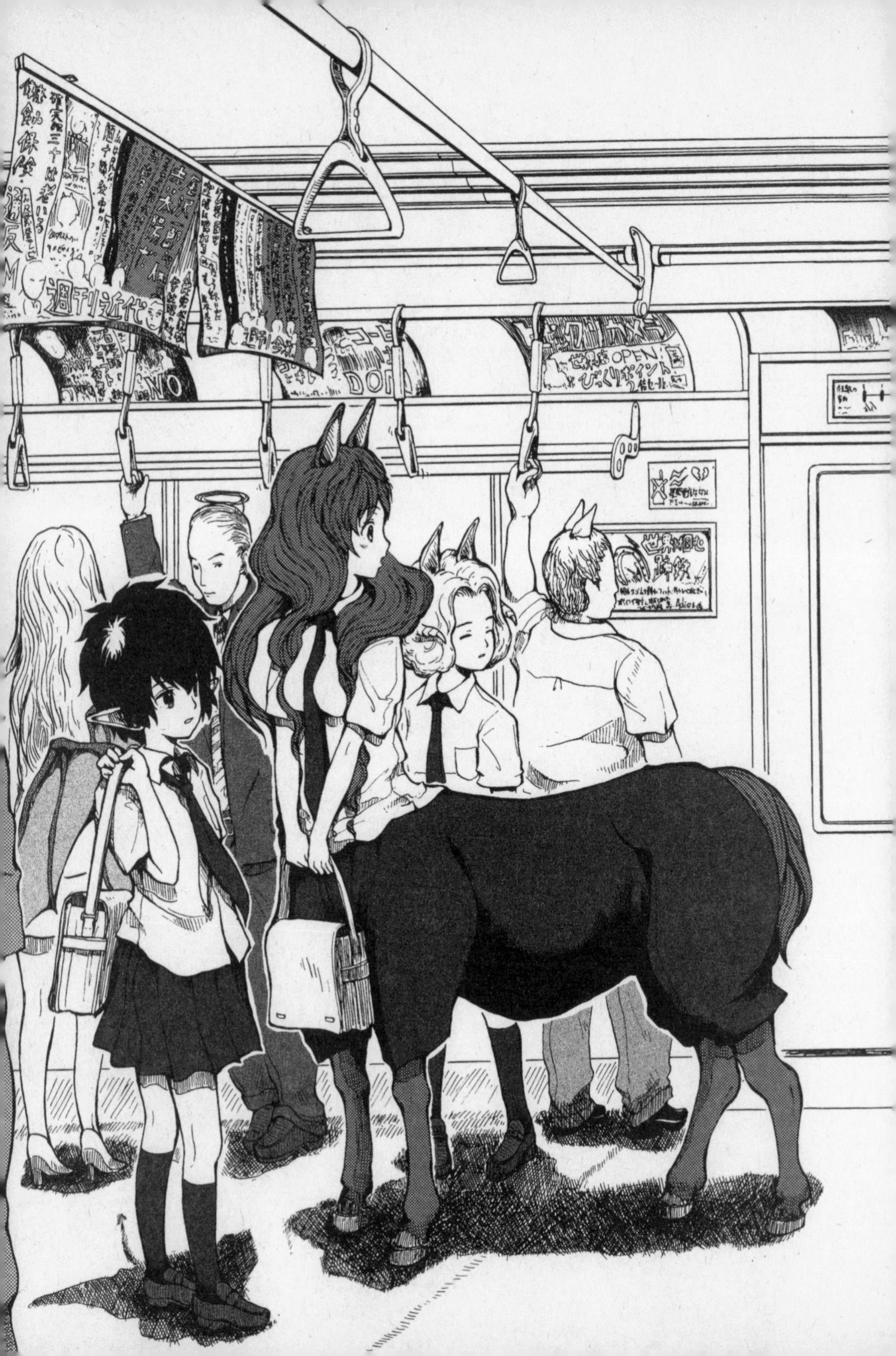
週刊近代
週刊今流
OPEN
びっくりポイント
2倍セール
DON
Adios

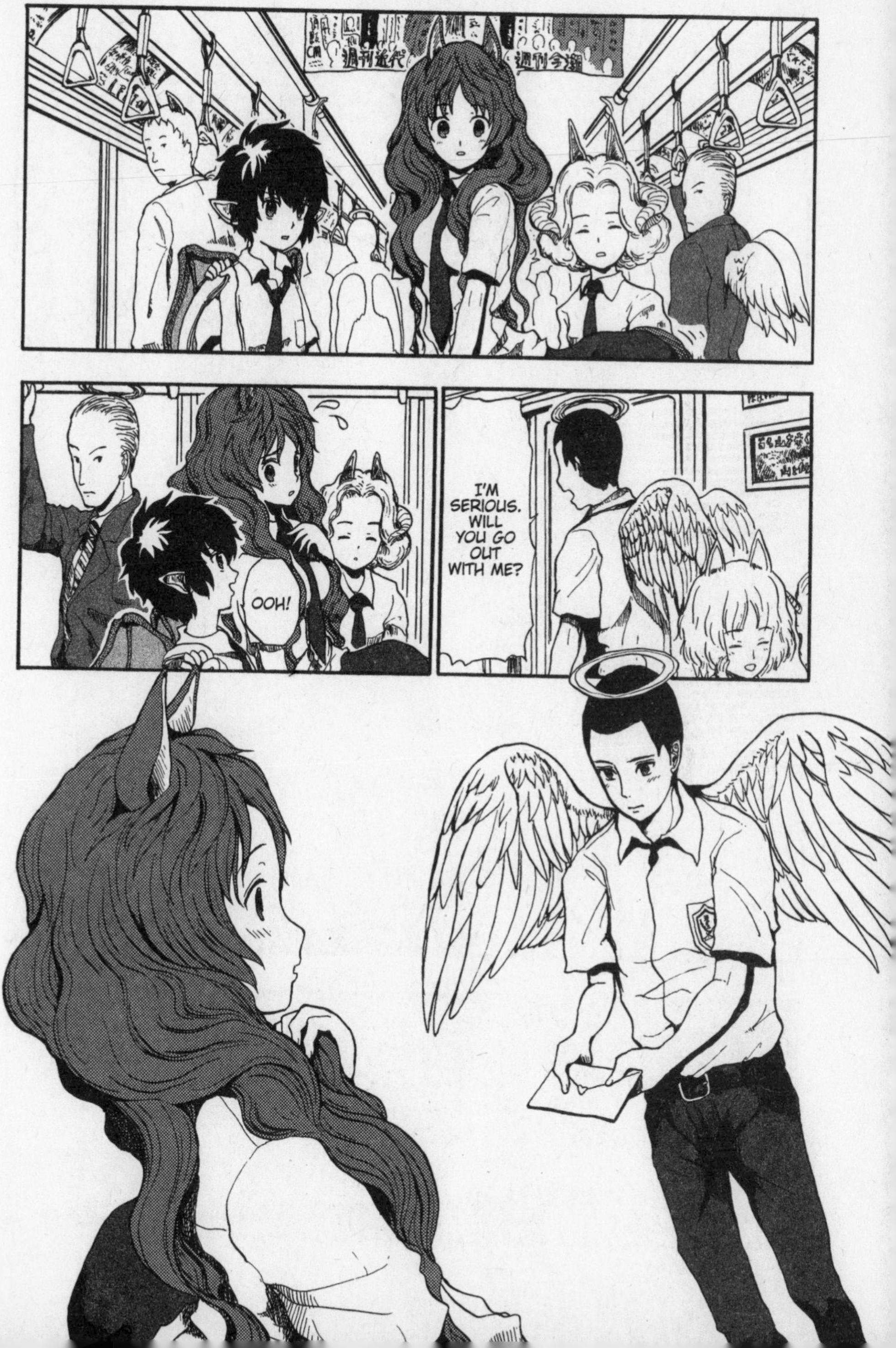
I'M SERIOUS. WILL YOU GO OUT WITH ME?
OOH!

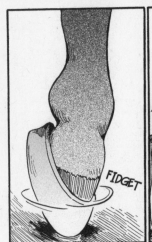

FIDGET

NGU-M

OOO!

NUDGE

NUDGE

SCREECH

WOBBLE

WHOA!

PSHH

NOW ARRIVING AT FURUKANATA STATION. THE DOORS ON THE LEFT WILL OPEN. PLEASE STAND CLEAR.

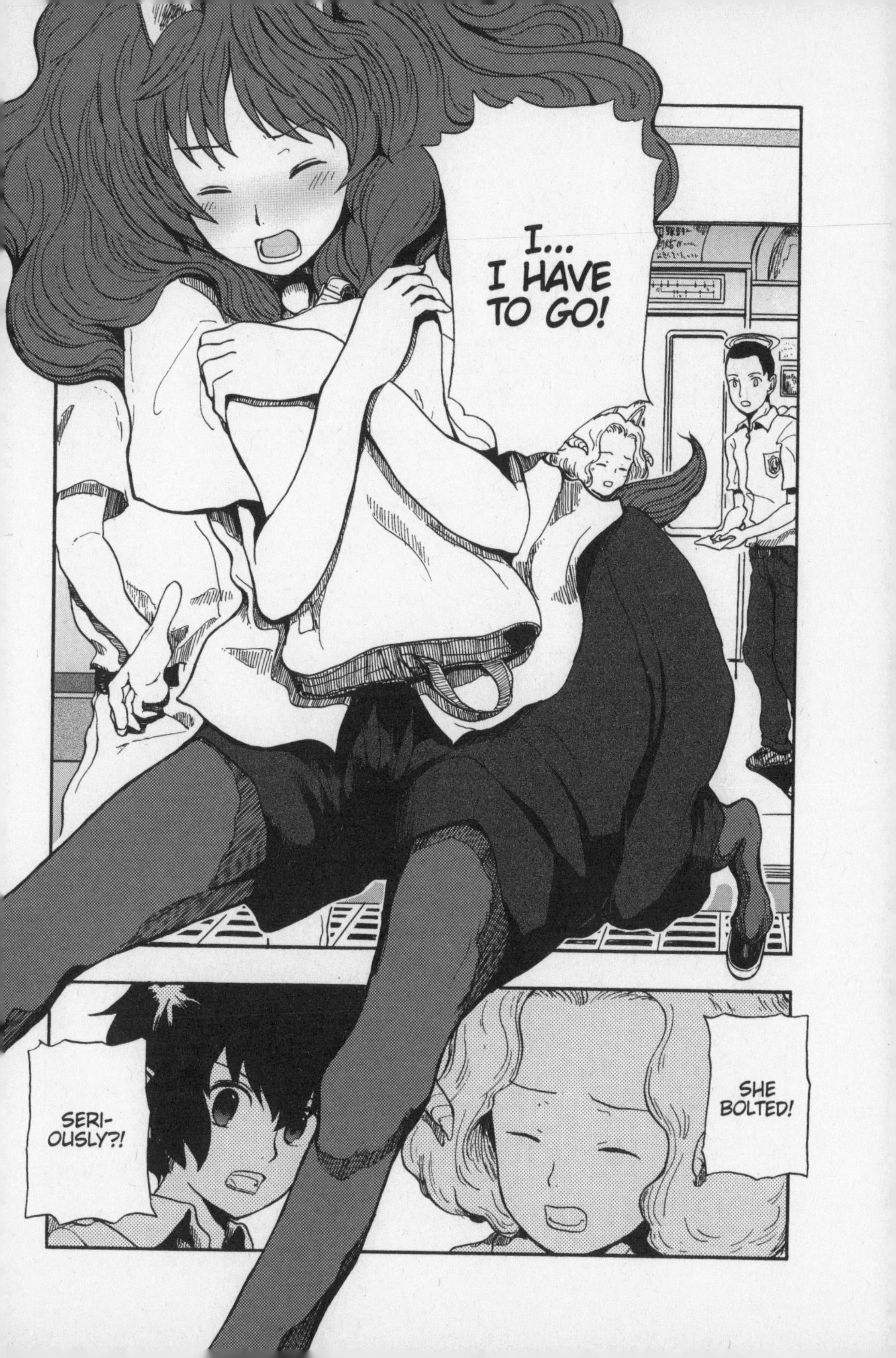
I... I HAVE TO GO!
SHE BOLTED!
SERI-OUSLY?!

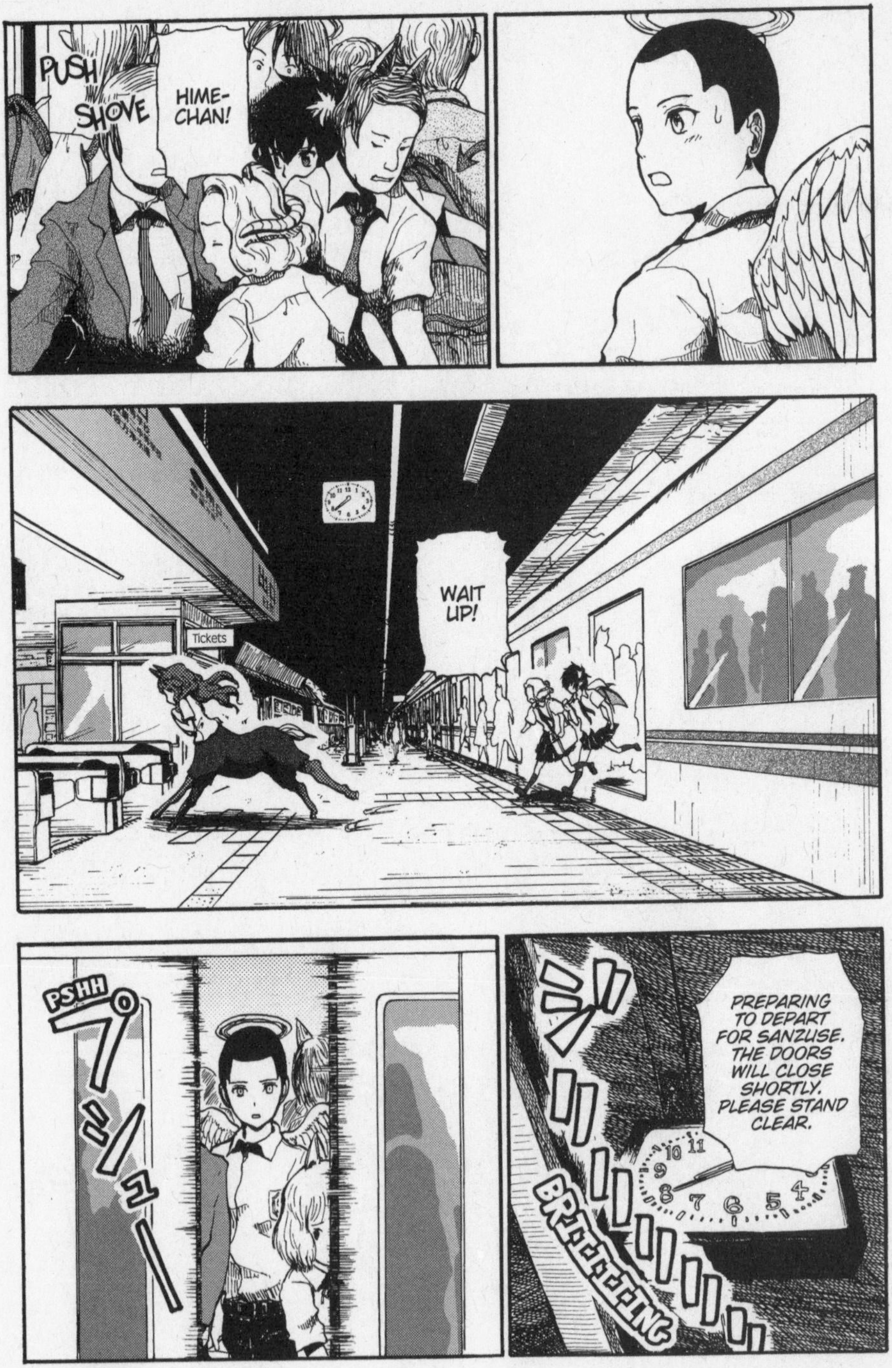
HIME-CHAN!
PUSH
SHOVE
WAIT UP!
Tickets
PREPARING TO DEPART FOR SANZUSE. THE DOORS WILL CLOSE SHORTLY. PLEASE STAND CLEAR.
PSHH

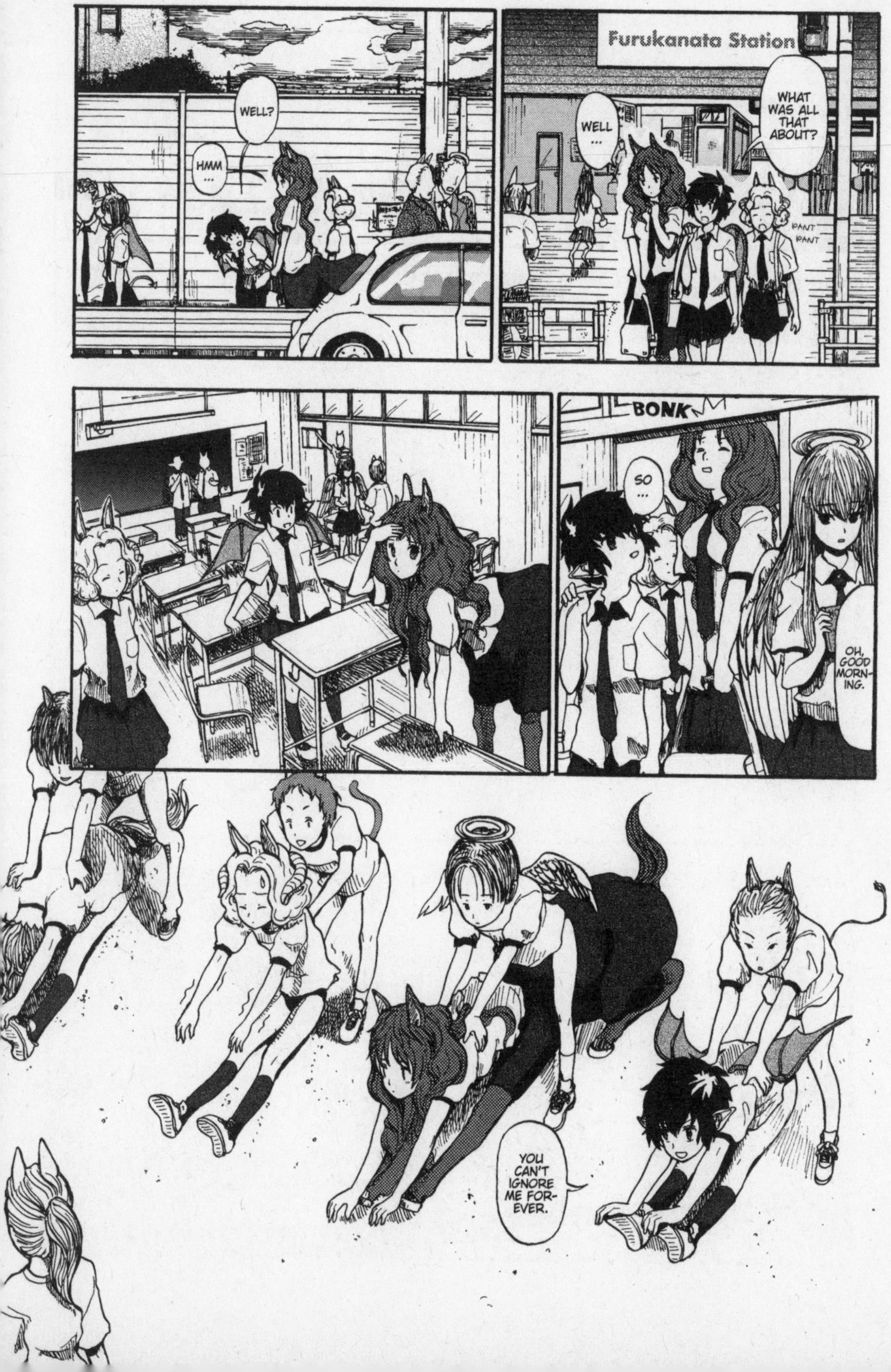
Furukanata Station
WHAT WAS ALL THAT ABOUT?
PANT PANT
WELL ...
WELL?
HMM ...
BONK
OH, GOOD MORN-ING.
SO ...
YOU CAN'T IGNORE ME FOR-EVER.

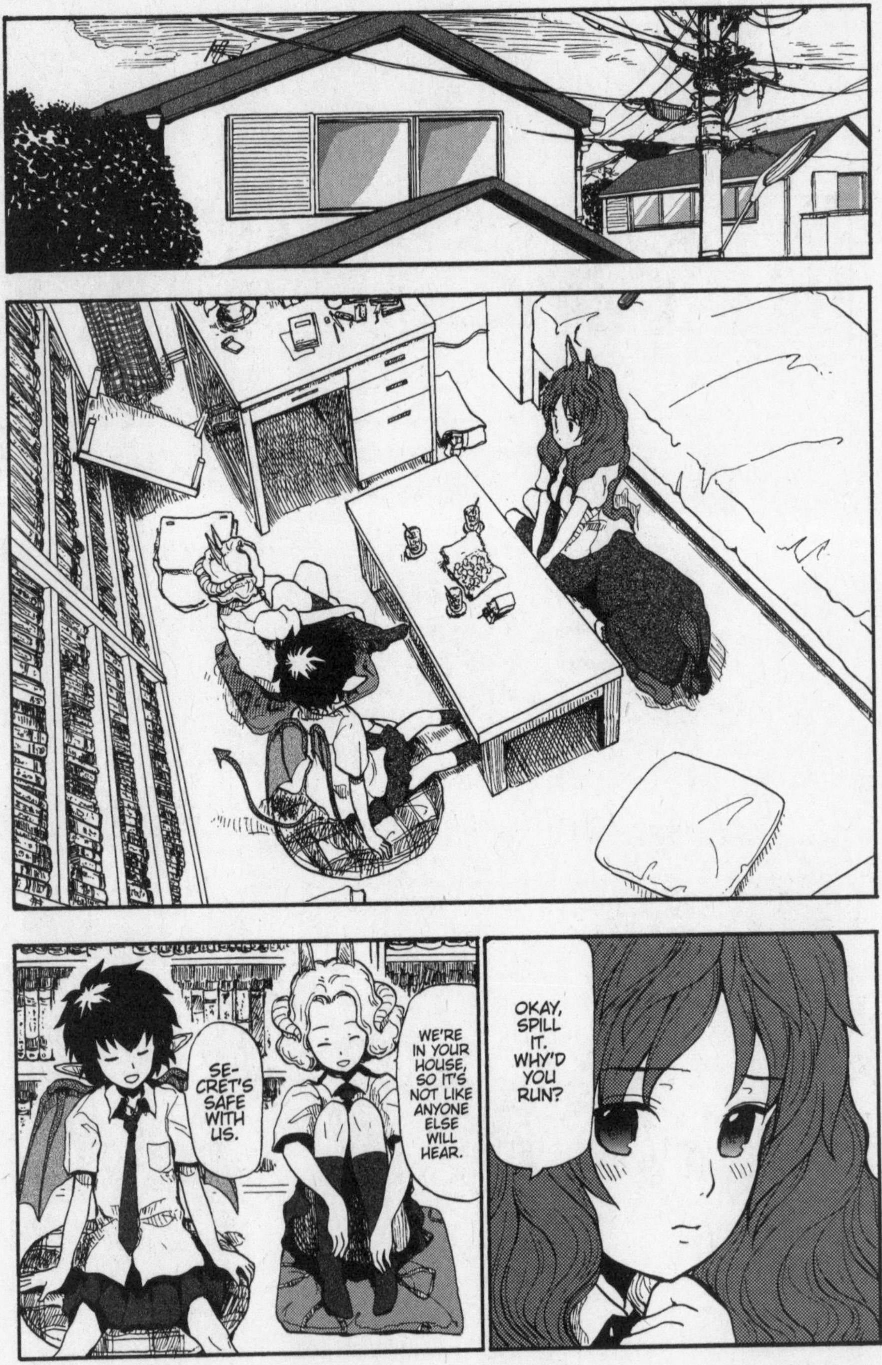
OKAY, SPILL IT. WHY'D YOU RUN?
WE'RE IN YOUR HOUSE, SO IT'S NOT LIKE ANYONE ELSE WILL HEAR.
SE-CRET'S SAFE WITH US.

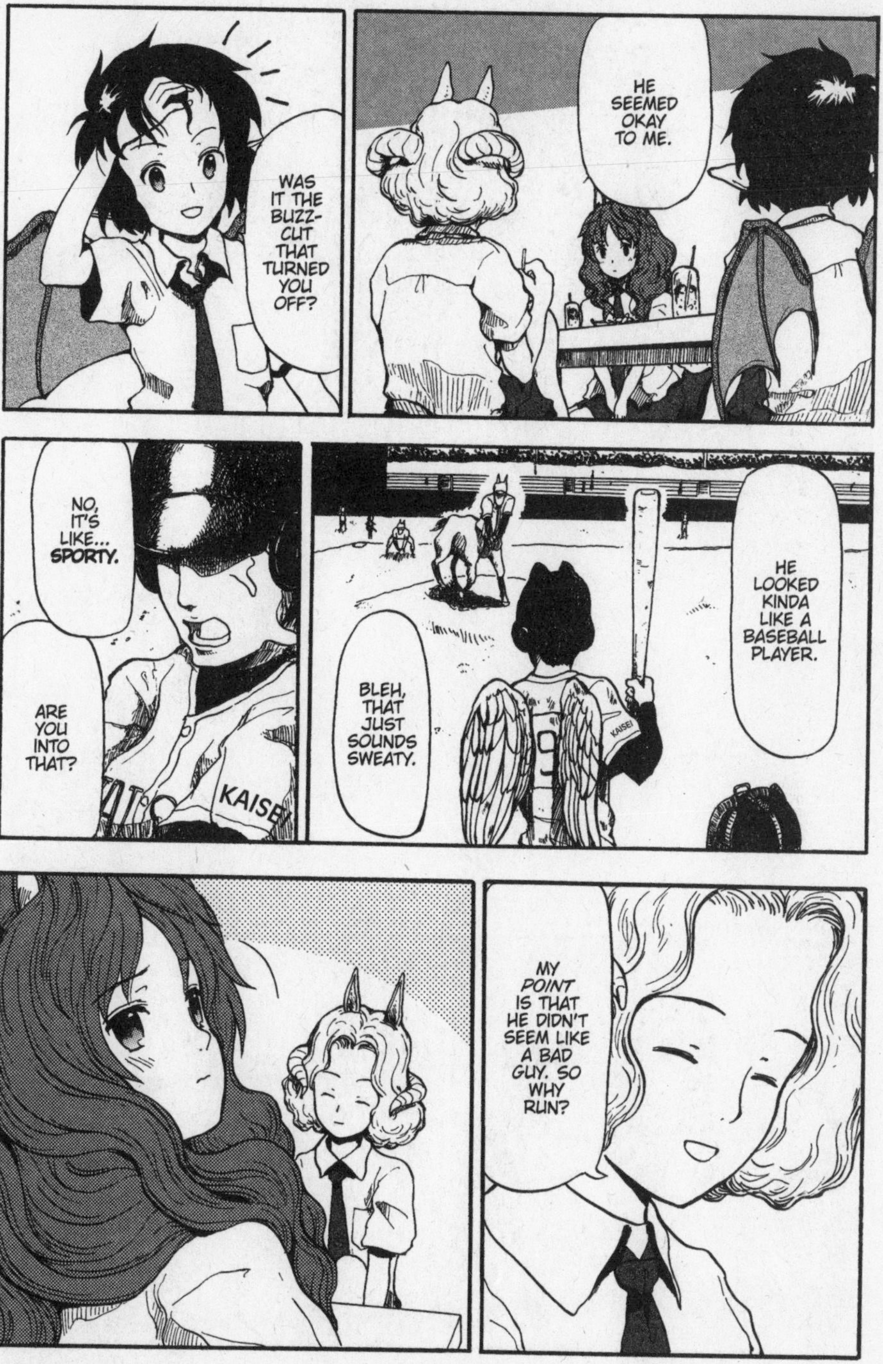
HE SEEMED OKAY TO ME.
WAS IT THE BUZZ-CUT THAT TURNED YOU OFF?
HE LOOKED KINDA LIKE A BASEBALL PLAYER.
BLEH, THAT JUST SOUNDS SWEATY.
KAISEI
NO, IT'S LIKE... **SPORTY.**
ARE YOU INTO THAT?
KAISEI
MY *POINT* IS THAT HE DIDN'T SEEM LIKE A BAD GUY. SO WHY RUN?

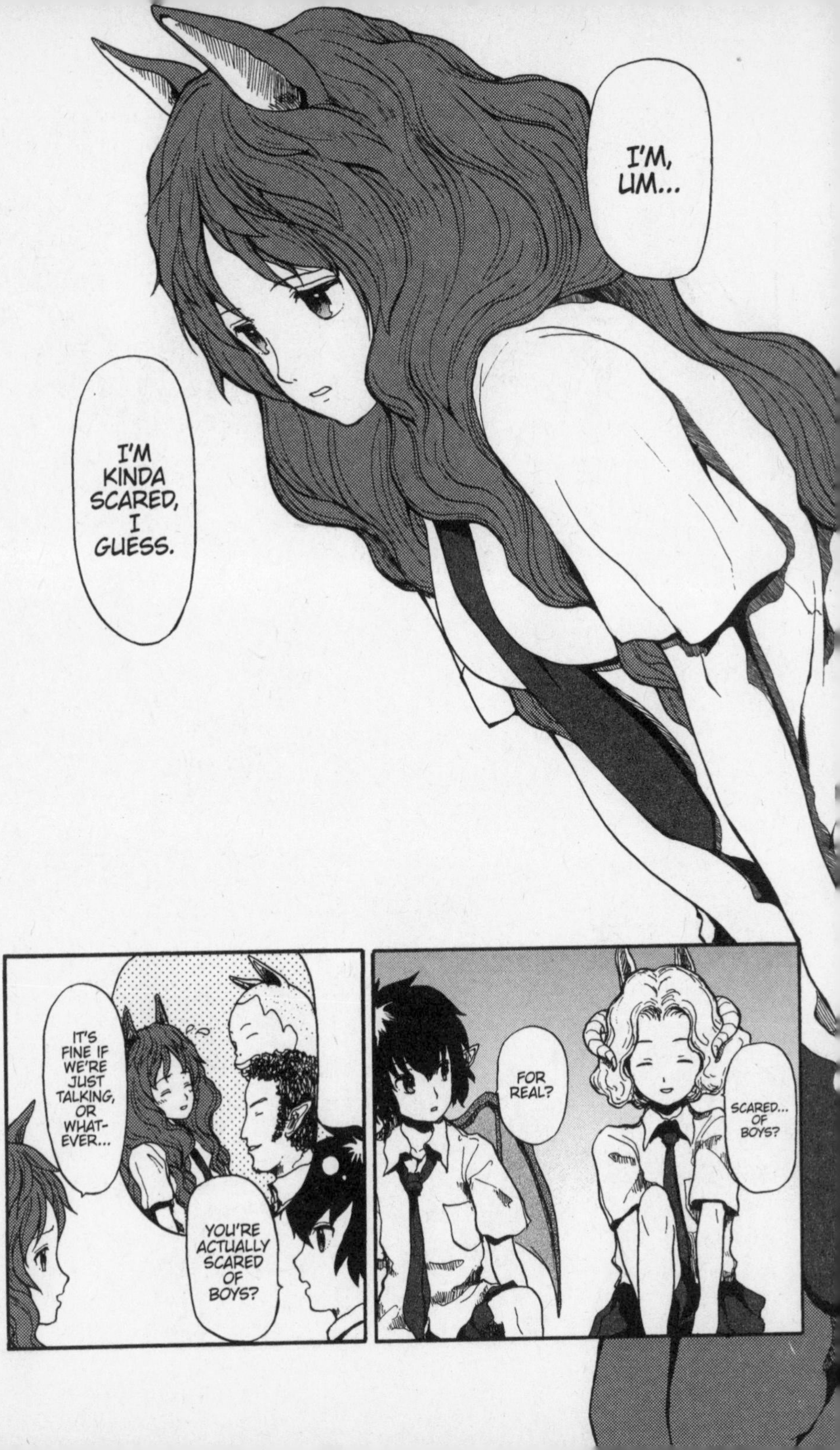
I'M, UM...
I'M KINDA SCARED, I GUESS.
SCARED... OF BOYS?
FOR REAL?
IT'S FINE IF WE'RE JUST TALKING, OR WHATEVER...
YOU'RE ACTUALLY SCARED OF BOYS?

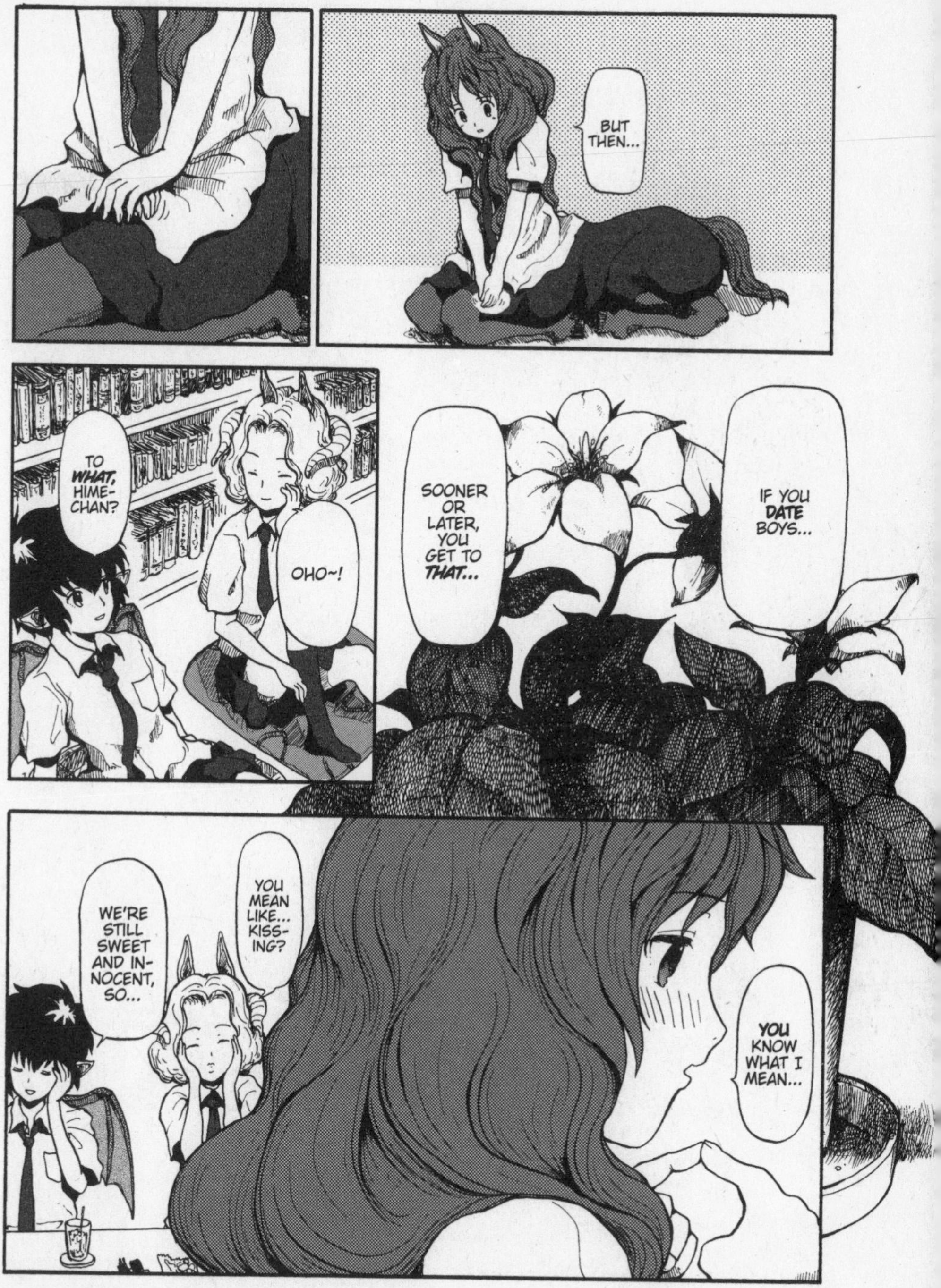
BUT THEN...
IF YOU DATE BOYS...
SOONER OR LATER, YOU GET TO THAT...
OHO~!
TO WHAT, HIME-CHAN?
YOU KNOW WHAT I MEAN...
YOU MEAN LIKE... KISSING?
WE'RE STILL SWEET AND INNOCENT, SO...

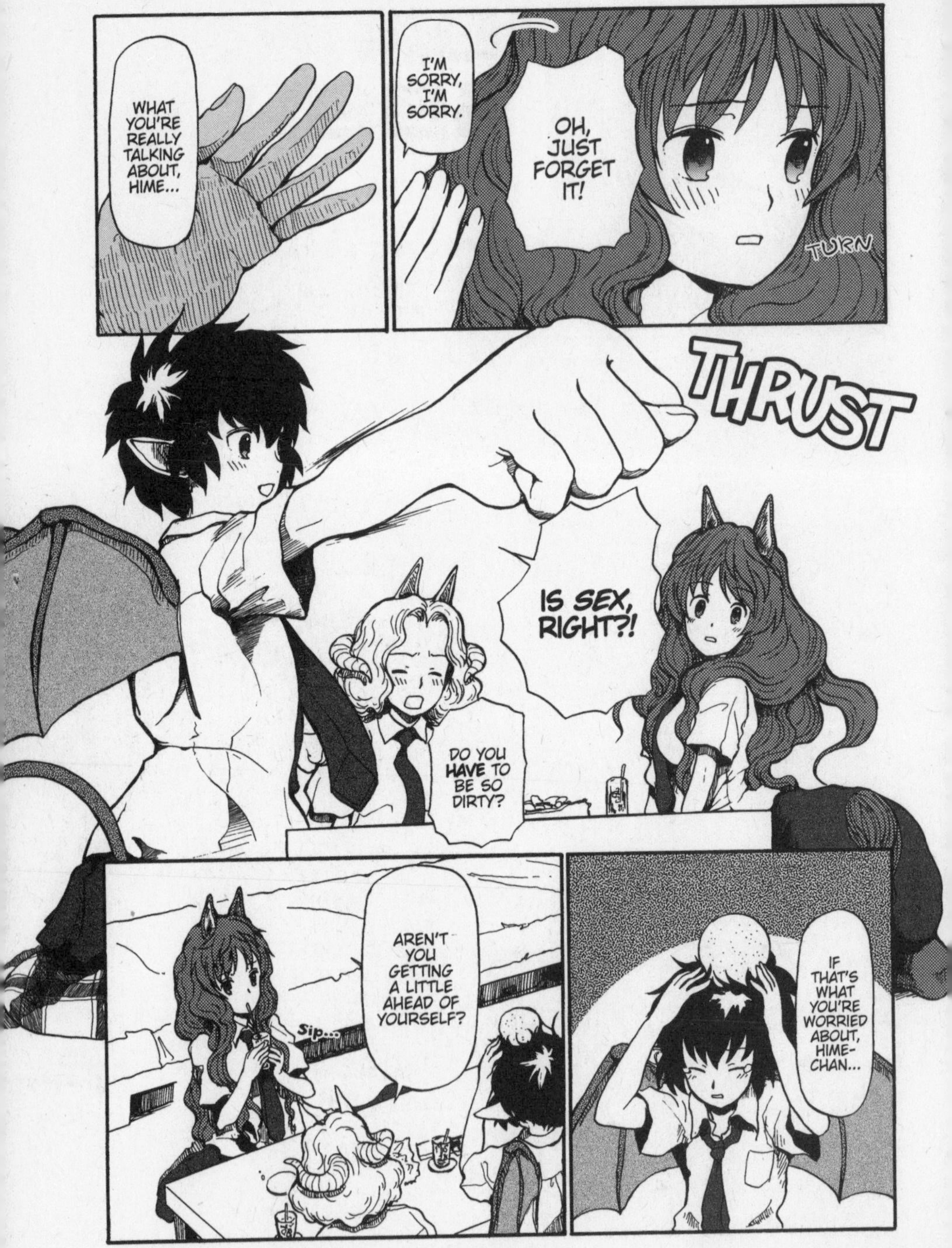
OH, JUST FORGET IT!
I'M SORRY, I'M SORRY.
TURN
WHAT YOU'RE REALLY TALKING ABOUT, HIME...
THRUST
IS SEX, RIGHT?!
DO YOU **HAVE** TO BE SO DIRTY?
IF THAT'S WHAT YOU'RE WORRIED ABOUT, HIME-CHAN...
AREN'T YOU GETTING A LITTLE AHEAD OF YOURSELF?
Sip...

Continued in *A Centaur's Life Vol. 1*!

COMING

NOVEMBER 2013

Alice in the Country of Clover:
Cheshire Cat Waltz Vol. 7

DECEMBER 2013

Alice Love Fables: Toy Box

Crimson Empire Vol. 3

JANUARY 2014

Alice in the Country of Hearts:
The Mad Hatter's Late Night
Tea Party Vol. 2